"... For 18 minutes the police moved in and got even for what they had been taking from the demonstrators for three days. After that, the police felt great. They were smiling and waving and you could see that it was a great psychological thing for them."

—Prosecuting Attorney, Thomas Foran

THE COURT   Are you saying that all evidence received in a criminal case as a result of a surveillance is inadmissible? If you are right, there are a lot of people languishing in the penitentiary who don't belong there.

WEINGLASS   I probably will have to agree with that.

THE COURT   If you can get a list of those people, maybe you can get some valuable clients.

WEINGLASS   I hope there aren't more added to that.

THE COURT   Don't be a pessimist.

The dignity of man lies in his ability to face reality in all its senselessness, to accept it freely, without fear, without illusions—and to laugh at it.

—Martin Esslin
The Theatre of the Absurd

ACKNOWLEDGEMENTS

The authors wish to acknowledge the help, kindness and consideration of the following people: Robert Lemon, NBC Vice President and General Manager WMAQ-TV; George Vaught, Director of News, NBC News, Chicago; Bernard Shusman, Executive Producer, NBC News, Chicago; Wallace Westfeldt, Executive Producer, The Huntley Brinkley Report; Jack Hakman, Art Director, NBC-TV, Chicago; John Ghilain, NBC Talent & Program Administration; and the consistent help of the National Broadcasting Company, Inc. and NBC News.

In addition, the publishers wish to thank Mark L. Levine, George C. McNamee, Daniel Greenberg and Bantam Books for access to the transcript of the trial; Joan Wiggins, Catherine Hinson, Jane Friedlander, Nenine Bilsky, Dr. Everett Parker, Mike Okpaku, Jim Leisy, Carter Smith, Paul Hush, Sidney Rosoff, Don Sheldon, Joan Adams, Wilbert LeMelle, Tom Cooney, Talton Ray, Charles Hobson, George Davis, all the beautiful people at Dial, Delacorte and Dell, and many others for their help and encouragement. We also wish to thank the Trustees of the Museum of Modern Art, for permission to reproduce Ben Shahn's poster, *This Is Nazi Brutality*. 1943, Offset Lithograph; *The New York Post* and *The New York Times* for clippings. and McGraw Hill publishers for the Eldridge Cleaver quote which is taken from *Conversation with Eldridge Cleaver/Algiers* by Lee Lockwood. The authors, and none others, are solely responsible for their respective contributions to this book. In no way may the expression of gratitude to the people above be construed as suggestive of concurrence with the views expressed or the logic applied to what are mainly standard American tenets.

drawings by arrangement with NBC-TV NEWS and WMAQ-TV, Chicago

millions who followed the events of the trial have seen many of the
drawings in this book on THE HUNTLEY-BRINKLEY REPORT.

First Printing

Cover design by Verna Sadock
Book design by Joe Okpaku
Type set by Terry Lintoyping, Inc., New York
Manufactured by Judd & Detweiler, Inc., Washington, D.C.
Library of Congress Catalog Card Number 79-129568

copyright © 1970 by The Third Press, Joseph Okpaku Publishing Co., Inc.
drawings copyright © 1970 by the National Broadcasting Company, Inc.
text copyright © 1970. by Joseph Okpaku

distributed by Dial/Delacorte Sales, 750 Third Avenue, New York, N. Y. 10017

Printed in the U.S.A.

VERDICT!

the exclusive picture story of the trial of the Chicago 8

drawings by
VERNA SADOCK

text by
JOSEPH OKPAKU
with the assistance of Ode Okore

THE THIRD PRESS
Joseph Okpaku Publishing Company, Inc.
444 Central Park West, New York, New York 10025

To Andy and Jonny for making the long hours in court worthwhile
Verna Sadock

To the young, and the young at heart
To all the beautiful people, and the beautiful at heart.

And to the disillusioned young American who, loving life, and loving his country, nurtures an ailing dream. He believes that at a time of seeming impending catastrophe, a great leader will emerge, and with a great vision, save a beautiful country from disaster.

He waits, watches the days go by, and, somehow, there's nothing in sight but mediocrity. Yet he waits; and in the meantime he murmurs painfully to himself and to his country:

Where have all the heroes gone?

Joseph Okpaku

PREFACE

A few words on what we have tried to do in this book. The drawings represent an artist's record of the court room experience throughout the trial. There is no distortion for purposes of humor or commentary. If all of the drawings of Julius Hoffman appear humorous it is because his appearance is, *per se,* humorous.

Excerpts from the transcript have been carefully chosen to record the nature of the trial itself. The purpose is to recreate, through the drawings and the excerpts, the experience of being at the trial. Complicated legal arguments as well as long monotonous narrations of who-told-who-what-and-where during the Democratic Convention have been left out. The result is an honest, brisk and vivid story by words and pictures.

The format of a picture story book for presenting a very controversial event is particularly fascinating. As a picture book, it carries a certain built-in pleasantness and relaxation which invites the reader without antagonising him. Consequently, the reader can, so to speak, join hands with the artist and the writer and in a friendly way take a quiet walk down the path of the experience. In so doing the reader is given a chance to feel at ease, and is therefore better prepared to take the ugly as well as the beautiful with an open mind. It is our belief that far too much unnecessary antagonism has been generated on all sides. As a result, it has become impossible to look honestly at the cold facts of a situation no one likes, no matter one's political stand, in order to genuinely search for a solution.

Throughout the main body of the book, we use a running commentary to tie the different episodes together as well as put the trial in the perspective of the overall situation in the country. We have left out such discussions as the merits and the demerits of the Vietnam War and the conduct of the defendants during the trial, simply because these issues have been thoroughly thrashed out and much of the present dialogue on them, sounding like a broken record, is repetitious and tedious. Our position on these issues can be expressed in short sentences.

The Indochina war is undesirable and should be ended. One finds it difficult to be convinced that those in authority are exercising the good faith necessary to bring about the termination of the war.

No one, under normal circumstances and in a system in which the courts are functioning fairly, would condone the antics of the defendants or the unprofessional comportment of their lawyers. But the illegal conduct of the trial itself is more reprehensible and the blatant denial of Bobby Seale's right to an attorney of his choice is an unpardonable travesty on even the most meager concept of justice. The implications of this vindictiveness more than justify the inevitable reaction of Bobby Seale, and the sympathetic response of his co-defendants.

As for constitutionality, the law simply could not be constitutional, if only because it is impossible to determine the prerequisite proof of guilt. Beyond that point, it is left to students of law to satisfy the professional concern for legal specifics. What is self-evident about the judicial system, however, is the glaring fact, as convincingly demonstrated by the trial, that no black man or even young white man, accused of anything that has the slightest resemblance of violence or any touch of social criticism can expect to find justice in an American court. The legal process is based on the mutual agreement that there are certain rules of the game for the police and the court, as well as for the ordinary citizen. Given the fact that the police do not exactly have an understanding of, or affection for, the young and the black, and the fact that there is effectively no consequence to a policeman for making an arbitrary arrest, there is nothing to prevent the police from using their powers to harass those they do not like or cannot understand. And this is what they do.

In the final chapter under the heading "THE RECKONING", we have tried to recreate for the reader the way many young people see the country today. By scraping off the obscenities and the rhetorical jargon, we have tried to penetrate the present confusion in order to articulate the basic validity of their criticism of the society. If the picture is disturbing, or the logic uncompromising, it is because this is the nature of the situation. It is not our purpose to indoctrinate or to convert. Nor is it our obligation to hide or sugar-coat unpleasant truths. Our objective is to identify the significant issues in order that the public may debate them. If we shall have identified one serious issue for one reader, our mission will have been more than accomplished.

It is also not our objective to upset or antagonize, nor is it our intention to rock the reader to sleep with soothing, therapeutic euphemisms. One does not play a match on violins, and the trial of the Chicago 8, especially the gagging and shackling of Bobby Seale, is not a love story.

If the reader finds this book unusually frank, it is because we, as young and black publishers, believe that a publisher should not go between an author and a reader, seeking to "tone down" the truth for him. If a publisher can understand or cope with a certain tenor, the reader most certainly can too. We believe that the duty of a publisher is to make it possible for all points of view to be presented to the reader in as articulate and succinct a manner as possible. Public debate of significant controversial issues is the lifeline of a free society. This is stifled when readers have no access to the viewpoint of a significant party to the issues, as expressed by that party rather than as represented by yet another member of the predominant group. Nigerian music played by the Boston Pops is not Nigerian music but a Boston Pops interpretation of Nigerian music.

It is the intention of *The Third Press,* in its modest way, to begin to correct the ills of a once artistic profession that has become highly biased and more rigid than even Wall Street organizations. Establishment publishers may say we are idealists, and we agree. But our reply is simple:

If a publisher is not idealistic, what will happen to the sensitivity of public thought?

Joseph Okpaku
Publisher

6

Once there was a man
and he had a court
and in the court there was a trial
and in the trial there were eight defendants
one was black, seven were white.

And across the country and throughout the world, people Young and Old,
listened with eagerness and read with astonishment the account of a trial that was,
to put it mildly, too absurd to be believable; too serious to be amusing; too amusing
to be disgusting; and too frightening to be dismissed.

Chicago was the scene of this saga.

the same Chicago that gave the world the memorable farce of the 1968 Democratic
National Convention.

On sober reflection, it had to be Chicago. The same Chicago that has meant
different things to all kinds of people.

From happy-go-lucky yippies to shoot-to-kill policemen; from Bertolt Brecht to
Norman Mailer.

Chicago that whimsically installed a monumental Picasso sculpture as if to make
amends for having given the history of Man, a phenomenon called Richard Joseph
Daley.

"Chicago is my kind of town," the one and only Spiro T. Agnew once said, "it's a
big city, but not arrogant. The people are warm and friendly, but not gushy."

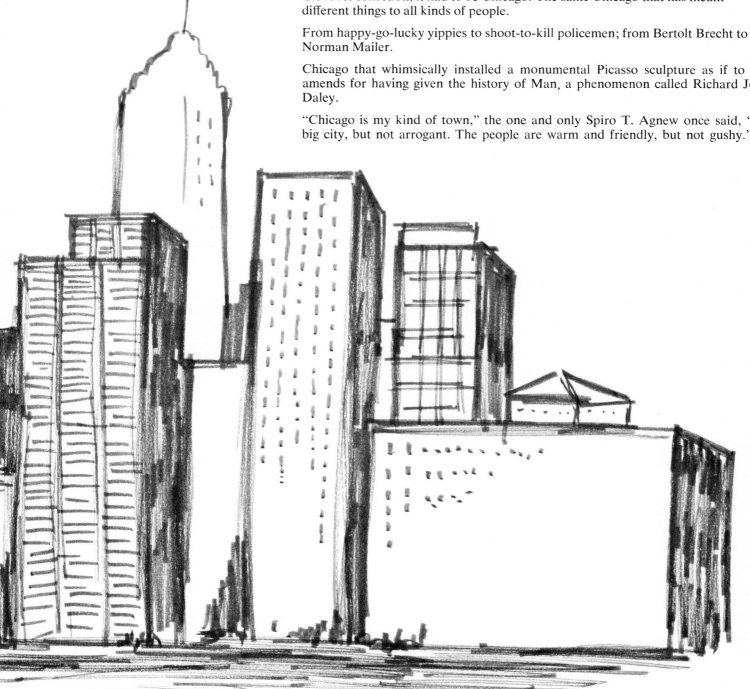

7

And the man was Julius Jennings Hoffman.

Thorny, spunky and quite a wit in his own rather restoration style. Perhaps a Wit-Would. With his glasses below his nose he would peer at one over the rims with a look that some say could be withering—which is rather hard to believe. Bony fingers, beautiful ties, handsome vest, quite expensively dressed. For his age, Julius Hoffman is thought to still consider himself a bit of a lady killer. As for his ego, story has it that someone once called him "that little son-of-a-bitch". "Me", Hoffman is said to have retorted, "I am not little". Towards the end of the trial he complained that an artist made him look like a prune on TV.

And on that day, in what looked like the year of our lord, one thousand, nine hundred and sixty-nine, on the twenty-sixth day of September, Julius Jennings Hoffman stood in his court, took a long spiralling look at his court and said:

I am the Judge

I am Judge Hoffman, sir

I am not a humorist.

I am not an obstructionist

I do not listen to the broadcasts of the defendants. I do not expect to hear anything nice about me on the air.

THE COURT   When you get to be as old as I am and have tried as many thousands of cases as I have, you will be able to rule properly—rapidly, too. And I don't rule too rapidly.

KUNSTLER   Your Honor, we have the same birthday, you and I. The difference between us is not that great.

THE COURT   You must have put an FBI man on me.

KUNSTLER   No, I compared our Who's Who in *Who's Who in America,* and I saw we had the same birthday.

THE COURT   Very brief, wasn't it?

KUNSTLER   No, yours was, I think, three lines shorter than mine.

THE COURT   I hope you get a better obituary.

KUNSTLER   Well, I know—all I know, your Honor, is I won't be able to read it, unfortunately.

8

And the court was the United States Federal Court, Northern District of Illinois, Eastern Division.

And the trial, No. 69 CR 180 United States of America vs David T. Dellinger, et al., came to be known variously as the Conspiracy Trial, the Trial of the Chicago 8 when it was still integrated and later, the Chicago 7 Trial after purification.

The cast for the Defendants was an unholy conglomerate of a Black Panther neo-Marxist intellectual, self-styled revolutionaries, so-called bushy-haired yippies and an elderly pacifist, a sociologist and a chemistry professor. Federal prosecuting attorney Honorable Thomas Foran was later to say of them in not exactly honorable language that all of them, except Bobby Seale, were fags—a hip expression for homosexuals.

Rabbi Arnold J. Wolf of the Solel Congregation, Highland Park, Illinois:

"I'll tell you why I am for these men: it is a Jewish law that a woman who is raped must yell—America is being raped and these men have been yelling."

JOHN R. FROINES
Acting Professor of Chemistry at the University of Oregon
His style was a T-shirt under a blue striped shirt.

RENNARD (Rennie) DAVIS
Brilliant, articulate, good organizer with charming boyish manners. Has a cold penetrating stare which warmed up as the trial did. With his plaid wool shirts, work shoes and terrible color coordination, Rennie has a perfect working class look.
"Davis", a reporter once said, "speaks with an underlined suggestion of humor as if the whole trial were some sort of mod joke which wryly amused him".

THOMAS HAYDEN
A Botticelli intellectual or perhaps an El Greco. Long hair, long face, long nose. A female prosecution witness described him, rather inaccurately, as "beady eyes and repulsive". Very eloquent. James Tuohy of the Chicago Sun-Times once described Hayden as "an extra-serious young man who would be a boring speaker if it were not for his stirring intelligence and ability to construct tight arguments . . . he tends to be somewhat doctrinaire". As a young intellectual, he is one of the last remnants of a dying breed of America—or the first of a new breed.

DAVID DELLINGER
"The old bear" but in clean shirts. A good in-fighter. A grandfather, and a pacifist since the 1930s when he drove an ambulance for the Quakers during the Spanish Civil War. Dave is not exactly like his fellow American grandfathers except perhaps that he is extremely verbose and rather moralistic. He missed no opportunity to point out for the benefit of Julius Hoffman the moral behind every significant event in the trial. He wore the same clothes throughout the trial and at the end, like the trial itself, it was rumpled and creazy but otherwise neat on the whole. Dave is one of those few people one feels like calling simply "good men".

9

ABBIE HOFFMAN

"My name is Abbie. I am an orphan of America. I live in Woodstock nation. It is a nation of alienated young people. We carry it around as a state of mind in the same way as the Sioux Indians carry the Sioux nation around with them.

Perfect court jester. Marvelous sense of humor but with hair-trigger temper. A man whose concept of ideas is very carefully thought out, Abbie can easily be mistaken for stupid by those incapable of his level of thought. Perhaps out of extended frustration he quickly shifts gears to semi-cynicism which is similarly lost on the same kind of audience. Far better read than a casual glance at him would suggest. His rather sloppy appearance could be quite misleading in that score.

JERRY RUBIN

Yippie patriarch. Extremely honest but inarticulate in impromptu situations. Absolutely wild-eyed. Product of the Berkeley Free Speech Movement, with an admirable, almost puerile idealism and an indefatigable determination. Rubin is ironically the perfect model of the contemporary all-American revolutionary—excessive determination but inadequate clarity of expression. Yet his concern for what is desirable for the country he so passionately loves is more than sufficient reason to praise a young man who has suffered jail and persecution in his attempt to awake the public conscience.

BOBBY SEALE

With much deeper experience and a concern far more complex than that of Julius Hoffman, Bobby Seale as a black man, and as the Chairman of the Black Panther Party, was the defendant most vulnerable to the commonly accepted idiosyncrasies of the judicial system. Of all the defendants, Bobby Seale was the only one who came to Chicago still believing in the potential of justice and the possibility of rectifying the inequites of a judicial system that manages to have more than eighty per cent of its prisoners come from less than twelve per cent of its population.

LEE WEINER

"I am a good Jewish middle-class boy and I am doing right, I tell them. And I really am. When I was indicted, CBS called me and said, 'Congratulations!' My mother-in-law was in the room at the time and she asked 'what's the matter?' 'You will find out', I said."

In his strand of little colorful beads, grey sweater, light blue unironed shirts and boots, Lee Weiner, in his Berkeley woven belt, leaves the impression of one who has read too many theoretical books.

Acting the roles of Defense attorneys were Kunstler and Weinglass.

WILLIAM KUNSTLER

"Although it is not yet clearly in focus, the shadow of the swastika is visible in America today," says William Kunstler, 50, the nation's pre-eminent defense lawyer in civil liberties cases. "Our Government fears and hates radical college students, the poor and the black, because they make us question the validity of our economic and political systems . . . And the fact that Attorney General John Mitchell now wants the power to wire-tap anyone he defines as a threat to our national interest shows how far we've advanced toward fascism."

Like a poet lost in a bullring, always in old rumpled brown suit, William Kunstler is a brilliant man whose tremendous commitment to the fair and the just does not protect him from being insensitive to errors of miscalculations on his part. He has not been so toughened by the painful experience of futility to be incapable of shedding a tear in response to the devasting impact of the shadow of utter hopelessness.

William Kunstler's wit is so complementary to that of Julius Hoffman that the pair could make a memorable team on Broadway. Without his resonance of wit, Julius Hoffman would not have succeeded in luring the defense to their doom like the Ancient Mariner to his. At the beginning of the defense's case he dubbed a very mod—double-breasted suit, blue shirt and a white polka-dot tie. But whenever the going got rough, he returned to his rumpled brown suit and old fashioned narrow tie.

KUNSTLER Your Honor, why can't the jury then have a view of the premises? Nothing is more important than to see what the premises looked like.

THE COURT Mr. —

KUNSTLER Kunstler.

THE COURT .....—Kunstler. I ought to know—you're

right—by now.

KUNSTLER No, names aren't important, your Honor. Whether you know my name or Mr. Weinglass' is completely unimportant—both "X" and "Y"—but let's look at the Amphitheatre.

THE COURT Names are important. They are to me.

LEONARD WEINGLASS

Every mother's dream child.

There is a story about Weinglass smoking a cigar while riding a court house elevator with Kunstler.

Kunstler: Does your mother know you are smoking that?

And those who bore the rather blunt sword of the Federal Government were Foran and Schultz.

RICHARD SCHULTZ

The good hard-working efficient boy you never really care to talk about. You may acknowledge his achievements but they never quite interest you. He will make a perfect civil servant but should never be a public leader in a position that requires the comprehension of social forces. Unfortunately there are one or two others like that who now hold national positions who should never be there—if only because, like Schultz, they lack the slightest sense of humor that is necessary for the comprehension of the complexities of human behavior. One cannot doubt his sincerity but, alas, like Spiro T. Agnew, he would be less dangerous if he were less sincere. But that is in anticipation of Richard Schultz. For the present, he is a good lawyer who has read his books thoroughly—almost too thoroughly.

11

THOMAS FORAN

Democrat in a Republican administration. Muscular, hard-hitting, rough midwesterner with a deep throated voice, and curly hair. Hard and tough, not exactly refined. Built like a bull; points his finger a lot and every muscle of his not quite robot frame strains with every movement.

One could easily monitor his mood by tracking the movement of his lips. Behind all that is a quick penetrating mind and an almost natural talent for being a prosecutor. One could even say he might enjoy a good laugh—once in a while. His language is far from eloquent and certainly not becoming of the decency he fought to uphold in court.

FORAN This crybaby stuff he goes through, your Honor, every time he asks a wrong question, is just—

KUNSTLER Crybaby? Did you ever hear Mr. Foran when he sinks into his seat—"So are we going through this again"—in his dying quail voice that I have pointed out on past occasions?

FORAN He has been remarkably contained, your Honor, in case—

THE COURT Try to go to a diction coach before tomorrow's session, Mr. Foran, so that you don't have a dying quail's voice.

THE JURY

And as for the shaky scale, it was left to ten women and two men to balance it as best they could.

THE COURT IN SESSION

And after the court had settled down, Judge Julius Jennings Hoffman, in a voice which William Kunstler compared to that of Orson Welles (how skeptical but pleased the judge must have been), called the case

NO. 69 CRIM. 180

the case of

United States of America, plaintiff

versus

David T. Dellinger, Rennard Davis, Thomas E. Hayden, Abbot H. Hoffman, Jerry C. Rubin, Lee Weiner, John R. Froines and Bobby G. Seale,

Defendants.

With that the curtain was drawn and the drama was in full swing.

OPENING STATEMENT ON BEHALF OF THE GOVERNMENT BY MR. SCHULTZ

. . . The Government, ladies and gentlemen of the jury, will prove in this case, the case which you will witness as jurors, an overall plan of the eight defendants in this case which was to encourage numerous people to come to the city of Chicago, people who planned legitimate protest during the Democratic National Convention which was held in Chicago in August of 1968, from August 26 through August 29, 1968. They planned to bring these people into Chicago to protest, legitimately protest, as I said, creat[ing] a situation in this city where these people would come to Chicago, would riot . . . [T]he defendants, in perpetrating this offense, they, the defendants, crossed state lines themselves, at least six of them, with intent to incite this riot.

. . . Ladies and gentlemen of the jury, the Government will prove that each of these eight men assumed specific roles in it and they united and that the eight conspired together to encourage people to riot during the Convention. We will prove that the plans to incite the riot were basically in three steps. The first step was to use the unpopularity of the war in Vietnam as a method to urge people to come to Chicago during that Convention for purposes of protest. The first was to bring the people here.

The second step was to incite these people who came to Chicago, to incite these people against the Police Department, the city officials, the National Guard and the military, and against the Convention itself, so that these people would physically resist and defy the orders of the police and the military.

So the second step, we will prove, was to incite, and the third step was to create a situation where the demonstrators who had come to Chicago and who were conditioned to physically resist the police would meet and would confront the police in the streets of Chicago so that at this confrontation a riot would occur. . . .

. . . The Government will not prove that all eight defendants met together at one time, but the Government will prove that on some occasions two or three of the defendants would meet together; on other occasions four would meet; on some occasions five of them would meet together to discuss these actions, and on several occasions six of the defendants met together to discuss their plans. . . .

In sum, then, ladies and gentlemen, the Government will prove that the eight defendants charged here conspired together to use interstate commerce and the facilities of interstate commerce to incite and to further a riot in Chicago; that they conspired to use incendiary devices to further that riot, and they conspired to have people interfere with law enforcement officers, policemen, military men, Secret Service men engaged in their duties; and that the defendants committed what are called overt acts in furtherance of the conspiracy—that is, they took steps, they did things to accomplish this plan, this conspiracy. . . .

* * *

OPENING STATEMENT ON BEHALF OF CERTAIN DEFENDANTS BY MR. KUNSTLER

Now the Government has given you its table of contents. I will present to you in general what the defense hopes to show is the true book. We hope to prove before you that the evidence submitted by the defendants will show that this prosecution which you are hearing is the result of two motives on the part of the Government—

SCHULTZ Objection as to any motives of the prosecution, if the Court please.

KUNSTLER Your Honor, it is a proper defense to show motive.

THE COURT I sustain the objection. You may speak to the guilt or innocence of your clients, not to the motive of the Government.

KUNSTLER Your Honor, I always thought that—

SCHULTZ Objection to any colloquies, and arguments, your Honor.

THE COURT I sustain the objection, regardless of what you have always thought, Mr. Kunstler.

* * *

KUNSTLER The evidence will show as far as the defendants are concerned that they, like many other citizens of the United States, numbering in the many thousands, came to Chicago in the summer of 1968 to protest in the finest American tradition outside and in the vicinity of the Convention, the National Convention of the party in power. They came to protest the continuation of a war in South Vietnam which was then and had been for many years past within the jurisdiction of the party in power which happened to be the Democratic Party at that time. . . .

There was, as you will recall, and the evidence will so indicate, a turmoil within the Democratic Party itself as to whether it would enact a peace plan, as part of its platform. This, too, would be influenced by demonstrators. The possibility of this plank was what motivated many of the demonstrators to come to Chicago. The possibility of influencing delegates to that National Convention to take an affirmative strong stand against a continuation of this bloody and unjustified war, as they considered it to be along with millions of persons, was one of the prime purposes of their coming to Chicago. . . .

At the same time as they were making plans to stage this demonstration and seeking every legal means in which to do so, the seeking of permits would be significant, permits in the seeking of facilities to put their plans into operation in a meaningful and peaceful way.

* *

At the same time as all of this was going on, the evidence will show that there were forces in this city and in the national Government who were absolutely determined to prevent this type of protest, who had reached a conclusion that such a protest had to be stopped by the—the same phrase used by Mr. Schultz —by all means necessary, including the physical violence perpetrated by demonstrators. These plans were

gathering in Washington and they were gathering here in this city, and long before a single demonstrator had set foot in the city of Chicago in the summer of 1968, the determination had been made that these demonstrations would be diffused, they would be dissipated, they would essentially be destroyed as effective demonstrations against primarily the continuation of the war in South Vietnam. . . .

We will demonstrate that free speech died here in the streets under those clubs and that the bodies of these demonstrators were the sacrifices to its death. . . .

* *

. . . [T]he defense will show that the real conspiracy in this case is the conspiracy to which I have alluded, the conspiracy to curtail and prevent the demonstrations against the war in Vietnam and related issues that these defendants and other people, thousands, who came here were determined to present

to the delegates of a political party and the party in power meeting in Chicago; that the real conspiracy was against these defendants. But we are going to show that the real conspiracy is not against these defendants as individuals because they are unimportant as individuals; the real attempt was—the real attack on the rights of everybody, all of us American citizens, all, to protest under the First Amendment to the Constitution, to protest against a war that was brutalizing us all, and to protest in a meaningful fashion, and that the determination was made that that protest would be dissolved in the blood of protesters; that the protest would die in the streets of Chicago, and that the protest would be dissipated and nullified by police officers under the guise of protecting property or protecting law and order or protecting other people. . . .

Dissent died here for a moment during that Democratic National Convention. What happens in this case may determine whether it is moribund.

15

FORAN Judge, the reason we were late this morning and then the reason for the request for the interruption was I was informed just about the time we were to come to court by the FBI that they had been informed that one of the jurors had received a letter or her family had received a letter that certainly could be of a threatening nature. . . . I have a copy of it here, your Honor, marked as Government's Exhibit A. It is addressed to the King family, 81 South Caroline, Crystal Lake, Illinois 60014. It is written in script, "You are being watched. The Black Panthers. . . ."

THE COURT Now my own marshal, gentlemen, was handed this morning this communication addressed to the Peterson family. . . .

It is not unlike Government's Exhibit A for identification. . . .

WEINGLASS I think this does raise the flag of caution that more than one has received a similar document. Perhaps we ought to ask all of the jurors.

THE COURT Defendant Derringer.

KUNSTLER I think your honor meant Dellinger.

THE COURT Dellinger, that's right.

FORAN [Mr. Kunstler] is in this argumentative fashion trying to once again play Perry Mason.

KUNSTLER He does pretty well, your Honor. If I can do half as well as Perry Mason—

FORAN As a television actor, you do, Mr. Kunstler.

FORAN Your Honor, will you let the man try to remember he has got a law degree?

KUNSTLER Your Honor, every time there comes this despairing anguished cry from Mr. Foran about the defense counsel for which I use the term dying quail, I believe, to describe it, and it occurs every time.

THE COURT I have never heard that. That is a new one.

* * *

KUNSTLER But you think that was a rather important thing that was said to you about tearing up the town?

FORAN Oh, your Honor, here we go again.

KUNSTLER Your Honor, if the remark "here we go again" is an objection, I never heard it.

FORAN I really am going to refer you to Wigmore's tonight, Mr. Counsel. Instead of watching yourself on TV, you can study evidence.

KUNSTLER . . . The proper way to object is to say "I object," not "Channel 7" or "Channel 5."

* *

FORAN . . . And by the way, your Honor, I would like to have your Honor tell counsel's group in the courtroom that they are not to respond by laughter and comments.

THE COURT I have already admonished the Marshal to see to it that order is maintained.

KUNSTLER Your Honor, a bit of laughter is not disorder, and I think sometimes—

THE COURT It is in this courtroom. This is either a serious case or it isn't. I don't waste my time.

KUNSTLER I know, but when your Honor makes a quip and makes people laugh, there is no such statement by the U.S. Attorney.

THE COURT It is not intended to provoke laughter.

KUNSTLER But it does, your Honor, and we all know that it does.

THE COURT I am not a humorist.

I am not a humorist

THE COURT   I can only use the voice the Lord gave me. This is the first time in about twenty-two years serving on state and federal benches that anybody has complained about my voice. They have complained about other things but nobody has complained about my voice. And it is amusing—you know, I am not forbidden to read the newspapers, I haven't forbidden myself, but I did see even some press friends of mine refer to my voice as being rasping. Then, on the other hand, I heard it referred to by your associate —what is the name of that actor—

KUNSTLER   Orson Welles, your Honor.

THE COURT   —as Orson Welles, who has a magnificently resonant voice.
    Now take your choice. It is either rasping or it is as resonant as Orson Welles'.

WEINGLASS   Well, I don't want to characterize the voice of the Court. However—

THE COURT   I do my best to use the vocal facilities the Lord has endowed me with.

THE COURT   You know Mr. Mies van der Rohe designed the lectern for the use of counsel and I wish you would stay behind it, sir.

KUNSTLER   Your Honor, sometimes for a free spirit, it is quite confining, so I move a little, and I am sorry.

17

But the question of the legal representation of Black Panther Party Chairman Bobby Seale had not been resolved. Try as hard as the judge did to solve it simply by threatening disciplinary action, those legitimate issues were to plague the trial for many days and haunt every twist and turn of the proceedings. The days saw Hoffman frustrate every last faint hope Seale had in the judicial system and the constitutional rights of the black American. It will not be too drastic to compare his outbursts in court to the last noble stance of many a Jew before succumbing to Nazi extermination. Julius Hoffman being Jewish ought to have had some sensitivity to that. Perhaps he did. Perhaps in so doing he saw the unavoidable parallel that compared him with Hitler's judges. Perhaps it is that devastating realization that provoked his panic, and his wanton vindictiveness. In punishment for Bobby Seale's outbursts, Judge Hoffman saw to it that Seale and other black Americans did not lose sight of their slave days in this country. "In chains you were born", he seemed to be saying, "and in chains you can always be put". And Julius Hoffman was soon to have Bobby Seale, a black man, publicly gagged and chained to the humiliation of all black people and the disgust of all men of decency.

Bobby Seale

Mickey

KUNSTLER But I want the record to quite clearly indicate that I do not direct Mr. Seale in any way. He is a free independent black man who does his own direction.

THE COURT Black or white, sir—and what an extraordinary statement, "an independent black man." He is a defendant in this case. He will be calling you a racist before you are through, Mr. Kunstler.

KUNSTLER Your Honor, I think to call him a free independent black man will not incite his anger.

18

KUNSTLER   How do you know an anti-police person when you see him?

MURRAY   I can't tell when I see him but when they open their mouth and yell, "Kill the pigs," I assume he is anti-police.

* * *

SCHULTZ   What, if anything, did Rubin say during the preceding ten minutes before the policemen were assaulted and during the time the policemen were assaulted which would encourage the crowd to assault the policemen?

MURRAY   He said "Let's get the m-f-en pigs out of here." He said, "Take off your guns and we'll fight you," and "you're shitheads," and "You're m-f-s" and "Your kids are f-n pigs."

* *

SEALE   Hey, you don't speak for me. I would like to speak on behalf of my own self and have counsel handle my case in behalf of myself.

How come I can't speak in behalf of myself? I am my own legal counsel. I don't want these lawyers to represent me.

THE COURT   You have a lawyer of record and he has been of record here since the 24th.

SEALE   I have been arguing that before the jury heard one shred of evidence. I don't want these lawyers because I can take up my own legal defense and my lawyer is Charles Garry.

* * *

SCHULTZ   . . . Now will you relate, please, to the Court and to the jury what you heard the Defendant Hoffman say.

DAHL   Yes, sir. He said, "Tomorrow we're going to meet in Grant Park, and we're going to storm the Hilton. We got to get there singly because if we go in groups the blank pigs are going to stop us."

SCHULTZ   You say "blank pigs." Did he say "blank pigs"?

DAHL   No, sir.

SCHULTZ   Did he use another word other than "blank"?

DAHL   Yes, sir.

SCHULTZ   Was it a four-letter word?

DAHL   Yes, sir.

SCHULTZ   What was the first letter of that four-letter word, please?

DAHL   "F."

THE COURT   I direct you, sir, to remain quiet.

SEALE   And just be railroaded?

THE COURT   Will you remain quiet?

SEALE   I want to defend myself, do you mind, please?

THE COURT   Let the record show that the Defendant Seale continued to speak after the Court courteously requested him to remain quiet.
Bring in the jury, Mr. Marshal.

19

William Kunstler

Judge Julius Hoffman

THE COURT I will let you speak as long as you want to on that question because your appearance is still of record.

KUNSTLER That is right, your Honor, but when a man stands up and says he wants to defend himself—

THE COURT That is not the law in the middle of a trial.

KUNSTLER That is the law. The constitution says any man that wishes to defend himself may do so.

THE COURT You may speak of the Constitution as though it were a document printed yesterday. We know about the Constitution way out here in the Middle West, too, Mr. Kunstler.

KUNSTLER Oh, your Honor, this is a little unfair, isn't it?

THE COURT We really do. You would be amazed at our knowledge of constitutional law.

KUNSTLER Isn't that a little unfair, your Honor? We are not here from different parts of the country—

THE COURT I am getting a little weary of these thrusts by counsel and I don't want any more of them. I had occasion to admonish you before.

KUNSTLER I know, but you said I could argue as long as I wanted.

THE COURT As long as you are respectful, sir.

KUNSTLER I am respectful.

THE COURT No, you haven't been.

KUNSTLER You implied, I thought, Chicago people didn't understand the Constitution, only Easterners understand it. That isn't true.

THE COURT Bring in the jury.

KUNSTLER You are not letting me argue as long as I want to.

THE COURT No. You haven't anything to say that is important right now.

* * *

20

DWAYNE OKLEPEK, undercover newspaper reporter

FORAN Would you state the conversation, Mr. Oklepek?

OKLEPEK Mr. Hayden told the group that this formation was the same type of formation that Japanese students had used to precipitate riots in Japan in 1960, which prevented then President Eisenhower from visiting that country. He said that "Getting people together in this kind of formation, getting the[m] moving and chanting and yelling, aroused their emotions, sustained their spirits, got them very excited."

He said that "This formation was very good for breaking through police lines and that in the event of an arrest situation, this formation would be used during the Convention Week to break police lines and to try to escape from Lincoln Park, for instance."

FORAN Did you ever see any person in Mobilization wearing a gun?

OKLEPEK Not that I could see, no.

FORAN You say not that you could see. Are you saying that you saw the outlines under their coats?

OKLEPEK I saw bulges under their coats.

FORAN Oh, you saw bulges. Did you say to yourself at that time, "Those are guns"?

OKLEPEK I said to myself at that time, "Those are bulges."

THE COURT [A]ll I get from your clients constantly is a laugh. Just this last second they sit there and laugh at a judge of the highest trial court in the United States. That is what I have been getting. Perhaps you think that is proper as a lawyer admitted to practice here by the courtesy of this court. . . .

KUNSTLER I just want to say, your Honor, for the record, I don't think that a laugh is always out of place in a Federal Court. I am not sure that your Honor is always interpreting these laughs as being directed at you. I think that that is your Honor's subjective reasoning.

THE COURT I am perfectly competent to know how they are laughing. You leave that to me.

FORAN I object to this, your Honor.

THE COURT I sustain the objection.

KUNSTLER Your Honor, I still say this is classic impeachment.

THE COURT . . . I don't know what you mean by "classic impeachment." To me impeachment is impeachment. We are not dealing with the classics, and that is not the way we do it.

THE COURT I don't want to assume a professional attitude, but you should know that your questions have been bad [as] a matter of form.

KUNSTLER I will try to redo them, your Honor.

THE COURT Borrowing your word, they are classically bad.

KUNSTLER In the Roman or Greek sense, your Honor, or in the modern sense?

THE COURT Just plain English.

THE COURT Ladies and gentlemen of the jury, good morning.

Mr. Feinglass, will you please continue with the cross-examination of this witness?

KUNSTLER Your Honor, so the record may be clear, I don't think Mr. Weinglass noticed the Feinglass. It is Mr. Weinglass.

THE COURT Oh, I did misspeak myself. I said Feinglass. I correct myself. I mean Weinglass. I am sorry I worked an F in there instead of the W that you deserve, Mr. Weinglass.

FORAN Did you see police and demonstrators in hand-to-hand wrestling and fighting?

OKLEPEK Yes, I did.

FORAN How big a crowd was there?

OKLEPEK I would say 5,000 people.

FORAN What was the crowd chanting?

OKLEPEK They were chanting, "Hell no, we won't go. Dump the Hump. Daley must go. NLF is going to win. Ho, Ho, Ho Chi Minh." Things like that.

JAMES TOBIN, Chicago police officer

SCHULTZ Did you hear Rubin say anything other than the things you have already related?

TOBIN Yes. As the march proceeded north, I heard Rubin use numerous obscenities. I heard obscenities in the crowd.

SCHULTZ All right. Would you relate the obscenities, please. Yes, you may relate the obscenities.

TOBIN I may? Rubin would yell to "Fu-- the pigs," "Off the pig."

SCHULTZ "Off the pig"?

TOBIN Yes.

SCHULTZ What is "Off the pig"? Have you ever heard that terminology before?

TOBIN Yes, I have. It's a street terminology for "Kill the pigs."

SCHULTZ Go ahead.

TOBIN He would yell—he was putting his finger up in the air and yelling, "Off the pig, off the pig," and he would use these obscenities back and forth to the people on the sidewalk, to the people in the cars, any police car that went by in the vicinity he would yell to them and he was jumping up and down, he was waving his arms, he was telling everybody, "Cheer it up, chant it up, chant it up."

* * * * * * * * * * * * * * * * * * * *

BOBBY SEALE

THE CLERK There is a motion here of Defendant Bobby Seale *pro se* to be permitted to defend himself.

THE COURT I will hear you, Mr. Seale.

SEALE I want to present this motion in behalf of myself and I want to place some statements concerning past—well, it is what has been described as in one manner and another interrupting the Court, but I am not and have not been—I am not a lawyer, but I do know that I "as one of the defendants" have a right to defend myself and I feel and know that it should be looked into by the Judge of this Court, Judge Hoffman, and I feel that it has not been looked into. . . .

Also I think my reasons should be clear that prior to the beginning of this trial my understanding of my legal representation here was so that this motion can have some validity and understanding to it. I understood quite a while back after arraignment, immediately after arraignment, in fact, the same day that I was arraigned on these charges, that Charles R. Garry would be the only one who would defend me here, that all other lawyers who would appear in court would appear in court only for pretrial motions and pretrial proceedings. There is where I stood and this has been my contention all along. . . .

I, Bobby Seale, demand and move the Court as follows:

Because I am denied this lawyer of my choice, Charles R. Garry, I cannot represent myself as my attorney would be doing, but because I am forced to be my own counsel and to defend myself, I require my release from custody, from the bail presently in force, so that I can interview witnesses, do the necessary investigating, do necessary factual research and all other things that being in custody makes impossible.

2. The right to cross-examine witnesses and examine witnesses of my choice.

3. The right to make all necessary motions that I as a layman can think of to help my defense and prove my innocence and to argue those motions. . . .

SEALE I know I have gotten some attacks from the Government saying we were playing games over here. I am not playing no game with my life, being stuck on the line, and I want to put that into the record to explain my situation.

THE COURT Mr. Schultz.

SCHULTZ May we briefly reply, your Honor?
Your Honor, this is a ploy. It's just a simple obvious ploy.

SEALE . . . I stated that it was my understanding and my agreement that only Mr. Charles R. Garry would represent me. Right after arraignment I saw all these other lawyers the defendants brought in, and it was my understanding and agreement that they would only represent me while I was in California, pretrial motions and proceedings, and that Charles R. Garry would represent me here. . .

THE COURT . . . Mr. Seale has moved to be allowed to act as his own counsel and for relief on bail in order to perform certain functions he deems necessary to his defense. . . .

In exercising its discretion, the Court should deny a motion to defendant *pro se* when such procedure would be disruptive of the proceedings and when denial would not be prejudicial to the defendant. . . .

I find now that to allow the Defendant Seale to act as his own attorney would produce the same disruptive effect. Moreover, the denial of the defendant's motion to appear *pro se* would not be prejudicial to his case. On the contrary, the complexity of the case makes self-representation inappropriate and the defendant would be more prejudiced were he allowed to conduct his own defense than if his motion were to be denied. . . .

[*As the defense is about to cross-examine Government Witness Robert Allen Tobin*]

SEALE I would like to say, Judge, that you denied my motion to defend myself and you know this jury is prejudiced against me.

THE COURT I will ask you to sit down.

SEALE   They have been made prejudicial against me. I know. I should be allowed to defend myself. I should be allowed to speak so I can defend myself.

THE MARSHAL   Be quiet.

SEALE   Don't tell me to shut up. I got a right to speak. I need to speak to defend myself.

THE COURT   Mr. Seale, I must admonish you that any outburst such as you have just indulged in will be appropriately dealt with at the right time during this trial and I must order you not to do it again.

SEALE   In other words, Judge—

THE COURT   If you do, you do it at your own risk, Sir.

SEALE   In other words, you are saying you are going to put me in contempt of court for speaking on behalf of myself?

THE COURT   I will not argue with you.
   Mr. Marshal—

SEALE   . . . Now you are saying you are going to put me in jail, you are going to put me in jail, that's one thing. You are going to put me in contempt of court because I am speaking in behalf of myself.

   The jury is prejudiced against me all right and you know it because of those threatening letters. You know it, those so-called jive threatening letters, and you know it's a lie. Now how can that jury give me a a fair trial?

THE COURT   Mr. Marshal will you go to that man and ask him to be quiet?

SEALE   You know, the black man tries to get a fair trial in this country. The United States Government, huh. Nixon and the rest of them.

   Go ahead and continue. I'll watch and get railroaded.

THE COURT   Gentlemen, I want to say just one word and my remarks are addressed particularly to Mr. Seale.

   Several times during this trial he has disobeyed the injunction of the Court not to stand and talk out. I feel that in fairness to him, I should admonish him and his lawyers as well, to the extent that they have any influence over him, that there is competent authority for dealing with a defendant who persists in talking out against the order of the Court and I want Mr. Seale to know that. I am sure the lawyers know it. I do this only in the interest of the other defendants. . .

October 22, 1969

KUNSTLER   . . . Mr. Seale informed me again on or about October 16th of this year that he was going to move before your Honor for permission to represent himself, and reiterated to me that he had discharged me and all other attorneys except Mr. Garry representing him, and that I should take no further action with reference to him and that I should withdraw formally. Accordingly, I am doing so through this

motion which I have filed with your Honor yesterday, and a copy has been served upon the United States Attorney. . . .

THE GOVERNMENT   . . . [I]t is then subject to the sound discretion of the court as to whether or not this prior right prior to the beginning of the trial of a client to defend himself is overcome in the Court's discretion by the strong likelihood that the discharge of a lawyer in the midst of a trial would result in total destruction of court proceedings—total disruption of court proceedings to the prejudice of a fair trial.

   On that basis, your Honor, the Government asks the Court to deny the motion.

KUNSTLER   Your Honor—

SEALE   Can I speak on that and answer his argument?

THE COURT   No. This is not your motion, sir. Your motion has been decided.

   [*Following eviction of a spectator from the court room*]

SEALE   You are a pig for kicking him out.

SPECTATORS   Right on. Right on.

THE MARSHAL   This Honorable Court will now resume its session.

THE SPECTATORS   Oink oink.

October 23, 1969

THE COURT   Ladies and gentlemen of the jury, good morning.

SEALE   Good morning. I hope you don't blame me for anything.

THE COURT   Ladies and gentlemen of the jury, it is my obligation to tell you that the parties to a lawsuit have no right to address the jury, and Mr. Seale just made a remark to you that was entirely out of order. I direct you to disregard it. . . .

SCHULTZ   He held up the newspaper for them [the jury] to see and—

HOFFMAN   It ain't a newspaper. It is the Berkeley Tribe and doesn't tell lies, so it isn't a newspaper.

October 27, 1969

SEALE   What about my constitutional right to defend myself and have my lawyer?

THE COURT   Your constitutional rights—

SEALE   You are denying them. You have been denying them. Every other word you say is denied, denied, denied, denied, and you begin to oink in the faces of the masses of the people of this country. That is what you begin to represent, the corruption of this rotten government for four hundred years—

THE MARSHAL   Mr. Seale, will you sit down.

SEALE   Why don't you knock me in the mouth? Try that.

THE MARSHAL   Sit down.

THE COURT   Ladies and gentlemen of the jury, I regret that I will have to excuse you.

SEALE   I hope you don't blame me for anything and those false lying notes and letters that were sent that said the Black Panther Party threatened the jury, it's a lie, and you know it's a lie, and the Government did it to taint the jury against me.

SEALE   You got that? This racist administrative Government with its superman notions and comic book politics. We're hip to the fact that Superman never saved no black people. You got that?

FORAN   Mr. Weinglass just asked me—

THE COURT   You just let me do my job, and you do yours properly, and we'll get along, Mr. Fein—Weinglass.

KUNSTLER   Your Honor, I think it is Weinglass.

THE COURT   Weinglass. I corrected it. I got in ahead of you. I corrected it.

* * * * * * * * * * * * * * * * * * * *

HOFFMAN   May I talk to my lawyer? There are 25 marshals in here now. . . .

KUNSTLER   Your Honor, we are objecting to this armed camp aspect that is going on since the begining of this trial.

THE COURT   It is not an armed camp.

KUNSTLER   It is not right, and it's not good, and it's not called for.

SCHULTZ   If the Court please, before you came into this courtroom, if the Court please, Bobby Seale stood up and addressed this group.

SEALE   That's right, brother.

SCHULTZ   And Bobby Seale said if he is—

SCHULTZ   —that if he's attacked, they know what to do.

SEALE   I can speak on behalf of my constitutional rights, too.

SCHULTZ   He was talking to these people about an attack by them.

SEALE   You're lying. Dirty liar. I told them to defend themselves. You are a rotten racist pig, fascist liar, that's what you are. You're a rotten liar. You're a rotten liar. You are a fascist pig liar.

. . . I hope the record shows that tricky Dick Schultz, working for Richard Nixon and administration all understand that tricky Dick Schultz is a liar, and we have a right to defend ourselves, and if you attack me I will defend myself.

SPECTATORS   Right on.

SEALE   A physical attack by those damned marshals, that's what I said.

THE COURT   Let the record show the tone of Mr. Seale's voice was one shrieking and pounding on the table and shouting. That will be dealt with appropriately at sometime in the future.

KUNSTLER   Your Honor, the record should indicate that Mr. Schultz shouted . . .

THE COURT   [I]f what he said was the truth, I can't blame him for raising his voice.

THE COURT   The last statement was made by the Defendant Abbie Hoffman.

HOFFMAN   I don't use that last name any more.

THE COURT   If you speak once again while the jury is in the box and I have to send them out, we will take such steps as are indicated in the circumstances.
Bring in the jury, Mr. Marshal.

SEALE   Good morning, ladies and gentlemen of the jury.

SEALE You have George Washington and Benjamin Franklin sitting in a picture behind you, and they were slave owners. That's what they were. They owned slaves. You are acting in the same manner, denying me my constitutional rights . . .

FORAN [N]ever have I been in a courtroom—again, for twenty years and for many years daily in courtrooms all over this state and in many instances all over the United States—have I seen the type of conduct that is not only constantly going on in this courtroom, with noise, with giggling, with laughter, with movement, with refusal to stand when the Court gets on the bench, with comments being made by defendants to a jury, with outbursts in front of the jury, with participation in this conduct not only by the defendants but by many of the spectators.

THE COURT Well, I have been called a racist, a fascist—he has pointed to the picture of George Washington behind me and called him a slave owner and —

SEALE They were slave owners. Look at history.

THE COURT As though I had anything to do with that.

SEALE They were slave owners. You got them up there.

THE COURT He has been known as the father of this country, and I would think that it is a pretty good picture to have in the United States District Court.

KUNSTLER We all share a common guilt, your Honor.

THE COURT I didn't think I would ever live to sit on a bench or be in a courtroom where George Washington was assailed by a defendant in a criminal case and a judge was criticized for having his portrait on the wall.

THE COURT I will not hear you now. I am asking you to be silent.

SEALE I want to know, will you—Oh, look—it's a form of racism, racism is what stopped my argument.

THE COURT Mr. Seale, do you want to stop or do you want me to direct the Marshal—

SEALE I want to argue the point about this so you can get an understanding of the fact that I have a right to defend myself.

THE COURT We will take a recess.
Take that defendant into the room in there and deal with him as he should be dealt with in this circumstance.

BOBBY SEALE I wasn't shackled because I called you a pig and a fascist, which I still think you are, a pig, and a fascist, and a racist, but I was denied my constitutional rights. When a man is denied his constitutional rights in the manner that you did, you will still be considered a pig, and a fascist, and a racist by me. You still denied me my constitutional rights.

Take that defendant into the room in there and deal with him as he should be dealt with in this circumstance.

Abbie's children visit in court and sketch the judge

By Bob Greene

The boy named Andrew ran up to his father, who was sitting in a big leather chair, said, "Daddy, someone said you're coming... is in Boston. When are you going to on?"

... is Abbie Hoff... for conspiring to ... National

scribbled away on a piece of paper. He was drawing what he saw going on. Amy, dressed in a blanket-type dress and red tights and wearing a Yippie button, drew a picture of U.S. District Court Judge Julius J. Hoffman on a file card.

The picture showed the judge saying "No." Perhaps Amy got that idea from what she saw during the afternoon session. Bobby Seale, the chairman of the Black Panther ... had filed a ... on his own,

Andrew even said that he thought the judge seemed like a pretty nice guy.

"He's already been in two fights at school about this thing," Abbie Hoffman said. "You know, about me being his father and all."

The children walked over to where the reporters sit, and Andrew asked a newspaperman if he thought the Boston papers would run a ... about the trial written by an 8-year...

... he marshals walked over ... as going to start again ... d have to go back to

age American father.

As Abbie Hoffman said last week wh... told someone his children were co... trial, "How am I going to expla... daughter? I'm only 4 myself."

The children ... to catch, so... out, a

Bobby Seale denounces Judge Hoffman as "racist" after request to conduct own trial is denied, Page 18.

In court to visit her father, Abbie, Amy Hoffman, 6, drew her version of Judge Hoffman.

And this is the way he was dealt with.

CHICAGO. October 29, 1969.
Bobby Seale, age 32, and black.

Ben Shahn
This Is Nazi Brutality
1943, Offset Lithograph
The Museum of Modern Art, New York
Gift of the Office of War Information

28

The man who ordered it. Julius Jennings Hoffman, age 74, white.
It was his retaliation for being called a racist pig.
But for the trial, this man would never have had the occasion to meet Bobby Seale.
Bobby's presence and what he stood for were sufficient to threaten the judge's very
existence. Scared like a little boy, Hoffman panicked, and like a tyrant, he made
Seale pay for exposing his own insecurity in public.

KUNSTLER I wanted to say the record should indicate that Mr. Seale is seated on a metal chair, each hand is handcuffed to the leg of the chair on both the right and left sides so he cannot raise his hands, and a gag is tightly pressed into his mouth and tied at the rear, and that when he attempts to speak, a muffled sound comes out as he has done several times since he has been bound and gagged.

KUNSTLER Your Honor, are we going to stop this medieval torture that is going on this courtroom? I think this is a disgrace. This is no longer a court of order, your Honor, this is a medieval torture chamber. It is a disgrace. They are assaulting the other defendants also.

RUBIN Don't hit me in my balls, motherfucker.

SEALE This motherfucker is tight and it is stopping my blood.

KUNSTLER I just feel so utterly ashamed to be an American lawyer at this time.

THE COURT You should be ashamed of your conduct in this case, sir.

KUNSTLER What conduct, when a client is treated in this manner?

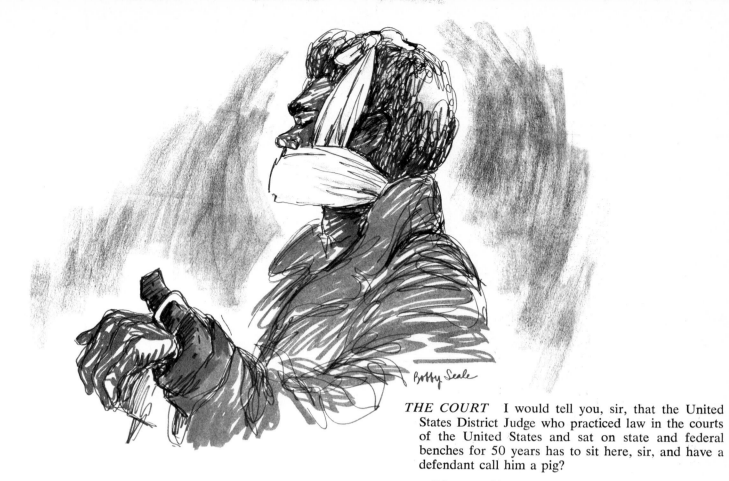

THE COURT I would tell you, sir, that the United States District Judge who practiced law in the courts of the United States and sat on state and federal benches for 50 years has to sit here, sir, and have a defendant call him a pig?

Listen to him now.

KUNSTLER Your Honor, we cannot hear him because of the binding and gag on him.

THE COURT You bring that to the Judicial Conference or wherever you want to bring it.

WEINGLASS I would be remiss in my duty to my client if I stood in this courtroom with fifteen marshals standing at the door, one man gagged and bound, the marshals striking at him and not asking the Court the simple question or not asking the jury if they could continue to deliberate in this trial. I see nothing improper with that. . . .

If my motion is now well founded in the law Mr. Foran can come to this lectern and cite case law. All he does is launch out on a personal attack and you have permitted it. Not only have you permitted it, you have added to it your own intimidation of me personally that I will be dealt with later.

THE COURT That wasn't intimidation, sir, that was—

WEINGLASS . I accepted that as intimidation.

THE COURT You are mistaken. This Court doesn't intimidate lawyers.

WEINGLASS What does your Honor intend—

THE COURT It cautions you not to repeat your conduct.

THE COURT I again caution you not to say—utter the kind of remark you have made here this morning.

WEINGLASS I would like to know what remark I have made that—

THE COURT I shall not answer your question, sir, because when I attempt to answer them you interrupt me.

WEINGLASS I give the Court my assurance that I will not.

THE COURT I wouldn't take your assurance because you have violated it on many occasions.

And, as Artie Seale of the Black Panther Party reported:

The chairman of the Black Panther Party was strapped and chained to a chair on the 24th floor of the Federal Building on October 31st, 1969 around 9:00 A.M. upon arriving from Cook County Jail. The incidents which follow all took place before 10:00 A.M. court time. Chairman Bobby Seale was told by the pig marshalls that they were going to put rags into his mouth to make sure that he wouldn't talk in court; and that this was going to be done whether he liked it or not. Bobby Seale protested such an act, and thus it was a struggle. He was trying to explain to the pig marshals that being strapped and chained as he was, and then to be gagged along with having surgical bandages around his face would cause him to run a high temperature. He also explained that he had tonsilitis and having to stay up 14 hours a day would make him very exhausted. At that point 2 marshals grabbed Bobby Seale's head and another one grabbed his nose attempting to stuff his mouth. He shut his mouth; and after a minute or so he began to lose his breath. He tried to jerk his head, and in process freed his head; but was quickly subdued by the marshals. One of the other marshals grabbed Bobby's head in one hand and his nose with the other. Another marshal pressed on Bobby's lips with the cloth until it began to hurt his teeth. Bobby held his mouth closed as tightly as possible. With his nose covered and his mouth covered he lost his breath again and surged backwards with all the weight he had. He jerked his head from side to side and finally he was able to free himself so that he could breathe. He was about to pass out!

32

At that point, the marshals decided because of his complaints about tonsilitis and his fever (which the Cook County doctors know about) to wrap his head up. These marshals wrapped Bobby's head up so tight that they saw Bobby choke. They saw Bobby lose his breath, and they saw him pass out. By this time it was near 10:00 A.M. and so the marshals rewrapped the surgical bandages, this time taking it away from the throat area, and putting it around his jaws, and around the back of his neck. The bandages were equally as tight as before. Bobby was brought into the court around 10:10 A.M. He became dizzy and almost passed out in court.

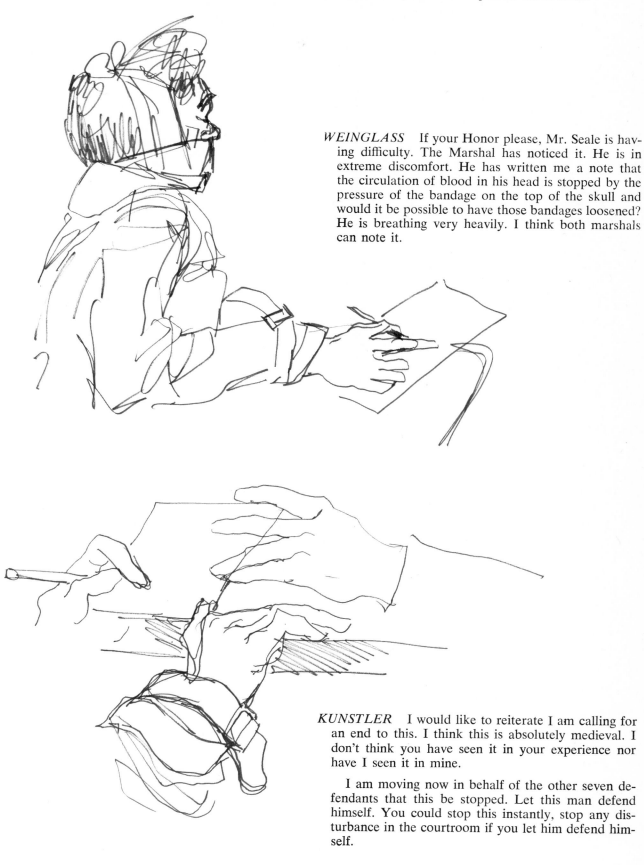

WEINGLASS If your Honor please, Mr. Seale is having difficulty. The Marshal has noticed it. He is in extreme discomfort. He has written me a note that the circulation of blood in his head is stopped by the pressure of the bandage on the top of the skull and would it be possible to have those bandages loosened? He is breathing very heavily. I think both marshals can note it.

KUNSTLER I would like to reiterate I am calling for an end to this. I think this is absolutely medieval. I don't think you have seen it in your experience nor have I seen it in mine.

I am moving now in behalf of the other seven defendants that this be stopped. Let this man defend himself. You could stop this instantly, stop any disturbance in the courtroom if you let him defend himself.

33

But at least one marshal would not let the strong insensitive hand of authority (wish one could have said the tender hand of justice) suffocate the defendant to death before scores of people just for the purpose of proving an irrelevant point. At least one marshal did not want a dead man on his conscience.

And like cracking popcorn while watching a boring Ronald Reagan western, Julius Hoffman's humor (or was it his undisguised contempt for the harmless defense Attorney Leonard Weinglass)—continued unperturbed.

THE COURT   What did you say?

SCHULTZ   The number was not disclosed.

THE COURT   . . . What is the number, Mr. Wein-stein—Weinramer—Weinberg—

WEINGLASS   Weinglass, your Honor.

THE COURT   All right. Then tell him who you are.

KUNSTLER   I am trying to find out if he knows.

THE COURT   That wastes time. He is Charles Kun-stler, the lawyer.

KUNSTLER   Your Honor, William Kunstler.

THE COURT   Oh, is it William?

KUNSTLER   Charles is the French author.

KUNSTLER If I were any kind of a lawyer I would protest against what is being done in this courtroom and I am so protesting . . .

THE COURT He is being treated in accordance with the law.

KUNSTLER Not the Constitution of the United States, your Honor, which is the supreme law. He has a right to defend himself.

THE COURT I don't need someone to come here from New York or wherever you come from to tell me that there is a Constitution in the United States.

KUNSTLER I feel someone needs to tell someone, your Honor. It is not being observed in this Court, if that is the treatment a man gets for wanting to defend himself.

THE COURT Read the books. You will find that the Court has the authority to do what is being done and I will not let this trial be broken up by his conduct.

THE COURT Why should I have to go through a trial and be assailed in an obscene manner.

KUNSTLER But, your Honor, that is a reaction of a black man not being permitted to defend himself. If you had said to him, "Defend yourself," none of this would have happened.

THE COURT I have had black lawyers in this courtroom who tried cases with dignity and with ability. His color has nothing to do with his conduct.

KUNSTLER But, your Honor, he feels—

THE COURT Not at all.

KUNSTLER He feels he is being denied a right which the Constitution gives him . . .

THE COURT If that is a motion, I deny the motion.

KUNSTLER Your Honor, before the jury comes in, the defendants would like to move to adjourn for the day until Monday so that we can have an opportunity to send the lawyers to California to consult with Mr. Garry, and we feel that we ought to do this both for humanitarian and for legal reasons . . .

. . . We feel as attorneys and so do the seven other defendants that it is impossible to continue as human beings with the trial of this case under the present circumstances; that it is impossible for essentially white men to sit in this room while a black man is in chains and continue—

THE COURT I wish you wouldn't talk about the distinction between white and black men in this courtroom.

KUNSTLER A lot of the seven white men—

THE COURT I lived a long time and you are the first person who has ever suggested that I have discriminated against a black man. Come to my chambers and I will show you on the wall what one of the great newspapers of the city said editorially about me in connection with [a] school segregation case.

KUNSTLER Your Honor, this is not a time for self-praise on either side of the lectern.

THE COURT It isn't self-praise, sir. It is defense. I won't let a lawyer stand before the bar and charge me with being a bigot.

KUNSTLER For God's sake your Honor, we are seeking a solution of a human problem here, not whether you feel good or bad or I feel good or bad.

THE COURT You can't solve a problem by vilifying people.

KUNSTLER I haven't vilified your Honor. I have asked for a day's adjournment so we can solve a problem that must affect every sensitive human being.

THE COURT That is one thing—

KUNSTLER —in the United States.

THE COURT Please don't raise your voice to me. I don't like that.

But as it turned out it was only a brief respite. Apparently, calling Julius Hoffman a racist pig was like throwing a Molotov cocktail at the backyard of a North Shore estate only to expose the neighbours having a Sunday barbecue in the nude. Such godfearing excessively wealthy good citizens, perfect disciples of law and order, could kill out of the embarrassment of being thus indecently exposed. This on-target offensive obviously hit a very soft spot and shook the poor man. If Julius Hoffman had been more exposed to the dynamics of contemporary American social rhetoric, he would have realized that Bobby Seale could not have spent one second to think of him. Bobby, and any of the other defendants for that matter, would have said it of any judge occupying the Bench. Julius Hoffman was rather conceited and presumptuous in believing that Bobby Seale would take the time to coin a name just for him. Hundreds of policemen throughout the country have been called racist pigs, just as millions of black people have been called nigger, including Foran. If these people were to react with a fraction of the intensity with which Julius Hoffman did, this country would have been reduced to a state that even the people of Sodom and Gomorrah would have called pitiful.

And so on November 3rd, Julius Hoffman as the plaintiff and the judge announced his punishment of a defenseless man to his court.

THE COURT   When the time comes when a federal judge is called a pig in open court before a hundred people, and publicized throughout the country and the Court can't do anything about it—and the contumacious conduct continues, courts whose judgement I must respect have held that this is a proper method of restraint. Now, it is the only time in my many years both in the practice of law and on the bench that I have seen anything like that happen, but it is the first time I have been called a pig.

KUNSTLER   Your Honor, I don't think that is really the issue, but we have argued it so many times.

THE COURT   Oh, of course not. I think that is just very pleasant for a judge to sit up here and be called a fascist, racist—I couldn't begin to recite all of the things that this man has said.

* *

(On November 3, Weinglass read a letter from Charles Garry, attorney for Defendant Seale. Mr. Garry had been unable to attend the trial because of illness. This is part of what the letter said:)

"The crisis in this trial has been precipitated by the gross violation by the Government and the trial judge of the fundamental constitutional rights of Mr. Bobby Seale, a black American citizen and national chairman of the Black Panther Party.

Mr. Seale's fundamental American constitutional right to counsel of his own choice was violated by the refusal of the Government and the trial judge to agree to adjourn the commencement of this trial until the seriously ill counsel of his own choice, the undersigned, Charles R. Garry, could attend. . . .

"Once the trial has started, Mr. Seale's fundamental American constitutional right to defend himself, which he demanded be afforded to him and was unlawfully and without any cause in law denied to him by the Government and the trial judge and in flagrant violation of the Constitution the Government and trial judge proceeded with the trial. . . .

"Meanwhile Mr. Seale must be immediately accorded by the Government and the trial judge his constitutional and statutory right to defend himself. He must be released forthwith from all physical bonds, gags and shackles. He must be released from all restraints upon his liberty so that he may defend himself and receive full and adequate apologies and compensation by the Government for the brutal, cruel, unusual and unconstitutional punishment inflicted upon him during the past two weeks of this trial. . . .

"[E]ven if I were physically and medically able to take part in a major trial, which I am not according to my physicians, my participation could in no way cure the fundamental constitutional infirmity with which it is already plagued. Accordingly, participation by me in this trial long after it is started would violate my basic professional responsibilities and might well be deemed malpractice."

36

November 4, 1969

SEALE . . . I don't know all of these formalities that the lawyers know in the courtroom. I could easily learn it if you would coach me and allow me to defend myself and cross-examine the witnesses and ask pertinent questions that directly relate to these charges against me because I am very well aware of those charges.

SEALE I wasn't shackled because I called you a pig and a fascist, which I still think you are, a pig, and a fascist, and a racist, but I was denied my constitutional rights. When a man is denied his constitutional rights—

THE COURT Will you sit down, please.

SEALE —in the manner that you did—

THE COURT Mr. Marshal, have that man sit down.

SEALE —you will still be considered a pig, and a fascist, and a racist by me. You still denied me my constitutional rights.

THE COURT Miss Reporter, did you get Mr. Seale's remarks?

KUNSTLER Your Honor, before you bring in the jury, I want to stand with Mr. Weinglass on this. I have heard now this remark "phony" and "two-

* * * * * * * * * * *

November 5, 1969

THE COURT Mr. Kunstler, do you have any cross-examination of this witness?

KUNSTLER Just one moment, your Honor.
Your Honor, since this witness only related facts relevant to Mr. Seale who has, as your Honor knows, discharged me, I have no questions.

SEALE Well, I think I have a right to cross-examine.

THE COURT No, you have no right in the circumstances of this case.

SEALE Why did you follow me, could you please tell me, Mr. Witness—

THE COURT Mr. Seale—

SEALE —at the airport?

THE COURT Mr. Seale, I ask you to sit down.

SEALE Have you ever killed a Black Panther Party member?

THE COURT Mr. Seale, I will have to ask you to sit down, please.

SEALE Have you ever been on any raids in the Black Panther Party's offices or Black Panther Party members' homes?

THE COURT Mr. Seale, this is the third time I am asking you to sit down as courteously as possible.

THE COURT We are going to recess now, young man. If you keep this up—

SEALE Look, old man, if you keep up denying me my constitutional rights, you are being exposed to the public and the world that you do not care about people's constitutional rights to defend themselves.

faced." It has been directed to my co-counsel. I can join him in asking your Honor, and I think you have an obligation to do something about that. I just can't understand how it can go on ad infinitum here without a word coming from you from that bench. I just— you know it is not right; to call a man phony and two-faced in oral argument is not right. We both know that. You don't say anything and you are countenancing the remark.

THE COURT For your information, maybe you don't know it, the word "phony" is in the dictionary.

KUNSTLER So is the word "pig," your Honor.

KUNSTLER I am moving, your Honor—

* * *

THE COURT I deny your motion.

KUNSTLER Thank you.

SCHULTZ May the record show that the Defendant Seale has been identified by the witness.

THE COURT The record may so indicate.

SEALE And may the record show that I am a black man, too, being railroaded.

* * * * * * * * *

THE COURT [I]t is therefore ordered that pursuant to the authority vested in the Court by Rule 42(a) of the Federal Rules of Criminal Procedure and by Title 18, United States Code, Section 401, the Defendant Bobby Seale be punished for contempt.

THE COURT Mr. Seale, you have a right to speak now. I will hear you.

SEALE For myself?

THE COURT In your own behalf, yes.

SEALE How come I couldn't speak before?

THE COURT This is a special occasion.

SEALE Wait a minute. Now you are going to try to— you were going to attempt to punish me for attempting to speak for myself before? Now after you punish me, you sit up and say something about you can speak? What kind of jive is that? I don't understand it. What kind of court is this? Is this a court? It must be a fascist operation like I see it in my mind, you know,— I don't understand you.

THE COURT You may speak to the matters I have discussed here today, matters dealing with your contemptuous conduct. The law obligates me to call on you to speak at this time.
I have tried to make it clear.

SEALE All you make clear to me is that you don't want me, you refuse to let me, you will not go by my persuasion, or my arguments, my motions, my requests to be, to the extent of even having to shout loud enough to get on that record for that record so that they can hear me half the time. You don't want to listen to me. You don't want to let a man stand up, contend to you that the man is not my lawyer, show you and point out to you that fact, in fact, I made motions and told you that I fired the man.

SEALE   If a black man stands up and speaks, If a black man asks for his rights, if a black man demands his rights, if a black man requests and argues his rights, what do you do? You're talking about punishing. If a black man gets up and speaks in behalf of the world—

THE COURT   Are you addressing me, sir?

SEALE   I'm talking. You can see I'm talking.

THE COURT   That's right, but if you address me, you'll have to stand.

SEALE   Stand? Stand now. Now let's see, first you said that I couldn't stand. I got my suit. It's going to a higher court, possibly the highest court in America.

* * * * * * * * * * * * * * * * * * *

THE COURT   I find that the acts, statements and conduct of the Defendant Bobby Seale constituted a deliberate and willful attack upon the administration of justice, an attempt to sabotage the functioning of the federal judiciary system, and misconduct of so grave a character as to make the mere imposition of a fine a futile gesture and a wholly insignificant punishment. Accordingly, I adjudge Bobby G. Seale guilty of each and every specification referred to in my oral observations, and the Court will impose—strike that—and the Defendant Seale will be committed to the custody of the Attorney General of the United States or his authorized representative for imprisonment for a term of three months on each and every specification, the sentences to run consecutively.

THE COURT   There will be an order in view of the disposition of this aspect of the case, there will be an order declaring a mistrial as to the Defendant Bobby G. Seale and not as to any other defendants.

SEALE   Wait a minute, I got a right—what's the cat trying to pull now? . . . I can't stay?

THE COURT   Now I will tell you this, that since it has been said here that all of the defendants support this man in what he is doing, I over the noon hour will reflect on whether they are good risks for bail and I shall give serious consideration to the termination of their bail if you can't control your clients, and you couldn't yesterday afternoon.

SEALE   I am not—I am not a defendant—he is not my lawyer. I want my right to defend myself. I want my right to defend myself.

KUNSTLER   Your Honor, they said this morning they supported fully his right to defend himself or have his lawyer of choice, and if that is the price of their bail, then I guess that will have to be the price of their bail.

And so Bobby Seale was sequestered and slammed in jail for four years on multiple contempt charges and led away to a cell. This cell must by now have become what the world looks like to a man condemned to perpetual imprisonment for having a courage and superior humanity that would not be silenced or destroyed by any degree of conceivable oppression. Such great men will continue to be a threat to any system that still has a remnant of conscience. This makes the possession of power a weakness and the disadvantage of it an embarrassment and a humiliation.

With Bobby Seale out of the way the only serious threat to the conscience and sanity of Judge Hoffman had been removed but the ghost of confrontation was to haunt him throughout the trial and probably for the rest of his life. Like a repentant husband caught redhanded in the act of unconsecrated adultery, Hoffman was to reassure every black witness that showed up that he was not a racist. At childhood we all have nightmares which include monsters. For Julius Hoffman his monster must have been a "pig". It seemed as if even his life itself was in great danger if he were called "pig" one more time. As if to prevent that, Bobby Seale was put out of the way. Little did he know that blacks did not have a monopoly of the expression. Little did he know that the white defendants would call him a fascist, racist pig. But that was in the future and Hoffman seemed to believe that sufficient unto the day was the best of all evils.

McTernan, assistant to Charles Gary, Bobby Seale's San Francisco lawyer and one of the few white Americans who have earned the right to be called by black men, "brother", tried to intercede.

McTERNAN Here is a layman, not trained as a lawyer, asking for what he considered his right to defend himself and discharge lawyers of record because the lawyer of his choice was not here. . . .

THE COURT You can disagree with the judge, laymen or lawyers—

McTERNAN A layman is not a lawyer.

THE COURT —but you don't call him a pig and a fascist in the process of disagreeing with him.

McTERNAN What I wanted to get to is this: You keep referring back to how contemptuous the conduct was and I am trying to say to your Honor, and I would like to develop the argument because I didn't get it all out, that we were dealing first with a layman and not a lawyer. Secondly, we were dealing with a black man who comes out of a black ghetto.

THE COURT Oh, I don't want to hear another thing about a black man. The only person who mentioned black men in this Court for the first time was your client.

JULIUS HOFFMAN You don't know me, sir, but I am as good a friend of the black people in this community as they have, and if you don't believe it, read the books.

True. That is why most black people say, "We ain't got no friends at all".

40

THE COURT   You are the one that brings up this black man thing again. I am weary of hearing about it because he has been discriminated against.

McTERNAN   I am not suggesting, your Honor, in this phase of my argument, that he was discriminated against.

THE COURT   Then why mention color?

McTERNAN   Because it has to do with the words he used, your Honor. It has to do with the culture from which he comes and the meaning ascribed to words. That is what I want to address myself to.

THE COURT   I have known literally thousands of what we used to call Negro people, and who are now referred to as black people, and I never heard that kind of language emanate from the lips of any one of them. I have had fine Negro lawyers stand at that lectern and at the lectern across in the old courthouse, and I never heard a lawyer, a Negro lawyer, use that kind of language, or any Negro defendant in a criminal case. I never did.

There is no evidence here in this case that it is part of a culture.

McTERNAN   Your Honor, that is precisely the point I am getting to. Of course there is no evidence here, but there should be. There should be before a man is sentenced to four years in jail for contempt for use of language. . . .

41

And the prosecution of the defendants continued—with what the Press now comfortably called the Chicago 7, almost as if it, too, like Julius Hoffman, was glad to forget that Bobby Seale was an integral part of the defense.

For the now Chicago 7, the period of the prosecution testimony was time out to catch up with correspondence, do some readings, check the court audience out or keep the nails clean as any good boy should.

BARBARA CALLENDER, policewoman

KUNSTLER   What drew your attention first to the man you say is Jerry Rubin, which is a half hour before he spoke, as I understand it?

CALLENDER   To be quite frank, I found him to be a very obnoxious man and—and this drew my attention to him and I just started to follow him.

KUNSTLER   Is your attention often drawn to obnoxious men?

*   *   *

KUNSTLER   Can you describe what Mr. Hayden looked like then?

CALLENDER   Yes. His hair was fairly close to regular length. He has kind of a pocked face. I don't remember any mustache or anything. Kind of beady eyes.

KUNSTLER   Beady eyes?

CALLENDER   Yes.

KUNSTLER   You don't like these defendants, do you, at all?

Even "friends" of the defendants who turned out to be undercover agents:

IRWIN BOCK

HOFFMAN I have a bladder problem.
(laughter)

THE COURT I suggest to the defendants that they refrain from loud laughter. This is a trial in the United States District Court, not a circus.

* * *

THE COURT This is a trial in the United States District Court: It is not a vaudeville theater.

KUNSTLER But, your Honor, we are human beings, too, and when remarks are made from the witness stand which evoke laughter, I don't think it can be helped. You can't make automatons out of us or robots; we are human beings and we laugh occasionally, and if it comes irrepressibly, I don't really see how that really becomes a court matter.

SCHULTZ Mr. Kunstler is laughing so he can influence the jury with the impression that this is absurd. That is why he is laughing aloud. . . .

KUNSTLER [S]ometimes when the absurdity becomes too much, I laugh . . . but we are not doing it just out of some calculation so the jury sees us laugh. They are far too intelligent to be misled by an occasional—

THE COURT I think they are, too.

KUNSTLER Mr. Schultz is implying they are not.

THE COURT I agree with you.

FIRST DAY

For the Defendants it was a painful shock and letdown.

DELLINGER I am very disappointed to see you here.

HOFFMAN And we all talked so much. We accepted him too easily.

SPECTATOR You blew your cover in New York, Bock.

RUBIN . . . I did not walk out on the trial. That is absolutely wrong. I like being here. It is interesting. I didn't intend to walk out. I have been here every day at 10:00 and 2:00 and stayed here to the end.

THE COURT That is the best—

RUBIN Let me finish.

THE COURT That is the best statement I have heard here during the trial. You said you enjoyed being here.

RUBIN It is good theater, your Honor.

45

THE COURT   Mr. Kunstler, there is a great architect, Mies van der Rohe, who lately left us. He designed that lectern as well as this building and it was a lectern, not a leaning post. I have asked you to stand behind it when you question the witness.

KUNSTLER   Your Honor, I think the U.S. Attorney questions from this table here—

THE COURT   I don't permit lawyers to lean on that thing. I don't want you to do it. I have asked you before. That was put there by the Government, designed by Mr. van de Rohe, and I want you to use it for that purpose.

KUNSTLER   Your Honor, the U.S. Attorney questions from the back of this table and leans on his material.

THE COURT   I don't care about that.

KUNSTLER   Why am I different?

THE COURT   I haven't seen the United States Attorney put his elbow on that thing and lean on it as though it was a leaning post and I wouldn't permit them to do it or you.

KUNSTLER   Perhaps I am tired, your Honor. What is wrong about leaning on it?

THE COURT   If you are tired then let Mr.—

KUNSTLER   Weinglass.

THE COURT   —Weinglass take over.
    Maybe I am tired, but I am sitting up here—

KUNSTLER   You are sitting in a comfortable chair.

THE COURT   I sit in the place where I should sit.

KUNSTLER   While I am standing up.

THE COURT   I will not permit you to lean on that.

KUNSTLER   May I place my hands like this, your Honor?

THE COURT   Yes. Yes. That is not leaning.
    Since you are tired, we will take a recess and you can go to sleep for the afternoon.

SCHULTZ   . . . Would you relate, please, Mr. Bock, what was stated at that meeting?

BOCK   . . . Tom Hayden said that "If the City doesn't give in to our demands, there would be war in the streets and there should be." . . .

BOCK   . . . Weiner said, "A good mobile tactic would be to pick a target in the Loop area and bomb that target." He said, "Such a diversionary tactic as bombing the fence across the street from the federal building, the high wooden fence, would burn very easily, and that this would draw police away from the demonstrators in the loop." . . .

    . . . Weiner then asked me if I could obtain the bottles necessary to make the Molotov cocktails. . . .

DAVIS   Why don't you arrest this lying police spy. He has filed an affidavit.

FORAN   I would like to have those remarks on the record, Miss Reporter.

KUNSTLER   I suggest to you, Miss Reporter, that no one has the authority to ask you to put those comments in the record.

DELLINGER   And that District Attorney who is teaching him to lie.

FORAN   Take that also, Miss Reporter.

DELLINGER   That is a fine way to get to be Senator.

By the end of the fourth day of questioning, Irwin Bock's disintegration was total. Perhaps to use friendship as a cover for spying was not that noble after all. Even as late as 1969 there must still be some human value in trust—if only purely sentimental. The pain and disappointment of those who took him for a close friend must have become obvious to him.

FOURTH DAY—the disintegration of an undercover agent.

And so must have become Abbie Hoffman's boredom with the entire goings-on.

47

KUNSTLER   On the tape during this speech particularly after the word "garbage" which appears on page 16, and after the references to Nixon, Humphrey and Wallace, which also appears on 16, there appears to be an animal sound on the tape. Was that a pig's oink?

SCHALLER   Yes.

KUNSTLER   And the pig oinked twice?

SCHALLER   I couldn't say if he did or not, sir.

KUNSTLER   You saw nothing subversive in that, did you?

SCHULTZ   Objection.

THE COURT   I have to rule, so I will sustain the objection.

KUNSTLER   Your Honor, the word "oink" has been used several times as implying something subversive.

THE COURT   Yes, I know it has been used several times; so has the word "pig."

JAMES ROCHFORD, Deputy Superintendent, Chicago Police Department

FORAN   May the record show the comment? Did you get that comment?

DELLINGER   He was speaking to his lawyer.

KUNSTLER   Your Honor, Mr. Foran I don't think even heard it, but Mr. Schultz whispered in his ear and then we have this little schoolhouse episode going on of reporting to your Honor what the bad boys are doing.

WEINER   Bill, the executioner is mumbling and I can't hear him.

KUNSTLER   Your Honor, is it possible to tell the witness to keep his voice up?

THE COURT   I think it is possible. I have demonstrated that because I have asked him two or three times already.

Although it would have taken a hopeless optimist to believe that the government, in pressing this trial, was merely carrying out its dispassionate duty of protecting the public interest, the sudden armed invasion of the Chicago Black Panther Party headquarters and the coldblooded assassination of Fred Hampton and Mark Clark could hardly be expected to reassure Bobby Seale and others that their appearance in Federal Court was anything but an unnecessary window dressing. These men are not exactly friends of the White House or pals of John Mitchell and J. Edgar Hoover. Even a United States Attorney, Cecil L. Poole, has said that there is a deliberate government conspiracy to wipe out members of the Black Panther Party. It is difficult to believe the absurd charge that a handful of Black Americans committed to self-defense in response to indisputable, incessant police brutality could be a serious threat to the world's most powerful nation. It is true that they carry guns for self-protection. But how many million white Americans carry guns for self-protection?

CHICAGO SUN-TIMES, Fri., Dec. 12, 1969

Hanrahan's photo of 'bullet holes' is nailed as mistake

Diagram of Hampton apartment at 2337 W. Monroe shows directions in which some shots were fired. Under one of the pictures the state's attorney released to Chicago Tribune Wednesday the caption identified it as inside of bathroom door through which a hall of lead was fired "from opposite bedroom." Actually the door pictured was in the front bedroom (circle) and because it was open it was riddled by bullets police fired through living room walls. (Diagram by Jack Ryan)

Bullet holes in north wall of Fred Hampton's bedroom were made by shots fired from the direction of the front bedroom. Ballistic rods show paths of bullets. State's attorney's police made no mention of firing from one bedroom to the other. (Sun-Times Photos by Bob Kotalik)

Tour of Hampton flat reveals errors

Continued from Page 1

descriptive material?"

"No," he responded, "We are not editors." Hanrahan would neither confirm nor deny that the marks were nail heads.

Richard Jalovec, chief of Hanrahan's special prosecutions unit, said after the press conference, however, that they were nails and ... asked the Tribune to ...

newspaper was faced with the decision whether to ignore a story of national significance — it was the first time police had given a full account of what they said happened during the raid—and the pictures used to support the story, or to reprint them. Attempts to reach Hanrahan failed and it was decided to reprint the kitchen door picture.

The tour by Sun - Times newsmen Thursday morning turned up the other discrepancy with regard to the pictures published by Tribune.

One of the four was said to be the bathroom door but ... head ...

The other two pictures were of a fr... showing a large hole said to have b... by a Panther shotgun blast. The ... door with the hole had been remo... apartment.

Asked if one of the ... a bathroom doo... was a pictur... bathro...

One does not need to be sympathetic to the Black Panther Party to feel revulsion at what common sense alone tells us does not make sense. It is indefensible when the police and the FBI reverse their role from the protection of *all* citizens, to the assassination of speciously defined dissidents. The very thought of protection from the police makes nonsense of any talk of law and order, or of justice.

And thinking about justice, one is reminded of a statement Dick Gregory once made at the University of Alabama; and I paraphrase:

"Richard Nixon says Clement Haynsworth is one of the most honest men he has ever known, and I agree with him." And no one asked the President how he could make such an evaluation when he had boasted that he had never met Mr. Haynsworth prior to his nominating him to the Supreme Court.

These and other similar thoughts ran through one's mind as one painfully observed the rallies outside the courthouse and read the simplistic and warped judgements passed on them by the police, and public officials.

FORAN Your Honor. I object to that, and I ask Mr. Kunstler to refrain from playing to his gallery.

KUNSTLER Your Honor, I think he said he took a serious offer, and he said Abbie Hoffman might have said Spiro Agnew offered him $200,000 to come to Chicago, and I asked whether he contacted Spiro Agnew.

THE COURT I would ask that you don't waste our time. I sustain the objection, sir.

ALBERT BAUGHER, Dept. of Human Resources, Chicago

KUNSTLER Now, you indicated that it was sometime around this time, that you met Lee Weiner, is that correct?

BAUGHER Yes, sir.

KUNSTLER And about what time was that?

BAUGHER Four o'clock, five o'clock.

KUNSTLER I think you describe the conversation something like this.
You said you said, "Hi," right?

BAUGHER Something to that effect, "Hello."

KUNSTLER Mr. Rubin then said, "Fascist pig"?

BAUGHER Yes, sir.

KUNSTLER Did he say "Hi" first?

BAUGHER No, sir.

KUNSTLER And then I think you resorted to a classic American expression, "Shove it."

BAUGHER I believe so, sir, yes.

PROSECUTING ATTORNEY What was the conversation?

BAUGHER Mr. Hoffman approached me, and we talked generally for a while. He gave me a copy of a booklet which he had printed in New York called "Fuck the System," which he said he was giving me free. He said that the city of New York had paid for it through an OEO grant that they had received from the city.

He then suggested that Chicago would be wise to cooperate, that they had first run into trouble in New York. I think he mentioned the Grand Central Station incident in March and said that since that time the city had been very cooperative and there had been no trouble, and they've gotten this money just to keep things cool.

PROSECUTING ATTORNEY Did he give any explanation of how they got the money or for what purpose?

BAUGHER He said that they had applied for a grant for venereal disease clinic, to the best of my recollection, and that they had used the money to print the booklet which had a small part on venereal disease, operate a free store, and use the money whichever way they saw fit.

THE COURT Have you gotten that—what is the name of that defendant speaking?

HOFFMAN Just Abbie. I don't have a last name, Judge, I lost it.

THE COURT   You may think these are schoolhouse episodes—

KUNSTLER   They are, your Honor, they are what we used to call tattletales.

THE COURT   If they are, you are going to be disillusioned.

The trial might as well have ended here. The message was clear. But perhaps Kunstler, Weinglass, the defendants and the rest of the nation needed the denouement of the two months that were to follow to realize the significant tragedy that this frank and gentle prophesy foreshadowed. In the weeks that followed, Abbie's antics were to turn into gestures of matyrdom. Kunstler was to talk about the cruelty of jails rather than the place of laughter in the courtroom; and for many it was to be the first time the significance of what happened to Bobby Seale struck a frightening chord.

Meanwhile, forces gathered in the streets for the first episode in the tragic melodrama of street democracy.

First, the police, in a fashion that would have been more befitting of Night Riders, held up the Black Panther Party headquarters in Chicago and shot and killed Fred Hampton and Mark Clark in cold blood.

There is a joke that many foreign visitors to Chicago still expect to find trigger-happy gangsters. It is a funny story— and a true story. Somehow, these gangsters have taken on a less colorful title, "policemen".

In the short-lived public uproar, Eastern liberals like Arthur Goldberg were to form a peoples' Tribunal to investigate the obviously government-enticed assassination and, more significantly, the Reverend Ralph Abernathy, a pacifist, was to stand over Fred Hampton's dead body eulogizing a slain so-called extremist.

In America, a day or two of concern is the most that any significant event can expect from the people. The society, it seems, has become too busy to spend time on important things.

The nation's blacks and sensitive whites called hopelessly for a meaningful investigation of an obvious plot to exterminate a section of society with which the government has been incapable of coming to terms. But their calls seemed like voices in the wilderness. And as for the deaf mute government that has thrown its lot with a nondescript mirage called "the silent majority"—what a travesty on the logic of the English language!—the only response was a foolhardy neon-sign obscenity, "LAW AND ORDER".

As if to make sure that the expressive minority got the point that Spiro T. Agnew in one giant step had abolished legitimacy of public opinion, the police hit the Black Panther Party again—this time in Los Angeles.

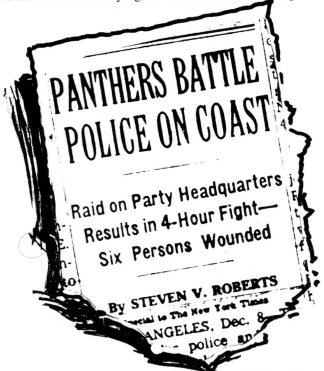

PANTHERS BATTLE POLICE ON COAST

Raid on Party Headquarters Results in 4-Hour Fight— Six Persons Wounded

By STEVEN V. ROBERTS
Special to The New York Times

ANGELES, Dec. 8
police an

And for the shock-proof silent majority, the old formula remained supreme: if it is done by the authorities, it must be justified.

Democracy—the rule of the most—began to resemble the law of the ignorant.

Abbie: *The system considers the streets to be contagious—so all of middle-class America is indoors somewhere in the closet.*

BARNACKE

THE NEW YORK TIMES, FRIDAY, APRIL 10, 1970

CONFLICTING DESCRIPTIONS: Photo above, released by | tian sources. Photographs at right were released in Tel
Egypt, is said to show a school bombed on Wednesday | Aviv. Taken before and during the raid, they are said
by Israeli planes. Thirty children died, assert the Egyp- | to show not a school but a military installation.

Israeli Planes Attack Near Area in Egypt Where 30 Pupils Were

Special to The New York Times
JERUSALEM, April 9—Israeli
bombers returned to the Suez
Canal region tonight, a day
after a raid there that the Egyptians said had killed 30 school-
children.

An army spokesman said the
raid was at 7:30 P.M. and an
hour in the "cen-
tral sectors of the

general area of
among whose
were said by
country in-
children

United States-made Phantoms
dropped five bombs and fired
two rockets at an elementary
school in the village of Bahr el
Bakar, near the Suez Canal.

When the bombs struck

of cynical indifference to the
killing of 30 Egyptian school-
children yesterday by Israeli
fighter-bombers.

The denunciation, made in
the form of a commentary by
the Government's Middle East
News Agency, was in reaction
to a statement by the State
Department calling the deaths
"deplorable and saddening" but
adding that they were "a consequence of the continuing disregard for the cease-fire."

The children were killed
when, according to the witnesses and official reports,

the one-story school, it was reported, burying 89 pupils, two
teachers and several school employes in rubble. An Egyptian
spokesman rejected Israeli con-
tentions that the school was in
a military camp.

"The school is surrounded by
open fields on all sides and
there are no military targets
anywhere near it," the semiof-
ficial newspaper Al Ahram said
today.

Foreign newsmen visited the
hospital at El Husseiniya yesterday, but were unable to go
to Bahr el Bakar, 10 to 15
miles to the east.

The attack on the State Department comment on the raid
as a consequence of the break-
down of the 1967 cease-fire
agreement came on the eve of
the arrival in Cairo

J. Sisco, Assistant Secret
State for Near Easter
South Asian Affairs, for
on the Arab-Israeli c
with President Gamal
Nasser and other Egypti
ficials.

The agreement by Ca
garded as an encouragi
velopment in the long ou
to work out a formula
settlement of the conflict.
ever, Cairo's attack o
State Department's atti
on the cease-fire
created a atmo:
mosphe.

ral Novel

Ten:
prepare to pacify guerr:

BEIRUT, Lebanon (AP) — Leb
political and military leaders
strategy Monday in preparation
Arab guerrillas about their
left some 30 dead and s

Tension eased in
cities but gunfire
City of Tri
guerrilla
orga

The
Arabia
southeast of
The firm carri
Oil Co.

President Ch
outgoing Prime Mini
commander in chief an
army, and his top poli
vance of Karami's ex
Cairo for talks with t
He will be accomp

A member of an Arab guerrilla unit, with heavily camouflaged uniform and
weapon, participates in a recent training exercise somewhere in Jordan.
Guerrillas claim they soon will launch a new phase in their conflict with Israel.

4 CHICAGO SUN-TIMES: Mon., Oct. 27, 1969

Ill. group is furious at 'I Am Curious'

By Sam Washington

Small Businessmen's Assn.
Sunday to stop the show-
of film 'I Am Curious
ice president of the

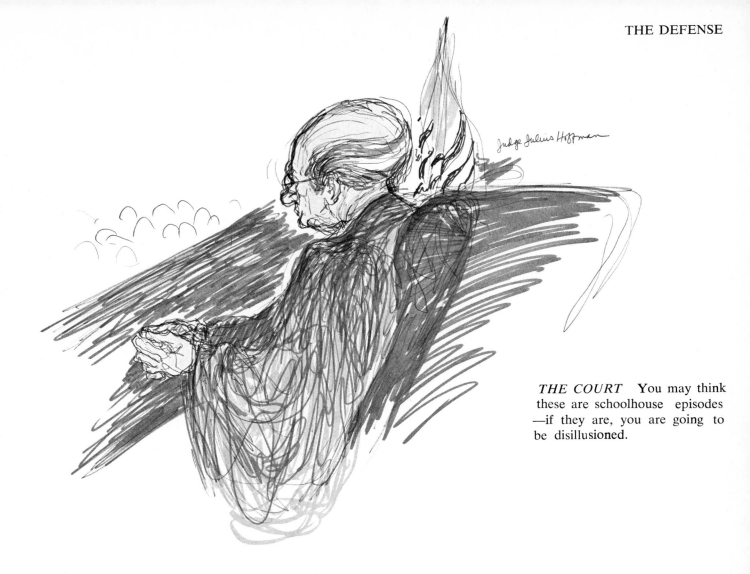

Judge Julius Hoffman

THE COURT You may think these are schoolhouse episodes —if they are, you are going to be disillusioned.

This chronicle can be characterized as Julius Hoffman's demonstration to his courtroom class that the trial in the United States District Court is not what he called "a schoolhouse play".

THE COURT Oh, I will let the witness tell whether he knows what an obscenity is. Do you know what an obscenity is?

SCHALLER I think I would, but I am sure. Counsel

and I have disagreement here and there.

SCHULTZ If the defense would try to expedite this trial instead of delaying it, we wouldn't be here now.

RUBIN We'd probably be in jail.

* * * * * * * * * * * * * * * * * * *

KUNSTLER . . . The main statute involved is 2101 and the defendants are accused of a conspiracy to travel in interstate commerce, to use the facilities of interstate commerce, with an intent to incite a riot and commit acts of violence in connection with or furtherance of such a riot and to aid and abet persons in committing acts of violence in furtherance of a riot, and to perform certain overt acts in furtherance thereof. . . .

Conspiracies are so easy to prove in the general sense because you don't have to prove anything. You never have had to prove the conspiracy in the routine case; all you have to prove is that the defendants had committed certain acts or one or two of them did and that they had some access to each other. Therefore this is why conspiracy is so often used, particularly in

cases like this.

The crime of conspiracy evolved in the court of star chamber crime as we know it today. It was formulated in the court of star chamber and used by that infamous court in order to prove in political cases primarily that acts of a certain type meant there must be agreement. But when you get into the type of case we have before your Honor, we are no longer in the routine conspiracy case . . . We are in the case of a so-called conspiracy in the First Amendment area . . . and the Government must be held to a standard of strictissimi juris which means that they must have established a prima facie case in the light of the rule of strictissimi juris—that is, they must be held to the strictest standard of the law in so establishing such a case.

In this particular case where we have a statute which is so suspect itself and which does involve First Amendment rights to an enormous degree, I don't think there is a legal scholar in the United States who, reading the statutes, would not say that it raises First Amendment problems. . . .

[T]he use or the evidence of public meetings, what they call mere public meetings, are not enough to prove a conspiracy. . . . Well, that is what we have in this case. You have mere meetings, all open. . . .

[T]here is nothing illegal about giving a speech. There is nothing illegal about conducting a self-defense marshals' session. There is nothing illegal about meeting in the Mobilization office or anywhere else. In fact, it is very difficult to find a single illegal act here attributable to any defendant. It is highly remarkable that in all of the illegality which was put on allegedly committed in Chicago, that with two ex-

ceptions you have no arrests of any defendant. . . .

* * *

. . . If anything, the Government has proved one thing in presentation of its evidence, that it has put together a mass of meetings, mainly public, a mass of speeches, all of which were public, a mass of statements in an earnest effort to prove that the defendants in this case committed some sort of a crime.

What they have really proved is essentially what we have argued throughout this case. What they have really proved is that the Government of the United States is out by any means necessary to destroy the First Amendment to the Constitution, and I think in that they have succeeded in so proving, and your Honor's judgment of acquittal granting our motion will be, I think, a refreshing breath of air in what is a case which has such onerous possibilities and dangers for the right of free speech in the United States.

FORAN Your Honor, there is a motion to exclude
witnesses from this courtroom that was made by that
man a long time ago.

KUNSTLER I am not "that man," Mr. Foran. I have
a name, William M. Kunstler.

FORAN Do you really? Do you really?

KUNSTLER And use my name. You use my name
when you call me and not "that man."

FORAN What I think of calling you I won't say before
ladies.

A QUAKER GIRL

JANE MEYERDING

A BRITISH MEMBER OF PARLIAMENT

ANNE PATRICIA KERR

THE COURT Just a minute, please. What do they call a member of Parliament in England? I want to address you properly.

KERR Just call me Anne.

THE COURT Well, now, we call our Senators here Senator. We call our Congressmen, Congressman.

KERR You can call me the Honorable Member for Rochester and Chatham.

THE COURT That is a little long. I will just have to call you Madame Witness. Read her last answer.

KERR I was trying to make it easy for you.

THE COURT Don't make it easy for me. That is not your responsibility.

KERR Mine is to tell the truth.

* * *

THE COURT   I am asking you whether you offered Defendants' Exhibit 145 for identification.

WEINGLASS   When I make my answer to the Court I borrow on what has gone before in this case with the expectation that the same rules will apply to us in that area.

THE COURT   Don't borrow on that. Your credit isn't good in that area. . . .

FORAN   Your Honor, if we could edit that film to eliminate the kind of title scenes, those line drawings and those individual pictures like the shot of a poster which I think is purely editorial and comment. The shot of the young man who looks like either Christ or Joshua, depending on which side we are standing on here.

THE COURT   I so hoped you would say Moses.

FORAN   All right, Judge, I will throw in Moses.
    If we could edit out those things, the Government would have no objection.

FORAN   We will limit [the objection] to the poster shot of Mayor Daley.

WEINGLASS   Another Biblical figure.

SARAH DIAMANT, Teaching Fellow at Cornell University

FORAN Well, from the time that the Poor People's wagon went through the police line, there were continuous chants from the crowd?

DIAMANT That is right.

FORAN And did you hear anything of those chants?

DIAMANT Sure.

FORAN Do you remember what they were?

DIAMANT They were yelling, "Dump the Humph," which I think referred to Hubert Humphrey.

Then there was, I am trying to remember what the "LBJ" one was. It wasn't that. "Hey, hey, LBJ, how many kids did you kill today?"

PHIL OCHS

"It is always the old to lead us to the wars; it is always the young to fall. Now look at all we've won with the sabre and the gun. Tell me, is it worth it all?"

"Now the labor leaders screaming when they close a missile plant; United Fruit screams at the Cuban shore. Call it peace or call it treason, call it love or call it reason, but I ain't marching any more. No I ain't marching any more."

SCHULTZ Now, in your plans for Chicago, did you plan for public fornication in the park?

OCHS I didn't.

THE COURT If you think I should tell the jury why this witness was directed to leave the stand, I will do it.

KUNSTLER I think they would be confused when the defense puts a witness upon the stand—

THE COURT Oh, trust me. You use the word so often.

I shall not confuse the jury, Mr. Kunstler. Don't worry about it.

KUNSTLER Your Honor, every remark you take as a personal affront. I am not saying that you would confuse them. I think without an explanation they would be confused.

KUNSTLER I think Mr. Hoffman has dropped his last name.

THE COURT What did you say?

KUNSTLER I think that Mr. Hoffman has dropped his last name as a protest against this court.

THE COURT He will have to do that in law. Here he is indicted as Abbie Hoffman. I know that he said that in court, Mr. Kunstler, but his mere saying of that doesn't deprive him of a last name.

KUNSTLER I know, but legally, your Honor, there is no requirement that you do have a formal change of name at all. A person can drop his last name.

THE COURT That is not an issue here. I do not share your view about that, but I think I will ask you to refer to your clients by their surnames.

KUNSTLER All right, I will rephrase the question, to change Abbie and Jerry to Abbie Hoffman and Jerry Rubin.

ALLEN GINSBERG

WEINGLASS   Could you indicate for the Court and jury what the area of your studies consisted of?

GINSBERG   Mantra Yoga, meditation exercises, chanting, and sitting quietly, stilling the mind and breathing exercises to calm the body and to calm the mind, but mainly a branch called Mantra Yoga, which is a yoga which involves prayer and chanting.

* * *

WEINGLASS   Now, calling your attention to the month of February 1968, did you have occasion in that month to meet with Abbie Hoffman?

GINSBERG   Yeah.

WEINGLASS   Do you recall what Mr. Hoffman said in the course of that conversation?

GINSBERG   Yippie—among other things. He said that politics had become theater and magic; that it was the manipulation of imagery through mass media that was confusing and hypnotizing the people in the United States and making them accept a war which they did not really believe in; that people were involved in a life style which was intolerable to the younger folk, which involved brutality and police violences as well as a larger violence in Vietnam, and that we ourselves might be able to get together in Chicago and invite teachers to present different ideas of what is wrong with the planet, what we can do to solve the pollution crisis, what we can do to solve the Vietnam war, to present different ideas for making the society more sacred and less commercial, less materialistic, what we could do to uplevel or improve the whole tone of the trap that we all felt ourselves in as the population grew and as politics became more violent and chaotic.

* * *

WEINGLASS   Would you explain what your statement was.

GINSBERG   My statement was that the planet Earth at the present moment was endangered by violence, overpopulation, pollution, ecological destruction brought about by our own greed; that the younger children in America and other countries of the world might not survive the next 30 years, that it was a planetary crisis that had not been recognized by any government of the world . . . [T]he more selfish elder politicians . . . were not thinking in terms of what their children would need in future generations or even in the generation immediately coming or even for themselves in their own life-time and were continuing to threaten the planet with violence, with war, with mass murder, with germ warfare. . . . The desire for preservation of the planet and the planet's form, that we do continue to be, to exist on this planet instead of destroy the planet, was manifested to my mind by the great Mantra from India to the preserver God Vishnu whose Mantra is Hare Krishna, and then I chanted the Hare Krishna Mantra for ten minutes to the television cameras and it goes:

"Hare Krishna, Hare Krishna, Krishna, Krishna . . .

KUNSTLER Your Honor, I object to the laughter of the Court on this. I think this is a serious presentation of a religious concept.

THE COURT I don't understand it. I don't understand it because it was—the language of the United States District Court is English.

KUNSTLER I know, but you don't laugh at all languages.

GINSBERG I would be glad to explain it, sir.

THE COURT I didn't laugh. I didn't laugh.

GINSBERG I would be happy to explain it.

THE COURT I didn't laugh at all. I wish I could tell you how I feel. Laugh, I didn't even smile.

FORAN Your Honor, of course the laughter came from everybody that Mr. Kunstler is usually defending for laughing.

KUNSTLER Your Honor, I would say—You mean from the press?

GINSBERG Might we go on to an explanation.

THE COURT Will you keep quiet, Mr. Witness, while I am talking to the lawyers?

*　*　*　*　*　*　*　*　*　*　*　*　*　*

There is a Jewish joke about a hostess, her guests and her cookies.

Guest: These cookies are great.
Hostess: I am glad you like them.
Guest: I have had only three.
Hostess: I have had 8 but who is counting?

KUNSTLER Now, do you recall what, if anything, occurred at 10:30?

GINSBERG There was a sudden burst of lights in the center of the park, and a group of policemen moved in fast to where the bonfires were and kicked over the bonfires.

KUNSTLER That what—

GINSBERG There was a great deal of consternation and movement and shouting among the crowd in the park, and I turned, surprised, because it was early.

KUNSTLER Without relating what you said to another person, Mr. Ginsberg, what did you do at the time you saw the police do this?

GINSBERG I started the chant, O-o-m-m-m-m-m-m, O-o-m-m-m-m-m-m.

FORAN All right, we have had a demonstration.

THE COURT All right.

FORAN From here on, I object.

THE COURT You haven't said that you objected.

FORAN I do after the second one.

THE COURT After two of them? I sustain the objection.

WEINGLASS If the Court please, there has been much testimony by the Government's witnesses as to this OM technique which was used in the park. Are we only going to hear whether there were stones or people throwing things, or shouting things, or using obscenities? Why do we draw the line here? Why can't we also hear what is being said in the area of calming the crowd?

FORAN I have no objection to the two Om's that we have had. However, I just didn't want it to go on all morning.

WEINGLASS Did you finish your answer?

GINSBERG I am afraid I will be in contempt if I continue to Om. . . .

WEINGLASS What did you do when you saw the policemen in the center of the crowd?

WEINGLASS Adrenalin ran through my body. I sat down on a green hillside with a group of younger people that were walking with me at about 3:30 in the afternoon, 4 o'clock, sat, crossed my leg and began chanting O-o-m—O-o-m-m-m, O-o-m-m-m,

O-o-m-m-m.

JUDGE Oh, no! no! no! no! Not one more O-m in this courtroom.

FORAN (jumping up and shouting): That's Four! I gave him four that time.

(As if to say, "but who's counting?"

At that point the entire court broke out laughing.)

JUDGE (as he spiralled up in his bench) Humm, Humm, what an indignity! Humm, what an indignity!

GINSBERG   I continued chanting for seven hours.

WEINGLASS   I am sorry, I did not hear the answer.

THE COURT   He said he continued chanting for seven hours. Seven hours, was it, sir?

GINSBERG   Seven hours, yes.

WEINGLASS   Now, when you left the Coliseum, where, if anywhere, did you go?

GINSBERG   The group I was with, Mr. Genet, Mr. Burroughs and Mr. Seaver, and Terry Southern, all went back to Lincoln Park.

WEINGLASS   What time did you arrive in the park?

GINSBERG   11:00, 11:30.

WEINGLASS   What was occurring at the park as you got there?

GINSBERG   There was a great crowd lining the outskirts of the park and a little way into the park on the inner roads, and there was a larger crowd moving in toward the center. We all moved in toward the center and at the center of the park, there was a group of ministers and rabbis who had elevated a great cross about ten-foot high in the middle of a circle of people who were sitting around, quietly, listening to the ministers conduct a ceremony.

WEINGLASS   After the ministers moved the cross to another location which you have indicated, what happened?

GINSBERG   After, I don't know, a short period of time, there was a burst of smoke and tear gas around the cross, and the cross was enveloped with tear gas, and the people who were carrying the cross were enveloped with tear gas which began slowly drifting over the crowd.

WEINGLASS   And when you saw the persons with the cross and the cross being gassed, what if anything did you do?

GINSBERG   I turned to Burroughs and said, "They have gassed the cross of Christ."

FORAN   Objection, if the Court please. I ask that the answer be stricken.

Terry Southern

THE COURT   I sustain the objection.

GINSBERG   I took Bill Burroughs' hand and took Terry Southern's hand, and we turned from the cross which was covered with gas in the glary lights that were coming from the police lights that were shining through the tear gas on the cross, and walked slowly out of the park.

FORAN   Now when you went out to the Coliseum and you met Abbie Hoffman, you said when you met him you kissed him?

GINSBERG   Yes.

FORAN   And you do consider him an intimate friend of yours?

GINSBERG   I don't see him that often, but I see him often enough and have worked with him often enough to feel intimate with him, yes.

FORAN   I call your attention to page 32 of the exhibit. Does that have on page 32 the poem, "The Night-Apple"?

GINSBERG   Yes. I wrote it in 1950. That was nineteen years ago. It still looks good.

FORAN   After refreshing your recollection, Mr. Ginsberg, could you recite that poem to the jury?

GINSBERG   Yes. "The Night-Apple."
"Last night I dreamed
of one I loved
for seven long years,
but I saw no face,
only the familiar
presence of the body:
sweat skin eyes
faces urine sperm
saliva all one
odor and mortal taste."

FORAN Could you explain to the jury what the religious significance of that poem is?

GINSBERG If you would take a wet dream as a religious experience, I could. It is a description of a wet dream, sir.

Be it a Guru or a Ginsberg, Daddy will always have the last word.

When the guru festival was over, the Defense confessed that it was at a loss as to which side Ginsberg's testimony helped.

Om! One thing was sure—Om! Allen Ginsberg did his own thing.

DICK GREGORY

KUNSTLER Would you describe to the jury where you saw Abbie Hoffman and what you saw him do.

GREGORY At 18th Street, lying under or directly in front of what I believe to have been a tank.

[W]hen I looked at Abbie, before we got to the crowd that started moving, I said, "Where are you going?" He said, "I don't know. The police is leading it." I said, "What do you mean by that?" He said, "The guy on the bullhorn." He said, "There is an undercover agent. He is leading it, so let him take them back to the park."

THE COURT . . . [O]ne of the defendants who we all remember, I think—he is no longer here—charged me with being a racist with absolutely no basis in fact.

KUNSTLER He said if your Honor didn't permit him to act as his own attorney you were—

THE COURT I would want this very nice witness to know that I am not, that he has made me laugh often and heartily.

KUNSTLER Your Honor, white people have always laughed at black people for a long time as entertainers.

THE COURT I want him to know I was the first judge in the North to enter a decree desegregating schools. But that is beside the point. There is no issue of racism in this case. . . .

68

Friends of the judge from the exclusive North Shore had their own day in court.

I saw red faced, blue helmeted, blue shirted or short-sleeve shirted men, their arms up, a club in one arm, coming out of the bus at full speed chanting, "Kill, kill, kill" and then go across the street and charge into the crowd and start beating heads.

—Defense witness, Ruth Migal, professor of fine art.

Stuart Ball, Sr., later appeared in court and told Judge Hoffman: I have reviewed the entire record. There is no act or conduct of my son of which I am ashamed.

HOFFMAN   I was laughing.   (pause)

KUNSTLER   . . . [Y]ou are depriving us of a lawyer at our defense table.

THE COURT   That is just too bad. You will have to suffer through without him. He is not a lawyer admitted to practice here.

KUNSTLER   He is a member of the bar of the District of Columbia. He has been assisting us for three months through this trial.

THE COURT   Let him go back to the District of Columbia. I will not have him here laughing at me while I am trying to rule—

THE COURT   . . . Mr. Marshal, will you remove that man sitting there? Ask him to leave. This man right here.

WEINGLASS   Your Honor, I don't believe Mr. Ball was—

THE COURT   He was laughing right at me while I was speaking.

WEINGLASS   I was standing here. Mr. Ball did not laugh.

THE COURT   Mr. Ball was laughing right at me.

DAVIS   Your Honor—

THE COURT   I ask Mr. Ball to leave.

HOFFMAN   I was laughing.

DAVIS   It was me that was laughing, your Honor.

THE COURT   I can't order you to leave. You are at trial.

*   *   *

THE COURT   Mr. Marshal, take Mr. Ball out.

DELLINGER   That is an injustice.

KUNSTLER   That is a lawyer who is part of our defense team.

THE COURT   He is not a lawyer admitted to practice in this Court.

KUNSTLER   You are removing a lawyer from the defense table.

THE COURT   No, he is not a lawyer admitted to practice here.

KUNSTLER   That doesn't matter, your Honor. He is—

DELLINGER   He wasn't laughing.

KUNSTLER   You have given him permission to sit here.

THE COURT   I withdraw the permission.

*   *   *

KUNSTLER   Your Honor, this is the second time you have picked the wrong man.

DELLINGER   Your Honor—

KUNSTLER   Mr. Davis has admitted he laughed.

THE COURT   That will be all, sir. Now I am making a ruling.

*   *   *   *   *   *   *   *   *   *   *

KUNSTLER   But he didn't laugh, your Honor. If he laughed, that is one thing, perhaps, but two defendants have admitted laughing.

THE COURT   My eyesight is good and my hearing is good.

KUNSTLER   You were wrong about Mr. Dellinger. You thought he made a noise. We have submitted an affidavit as to that.

THE COURT   I suppose I didn't hear him call me a liar in open court.

KUNSTLER   That is a different matter, your Honor.

U.S. Marshal

Lloyd Dellinger

THE COURT Oh—

DELLINGER I said if you said I was talking, that that was a lie, that you were calling me a liar.

THE COURT You didn't—you said, "You are a liar."

KUNSTLER No. Read the transcript.

DELLINGER You accused me of being a liar and I said that was a lie.

DELLINGER And you are very prejudiced and unfair and I state that in open court. It is not a fair trial and you had no intention of giving us a fair trial and when I speak throughout the country, I say that you are the Assistant Prosecutor or maybe the Chief Prosecutor and it is true and the people of this country will come to learn that about you and about some other judges in this Court.

A SPECTATOR RIGHT ON!

DELLINGER That's why I called it a fascist court before.

A SPECTATOR RIGHT ON!

* * *

KUNSTLER Your Honor, what is happening? The marshals are taking people out.

A SPECTATOR Why don't you clear the whole courtroom?

THE COURT Will you—

DELLINGER You see, we are interested in the truth. That is what the conflict is here.

THE COURT No, Mr. Ball will not be readmitted. He is not admitted to practice here and for good and sufficient reasons I order him out.

KUNSTLER Your Honor, put him on the stand and ask him whether he laughed.

THE COURT Will you sit down, please?

KUNSTLER I guess I have no alternative, your Honor.

* * *

SCHULTZ Your Honor, this tactic of one jumping up and then the other, this disruption that is slowly escalating is becoming quite eviden[t] and I would ask your Honor to order these—

HOFFMAN Why don't you call out the National Guard.

RIGHT ON!

Richard Schultz

71

LINDA MORSE, the girl next door

Act 1—The Initiation

December 16, 1969

LINDA MORSE, FORMER OFFICE MANAGER OF THE
FIFTH AVENUE PEACE PARADE COMMITTEE, BY
DEFENSE ATTORNEY KUNSTLER

THE COURT . . . Miss Morse, please listen to the
question of Mr. Kunstler.

THE WITNESS I am sorry, your Honor. It is the first
time I have ever testified. It is very confusing.

KUNSTLER I know it is difficult.

SCHULTZ It is not difficult at all, and Mr. Kunstler
has so very carefully told all his witnesses say what
you please, and when you are cut off, your Honor, this
is the first time. . . .

KUNSTLER Your Honor, Mr. Schultz has made a
statement, which I think is quite a serious one. . . .
He has implied that I have coached a witness to
come into this courtroom and make statements that
will be objectionable.

KUNSTLER I think the jury ought to be told that is an
improper statement, to imply that counsel has in some
way coached a witness that she will make statements
that will be objectionable.

THE COURT I will direct the jury that the statement
of Mr. Schultz is not well founded in fact, and to disregard it.

Act 2—Telling it like it is

MORSE [T]he Government of the United States has
lost its credibility today; there is fighting in the United
States today going on in cities in this country today.
People's Park in Berkeley, the policemen shot at us
when people were unarmed, were fighting, if you wish,
with rocks, the policemen used double-load buckshot
and rifles, and pistols against unarmed demonstrators.
That is fighting. OK? There is fighting going on in the
United States right now. People are fighting to regain
their liberty, fighting to regain their freedom, fighting
for a totally different society, people in the black community, people in the Puerto Rican community, people in the Mexican-American community and people
in the white communities. They are fighting by political means as well as defending themselves.

SCHULTZ Your Honor, that is not an answer to my
question. . . .

KUNSTLER Your Honor, they are intensely political
questions and she is trying to give a political answer
to a political question.

THE COURT This is not a political case as far as I
am concerned.

KUNSTLER   Well, your Honor, as far as some of the rest of us are concerned, it is quite a political case.

THE COURT   It is a criminal case. There is an indictment here. I have the indictment right up here. I can't go into politics here in this Court.

KUNSTLER   Your Honor, Jesus was accused criminally, too, and we understand really that was not truly a criminal case in the sense that it is just an ordinary—

THE COURT   I didn't live at that time. I don't know. Some people think I go back that far, but I really didn't.

KUNSTLER   Well, I was assuming your Honor had read of the incident.

*   *   *

Act 3—The Revolution

SCHULTZ   With regard to the revolution that we are talking about, you are prepared, aren't you both to die and to kill for it, isn't that right?

MORSE   Yes.

SCHULTZ   And the more you realize our system is sick, the more you want to tear it from limb to limb, isn't that right?

MORSE   The more that I see the horrors that are perpetrated by this Government, the more that I read about things like troop trains full of nerve gas traveling across the country where one accident could wipe out thousands and thousands of people, the more that I see things like companies just pouring waste into lakes and into rivers and just destroying them, the more I see things like the oil fields in the ocean off Santa Barbara coast where the Secretary of the Interior and the oil companies got together and agreed to continue producing oil from those off-shore oil fields and ruined a whole section of the coast; the more that I see things like an educational system which teaches black people and Puerto Rican people and Mexican-Americans that they are only fit to be domestics and dishwashers, if that; the more that I

see a system that teaches middle-class whites like me that we are supposed to be technological brains to continue producing CBW warfare, to continue working on computers and things like that to learn how to kill people better, to learn how to control people better, yes, the more I want to see that system torn down and replaced by a totally different one; one that cares about people learning real things in school; one that cares about people going to college for free; one that cares about people living adult lives that are responsible, fulfilled adult lives, not just drudgery, day after day after day going to a job; one that gives people a chance to express themselves artistically and politically, and religiously, and philosophically. That is the kind of system I want to see in its stead.

SCHULTZ   Your Honor, the answer is not responsive. I move it be stricken.

KUNSTLER   The answer could not have been more responsive to his question.

THE COURT   Not much more, I strike the answer and direct the jury to disregard it as being unresponsive to the question.

73

KUNSTLER Miss Morse, I want to read you something from the Declaration of Independence, which I think the Court can take judicial notice of, and then ask you a question about it.

SCHULTZ Objection to reading from the Declaration of Independence.

THE COURT I can think of nothing in the cross-examination that makes the Declaration of Independence relevant on redirect examination.

KUNSTLER Your Honor, if the Declaration of Independence isn't relative to what is going on in the courtroom here, I can hardly think of anything more relevant.

THE COURT I didn't say that. I said to the redirect examination. I wouldn't let you read the entire Constitution or one of Mr. Ginsberg's poems. It must be relevant to the examination which precedes it.

KUNSTLER But your Honor, the cross-examination went into great lengths on Miss Morse's philosophy of change of government, of change of the way a society exists, and since the Declaration has relevant statements on that, I wanted to read them to her and have her comments on them.

THE COURT I will not permit you to read from the Declaration of Independence. I sustain the objection.

* * *

Artie Seale: Madonna and Child

Bobby Seale: Father and Son

The Yippies wanted to run a pig for President

HOW IT ALL BEGAN

The National Convention of the Democratic Party, Chicago, August 1968.

Sound-track from a news film on the melee outside the Hilton Hotel during the Democratic Convention.

They are forcing, the police are forcing the crowd back and now, and it is going to be a difficult job. A big police van has pulled into the intersection, and its role, I assume its role is just to clear a way. Here come the police. Step up here. The police are pushing and shoving. Here they come. We're going to get it. We're going to get it. They are clear, and we are out of the way. Watch the wire.

Now the police are clubbing this young man, clubbing him. This is a real police charge. Now I have seen them club at least three young people. Now they are moving into the crowd and beating them with the night sticks. The beatings are going on. Here they come. There are glasses and bottles being thrown. These police mean business. Watch the wire. Here come the police. There are a lot of young people on the ground now. This is a real bedlam.

This is the worst it has been so far in Chicago. Police running across here. There's another one hit the ground, and he is screaming. They are really letting them have it now. Here they come.

There the police go. They are clubbing these young people. Our truck is down there. They are dragging them across the intersection. They are dragging them across the intersection.

This is the most amazing thing that has ever occurred in the Loop of Chicago in modern history. A firecracker went off there. They have turned Michigan and Balbo into a war zone.

THE OBSERVER REVIEW
1 SEPTEMBER 1968
INSIDE CHICAGO, CITY OF
VIOLENCE
COLIN McGLASHAN writes from Chicago: 'America's police forces are preparing to fight guerrilla warfare in the streets. They are ready for civil war.'

They have cleared part of the intersection. They have young people off on the sidewalk now. I have seen dozens of them being beaten, and the police really mean business here in front of the Hilton Hotel.

The whole world watches. The whole world watches.

They are shouting, 'The whole world watches.' The police are regrouping.

75

Here comes another skirmish on the other side. They are moving these people back, chasing them up the bridge, moving them in full force. As you can see, they are chasing them up the bridge, across the bridge, back into the Grant Park area.

Debris is flying here. It is really flying. Here comes a bottle. It is a film can of some kind, a metal can.

Now the police are going to hold the line right here by our cameras, and it is truly amazing here. There's some young people fallen into the street now by the Hilton Hotel. Some of the Red Cross Peace people are picking them up and moving them on to the sidewalk, and the police van is now moving back to the west, away from Michigan Avenue.

Now there are some things being thrown out of the hotel window of the Sheraton-Blackstone just north of the Hilton, and these young people mean business, and so do the police,

. . . and it's not over yet.

FORAN   A director of plays and writer of plays?

LEVY   Director and writer.

FORAN   Now, this "Oh, Calcutta!" that you directed is rather famous, isn't it?

LEVY   "My Learns are Goided."

FORAN   It was shut down in a number of cities?

LEVY   No. Wrong. Wrong. Wrong. It never was shut down.

FORAN   It was shut down last night in Los Angeles, wasn't it?

LEVY   Not that I know of. Was it shut down last night? Was it shut down last night? No, I didn't know about that.

FORAN   It is a kind of a tribal celebration of nudity?

LEVY   No, absolutely not.

FORAN   A lot of nudity?

LEVY   I wouldn't have anything to do with a tribal celebration of anything.

FORAN   There is a lot of nudity in it, isn't there?

LEVY   It depends on what you mean by a lot.

FORAN   Well, how many—

LEVY   Compared to what is a lot— object to that, somebody.

FORAN   How many at various times?

LEVY   How many what?

FORAN   Characters on the stage are in the nude?

LEVY   Ten people on the stage in the nude.

FORAN   In the nude. And what are they doing on the stage?

LEVY   Dancing, singing.

FORAN   In the nude?

LEVY   Gliding, improvising, having what they describe as a terrifically good time and what the audience feels is a good time.

FORAN   In the nude?

LEVY   The audience isn't in the nude.

FORAN   Ten, is that it? Is that at one time or individually that they show up in the course of the play?

LEVY   Well, they are there sometimes at one time and sometimes again—

FORAN   Individually?

LEVY   No. that means at one time; sometimes together.

FORAN   Sometimes there are as many as ten on the stage at one time?

LEVY   Yes.

KUNSTLER   Your Honor, that has been asked and answered, as I recall.

THE COURT   No, I don't believe it has been.

FORAN   There are other times when there is just one person in the nude on the stage, two people, or three people?

LEVY   Three or four, right.

JACQUES LEVY

FORAN   How many acts are there?

LEVY   In the nude?

FORAN   Yes.

LEVY   Four.

FORAN   In four of the acts. How many acts are there altogether.

LEVY   Twelve.

FORAN   So that in a third of the acts, there are nude demonstrations on the stage of various kinds?

LEVY   Yes. Is that really true, that it was closed down in Los Angeles?

FORAN   Do you want to read the paper?

LEVY   It is still running in New York and in San Francisco.

THE COURT   There is no question for you to answer.

FORAN   By the way, at Grand Central Station, the whole station was shut down, wasn't it, and the ticket vending stopped, and everything stopped for four hours there?

LEVY   The station wasn't shut down. I saw people getting on trains and getting off trains. I don't know about the ticket vending. I have no idea. I wasn't over by the ticket vending, but I know people were coming in and going out.

FORAN   Now, this big, what do they call it, this Festival of Life, that is what I wanted to say, I knew there was a name for it, had you participated in the ideas for that Festival of Life? I mean, you were asked to give them some direction on how to conduct a Festival of Life?

LEVY   What I was asked about was not to give them some direction, but was to give my opinion on the various possibilities, and to bring up any possibilities that I thought might be feasible.

FORAN   Did you suggest as a possibility giving it a heading of, "How to Fuck the System"?

LEVY   No.

FORAN   Did you suggest that one of the things they should learn at this Festival would be how to disrupt the university?

LEVY   No.

FORAN   How about "How to Fuck the Draft"? Was that one that you suggested?

LEVY   No.

FORAN   How about one "How to Fornicate"? How is that? Did you suggest that one?

LEVY   No, but you are getting closer. No, I didn't suggest any of those things.

FORAN   Did you suggest that in the Yippie Olympics, they have a game called, "Pin the Rubber on the Pope"?

LEVY   Can I say something about that, or just answer yes or no?

79

My wife, whose name is Mrs. Leary, had a lantern by a cow, and we were announcing that we were going to come to Chicago in August, not with fire, but to bring light and peace.

HE TUNED IN

THE COURT "Erotic," did you say?

LEARY Erotic

THE COURT E-r-o-t-i-c?

LEARY Eros. That means love, your Honor.

THE COURT I know; I know. I wanted to be sure I didn't mishear you.

LEARY Because Mr. Rubin pointed out that Mr. Robert Kennedy did represent a youthful, healthy, masculine approach that was lacking in most of our other politicians, and we felt that young people would respond to a person like Mr. Kennedy, who seemed to enjoy life as opposed to the pessimistic uptight older politicians.

TURNED ON

KUNSTLER Your Honor, sometimes it is hard because we work together in this case, we use first names constantly.

THE COURT I know, but if I knew you that well, and I don't, how would it seem for me to say, "Now Billy . . ."

KUNSTLER I was just thinking I hadn't been called "Billy" since my mother used that word the first time.

THE COURT I haven't called you that.

KUNSTLER I know, but you used it.

THE COURT I used it . . .

KUNSTLER It evokes some memories.

THE COURT I was trying to point out to you how absurd it sounds in a courtroom.

KUNSTLER It didn't sound . . .

THE COURT Oh, let's get on. Let's examine this witness. He seems eager to get away.

And a few weeks later

They contended that these re- / cutor were solely responsible for that investigation.

Leary Found Guilty Again On Marijuana Charges

LAREDO, Tex., Jan. 20 (UPI) —A Federal Court jury found Dr. Timothy Leary guilty today of helping import three ounces of marijuana into Texas four years ago in his teen-age daughter's underwear.

It was the second time that Leary, sometimes called "the high priest of pot," had been convicted in Federal Court in this Mexican border town.

Leary, 49 years old, dressed in gray bellbottom trousers and

a magenta shirt, said he would "just stay loving and keep cool."

Federal Judge Ben C. Connally continued Leary's $5,000 bond and set sentencing for 10 A.M. Feb. 16 in Federal District Court at Houston.

Leary was convicted March 11, 1966, in Laredo of the same charge and appealed. The Supreme Court overturned the verdict and ordered a new trial.

"I'm very sorry that I hasn't learned a thing in five years," Leary said after today's verdict.

DROPPED OUT

THE COURT   He said "s.o.b." and other profanities.

KUNSTLER   No, he said "pig, fascist—"

THE COURT   "s.o.b. and other profanities."

KUNSTLER   Right, but I am not sure that the word "pig" or the word "fascist" is a profanity.

THE COURT   I am not sure. I am not sure about that, Mr. Kunstler. I never looked up the word in that connotation.

KUNSTLER   It is a common word. It is in the dictionary, your Honor. It is in any dictionary.

SCHULTZ   I didn't call it a profanity. I said "pig, fascist, s.o.b., and other profanities."

THE COURT   I am not prepared to rule on that at this time, Mr. Kunstler.

KUNSTLER   If Mr. Schultz is relating that the only word he classified as a profanity among those is s.o.b., then I have no objection.

THE COURT   To call a man a fascist may be contemptuous, but it may not be profane.

KUNSTLER   But it may be accurate.

THE COURT   What do you say?

KUNSTLER   But it may be accurate.

SCHULTZ   I don't think Mr. Kunstler is very funny. He is trying to be very humorous.

THE COURT   Oh, he is trying to be humorous? I thought he was making a legal argument.

KUNSTLER   I am making an argument. Mr. Schultz is categorizing it, and I am not going to argue about his feelings.

SCHULTZ   Your Honor was obviously referring to having been called a fascist and Mr. Kunstler is saying it might be accurate.

THE COURT   Oh, I have been called worse than that. We will take care of that. I am not sure but that the word "fascist" used as it has been used on occasion is not even worse than profanity.

KUNSTLER   Your Honor, it is used in many contexts every day. It is used in the newspaper one way or another. That is what I am referring to.

THE COURT   Not every day. I read the newspapers every day. I can't remember when I have seen the word "fascist" in the newspapers except in connection with this trial.

KUNSTLER   Then I recommend today's New York Times to your Honor.

THE COURT   Am I called a fascist in that paper?

KUNSTLER   No, your Honor. Every time the word "fascist" is used it doesn't necessarily mean Judge Julius Hoffman.

THE COURT   Well, that is reassuring. That is so reassuring.

KUNSTLER   You are taking it so personally every time it is used—

THE COURT   Oh, no, not at all. I haven't said anything about myself personally.

KUNSTLER   Well, your Honor, I got the strong drift that you were taking it quite personally this time. If I am wrong, I am sorry.

THE COURT   Don't drift so easily.

KUNSTLER   I will fight against the tide winds.

ABBIE minus HOFFMAN

WEINGLASS   Will you please identify yourself for the record.

HOFFMAN   My name is Abbie. I am an orphan of America.

WEINGLASS   Where do you reside?

HOFFMAN   I live in Woodstock Nation.

WEINGLASS   Will you tell the Court and jury where it is.

HOFFMAN   Yes. It is a nation of alienated young people. We carry it around with us as a state of mind in the same way the Sioux Indians carried the Sioux nation around with them. It is a nation dedicated to cooperation versus competition, to the idea that people should have better means of exchange than property or money, that there should be some other basis for human interaction. It is a nation dedicated to—

THE COURT   Excuse me, sir.
Read the question to the witness, please.
(Question read)

THE COURT   Just where it is, that is all.

HOFFMAN   It is in my mind and in the minds of my brothers and sisters. We carry it around with us in the same way that the Sioux Indians carried around the Sioux nation. It does not consist of property or material but, rather, of ideas and certain values, those values being cooperation versus competition, and that we believe in a society—

SCHULTZ   This doesn't say where Woodstock Nation, whatever that is, is.

WEINGLASS   Your Honor, the witness has identified it as being a state of mind and he has, I think, a right to define that state of mind.

THE COURT   No, we want the place of residence, if he has one, place of doing business, if you have a business, or both if you desire to tell them both. One address will be sufficient. Nothing about philosophy or India, sir. Just where you live, if you have a place to live.

Now you said Woodstock. In what state is Woodstock?

HOFFMAN   It is in the state of mind, in the mind of myself and my brothers and sisters. It is a conspiracy.

WEINGLASS   Can you tell the Court and jury your present age?

HOFFMAN   My age is 33. I am a child of the 60's.

WEINGLASS   When were you born?

HOFFMAN   Psychologically 1960.

WEINGLASS   Can you tell the Court and jury what is your present occupation?

HOFFMAN   I am a cultural revolutionary. Well I am really a defendant—

WEINGLASS   What do you mean?

HOFFMAN   —full time

* * *

THE COURT   The witness turned his back on me while he was on the witness stand.

KUNSTLER   Oh, your Honor, aren't—

SCHULTZ   Mr. Kunstler went out of his way, out of his way the other day to explain to the jury that the defendant Hoffman had eliminated his last name.

THE COURT   I will have no further argument on your motion. I will ask you to sit down.

HOFFMAN   I was just looking at the pictures of the long-hairs up on the wall.

* * *

WEINGLASS   During the year 1967, were you living a totally private life?

SCHULTZ   Objection to the form of the question.

HOFFMAN   I understand that one.

THE COURT   I sustain the objection.

HOFFMAN   I didn't understand the other one, but I understand that question.

THE COURT   I heard the objection. I sustain the objection. I relieve you of the obligation of answering it.

HOFFMAN   Oh, thanks. Gee.

HOFFMAN   Jerry Rubin, I believe, said that it would be a good idea to call it the Festival of Life in contrast to the Convention of Death, and to have it in some kind of public area, like a park or something, in Chicago. . . .

At one point, I believe it was Mr. Krassner, when we were talking about the Hippie community, Mr. Rubin asked how come we are called Hippies when we never called each other that?

PAUL KRASSNER

KUNSTLER   Your Honor, this is not playing around. This is a deadly serious business. The whole issue in this case is language, what is meant by—

SCHULTZ   This is not—

THE COURT   Let Mr. Weinglass defend himself.

WEINGLASS   Your honor, I am glad to see Mr. Schultz finally concedes that things like levitating the Pentagon building, putting LSD in the water, 10,000 people walking nude on Lake Michigan, a $200,000 bribe attempt are all playing around. I am willing to concede that fact, that was all playing around it was a play idea of the witness, and if he is willing to concede, we can all go home.

THE COURT   I sustain—

WEINGLASS   Because he is treating all these things as deadly serious.

WEINGLASS   What equipment, if any, did you personally plan to use in the exorcism of the Pentagon?

HOFFMAN   I brought a number of noisemakers—

SCHULTZ   Objection if the Court please.

THE COURT   I sustain the objection.

On Christmas Day Santa Claus and his reindeer stood outside Chicago, waiting for a permit to enter the city with intent to celebrate the festival of life. Not even good old Saint Nicholas would risk a conspiracy charge and a bonus contempt sentence. But Weinrob—or is it Weingrass—oh!—Feingrass—anyway, what's his name—still hoped to find one point of agreement with Julius Hoffman.

Poor Len, he should have listened instead to the little angels singing their first Noel in the basement of Richard J. Daley's well-guarded mansion.

WEINGLASS I ask the Court to adjourn to Room 406A of Michael Reese Hospital where your Honor could for yourself talk to Abbie and see his condition with doctors present and make a determination right at that point.

THE COURT You know despite the complaints that have been made by representatives of the defendants about the size of this courtroom, I find it pretty nice.

I don't feel that I am living in squalor here. I think I will refrain from going to Michael Reese. It is really very depressing, hospitals are depressing, especially in their crowded conditions now.

Present my compliments to Mr. Hoffman and thank him for the invitation. Tell him that I decline it with regrets.

AWAY IN A PRISON

Away in a prison, no crib for a bed
Little Lord Abbie laid down his bushy head
The guards in the dark corridors looked down where he lay
The little troubled Abbie asleep on the hay.

The pigs are oinking, the yippie awakes
But little Lord Abbie no yielding he makes
I watch thee, Lord Abbie! Look down from the cell
And play by my cradle till the clouds dissipate.

Will Santa Claus come looking like Richard Daley or will Richard Daley come looking like Santa Claus?

Next time they won't keep me here too long because, the last time I was in the hospital, I organized all the doctors and about five of them went to Cuba.

HOFFMAN They said they arrested me because I had the word "fuck" on my forehead. They called it an "obscenary" they said it was an "obscenary."

WEINGLASS Mr. Schultz has indicated to the jury that we are afraid of this book, and—

THE COURT If you will listen to me, sir. I am the one who determines what the jury sees. Those books are not in evidence.

WEINGLASS Then you should admonish the U.S. Attorney not to say that we are afraid of this book.

THE COURT I will admonish the jury—the United States Attorney—

HOFFMAN Wait until you see the movie.

THE COURT If it is required that he be admonished.

HOFFMAN Wait until you see the movie.

THE COURT And you be quiet.

HOFFMAN Well—the movie's going to be better.

SCHULTZ Did you see some people urinate on the Pentagon?

HOFFMAN On the Pentagon itself?

SCHULTZ Or at the Pentagon?

HOFFMAN In that general area in Washington?

SCHULTZ Yes.

HOFFMAN There were in all over 100,000 people. That is, people have that biological habit.

SCHULTZ And did you?

HOFFMAN Yes.

SCHULTZ Did you symbolically—

HOFFMAN Did I go and look?

SCHULTZ Did you symbolically and did you—did you symbolically urinate on the Pentagon, Mr. Hoffman?

HOFFMAN I symbolically urinate on the Pentagon?

SCHULTZ Yes.

HOFFMAN Nearby yes, in the bushes, there, maybe 3,000 feet away from the Pentagon. I didn't get that close. Pee on the walls of the Pentagon?

You are getting to be out of sight actually. You think there is a law against it?

SCHULTZ Are you done, Mr. Hoffman.

HOFFMAN I am done when you are.

SCHULTZ Did you ever on a prior occasion state that a sense of integration possesses you and comes from pissing on the Pentagon?

HOFFMAN I said from combining political attitudes with biological necessity, there is a sense of integration, yes. I think I said it that way, not the way you said it, but—

SCHULTZ You had a good time at the Pentagon, didn't you, Mr. Hoffman?

HOFFMAN Yes, I did. I am having a good time now. Could I—I feel that biological necessity now. Could I be excused for a slight recess?

THE COURT We will take a brief recess, ladies and gentlemen of the jury.

Ladies and gentlemen of the jury, we will take a brief recess.

HOFFMAN Just a brief—

SCHULTZ Do you want to do any headstands for us?

HOFFMAN No, but I think I might like to go to the bathroom, if I could.

SCHULTZ Your Honor, we only have about ten more minutes. I'd like very much to get this finished.

HOFFMAN Ten more minutes?

STUART MEACHAM   CARL OGLESBY   PAUL SILLS

ED SANDERS

FORAN   Oh, your Honor, I object.

SANDERS   I am a poet, songwriter, leader of a rock and roll band, publisher, editor, recording artist, peace-creep—

SCHULTZ   What was the last one, please, I didn't hear the last one.

THE COURT   Miss Reporter, read the last words of the witness. I think there were two words and they were hyphenated.

THE COURT   Peace-creep?

SANDERS   Yes, sir.

THE COURT   Will you please spell it for the reporter.

SANDERS   P-e-a-c-e, hyphen, c-r-e-e-p.

THE COURT   Peace-creep, Mr. Schultz.

And Yodeler

KUNSTLER Mayor Daley, on the 28th of August, 1968, did you say to Senator Ribicoff—"Fuck you, you Jew son-of-a-bitch, you lousy mother fucker, go home"?

MAYOR RICHARD J. DALEY, Power Inc.

Abbie: *Why don't you and I settle this thing right now?*

With so many of Mayor Daley's bodyguards in court, one wondered if it was actually Julius Hoffman's Court, or Daley's Court

Richard Daley sat, impassive

While his men disciplined the hissing audience

Richard Daley—God did not make a duplicate of him. Thank God.

Perhaps that is why Judge Hoffman would not declare him a hostile witness

TEMPEST OF THE TOILET

There is an old saying
That the only place where men are truly equal is in the toilet
If there isn't such a saying,
There ought to be.

KUNSTLER   Your Honor, may I have the Court's permission to attend the men's room?

THE COURT   You may go.

KUNSTLER   Thank you.
(Brief intermission)

KUNSTLER   I have returned, your Honor.

THE COURT   Oh, let's be done with that. Really that doesn't amuse me at all.

KUNSTLER   Your Honor, I am just trying to live up to what Mr. Schultz apparently thinks we ought to do like in a schoolhouse, check in and check out.

THE COURT   My eyesight is not impaired. When you walk in here, I can see, sir.
Bring your next witness to the stand.

THE MARSHAL   Excuse me, Mr. Kunstler. [to Rubin] Will you sit down, sir.

KUNSTLER   Your Honor, Mr. Rubin is, I think, seeking to go to the men's room.

THE COURT   We made an order on that yesterday.

KUNSTLER   But that's a jail cell, your Honor, with an open, uncovered toilet.

THE COURT   I know. That was my order, and that order will be in effect.

KUNSTLER   But, your Honor, they are not convicted yet. They don't have to go into a jail cell.

THE COURT   That is not a jail cell. It's a men's room, and he may use that.

KUNSTLER   It's the first men's room I ever saw with bars, your Honor.

THE COURT   There are locks on the doors.

KUNSTLER   But—

THE COURT   They will use that, Mr. Kunstler.

KUNSTLER   It is an open, unseated toilet in a cell.

THE COURT   He may use that because they violated the privilege I have given them before. The marshals report that they have gone out and held conferences in the hall, they've gone places other than the regular public men's room. That is a place they will use when they have to go.

KUNSTLER   Your Honor—

THE COURT   There will be no argument about it.

KUNSTLER   —there is something ignominious about being in a jail cell.

THE COURT   There will be no argument about it.

THE COURT   Mr. Marshal, will you have those men at the table remain quiet. Their lawyer—

THE MARSHAL   Sit down, Mr. Rubin.

RUBIN   I want to go to the bathroom. That's a jail. I spent time in there when I was in jail. That is going behind locked doors, bars.

THE COURT   Then you may sit down if you don't want to use the facilities there.

RUBIN   I want to go to the bathroom.

DELLINGER   Convicted us already.

DAVIS   Guilty until proven innocent.

KUNSTLER   There is no argument on that, your Honor.

RUBIN   Your Honor, could Mr. Schultz be directed not to make remarks? He sarcastically pointed to the bathroom in there and said "Go to the bathroom" to me.

SCHULTZ   As I walked back to the counsel table, your Honor, Mr. Rubin was laughing at me and snickering at me, and I pointed to the bathroom. I did that, your Honor—

RUBIN   He said, "Go to the bathroom."

SCHULTZ   Your Honor—

RUBIN   —like it was a victory for you to force us to go to the bathroom in jail.

SCHULTZ   I said that. It was not very professional of me, your Honor. Apparently I succumbed a little bit to Mr. Rubin's harassment that started four months ago and of the defendants that started four months ago, a procedure and technique they have been using on authorities and policemen all of their lives. They have been trying it on your Honor and on Mr. Foran and myself, and I did, I succumbed, and I pointed to the bathroom, and that was improper, and I'm sorry, very sorry, that I did that.

KUNSTLER   Do you want to be a witness? You can sit up there.

Your Honor, can I call Mr. Schultz for a few moments? If he'd like to testify, I have no objection.

THE COURT   No, you may not. You may not, and we won't have—

KUNSTLER   Then I would like to have the record contain a motion for a mistrial at this time. Mr. Schultz—

THE COURT   And the record may contain the Court's order denying it, Mr. Kunstler.

KUNSTLER   You haven't even heard my argument.

THE COURT   What did you say?

KUNSTLER   You haven't even heard my argument.

THE COURT   Oh, it had so little basis—

KUNSTLER   No basis when a prosecutor stands in front of a jury and accuses us of harassing everybody?

THE COURT   I don't want to hear anything further. Will you be quiet, sir.

SCHULTZ   Today as I walked back to the counsel table—this morning as I walked back Rubin was making additional comments to me and I did as I stated to your Honor, simply pointed out the bathroom, and then he told me that he was going to do it on me. That is what he said. Then we—instead of going to the bathroom. That was the colloquy. I said nothing.

KUNSTLER . . . I think Mr. Lane can take care of himself.

THE COURT Oh, I'm sure that he can. I am sure that he can be taken care of, too.

KUNSTLER Well, that is threat No. 96, I guess, against lawyers.

JOHN SACK

SACK The kids would also come by and give the police the V for victory sign and one or two of the policemen would reply with a W for Wallace sign. . . .

FORAN I object to this. I never heard that before in my life.

WEINGLASS Who told you the three fingers stood for Wallace?

FORAN I object to that, your Honor.

SACK The police.

THE COURT Now, Mr. Weineruss—Weinglass.

WEINGLASS Weinglass, your Honor.

THE COURT Whatever your name is. Continue with the examination of this witness. Mr. Weinglass. Somebody held up the name.

KUNSTLER We have the name here, your Honor.

THE COURT Yes.

HOFFMAN Here it is. Shall we put it on him?

* * *

KUNSTLER Would you state to the jury what Mr. Rubin said while you were listening at this demonstration?

KUNEN Yes. Well, he began by saying that Hubert Humphrey was an ass hole, and he meant that very specifically—or he went on to elaborate that he meant that very specifically, not the buttocks or the anal sphincter, but the hole, that he was nothing, you know, and the reason he was nothing was because he had long since sold his soul to the great corporation which is the United States of America and said that Mr. Humphrey had done this because for anyone to arrive at any position of political power in this country, he has to kiss asses all the way up and he said that since the country was like a giant corporation and was run from the top down, that the elections which were to follow that November were meaningless and that the people would not fall for them. . . .

SCHULTZ And he made an obscene statement, did he not?

94

JULIAN BOND

Arlo's Restaurant

GUTHRIE   Abbie told me that he was interested in having a Festival of Life, and he was working with Jerry, and they wanted me—

THE COURT   Now, you're—

GUTHRIE   Oh, excuse me.

KUNSTLER   Try to relate it to the person. If you can't remember the person, then say so.

GUTHRIE   Right.

KUNSTLER   But try to relate it to the person.

GUTHRIE   I think it was Abbie because I was talking mostly to Abbie, and he wanted me to come down and sing at a Festival of Life here in Chicago, and we were talking about the purposes of it, which were—and what my own—and what I said to Abbie was that it would be rather difficult, you know, for me to get involved in that kind of thing because we had a lot of trouble before with festivals and gatherings because of police violence, and so we—Abbie asked me if I had any song or any kind of theme song for the festival, and I said yes. *Alice's Restaurant,* and Jerry said *"What's that?"* He had never heard it, and I proceeded to tell him about *Alice's Restaurant,* that it—

KUNSTLER   What did you tell him?

GUTHRIE   Well, I told him that it was about Alice and Ray Brock, who live in a church in Stockbridge, Massachusetts, that she ran a restaurant and that the song was not called *Alice's Restaurant* because—excuse me—the restaurant was not called *Alice's Restaurant,* but the song was, and that they lived in a church and they had a lot of room in the church, and having all the room in the church, they decided that they didn't have to take out their garbage, so—I thought it was funny, too—but anyway, they had a lot of room, and we had a big Thanksgiving dinner, and after we took out the garbage and we went to the garbage dump, but it was closed. There was a sign across the entrance saying, CLOSED ON THANKS-GIVING, and we drove around looking for another place to put the garbage. We found one and dumped it. We went back to the church, ate some more.

ARLO GUTHRIE, Julius Hoffman loved him as he would his own son. Poor Arlo!

95

The next morning I got up, we got a 'phone call from a police officer who wanted to know who had dumped the garbage. He had found my name on a piece of paper in the middle of the pile, said it was illegal to dump it there, to come down to the police station and pick up the garbage, so I went down, and he arrested me, and I went with my friend, and we all went over to the garbage, looked around. We went to court, got fined 25 bucks, and eventually picked up the garbage and it was after that I went down for my induction office physical examination thing in New York City at Whitehall Street, and I went through a lot of tests and vision examinations, I had examinations and all kinds of things. I eventually went to see a psychiatrist.

THE COURT   Did you pass?

GUTHRIE   Excuse me?

THE COURT   Did you pass the examination?

GUTHRIE   Not yet.
Anyway—

KUNSTLER   Your Honor, this is a story of *Alice's Restaurant.*

THE COURT   Oh, this didn't happen to him?

GUTHRIE   Yes, it did.

THE COURT   Oh. You're mistaken. You're mistaken, Mr. Kunstler.

GUTHRIE   It did happen to me.

THE COURT   The witness says, "This is what happened to me."
Did you pay the $25 fine?

GUTHRIE   Yes, I did.
Anyway, I finally came to see the very last person in the induction center who had asked me if I had ever been arrested. I told him yes, I was. He said, *"What for?"* I said, *"Littering,"* and he said, *"Did you ever go to court?"* and I said, *"yes",* and I was unacceptable to the draft because I had been a litterbug in Stockbridge, Massachusetts.

The end of the song is the chorus which goes: *You can get anything you want—*

THE COURT   Oh, no, no. No. I am sorry.

KUNSTLER   Your Honor, that's what he sang for the defendants.

THE COURT   I don't want the theater owner where this picture is shown to sue me.

KUNSTLER   We'll represent you, your Honor.

THE COURT   No singing. No singing. No singing, sir.

KUNSTLER   Mr. Weinglass and I, free of charge, will represent you. Then you'll have to be represented by Mr. Foran—

THE COURT   I will reserve my comment on that one. You please don't sing.

GUTHRIE   All right.

KUNSTLER   Your Honor, he did sing it to Jerry Rubin.

THE COURT   What did you?

KUNSTLER   So Jerry Rubin could ascertain whether this could be a proper song for the festival.

THE COURT   I have had everything else. I think I will forego that pleasure.

KUNSTLER   Could you say the end of the song rather than sing it?

GUTHRIE   Well, the end of the song is basically about how if one person sang the song, it wouldn't really mean anything. If two people sang it in the induction center in harmony, they might think that they were both homosexuals, and not take them. If three people sang it, they might think it was an organization, and if 50 people a day sang it or a large number of people sang it, it would be a movement, and that was the basis for my wanting it to be sung here in Chicago.

KUNSTLER   Can you say the words of the chorus?

GUTHRIE   *You can get anything you want at Alice's Restaurant*

You can get anything you want at Alice's Restaurant

*Walk right in—it's around the back
About half a mile from the railroad track, and
You can get anything you want at Alice's Restaurant*

KUNSTLER   Now, Mr. Guthrie, I show you D-222 in evidence and ask if you can tell us what that document is?

GUTHRIE   Yes. I was shown this at the meeting at the radio station, and I was asked if I would sign it, which I did.

KUNSTLER   That is, is it not, the Yippie call to the Chicago convention?

GUTHRIE   Yes, it is.

KUNSTLER   And your name appears upon it, is that correct?

GUTHRIE   Yup.

KUNSTLER   Now, in connection with D-222 which you have just been shown, did Abbie and Jerry ask you to come to Chicago?

GUTHRIE   Yes, they did.

KUNSTLER   And did you agree to come?

GUTHRIE   Yup.

KUNSTLER   Now, I call your attention to the middle of March, approximately, of 1968. Did you have a conversation with either Abbie Hoffman or Jerry Rubin?

GUTHRIE   Yes, I did. I got a 'phone call from Jerry. I was in the Tropicana Motel on Santa Monica Boulevard in Los Angeles, and I was rather angry because my name had appeared, I think, in the *New York Times* or something like that as the leader of the Yippie movement, and my concern was—

FORAN   Your Honor, would you ask the witness to give the conversation.

THE COURT   Yes. I sustain the objection. I am not concerned with his concern. I sustain the objection.

KUNSTLER   Just state what you said.

ARNOLD WASKOW

THE COURT   Are you a clergyman, sir?

WASKOW   No, sir.

THE COURT   You will have to remove your hat.

SCHULTZ   Your Honor, we don't object. I know that he—

THE COURT   I object.

WASKOW   Your Honor, I am observant and religious, too; I cannot remove my hat.

THE COURT   I will not permit him to remain on the witness stand.

KUNSTLER   Oh, your Honor—

THE COURT   I will not permit him— I've had that before. You and I have argued that.

KUNSTLER   I know, but we have argued only about spectators, your Honor. This is a witness.

RICHARD GOODWIN   A FORMER KENNEDY ADVISER

FORAN   Did Hayden tell you at that time at that place, Mr. Goodwin, or ever, that the political confrontation in Chicago was going to be the first step of the revolution? Did he tell you that in that specific statement? Did he say that to you?

GOODWIN   No. He never talked in such grandiose terms.

TWO FORMER AIDES TO EX-ATTORNEY GENERAL, RAMSEY CLARK

WESLEY POMEROY

ROGER WILKINS

But not Ramsey Clark, the one man whose story had to be relevant if only because he, and not John Mitchell, was in the government driver's seat at the time of the alleged conspiracy.

"This witness," said Judge Hoffman "could not testify to anything material or relevant."

Meanwhile among the spectators

DUSTIN HOFFMAN

JUDY COLLINS

COLLINS   There were a number of people who were singers, entertainers. There was also Jerry Rubin who was there, Abbie Hoffman was there. Allen Ginsberg was there, and sang a mantra. Some people from the United States of America were there — that's a group. . . .

KUNSTLER   Now, what did you do at that press conference?

COLLINS   Well, where have all the flowers—

THE COURT   Just a minute, young lady.

COLLINS   —where have all the flowers gone?

DEPUTY MARSHAL JOHN J. GRACIOUS   I'm sorry. The Judge would like to speak to you.

THE COURT   We don't allow any singing in his court. I'm sorry.

COLLINS   May I recite the words?

KUNSTLER   Well, your Honor, we have had films. I have not objected strongly every time a person who sang at some occasion has attempted to do so and was stopped, but I think it is as legitimate as a movie. It is the actual thing she did. . . .

98

KUNSTLER   Your Honor, this is what she said at the press conference. It was in singing. She's going to say it.

FORAN   It is not relevant to the charges in this indictment.

THE COURT   I sustain the objection.

KUNSTLER   All right.

KUNSTLER   What did you say at the press conference?

COLLINS   I said a great deal. I said at the press conference that I want to see a celebration of life, not of destruction. I said that I personally, as a singer, which is, by the way, my profession, as your profession is a lawyer, sir, that my soul and my profession and my life has become part of a movement toward hopefully removing the causes for death, the causes for war, the causes for the prevalence of violence in our society, and in order to make my voice heard, I said that I would indeed come to Chicago and that I would sing. That is what I do, that's my profession.

I said that I wanted to participate in a festival of life. I feel that as I spoke at that press conference and I stated what I wanted to do, I expressed the feelings of other people, not only of myself, because I do have an audience and I am a singer. I said that I was there because life was the force that I wished to make my songs and my life known for.

I said:

"Where have all the flowers gone? Long time passing.

"Where have all the flowers gone? Long time ago.

"Where have all the flowers gone? Young girls have picked them.

"Every one. Oh, when will they ever learn?

"When will they ever learn?

"Where have all the young girls gone? Long time passing. . . .

"Where have all the young girls gone? Long time ago.

"Where have all the young girls gone? Gone for husbands, every one.

"Oh, when will they ever learn?

"When will they ever learn?

"Where have all the young men gone? Long time passing.

"Where have all the young men gone? Long time ago.

"Where have all the young men gone? Gone for soldiers, every one. Oh, when will they ever learn?

"Where have all the soldiers gone? Long time passing.

"Where have all the soldiers gone? Long Time ago.

"Where have all the soldiers gone? Gone to grave yards. Every one? Oh, when will they ever learn?"

"When will they ever learn?"

I said that I would give my music and my voice to a situation in which people could express themselves about life with a permit, of course, from the City of Chicago.

DEFENDANT RENNIE DAVIS, a frustrating witness. Such a witness could give a prosecutor an ulcer.

MARSHAL JONESON Will you be quiet, Mr. Dellinger.

DELLINGER After such hypocrisy I don't particularly feel like being quiet. I said before the Judge was the chief prosecutor, and he's proved the point.

THE COURT Will you remain quiet. Will you remain quiet, sir.

DELLINGER You let Foran give a foreign policy speech but when he [Kunstler] tries to answer it, you interrupt him and won't let him speak,

There's no pretense of fairness in this Court.

MARSHAL JONESON Be quiet, sir.

DELLINGER —just like you gagged Bobby Seale because you couldn't afford to listen to the truth that he was saying to you. You're accusing me. I'm a pacifist.

JONESON Sit down, please, and be quiet.

DELLINGER I am employ[ing] non-violence, and you're accusing me of violence, and you have a man right here, backed up by guns, jails, and force and violence. That is the difference between us.

* * *

KUNSTLER By Attorney General Mitchell's press conference—

SCHULTZ The rules of the court prohibiting every attorney in this case from making press conferences, and he has been doing it and he stands before this Court and says the Government has.

DELLINGER And they had rules like that in Nazi Germany.

FORAN   And what you want to urge young people to do is to revolt, isn't that right?

DAVIS   Yes, revolt. That is probably right.

FORAN   And you have stated, have you not, "That there can be no question by the time that I am through that I have every intention of urging that you revolt, that you join the movement, that you become a part of a growing force for insurrection in the United States." You have said that, haven't you?

DAVIS   I was standing right next to Fred Hampton when I said that, and later he was murdered.

FORAN   You said that, did you not, sir? You stated that, did you not?

DAVIS   Side by side with Fred Hampton who was murdered in this city by policemen.

*   *   *

THE COURT   This trial is going on. Call your next witness. Three of the defendants have gone out.

KUNSTLER   They are bringing him in.

THE COURT   Oh, it takes three to bring the next witness in?

KUNSTLER   No, but he likes company.

THE COURT   Does he want to hug the witness too, the way they hugged this witness? I have never presided at a trial where there was so much physical affection demonstrated in the courtroom.

VOICES   RIGHT ON.

THE COURT   Perhaps that is part of the love-in, I don't know.

KUNSTLER   Maybe this not a bad place for it to happen, in the United States District Court.

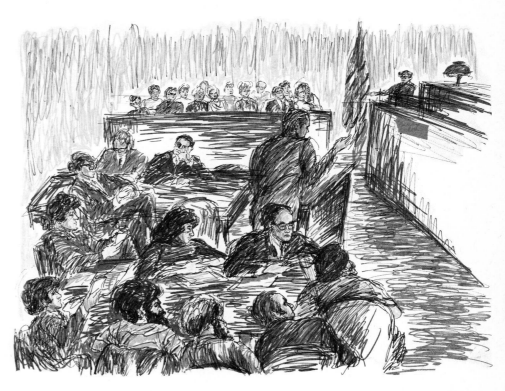

Foran was later to say that Rennie Davis was the toughest witness he ever cross-examined.

And his fellow defendants must have thought so too.
At last, one point on which Foran and his foes agreed. Perhaps things are not that hopeless afterall.

THE COURT   Mayor Daley, as far as I am concerned, and so I am told, is a good mayor. I don't think I have ever spoken three sentences to him other than— I don't know whether I spoke to him when he was on the stand here or not. Perhaps I did direct him to answer some question, I don't know.

* * *

THE COURT   I didn't want anybody to get the impression that anybody but President Eisenhower nominated me for this position on the bench and that I was confirmed by the Senate of the United States unanimously. I want the witness to feel easy.

Rennie: *Take your hands from your pocket, Schultz.*

NORMAN MAILER

Schultz: *We are to determine facts here.*

Mailer: *Facts are nothing without their nuance, sir.*

MAILER   I said that Chicago was a city run by a man who had been a giant and had ended as a beast. I was referring to Mayor Daley. And then I went on and said that the country was being run or had been run by a man from Texas who begun as a giant and ended as a beast.

* * *

KUNSTLER   Now, Mr. Mailer, can you give us some idea of your experience in the political arena? Have you run for public office?

MAILER   Yes, I ran in the Democratic Primary for Mayor last spring, and I came in fourth in a field of five.

THE COURT   You didn't say what city, sir.

MAILER   I am sorry, Judge, in New York City.

THE COURT   I knew I haven't seen your name on our ballot.

At last, even Foran and Schultz finally tried a little—humor? But by comparison with "Julie" Hoffman and "Billy" Kunstler, the Tom-'n-Dick humor, if that is what it was, was elementary at its best.

PETE SEEGER

KUNSTLER   Mr. Seeger, recently you conducted your singing on board a vessel, did you not?

FORAN   Objection, your Honor.

SCHULTZ   Objection.

THE COURT   I sustain the objection.

KUNSTLER   Who is going to do it?

SCHULTZ   We haven't decided yet.

FORAN   Flip a coin.

SCHULTZ   I'm taller, your Honor. I object.

THE COURT   I sustain the objection.

FORAN   He's only an inch, Judge. I'm smarter.

103

STAUGHTON LYND, Professor of American History

PROFESSOR LYND   I have the opinion that the right which is enumerated in the First Amendment, adopted shortly after the ratification of the United States Constitution, the right to petition for redress of grievances, had a much broader meaning to the men who made the American Revolution and who wrote the United States Constitution than we ordinarily assume. . . .

And what they were doing in this petitionary process prior to the American Revolution was not asking for the passage of a particular law, but crying out against what the Declaration of Independence called a long train of abuses evincing the design of the attempt to create an absolute despotism. . . .

This is what the petitioning meant to them, and the reason that I think this concept of petitioning is relevant to the situation before this Court is that it seems to me that the First Amendment was involved in what happened in Chicago in 1968 in a far broader sense than in its particular senses of the right to march, the right to use a public park, the right to free speech, and the right of free press. It seems to me that the jury might wish to consider the entire process of the demonstration, that which made people come to Chicago, as a kind of petitioning process in which people who felt that their elected government was no longer responsive to them, felt themselves to be in the same position as the colonists before the American Revolution and came to Chicago to make one last direct appeal to the men of power who were assembled in the Democratic Convention . . .

I don't see how we can say that the American people have a right to revolution as a last resort against total oppression and say that they lack a right of resistance short of revolution to a partially oppressive situation. . . .

. . .This is a form of intermediate resistance full of precedent from the American Revolution, very much in the American tradition, and it seems to me at least quite appropriate in the circumstances of 1968.

WEINGLASS If the Court please, that completes the offer of proof.

THE COURT What is the position of the Government in respect to what has been described here by Mr. Weinglass as an offer of proof?

FORAN The Government objects.

THE COURT I sustain the objection. . . .

SUDDENLY, THINGS ARE NO LONGER AT EASE

DELLINGER   I made the speech.

THE COURT   What did you say?

DELLINGER   I made the speech. Was there anything in the speech that suggested I won't show up for trial the next day or simply that I criticized your conduct of the trial?

THE COURT   I didn't ask you to rise, sir, and I am certainly not going to be interrogated.

DELLINGER   Why are you threatening me with revocation of bail for exercising my freedom of speech? What has that got to do with it? I am here, aren't I?

A VOICE   RIGHT ON.

HOFFMAN   We all give the same speech.

WEINGLASS   Another spectator was physically carried by the marshals from the courtroom.

THE COURT   Yes. From what I have observed here, I think that that sort of thing should have been done before.

WEINGLASS   I repeat, I have never seen or heard anything in the many, many years such as occurred during this trial.

KUNSTLER   I want to comment on this your Honor, because I think what you have just said is about the most outrageous statement I have ever heard from a bench, and I am going to say my piece right now, and you can hold me in contempt right now if you wish to.

You have violated every principle of fair play when you excluded Ramsey Clark from that witness stand. The *New York Times*, among others, has called it the ultimate outrage in American justice.

VOICES   RIGHT ON.

KUNSTLER   I am outraged to be in this Court before you. Now because I made a statement on Friday that I had only a cameraman, and I discovered on Saturday that Ralph Abernathy, who is chairman of the Mobilization, is in town, and can be here, and because you took the whole day from us on Thursday by listening to this ridiculous argument about whether Ramsey Clark could take that stand in front of the jury, I am trembling because I am so outraged. I haven't been about to get this out before, and I am saying it now, and then I want you to put me in jail if you want to. You can do anything you want with me, if you want to, because I feel disgraced to be here, to say to us on the technicality of my representation that we can't put Ralph Abernathy on the stand. He is co-chairman of the MOBE. He has relevant testimony. I know that doesn't mean much in this Court when the Attorney General of the United States walked out of here with his lips so tight he could hardly breathe, and if you could see the expression on his face, you would know, and his wife informed me he never felt such anger at the United States Government as at not being able to testify on that stand.

* *

KUNSTLER   . . . I have sat here for four and a half months and watched the objections denied and sustained by your Honor, and I know that this not a fair trial. I know it in my heart. If I have to lose my license to practice law and if I have to go to jail, I can't think of a better cause to go to jail for and to lose my license for—

A VOICE   RIGHT ON.

KUNSTLER   —than to tell your Honor that you are doing a disservice to the law in saying that we can't have Ralph Abernathy in the stand. You are saying truth will not come out —

— then I think there is nothing more for me to say.

THE COURT   There is not much more you could say.

KUNSTLER   I am going to turn back to my seat with the realization that everything I have learned throughout my life has come to naught, that there is no meaning in this Court, and there is no law in this Court—

VOICES   RIGHT ON.

KUNSTLER   —and these men are going to jail by virtue of a legal lynching—

VOICES   RIGHT ON.

KUNSTLER   —and that your Honor is wholly responsible for that, and if this is what your career is going to end on, if this is what your pride is going to be built on, I can only say to your Honor, "Good luck to you."

THE COURT   Out with those applauders.

DAVIS   I applauded, too, your Honor. Throw me out.

THE COURT   Unfortunately, you have to remain, Mr. Davis, but we note that you applauded. . . .

KUNSTLER   We have a right to state our objection to resting before the jury.

THE COURT   Don't do it.

KUNSTLER   I am going to have to put my liberty in your hands on that score.

SCHULTZ   Mr. Kunstler is simply inviting it.

KUNSTLER   Oh, of course I am inviting it because what your Honor is doing is a disgrace in this Court.

THE COURT   He did more than invite.

*   *   *

He could not testify because he was fifteen minutes late.

I have just returned from abroad as an ambassador of goodwill for my country. When I was asked difficult questions about my country's system of justice and equality, I groped for words to explain that both existed. When foreigners said, "You have no democracy, no justice, in America", I attempted to prove that we did. After my experience yesterday in this court, I can no longer defend my country against such attacks.

He offended Julius Hoffman because he and Kunstler embraced each other in the U.S. District Court.

I have been informed that my embracing Bill Kunstler prejudiced the government's case against my brothers on trial. The least I can do for a man who has been my friend and lawyer for ten years is to embrace him warmly when I see him, and if this prejudices the government's case against his clients, then I hope that I will have the opportunity to do it again.

THE REBUTTAL

KUNSTLER You miss no opportunity in front of the jury to deride the defense table.

THE COURT I am not the janitor. I told you that before. I have a lot of responsibilities; among them is not tending to the furnace.

KUNSTLER Your Honor, I am not asking you to stoke the furnace; I am merely asking you to find someone to—

KALE

RICHARD PHILLIPS

IRWIN BOCK

U.S. MARSHAL,
RON DOBOWSKI

UH! I MEAN . . . LBJ, YES, BUT NOT . . . NO!

KUNSTLER   What about Mr. Hoffman?

PHILLIPS   Which one is Mr. Hoffman?

KUNSTLER   You are the first one who hasn't identified him. This is Mr. Hoffman over here.
(*laughter in the courtroom.*)

THE COURT   Let the record show that Mr. Hoffman
stood up, lifted his shirt up, and bared his body
in the presence of the jury—

KUNSTLER   Your Honor, that is Mr. Hoffman's way.
(*More laughter in the courtroom*)

KUNSTLER   Your Honor, that is Mr. Hoffman's way.

THE COURT   It is a bad way in a courtroom.

KUNSTLER   I remember President Johnson bared his
body to the nation.

THE COURT   Well, that may be.

KUNSTLER   Over national television.

THE COURT   Maybe that is why he isn't President
any more.

To Dellinger, it was "BULLSHIT",

To Julius Hoffman, a "BARNYARD VULGARITY"

THE COURT This morning I was asked by Mr. Kunstler whether I wasn't taking things too seriously. I certainly do take them seriously.

SCHULTZ Did you see where he went?

RIORDAN He left with the head of the group that were carrying the flags.

JAMES RIORDAN, Deputy Chief of Police, Chicago.

DELLINGER Oh, bullshit.

THE COURT Did you get that, Miss Reporter?

KUNSTLER Sometimes the human spirit can stand so much, and I think Mr. Dellinger reached the end of his.

THE COURT I have never heard in more than a half century of the bar a man using profanity in this court or in a courtroom.

HOFFMAN I've never been in an obscene court, either.

THE COURT I never have as a spectator or as a judge. I never did.

KUNSTLER You never sat here as a defendant and heard liars on the stand. . . .

SCHULTZ Your Honor, we had to sit with our lips tight, listening to those defendants, to those two de- fendants, Mr. Hayden and Mr. Hoffman, perjure themselves.

DELLINGER You're a snake. We have to try to put you in jail for ten years for telling lies about us, Dick Schultz.

MARSHAL JONESON Be quiet, Mr. Dellinger.

DELLINGER When it's all over the Judge will go to Florida, but if he has his way, we'll go to jail. That is what we're fighting for, not just for us, but for all the rest of the people in the country who are being oppressed.

A SPECTATOR Damn right, Assert ourselves.

VOICES RIGHT ON.

* * *

THE COURT   May I say that I think I have demonstrated great patience during this trial in trying to insure a fair trial both for the Government and for the defendants. Some people have the notion that there is only one party to a case and that is the defense. There are two parties. The title of this case is "United States of America vs. Dellinger and others."

I have up here a transcript of what was said and done this afternoon. I do not intend to use the obscenities engaged in or used or applied by Mr. Dellinger. I don't use that kind of language myself. And I don't even like to use it in court here to quote a defendant. I shall turn over this transcript which has been prepared by the official reporter for me to the United States Attorney, and I hereby, Mr. Clerk, terminate the bail of the defendant David Dellinger and remand him to the custody of the United States Marshal for the Northern District of Illinois for the remainder of this trial.

DAVIS   Mr. Rubin's wife they are now taking—

RUBIN   Keep your hands off her. You see them taking away my wife?

DAVIS   Why don't you gag the press, too, and the attorneys, gag them?

* * *

KUNSTLER   Your Honor, is there no decency left here? Can't we just argue the point?

THE COURT   Oh, wait a minute. I have another contempt matter here, or, rather, it is a contempt matter as distinguished from the last, and you will have to go away from that lectern. You can't stand there and insult the United States District Court.

KUNSTLER   I am not insulting you. I am asking for argument. Everything you characterize as such an insult—

THE COURT   Yes, you are.

KUNSTLER   Everything in this case is an insult.

THE COURT   You just insulted me again and you have done it often.

KUNSTLER   Every argument is not an insult.

THE COURT   This case is recessed.

KUNSTLER   I would like to say my piece. He is my client, and I think this is an utterly—
(Disorder in the courtroom.)

I would like to—
You brought this on, your Honor. This is your fault. This is what happened in Chicago. You made the power move. You exerted the power, and I would like to argue the point.

THE COURT   You won't argue that point.

KUNSTLER   I will argue, your Honor, that your Honor's action is completely and utterly vindictive, that there is no authority that says because a defendant blurts out a word in court—

THE COURT   This isn't the first word, and I won't argue this.

DAVIS   This Court is bullshit.

113

DAVIS You can jail a revolutionary, but you can't jail the revolution.

HOFFMAN You are a disgrace to the Jews. You would have served Hitler better. Dig it.

THE MARSHAL That was Mr. Hoffman, your Honor.

THE COURT I saw him and I heard him.

* * *

HOFFMAN Your idea of justice is the only obscenity in the room. You *schtunk. Vo den? Shanda fur de goyem?* Huh.

(The not exactly flattering Yiddish can be translated as "You skunk. What next? Playing up to the gentiles?" i.e. the Establishment.—J.O.)

RUBIN You are a fascist, Hoffman—

HOFFMAN I heard you haven't let anybody free in four years. That's right, stop me.

THE MARSHAL That was Mr. Rubin the last time your Honor.
Clear the court.

THE COURT Clear the courtroom, Mr. Marshal.

DAVIS Get as many people as you can. Just like the Convention all over again.

THE MARSHAL Clear the court.

THE COURT Clear the court.

A FEMALE VOICE You little prick.

114

WEINGLASS Your Honor will not permit me to continue a legal argument?

THE COURT You heard what I said. I deny the motion.

DAVIS May we defend ourselves if our lawyers can't?

KUNSTLER I think the Marshal is going to have this.

THE COURT Mr. Marshal, will you ask the Defendant Hoffman to—

HOFFMAN This ain't the Standard Club.

THE MARSHAL Mr. Hoffman—

HOFFMAN Oh, tell him to stick it up his bowling ball. How is your war stock doing, Julie?

RUBIN You are the laughing stock of the world, Julius Hoffman; the laughing stock of the world.

HOFFMAN Mies van der Rohe was a Kraut, too.

RUBIN Every kid in the world hates you, knows what you represent.

DOBOWSKI Be quiet, Mr. Rubin.

RUBIN You are synonymous with the name Adolf Hitler. Julius Hoffman equals Adolf Hitler today.

HOFFMAN You know you cannot win the fucking case. The only way you can is to put us away for contempt. We have contempt for this Court, and for you, Schultz, and for the whole rotten system. That's the only justice. That is why they want this because they can't prove this fucking case.

THE COURT I order the defendants and their counsel not to make reference to this motion made.

RUBIN And the reason is because it is a hung jury, and you know it. You want to get us in jail anyway. That is the reason because you know you are losing the jury trial, but you have got to get us in jail, because the people will decide that we are not guilty, so you are going to railroad us into jail.

* * *

RUBIN Gestapo.

HOFFMAN You put him [Dellinger—ed.] in jail because you lost faith in the jury system. I hear you haven't lost a case before a jury in 24 trials. Only the Krebiozen people got away. We're going to get away, too. That's why you're throwing us in jail this way.

Contempt is a tyranny of the court, and you are a tyrant. That's why we don't respect it. It's a tyrant.

HOFFMAN The judges in Nazi Germany ordered sterilization. Why don't you do that, Judge Hoffman?

THE COURT Mr. Marshal, will you have Mr. Hoffman remain quiet, please? Order him to remain quiet.

HOFFMAN Order us? Order us? You got to cut our tongues out to order us, Julie.

115

You railroaded Seale so he wouldn't get a jury trial either. Four years for contempt without a jury trial.

THE MARSHAL   Mr. Hoffman. Will you shut up.

HOFFMAN   No, I won't shut up. I ain't an automaton like you. I don't want to be a tyrant and I don't care for a tyrannical system.
   Best friend blacks ever had. Huh. How many blacks are in Drake Towers? How many are in the Standard Club. How many own stock in Brunswick Corporation?

THE COURT   May the record show defendants Hoffman and Rubin came in at 1:28 with their—

RUBIN   The Marshal just came and asked us to come in. We came as soon as we were asked.

THE COURT   And also attired in what might be called collegiate robes.

RUBIN   Judges' robes, sir.

A DEFENDANT   Death robes.

THE COURT   Some might even consider them judicial robes.

RUBIN   Judicial robes.

THE COURT   Your idea, Mr. Kunstler? Another one of your brilliant ideas?

KUNSTLER   Your Honor, I can't take credit for this one.

THE COURT   That amazes me.

THE COURT   Mr. Marshal, the Court will be in recess until Monday morning.

DOBOWSKI   Everyone please rise.

DELLINGER   You now have my respect, Judge, I am sure you know.

DAVIS   Have a good weekend, Judge.

DOBOWSKI   Everyone please rise.

THE COURT   You have got all of that, have you?

THE REPORTER   Yes, your Honor.

A DEFENDANT   One more, Julie, and you'll be a saint.

116

KUNSTLER I am glad your Honor is laughing because you know I have always advocated that there is room in the courtroom for a little laughter.

THE COURT I am laughing now. I don't promise to laugh the rest of this trial. . . .

THE COURT And I guess I am laughing because of what I was about to say. I am not even certain that you understood the references that were made here by one of the defendants in one of the most ancient languages. I don't think it was a dead language, but the language out of which the language came was a dead language.

KUNSTLER The defense would have no objection, your Honor, if you used that language for your charge.

THE COURT Referring to who?

KUNSTLER You mean Mr. Hoffman's Hebraic expressions?

THE COURT Yes. Well, if you can call them Hebraic.

KUNSTLER We would even consent to that, your Honor.

THE COURT I would think the authorities would call that Yiddish, wouldn't they? I don't know whether you understand that or not.

KUNSTLER I understand the intonation of it, your Honor, and then Mr. Hoffman explained it to me later.

THE COURT Oh, he translated it?

KUNSTLER He translated some of it, some of the more esoteric—

THE COURT I had the benefit of a not too accurate translation in one of the newspapers.

KUNSTLER Schtunk I heard before. The other expression I had to have translated for me.

*   *   *   *   *

After the summation, the judge called the press to his chambers for a tete-a-tete. He briefed them on his instructions to the Jury.

"You", he said kindly to one of the press artists, *"You make me look like a prune on TV."*

He who would laugh last, but has laughed all along, should never have laughed in the first place.

Within minutes of sending the Jury in to deliberate on their VERDICT, Judge Julius Hoffman began sentencing the defendants and their lawyers for contempt of court. The citations were minute but so numerous that most of the defendants had long jail sentences; long enough that, as far as going to jail was concerned, it hardly mattered whether the Jury found them guilty or innocent.

THE COURT   This was a long trial. The behavior of the defendants and Defense Counsel was prepared with direct and defiant contempt for the Court and the federal judicial system as a whole. Here is a record of exceptional circumstances which were disruptive of the proceedings.

. . . I will first consider the conduct of the Defendant David Dellinger. . . .

DELLINGER   You want us to be like good Germans supporting the evils of our decade and then when we refused to be good Germans and came to Chicago and demonstrated, despite the threats and intimidations of the establishment, now you want us to be like good Jews, going quietly and politely to the concentration camps while you and this Court suppress freedom and the truth. And the fact is that I am not prepared to do that. You want us to stay in our place like black people were supposed to stay in their place—

THE COURT   Mr. Marshal, I will ask you to have Mr. Dellinger sit down.

DELLINGER   —like poor people were supposed to stay in their place, like people without formal education are supposed to stay in their place, like women are supposed to stay in their place—

THE COURT   I will ask you to sit down.

DELLINGER   Like children are supposed to stay in their place, like lawyers—for whom I thank—I thank you—are supposed to stay in their places.

It is a travesty on justice and if you had any sense at all you would know that that record that you read condemns you and not us.

THE COURT   All right.

DELLINGER   And it will be one of thousands and thousands of rallying points for a new generation of Americans who will not put up with tyranny, will not put up with a facade of democracy without the reality.

* * *

DELLINGER   . . . People no longer will be quiet. People are going to speak up. I am an old man and I am just speaking feebly and not too well, but I reflect the spirit that will echo—

THE COURT   Take him out—

DELLINGER   —throughout the world—
(*applause.*)

DELLINGER   —comes from my children who came yesterday—
(*Complete disorder in the courtroom.*)

118

KUNSTLER My life has come to nothing, I am not anything any more. You destroyed me and everybody else. Put me in jail now, for God's sake, and get me out of this place. Come to mine now. Come to mine now, Judge, please. Please. I beg you. Come to mine. Do me, too. I don't want to be out.

* * *

I am sorry I do not have the complete transcript with me so that I could report on each of the 23 counts in detail.

This morning you said that the only alternative to what I have done here in the courtroom is anarchy, and perhaps you are right. You have said as well that as a matter of law, there is no defense for what we have done, and I believe that there is a defense for what we have done.

DAVIS . . . Judge, you represent all that is old, ugly, bigoted and repressive in this country, and I will tell you that the spirit at this defense is going to devour your sickness in the next generation.

* * *

THE COURT It is the spirit of rebellion against the orders of the Court. I know you don't like courts, but you are going to have to like them or deal with them and you had better decide to just respect them. If you don't want to, that is, [of] course, your privilege, but you are going to have to somewhere along the line take the consequences. That is all. . . .

THE COURT To be characterized as a racist was an absolute absurdity. There is nothing here that shows me a racist. Is there now? Now is there anything that shows me a racist? You think I disciplined Mr. Seale because of his color? It's what he said and what he did. And a white man would have been disciplined in the same way.

DAVIS You have just jailed one of the most beautiful and one of the most courageous men in the United States.

THE COURT All right. Now we will talk about you Mr. Davis. . . .

THE COURT Mr. Davis, do you care to be heard?

DAVIS Yes.

Rennard Davis: 25 months and 14 days on 23 counts of contempt

119

HAYDEN So, your Honor, before your eyes you see the most vital ingredient of your system collapsing because the system does not hold together.

THE COURT Oh, don't be so pessimistic. Our system isn't collapsing. Fellows as smart as you could do awfully well under this system. I am not trying to convert you, mind you.

HOFFMAN We don't want a place in the regiment, Julie.

Abbot Hoffman: 8 months on 24 counts of contempt

* * * * *

HOFFMAN Furthermore, you have asked us to respect the law but this is a law—I sat there on the witness stand and Mr. Schultz said, "What were you wondering?" as he quoted from my book and speeches. "What were you wondering that night when you stood before a building?"

And I said, "Wonder? Wonder? I have never been

HAYDEN [F]or a lot of people who feel the way I do, we are in the movie "Z," I mean there is not going to be a higher court.

THE COURT You are going to shout them down right here at the trial level, is that right?

HAYDEN I am not raising my voice. But I find this is the only place I may have or I may in the next ten years be allowed to speak to these people, to them and to the press. But the point that I wanted to make about punishment is that the problem that I think people have who want to punish us—Mr. Foran who calls us evil, people who want to punish us, is that what must cause a great problem for the understanding of people like that is why the punishment does not seem to have effect. Even as the elder Dellinger is taken off for two years, a younger Dellinger fights back.

* * * * *

THE COURT [Y]ou are going to have to abide by the system, the rules of the system, the federal system, when you get into trouble. . . .

* * *

HAYDEN I think the difficulty is trying to try people for political crimes or crimes of consciousness or ideological crimes. That is what brings politics and consciousness into the courtroom. . . .

* * *

THE COURT . . . I will hear from Mr. Hoffman if he wants to be heard.

HOFFMAN You have always referred to—they were my remarks—you said that we did not pay tribute to the highest court in the land, but to us the Federal Court is not the highest court in the land.

THE COURT I didn't hear myself say that.

HOFFMAN Oh, yes, you did. You always call it the highest court in the land. Sure.

THE COURT The Supreme Court is.

HOFFMAN We don't consider it the highest. We consider the people the highest court in the land.

HOFFMAN When decorum is oppression, the only dignity that free men have is the right to speak out. Furthermore, you said we do not honor your authority, but we recognize that authority as illegitimate in the same way that the authority that decided the political decisions in that heavy week in August of 1968 was illegitimate and did not represent the will and the desire of the people.

So we cannot respect an authority that we regard as illegitimate authority.

on trial for wondering. Is that like a dream?"

He said, "Yes, that's like a dream."

And I have never been on trial for my dreams before. How can I respect the highest court in the land or a Federal Government that puts people on trial for their dreams. I can show it no respect.

120

RUBIN I want to discuss the contempts and the motivation behind them, which would affect your punishment and I want to start with the references that I have made on a number of occasions to Gestapo, fascism and Hitler, and I want to explain what motivated me to say that.

Everything that happened in Nazi Germany was legal. It happened in courtrooms, just like this. It was done by judges, judges who wore robes and judges who quoted the law and judges who said, "This is the law, respect it."

We saw Nazi Germany [as] immoral, and I think that this is the closest thing that I personally experienced to what happened in Nazi Germany, and it was the closest thing in my experience to say to you, to communicate to you, that just quoting law is no answer, because the law in the courtroom gagged and chained Bobby Seale and I refuse to stand up and say, "Heil Hitler" when a black man was gagged and chained and I think that any human being sitting in that courtroom refused to stand up and that's why I refused to stand up because *I* came to this trial. I wanted to be indicted.

I issued a statement I was indicted upon the Academy Award protest. I was ready for a trial with lawyers, a full defense. The moment you walked in, I don't know what day it was, for the arraignment, we got from you instantly the message we were going to jail, and I think it's interesting that while the jury is out, before it reaches a verdict, the 10 of us are going to jail. Who has respect for the law?

* * *

By punishing us, you are going to have ten million in two weeks. Deterrent? Putting us in jail is just going to produce more trials like this. You have done more to destroy the judicial system. That's what punishment is going to be; that's what punishment is going to be. Revenge never got you anywhere. By having to punish us, you have shown the world that this judicial system has lost the respect of the youth, and the youth will free us. We're going to jail with smiles on our faces because we know that in jail, there are millions of kids, young kids out there who identify with us, and are going to fight to free us, and that's the revolution. And your jailing us is a vindictive, revengeful act. . . .

121

Lee Weiner: 2 months and 18 days on 7 counts of contempt

WEINER   I think the judicial system as an idea, an abstract idea, is a fairly reasonable one, and so I have a great deal of sympathy, and I guess, pity for Lennie and Bill who have worked so hard to gain some expertise in a system which should, if it functioned adequately, provide some opportunity for some kind of abstract notion of justice to come at least close to, but I think here, you, not necessarily because you are anything necessarily evil, but simply because you are what you are, who you are—you are older than us—

* * *

Like a naughty pupil brought before his boarding school headmaster—defiant in intention, humble and obedient in effect

John Froines: 5 months and 15 days on 10 counts of contempt

THE COURT   I will next consider the conduct of the lawyers in this case—oh, I beg your pardon. We have —I almost forgot to take care of Mr. Froines. Mr. Kunstler has finished. Mr. Froines, I give you the same opportunity I accorded all of the others to speak in mitigation of punishment here, but without saying offensive things to the Court.

FROINES   It's part of being a media unknown that even the Judge finally forgets you're here.

In the Oregon Constitution there is an article which I think describes some of what we do and that is entitled "Natural Rights Inherent in the People." It says that we declare all men, when they form as a social compact, are equal in right, that all power is inherent in the people, and all free governments are founded on their authority and instituted for their peace, safety and happiness and they have at all times a right to alter, reform or abolish the government in a manner as they may think proper. And I think that's what we did.

122

THE COURT This matter now involves the conduct of Mr. William Kunstler, counsel for some of the defendants here, who has participated in this trial from the very beginning.

I have said here frequently that the Court has never had the occasion to hold a lawyer in contempt, and only on one occasion did the Court hold someone who is not a lawyer in contempt. . . .

I recognize the obligation of a lawyer to defend a client with vigor, and secure for his client the full benefits under the law. Nevertheless, if he crosses the bounds of legal propriety, the Court must deal appropriately with that conduct.

KUNSTLER I just have a few words, your Honor. Your Honor, I have been a lawyer since December of 1948, when I was first admitted to the bar in the state of New York. Since that time, I have practiced before, among other courts, the Supreme Court of the United States, the United States Court of Appeals for the First, Second, Third, Fourth, Fifth, Sixth, Seventh, Tenth, District of Columbia Circuits, Federal District Courts throughout a great deal of the United States, and the United States Court of Military Appeals. . . .

Until today I have never once been disciplined by any Judge, federal or state, although a large part of my practice, at least for the last decade, has taken place in hostile southern courts where I was representing black and white clients in highly controversial civil rights cases.

Yesterday, for the first time in my career, I completely lost my composure in a courtroom, as I watched the older daughter of David Dellinger being rushed out of the room because she clapped her hands to acknowledge what amounted to her father's farewell statement to her.

I felt then such a deep sense of utter futility that I could not help crying, something I had not done publicly since childhood.

I have tried with all my heart to represent my clients in the face of what I consider—and still consider—repressive and unjust conduct toward them. If I have to pay with my liberty for such representation, then that is the price of my beliefs and my sensibilities.

I can only hope that my fate does not deter other lawyers throughout the country, who, in the difficult days that lie ahead, will be asked to defend clients against a steadily increasing governmental encroachment upon their most fundamental liberties. If they are so deterred, then my punishment will have effects of such terrifying consequences that I dread to contemplate the future domestic and foreign course of this country. However, I have the utmost faith that my beloved brethren at the bar, young and old alike, will not allow themselves to be frightened out of defending the poor, the persecuted, the radicals and the militants, the black people, the pacifists, and the political pariahs of this, our common land.

But to those lawyers who may, in learning of what may happen to me, waver, I can only say this, stand firm, remain true to those ideals of the law which even if openly violated here and in other places, never desert those principles of equality, justice and freedom without which life has little if any meaning.

I may not be the greatest lawyer in the world, your Honor, but I think that I am at this moment, along with my colleague, Leonard Weinglass, the most privileged. We are being punished for what we believe in.

Your Honor, I am ready, sir, to be sentenced, and I would appreciate it if I could be permitted to remain standing at this lectern where I have spent the greater part of the past five months, while you do so.

123

KUNSTLER Your Honor, I am glad your Honor spoke because I suddenly feel nothing but compassion for you. Everything else has dropped away.

For perhaps the first time in twenty weeks, Julius Hoffman was polite enough to call Weinglass by the correct name.

WEINGLASS This has been a long, difficult, highly contested proceeding in which all of us at one time or another have lost our sense of professional control and judgment. I only have to cite to the court Mr. Schultz' reference to the bathroom in front of the jury, for which he later apologized. There were unlawful references to the fact that two of the defendants took the stand and perjured themselves for which he apologized; Mr. Foran's statements that Tom Hayden and Rennie Davis were guilty of a crime for which they had neither been charged nor were before a grand jury, for which he later apologized.

But I have no quarrel with either Mr. Foran or Mr. Schultz. They were attorneys involved in a very difficult adversary proceeding and they are entitled to errors of judgment, to loss of control, which they committed in the course of this four and a half months.

For the same understandable defects, Mr. Kunstler and myself will have to serve time in jail. . . .

*   *   *

WEINGLASS With respect to our different understandings of respect, I was hopeful when I came here that after 20 weeks the Court would know my name and I didn't receive that which I thought was the minimum—

*   *   *

THE COURT Well, I am going to tell you about that. . . .

THE COURT I have got a very close friend named Weinruss and I know nobody by the name of Weinrob—and somehow or other the name of Weinruss stuck in my mind and it is your first appearance here. You have seen lawyers pass before this bar all during your four to five months here whom I know intimately and I scarcely ever forget a lawyer's name even when he hasn't been in for 20 years.

* *

WEINGLASS My natural instincts are and have always been to avoid, if possible, a protracted fight. I am not as strong a man as Bill Kunstler by far, and I think I am more vulnerable to what I perceive to be intimidation—whether it is or not. And I have had to fight that instinct here in court, not only because of the inspiration I drew from Bill Kunstler as well as the other persons who have worked with me.

THE COURT Did you ever feel like tapping one of those defendants, one or more of them, on the hand when they were assailing me with vile epithets to say, "Hey, hey, be quiet?"

WEINGLASS Does your Honor seriously believe that what was in conflict here in this courtroom could have dissipated by an admonishment from Bill Kunstler or myself?"

THE COURT I judge your whole attitude toward the Court by your omission to do that. But I am obligated under the law to particularize these items of contempt which I have.

WEINGLASS I only need point out to the Court one thing in answer to that. Those men are upstairs now, they are serving long prison terms, the Court made it known to them throughout this trial that they would, and your Honor failed in your attempt to silence what they felt was their right to speak out when they just couldn't stand it any more, to sit and be silent.

Meanwhile the Jury deliberated, while the press and the general public waited with eagerness.

125

The jury of the defendants' peers—young Americans with no powerful national figure to turn to for redress and no political party noble enough to transcend its petty chauvinism—took to the streets to express their verdict as best they knew how. Their old friends—the law enforcement officers or the "pigs" (depending on where you stand)—were there once again to meet them with guns, clubs and tear gas.

Weary, tired, with meagre salaries, little protection and no independent control of their own behavior, many of these policemen-soldiers, some of them young, were probably capable of gentleness and understanding, and probably no less honest and disillusioned than the young people whose heads they must clobber and some of whom they must perhaps kill in order to keep their jobs—and make ends meet.

For now and for what looks like years to come, these young Americans will have no valid and meaningful representation in Congress or in the White House. Their leaders will be in jail, and their true heroes are mostly dead and gone. As for the few who still care and understand, if only in part, they have no real power. But they did the only thing they can do . . . They sent cables of protests, made speeches and promised to be heard from sometime soon.

NEW YORK POST, FRIDAY, FEBRUARY 20, 1970

Chi 5 Face Key Ruling, Sentencing

CHICAGO (AP — The convicted defendants in the Chicago riot trial take their first step on a lengthy appeals path today, and Federal Judge Julius J. Hoffman may hand down their sentences.

Five of the seven defendants were found guilty Wednesday of inciting riots at the time of the 1968 Democratic National Convention. Each faces a possible maximum of five years imprisonment and a fine up to $10,000.

Judge Hoffman was expected to rule today on whether the government used wiretapped conversations of several defendants to bulwark its case

The judge spent most of yesterday studying the wiretapping logs, impounded before that start of the trial.

If the judge rejects the no that the illegally ob conversations helped t ernment, he would be impose sentences.

Defense attorn Kunstler said y ports that th mised on a v desire to f over with pealin he

late Tuesday House Hotel, v. had been seq Sept. 24.

Kunstler said atmosphere of what he callec Judge Hoffma: fendants and the question of federal a be key app

The five David T. C. Rubi 31; Tho Rennie John er, t

Washington demonstrators who marched on Attorney General Mitchell's home to protest Chicago trial convictions help injured girl away from skirmish with police who broke up the march with clubs and tear gas. Four were injured and 123 arrested. There were other protests in Boston, Los Angeles, Baltimore and E. Lansing, Mich., and a jail riot in San Jose, Cal.

Associated Press Wirephoto

All 7 Settle Into Cells; Abbie May Be 'Floored'

MAS J. DOLAND
O (CS-T)—The Chi-
n have settled down
y life in Cook
pt for Abbie
or of

prisoner's reference to him as a pig.

"He doesn't like me too well," the chief officer said. "But I guess that's an occupational hazard."

Paired in other cells on the G-4 tier were John Froines and who were found nts growing

queried, "Are you the public defender?"

Finkbeiner identified him and the prisoners see lose interest in his vis)

In the next cell, stirring a cup visitors an "Ho

COURTS OF INJUSTICE CANNOT PREVAIL!

FREE THE CONSPIRACY 10 AND THE NY PANTHER 21!

VIETNAM PEACE PARADE COMM.

ON THE MARCH: Peace demonstrators on 42d Street yesterday before march to Madison Square Park. Sign refers to Chicago case and to Black Panthers accused of bomb plot.

OBSERVE WASHINGTON'S BIRTHDAY: Knights of Columbus entering St. Patrick's Cathedral yesterday. The organization conducted its annual parade up Fifth Avenue.

Knights of Columbus Honor Washington; Other Marchers Protest Chicago Trial

By ARNOLD H. LUBASCH

Two parades—one of devotion, and one of dissent—marked the observance of George Washington's Birthday here yesterday.

With flags flapping smartly in the breeze of a brisk morning, the Knights of Columbus marched up Fifth Avenue from 35th Street to St. Patrick's Cathedral at 50th Street in a display of pageantry, prayer and patriotism.

The parade of 500, accompanied by the cadence of a fife and drum corps of youngsters in colonial costumes and tri-cornered hats, moved up the avenue past small clusters of silent spectators who seemed more interested in shops than marching.

The marchers, climbing the cathedral's steps double row of flags [...]

were convicted.

More than 1,000 marchers assembled by the committee moved from Bryant Park, at 42d Street, west on 42d Street, down Fifth Avenue, east on 34th Street, south on Broadway, east on 28th Street, down Fifth again to Union Square Park, at [...]

The predominantly youthful marchers, who included many long-haired boys and short-skirted girls [...]

AT PEACE RALLY: William M. Kunstler, defense lawyer in the Chicago conspiracy case, at Madison Square Park.

SEATTLE, Wash., Feb. 18—ARRESTS ARE MADE—Riot equipped police close in on a youth and a girl during a melee that erupted Tuesday in front of the Federal Courthouse here. More than 1,000 demonstrators gathered, smashing windows and the glass doors, in protest of its contempt-of-court sentences against seven defendants at the Chicago conspiracy trial. (AP WIREPHOTO)

Chi 7 Defense Eyes Writ to Dismiss Jury

Arraign Protesters Here Under Tight Security

The 15, who face charges of disorderly conduct, harassment [...] of government [...]

police rescued him from his perch, they too were hit with snowballs.

QUIET CONTENT POWER

With the end of the trial of the Chicago 7 and Judge Julius Hoffman's sentencing of the defendants and their lawyers to long jail terms for contempt of court, demonstrators, like these in New York, took to the streets in a number of American cities to protest the judge's actions.

How Can You Handle Unruly Defendants?

authority of the law, the legal system as such. Judges have always been eager to view their extraordinary power in these abstract terms. A Mississippi court is reported to have said in 1858: contempt against these courts administration of their [...] offered to the [...] them-

May he be judge in what is his own case? Justice Frankfurter emphatically denied this strange possibility in his dissent in the Sacher case of 1952. In that case, involving attorneys of Communists who had been prosecuted under the Smith Act, Judge Harold Medina of New York had restricted himself to six-month terms. It goes [...] saying that at the end of [...] there is no need to pro-[...] before

youth said. "I don't [...] court, I'll say what [...] saying."

In a steely voic[...] tagh pronounce[...] contempt of [...] that "you[...] county [...] judge [...] time [...]

General view from above overlooking Foley Square as the march moved along Center St. to the Federal Court Square.

And what of the man for whose aspirations these young Americans
swarmed to the city of Chicago in the first place?

Like a broken record, Eugene McCarthy continues to talk about Vietnam.

Once there was an old comedian who lived down the road from the village church.
One day, after many years of painful effort, he finally came upon a joke that made
people laugh
"Thank God," he said, "I can't believe this."
And who could blame him for it?
And so, for years later, the old man stuck to his lone joke
And would not try anything new for fear he might once again fail.
Poor man, what he would not face was that his successful joke ceased to be funny
a long time ago.

The times had changed, but he was too busy to take notice.

Eugene McCarthy wanted the Vietnam war brought to an end so that the efforts wasted there might be usefully spent at home. But when the battle shifted to the home front, he drifted and foundered. It was for his political aspirations that many of the young people went to Chicago in 1968. But he had nothing to say when they got into trouble with the courts. Perhaps if Establishment men like McCarthy defended the rights and privileges of the young and the disenchanted, they would not feel the need to defend themselves. And some of this confrontation might be avoided.

Incidentally, if you want to see the old comedian
And wish to hear his old joke
Look down the road from the village church
That's where I last saw him — I think
It's been so long now
And actually I don't remember if I ever knew him in the first place
But if you do find him, let me know

128

The lone voice from the polluted wilderness of New York City was that of one who was orphaned by his party.

Before the New York Bar Association gathered for its Centennial Program on February 17, John V. Lindsay, Mayor of New York City, delivered the following speech:

This is a landmark for New York. For 100 years, the Association of the Bar has had a single client—the people of this city. And you have served them well.

From its birth, the Bar Association has fought the good fight for judicial reform for an end to the municipal corruption—and for a legal system that reaches to the least as well as to the highest among us. This city can be thankful for your determination and your achievement.

This is, unhappily, a time when another obligation of the legal world is growing increasingly important. I say unhappily because it is time to remind ourselves of our obligation as lawyers to protect our citizens' rights and liberties from threats and infringements.

The blunt, hard fact is that we in this nation appear headed for a new period of repression—more dangerous than at any time in years. The frenzy, the bitterness, the tumult of the last few years have led many people—including many in positions of power—to expect peace and order to come by whittling away at the Bill of Rights of our Constitution.

And this new threat of repression imposes on all of us an obligation to stand and be heard.

Think back to last year at this time—when dozens of colleges were being hit by student disorders and disruptions. Few denied that there were real grievances. But all of us were shocked at the means of pressing those grievances—most especially the smothering of free speech by shouting down speakers with unpopular views on the campus. All across public life, we rightfully heard angry attacks on such repressive means to achieve ends, however important those ends might be.

Now look at events of recent weeks. Not long ago, the Senate passed a drug law. It would permit federal agents to enter the home of a private citizen with no warning whatsoever. This is at least a sharp extension of traditional fourth amendment limits. Not one Senator voted against that bill.

At almost the same time, the Senate passed a crime bill which drastically limited a defendant's right to examine possibly illegal sources of evidence; which imposed a statute of limitations on the right to be free of illegal searches. Only one man stood up against that bill.

And a week later, the House passed a "Defense Facilities Bill"—which would extend to private industry broad government investigatory powers. It would authorize federal agents to examine the political associations, and acts of people in private industry—and it would permit these private citizens to be fired from their jobs without even being told the basis for that dismissal. It passed by an overwhelming margin.

And while this bill was being passed, the Justice Department issued—then retracted—a startling series of subpoenas, asking for the notes and tapes of newsmen — a step which could basically endanger the traditional independence of our news media.

All of this has happened within the last few weeks. Yet where are the declarations of opposition? Where are the leaders, in politics, the Bar, and academic life, speaking out against these new threats to our constitutional freedoms?

Of course these are controversial areas. The most dangerous threats to freedom always are. When government intrudes in a trivial field, we all enjoy laughter aimed at the clumsy workings of bureaucrats.

But—it is precisely when government treats real dangers—like crime, drugs, and security—with dangerous means that government is most likely to endanger our freedoms by increasing repression. And it is at this point that the defense of freedoms must be made.

There is a similar duty, too, to speak out in defense of the judicial process itself. We all know the danger of using courtrooms as political forums. And it is important to oppose political extremists who make illegitimate use of our courts.

But that is exactly why we must speak out when officials and when governments do the same thing.

All of us, I think, see the recent Chicago trial as a defeat for the integrity of the judicial process. All of us, I think, see in that trial a tawdry parody of our judicial system.

But it is important to understand the roots of this disaster. When you try political activists under a conspiracy charge—long considered to be the most dubious kind of criminal charge—difficult to define or to limit—and when a trial becomes fundamentally an examination of political acts and beliefs—then guilt or innocence becomes almost irrelevant. The process becomes a matter of political opinion instead of legal judgment, and the sense of a courtroom as an independent, open and judicious tribunal becomes lost.

And we lost something else, too. Whatever the ultimate verdicts, who has really won in this case? Think of yourself as a young man or woman, emerging into political concern. If you had witnessed what happened in Chicago, which of you would believe that our system was open, fair-minded, and humane? Which of you would come away from this trial with a renewed faith in our judicial system?

With this matter now on us—with the range of new laws of dubious value or legitimacy—what must concern us all as lawyers is this growing evidence of encroachment on our most cherished rights and liberties. And this concern must remain, whether the threat comes from our executive, legislative or judicial branches of government—or from individual citizens under the false notion that violence, disruption, and repression of their own is the way to a better society.

This Association has always had the courage to stand up for its beliefs, even at great cost. Exactly 50 years ago, led by Charles Evans Hughes, this very Association spoke out against the unseating of five Socialist Legislators by the State Assembly. The men who led this fight had nothing in common politically with the victims of that repression. But they did have a faith in freedom—and they acted on that faith.

Today, when the turmoil of the last few years has made repression a politically popular step, it is our obligation as lawyers to stand against it—in whatever form it takes.

It is time again to put our faith in the system of open and free debate—and in full constitutional protection for those accused of crimes. It is time again to speak out in defense of these precious barriers between tyranny and liberty.

This is not an easy task. But there is none more vital today. And there is none more noble to begin your second century of life.

* * * * * * * * * * * * * * * * * * *

The "punishment" was immediate. Ronald Reagan, cow poke turned politician, the California governor whose ambition seems to have been to destroy all that is unique and beautiful about the San Francisco Bay Area, especially Berkeley, simply because youth is incomprehensible to him and will not succumb to his whims, acted swiftly:

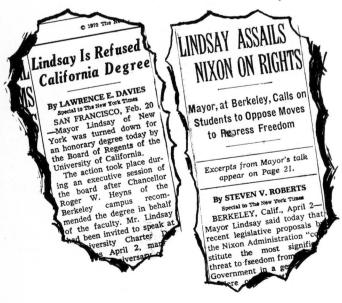

Somehow, John Lindsay becomes California's chief headache

Meanwhile, back in Chicago, the jury continued its deliberation under armed guard

And the streets continued to rumble, banks burn, bombs explode

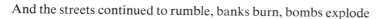

FOUR BOMBS AT MURTAGH HOME

But as for the President, there were more important things to do

And from John Mitchell, the chief architect of all this anti-catastrophe catastrophe, no word.

The defendants, convinced before the trial began that they would be jailed anyway, took time out just before the contempt sentencing to say goodbye to old friends.

On February 17, four days of Jury deliberation, and yet no verdict. The rather pleasantly surprised defendants formed their hopes for a hung jury, and William Kunstler asked for a mistrial.

And the motion was promptly denied.

On February 19th, the court was back in session

The defendants were brought in from the jail where they were already serving their contempt sentences.

A Voice: *We will dance on your grave, Julie, and the graves of the pig empire.*

The families of the defendants were removed from the courtroom on prosecuting attorney, Richard Schultz's request—over William Kunstler's objection.

And the jury brought in

The verdict

THE CLERK   "We, the jury, find the Defendant David T. Dellinger guilty as charged in Count No. 2 of the indictment and not guilty as charged in Count No. 1. ". . .

". . . the Defendant Rennard Davis guilty as charged in Count No. 3 of the indictment and not guilty as charged in Count No. 1." . . .

". . . the Defendant Thomas E. Hayden guilty as charged in Count No. 4 of the indictment and not guilty as charged in Count No. 1 of the indictment." . . .

". . . the Defendant Abbot H. Hoffman guilty as charged in Count No. 5 of the indictment and not guilty as charged in Count No. 1 of the indictment." . . .

". . . the Defendant Jerry C. Rubin guilty as charged in Count No. 6 of the indictment and not guilty as charged in Count No. 1 of the indictment." . . .

". . . the Defendant Lee Weiner not guilty as charged in the indictment." . . .

". . . the Defendant John R. Froines not guilty as charged in the indictment."

Signed by Edward F. Kratzke, Foreman, and eleven other jurors.

*   *   *

In other words, the seven defendants who survived the trial were acquitted of conspiring to incite a riot in Chicago during the 1968 Democratic National Convention.

But five men, David T. Dellinger, Rennie C. Davis, Thomas E. Hayden, Abbie Hoffman and Jerry Rubin, were found guilty of crossing state lines with intent to incite a riot and giving inflammatory speeches for that purpose.

The other two defendants, John R. Froines and Lee Weiner, were acquitted on both the conspiracy and the individual counts.

Earlier in the trial, Bobby Seale had been given a mistrial and will have to stand a new trial, sometime in the future.

THE SENTENCING

THE COURT . . . I now proceed with the imposition of sentence. I will hear you for your clients, Mr. Kunstler. . . .

KUNSTLER Well, your Honor, I say this. One, the defendants had no way of knowing they are going to be sentenced today. Their families are not even present, which would seem to me in common decency would be permitted.

THE COURT The reasons—

KUNSTLER Unless those words are contemptuous too.

THE COURT The reason they were kept out is my life was threatened by one of the members of the family. I was told they would dance on my grave in one of the hearings here within the last week.

KUNSTLER Your Honor, are you serious?

THE COURT Mr. Dellinger, you have the right to speak in your own behalf.

DELLINGER First, I think that every judge should be required to serve time in prison, to spend time in prison before sentencing other people there so that he might become aware of the degrading and anti-human conditions that persist not only in Cook County jail but in the prisons generally of this country. . . .

Like Mr. Kunstler I feel more compassion for you, sir, than I do any hostility. I feel that you are a man who has had too much power over the lives of too many people for too many years. You have sentenced them to those degrading conditions that I am talking about without being aware fully of what you are doing, and undoubtedly feeling correct and righteous, as often happens when people do the most abominable things.

* * * * * * * * * * * * * * * * * *

DELLINGER I want to say that sending us to prison, any punishment the Government can impose upon us, will not solve the problems that have gotten us into "trouble" with the Government and the law in the first place; will not solve the problem of this country's rampant racism, will not solve the problem of the economic injustice, it will not solve the problem of the foreign policy and the attacks upon the underdeveloped people of the world. . . .

The Government has misread the times in which we live just like there was a time when it was possible to keep black people in slavery, and then it became impossible. So, this country is growing out of the time when it is possible to keep young people, women, black people, Mexican-Americans, anti-war people, people who believe in truth and justice and really believe in democracy, when it is going to be possible to keep them quiet or suppress them.

David Dellinger, Age 54.

DELLINGER Our movement is not very strong today. It is not united, it is not well organized. It is very confused and makes a lot of mistakes, but there is the beginning of an awakening in this country which has been going on for at least the last fifteen years, and it is an awakening that will not be denied. Tactics will change, people will err, people will die in the streets and die in prison, but I do not believe that this movement can be denied because however falsely applied the American ideal was from the beginning when it excluded black people, and Indians and people without property, nonetheless there was a dream of justice and equality and freedom, and brotherhood, and I think that that dream is much closer to fulfillment today than it has been at any time in the history of this country.

* *

Rennard Davis, Age 29, born in Lansing, Michigan

DAVIS . . . I do not think that it is a time to appeal to you or to appeal to the system that is about to put me away.

I suppose if I were to make any appeals, it really should be to Agent Stanley or to J. Edgar Hoover, because the sentence that I am about to receive comes not from you in my judgment but from the FBI. This trial has been controlled by the police and the FBI and undercover agents from the beginning, from the witnesses that have been paraded with their lies to that witness stand day after day after day right up to the last sentence that is going to be delivered, comes from the FBI, and I don't think the FBI is interested in speeches. I don't think the FBI is interested in words. I think that what moves a government that increasingly is controlled by a police mentality is action. It is not a time for words; It is a time that demands action. And since I did not get a jury of my peers, I look to the jury that is in the streets. My jury will be in the streets tomorrow all across the country and the verdict from my jury will keep coming in over the next long five years that you are about to give me in prison.

I guess if I have any hope at all it is that I am allowed out of prison by 1976 because in 1976 the American people are not going to recount their history, they are going to relive their history, and when I come out of prison it will be to move next door to Tom Foran. I am going to be the boy next door to

Tom Foran and the boy next door, the boy that could have been a judge, could have been a prosecutor, could have been a college professor, is going to move next door to organize his kids into the revolution. We are going to turn the sons and daughters of the ruling class in this country into Viet Cong.

* *

Thomas Hayden, Age 29, born in Michigan

HAYDEN Our intention in coming to Chicago was not to incite a riot. Our intention in coming to Chicago was to see to it that certain things, that is, the right of every human being, the right to assemble, the right to protest, can be carried out even where the Government chooses to suspend those rights. It was because we chose to exercise those rights in Chicago in the jaws of a police state that we are here today. . . .

We have known all along what the intent of the Government has been. We knew that before the famous events of August 28, 1968. If those events didn't happen, the Government would have had to invent them, as I think it did for much of its evidence in this case, because they were bound to put us away. They had to put us away in some way that would preserve the image of the system.

* * *

HAYDEN We would hardly be notorious characters if they had left us alone in the streets of Chicago last year. It would have been a few thousand people. It would have been testimony to our failure as organizers. But instead we became the architects, the master minds and the geniuses of a conspiracy to overthrow the government. We were invented. We were chosen by the government to serve as scapegoats for all that they wanted to prevent happening in the 1970's. We were chosen because we had a history in the 1960's of doing things that had to be stopped. . . . So the Government has had every reason to eliminate us because the Government operates from the theory that somebody must be behind these things and because we have been so active and aggressive, it must be us, and by putting us away, that will put an end to the problems.

137

HAYDEN I want to press to try to understand how we view the structuring [of] our indictment. First of all pick Weiner and Froines, innocent young men, so if they are found guilty, that will scare every innocent young person who might associate with leaders, who might go to a demonstration, because they are average people, and when people saw them indicted, they said, "Well, that could have been me."

Also it gives you plenty of room to negotiate if the jury doesn't want to feel that it's putting everybody away, the jury can always negotiate over Froines and Weiner—why not, because they'll obviously show up to be much less guilty than the others.

Then give us two counts instead of one so you have a maximum and a minimum. Ten years, that will be nice, but if the jury finds us guilty on one and not guilty on the other, that will look to people like the whole thing came out fairly.

* * *

HAYDEN I think we will not be given bail which is the ultimate example, the ultimate example of the suspension of constitutional rights to people who might use them effectively.

It is all right to let Mafia people out on bail. It is all right to let murderers out on bail. It is all right to let DeSapio out on bail. They walked right out of the courtroom; it is not going to be all right to let us out on bail because they will say, there is an incendiary situation.

HAYDEN People have tried through the system, people have tried through all of the avenues to register their feelings. Then they have gone home to watch color TV and have oxtail soup, and to see their four-year-old poodle hoping that nobody blames them. . . .

The tragedy is that people of that older generation do not know yet how to hold out, and probably never will, do not know how to fight to the end. . . . I have no doubt that if we had a jury of our peers, by any definition anybody wants to give to the word peers, if we had a jury of our peers we would have walked out of this place, or we would have had an absolutely hung jury because younger people in the country today know what principles are, and know what bullshit is, and know how to stand up and are not in the least afraid of expressing their convictions in the face of the state, in the face of the troops, in the face of police.

HAYDEN If you didn't want to make us martyrs, why did you do it? If you wanted to keep it cool, why didn't you give us a permit? You know. You know if

you had given us a permit, you know if you had given slightly different instructions, very little would have happened last year in Chicago. Ramsey Clark knows it. He survived many more street confrontations than most people in this room, no matter how much you want to call him an intellectual from Washington. . . .

. . . You don't believe it but we have to do this. We have no choice. We had no choice in Chicago. We had no choice in this trial. The people always do what they have to do. Every person who is born now and every person under thirty now feels an imperative to do the kind of things that we are doing. They may not act on them, they may not act on them immediately, but they feel the same imperatives because they are part of the same generation. They are part of the same body of people that came to life in the 1950's and 1960's and saw things differently from the older people. So they feel an imperative. They proclaim that imperative from the streets. Some day they are going to proclaim the imperative from the bench and from the courthouse. It's only a matter of as a slaveholder because he was. All men and children of their times, even revolutionaries. We are children of our times.

* * * * * * *

Abbot Hoffman, Age 31

THE COURT Mr. Hoffman, the law gives you the right to speak in your own behalf. I will hear you if you have anything to say.

HOFFMAN Thank you.

I feel like I have spent 15 years watching John Daly shows about history: You Are There. It is sort of like taking LSD, which I recommend to you, Judge. I know a good dealer in Florida. I could fix you up.

* * *

HOFFMAN Right from the beginning of the indictment, up until the end of the trial, I always wanted to change my plea. I had just a great urge to confess; say, "I am guilty," because I felt what the State was calling me was an enemy of the State and I am an enemy of the State, I am an enemy of the America as it is now, with a K. . . .

138

Mr. Foran says that we are evil men, and I suppose that is sort of a compliment. He says that we are unpatriotic. Unpatriotic? I don't know, that has a kind of jingleistic ring. I suppose I am not patriotic.

But he says we are un-American. I don't feel un-American. I feel very American. I feel very close to the vision of America in that film, the Yippie film you wouldn't allow into evidence, because it didn't go into our intent.

It said it is not that the Yippies hate America. It is that they feel the American dream has been betrayed. That has been my attitude.

* * *

I know those guys on the wall. I know them better than you, I feel. I know Adams. I mean, I know all the Adams. They grew up 20 miles from my home in Massachusetts. I played with Sam Adams on the Concord Bridge. I was there when Paul Revere rode right up on his motorcycle and said, "The pigs are coming, the pigs are coming. Right into Lexington." I was there. I know the Adams. Sam Adams was an evil man.

Thomas Jefferson. Thomas Jefferson called for revolution every ten years. Thomas Jefferson had an agrarian reform program that made Mao Tse-tung look like a liberal. I know Thomas Jefferson. . . .

* * * * * * * * * * * * * * * * * * * *

Washington? I now respect Bobby Seale's opinion of him as a slaveholder because he was. All men are children of their times, even revolutionaries. We are children of our times and we are not perfect.

Washington grew pot. He called it hemp. It was called hemp then. He was probably a pot head. . . .

Abraham Lincoln? There is another one. In 1861 Abraham Lincoln in his inaugural address said, and I quote, "When the people shall grow weary of their constitutional rights to amend the government, they shall exert their revolutionary right to dismember and overthrow that government."

He gave that speech. If Abraham Lincoln had given that speech in Lincoln Park, he would be on trial right here, right here in this courtroom, because that is an inciteful speech. . . .

HOFFMAN It wasn't funny last night sitting in a prison cell, a 5x 8 room, with no light in the room. . . .

There's no light. It's not a nice place for a Jewish boy to be, with a college education. I'm sure my mother would say that.

Speaking about that, I remember when we were speaking before, you said, "Tom Hayden, you could have had a nice position in the system, you could have had a job in the firm." We have heard that for the past ten years, all of us have heard that. And our only beauty is that we don't want a job. We don't want a job there, in that system. We say to young people, "There is a brilliant future for you in the revolution. Become an enemy of the State. A great future. You will have your soul."

* * * * * *

Jerry Rubin, Age 31

THE COURT The next defendant, Mr. Rubin, so you desire to speak in your own behalf? You have that privilege.

RUBIN You see, you are not jailing five individuals. You can read the paper and see what is happening. . . .

. . . I am going to jail because I am part of a historical movement and because of my life, the things I am trying to do, because, as Abbie said, we don't want to be—we don't want to have a piece of the pie.

We don't just want to be part of the American way of life. We don't want to live in the suburbs. We don't want to have college degrees.

139

We don't want to stand before the Judge and say, "Yes, we respect you, Judge, no matter what happens." We don't want that. We are moved by something else. . . .

RUBIN There is a family around this table. We have called this the life versus death culture. Anybody walking in the courtroom could see this life versus death culture. People in this courtroom were a family, together like this. The people here were like machines, machines, and so the machines are sentencing the human beings to jail. . . . My gosh, what is happening in this courtroom? What is happening in this country? What is going on? The five of us are to blame for what happened in August of 1968. Incredible. . . .

* * *

RUBIN A father tells his son, "Respect me or else." That's what America told its youth. America told its youth, "Respect us or else." The kids grow up saying, "I am not going to respect you or else. When you are killing black people, I am not going to respect you." . . .

* * *

RUBIN We are on trial because we are trying to wake America up. We are on trial because we are trying to wake it up emotionally, because it turned us all into machines, it turned us all into marshals, reporters, judges, prosecutors; it's destroyed our humanity. So the people at this table are trying to wake it up, and the only way we can wake it up is by screaming, yelling, standing on our heads, doing whatever we can do. That's what we tried to do during this trial. That's what our defense was.

Our defense was trying to present our life to this jury. We are doing—we acted in this trial just the way we always act. We didn't do a single thing to try and get a not guilty verdict; to try and get someone's respect. We were ourselves. And you are sentencing us for being ourselves. That's our crime: being ourselves.

Judge, I want to give you a copy of this book. I want you to read it on your vacation in Florida, be-cause this is why I am on trial. I inscribed it . . . "Julius, You radicalized more young people than we ever could. You're the country's top Yippie." . . .

. . . [W]e are going to jail with smiles on our faces because we are the happiest people in the courtroom because we know what is happening because you are jailing your youth, America. And you are jailing it for the crime of dreaming, dreaming of an alternative. You are jailing it for the crime of idealism. Our crime is idealism. That's the only thing. And there is this slogan, you can jail the revolutionary but you can't jail a revolution. . . .

What you are doing out there is creating millions of revolutionaries, millions of revolutionaries. Julius Hoffman, you have done more to destroy the court system in this country than any of us could have done. All we did was go to Chicago and the police system exposed itself as totalitarian. All we did is walk into the courtroom and the court system exposed itself as totalitarian. . . . Maybe now people will be interested in what happens in the courthouse down the street because of what happens here. Maybe now people will be interested.

This is the happiest moment of my life.

The Court then sentenced Defendants David Dellinger, Rennie Davis, Tom Hayden, Abbie Hoffman and Jerry Rubin to prison for individual terms of five years and fines of $5,000 each, the maximum penalties permitted.

THE COURT —the defendant[s] are to stand committed until the fine and costs have been paid, the prison terms to run concurrently with the prison term or prison sentence previously imposed for direct contempt of Court in the presence of the Court.

Not only on the record in this case, covering a period of four months or longer, but from the remarks made by the defendants themselves here today, the Court finds that the defendants are clearly dangerous persons to be at large. Therefore the commitments here will be without bail.

KUNSTLER Your Honor, couldn't I say my last words without cutting me off?

THE COURT You said you didn't want to speak.

KUNSTLER Your Honor, I just said a moment ago we had a concluding remark. Your Honor has succeeded perhaps in sullying it, and I think that maybe that is the way the case should end, as it began.

141

MENE MENE TEKEL UPHARSIN

THE RECKONING

Kunstler wept

And so the society is blowing up in upheaval and anger. The system shows signs of decadence and unreality. Old truths suddenly yield to false dreams. The once great, reputable, life-inspiring and almost sacred institutions of learning and justice suddenly become places of disillusionment and rage among the youth. Politics becomes, for the competent and the qualified, a disenchanting field where only the avowedly ignorant and the loud-mouthed are acclaimed, and only the stubborn, insensitive and mediocre survive. Liberalism connotes communism and dissent becomes rebellion. Traditional liberalism now scared takes cowardly refuge behind the excuse of survival while silencing the bravery of commitment with an appeal for restraint; an obvious suicide in the face of a powerful, unrestrained rightwing offensive. Patriotism becomes indefinable because disagreement is taken for disloyalty. Moral confusion sets in and honor disappears. The great American Dream becomes a nightmare. Enlightenment becomes an anachronism.

The government has gradually become a secret cult with its machinery and method of operation hidden from the observation and comprehension of the ordinary citizen. It has public standards of its own and projects a social image according to its own values. Either as a result of a complete lack of grasp of the fundamental problems of the society or a gross insensitivity and apathy towards them, a government which takes pride in its mediocrity has evolved a strange set of values that only serve to polarize the country. But rather than admit the dangers caused by its own shortsightedness or ineptitude, the Government seems more interested in the redefinition of patriotism and the re-interpretation of the American Dream. As far as it is concerned. the fundamental issue is patriotism. And in deciding what is patriotic and what is not, the government becomes both the litigant and the arbiter. There is a nauseating attitude of self-righteousness that seems to emanate from crass ignorance. And suddenly the government finds unexpected glory in combing the society, seeking to kill every voice of dissent and dubbing every thinking person as a traitor or communist.

Meanwhile the armed police massacre disenchanted blacks, and bombs explode from coat pockets in department stores. The Ku Klux Klan poisons the cattle of Black Muslim farmers with cyanide and the law and order government does not as much as scratch its head. The President pulls the blanket over his head, hoping that when he pulls it down again, the problems of the society shall have voluntarily disappeared. As for the people, they stay mute, inarticulate and shockproof. But above all, business goes on as usual.

Is this the Apocalypse?

This is the background against which the Conspiracy Trial took place. And this is the context in which the verdict and its ramifications must be discussed. Many— liberal, neutral and conservative alike—have taken comfort in the safe but meaningless theory that both sides, the court and the defendants, were wrong. This noncommital position only avoids the responsibility of conscience and judgement. Not both sides in the trial were wrong.

143

It is not simply for the purpose of argument that one feels compelled to defend at least the objectives of the defendants and condemn those of the government and the Court. The theory of equal blame is useful only when both sides are either equally powerful and have equal access to legal recourse, or when the issue is so trivial that the outcome has no significance in influencing the state of affairs. These two conditions do not exist in the trial and the theory is therefore invalid. Julius Hoffman could punish Bobby Seale for calling him a "racist pig", but Bobby Seale could not punish Hoffman for having him gagged and chained in public. Secondly, the trial reveals far too much about the present state of affairs in the country for it to be regarded and dismissed as merely a distasteful and unfortunate accident. The truth of the matter is that we have a government using the courts for a political *offensive* against a carefully selected company of scapegoats who are anxious not to be quietly jailed and destroyed.

The Government went to court to stifle legitimate dissent on issues it has been extremely incompetent to cope with. This is the characteristic case of a teacher who punishes a pupil for daring to raise a question the teacher cannot answer. This is outright wrong. The defendants went to court to arouse the national conscience to the reality of the judicial system—one which has railroaded thousands of black people to jail for years without the public being aware of it.

But for the methods used by the defendants, not much attention would have been focused on the trial and the public would have lost one of its last chances of controlling the institutions intended to serve and not to dominate it. This action was not only absolutely right but revealed an unquestionable if paradoxical sense of courage and patriotism on the part of the defendants.

For most white Americans what happened in Chicago was unusual and exceptional. But for most black Americans and people like William Kunstler and Charles Garry who have had to defend them before highly obstructionist judges, it was routine. So the difference between a liberal editorial writer who is "upset" by the *antics* of the trial and a Charles Garry who is "bitter" about the *cruelty and the vindictiveness* of the same trial is the difference between the reaction of a man who is fascinated by the seeming nuance of a slightly irritating phenomenon and that of a man who is hurt by the cold reality of a painful and unabating process of outright inequity.

"I am bitter, I am angry, I am raising my voice," Charles Garry once said on a TV show, "because the American judicial system today is irrelevant to sixty million Americans".

The trial of the Chicago 8 is a microcosm of the state of the nation at large. But before we look at the society, let us examine some of the shallow answers given to questions raised concerning the conduct of the trial itself.

First, let us take the question of decorum. When the charge is made that certain people have not behaved according to certain standards, there is the implicit assumption that these standards do exist and that they are being lived up to by other segments of society (generally referred to as "proper and law-abiding"). If, however, these models of good behavior do not exist, then the charge is invalid. This is precisely the case with the over-all decorum in this trial. First, Julius Hoffman did not behave any better than the defendants and in not so doing, failed to establish in fact the standard he kept glorifying every blessed day of the trial. Second, on a much wider scale, nowhere in the country is this standard adhered to. For example, protocol requires an even higher level of good manners than does court decorum. A few days after the end of the trial, French President, Georges Pompidou, addressed a joint meeting of the United States Senate and House of Representatives. Some Congressmen walked out on the distinguished visitor. Many will quickly rush to say that this is an unfair comparison. They would argue that the Congressmen had reason for their behavior: that they were angry; that it was a moral issue; that it was a far more fundamental issue and that, most sentimentally, it had to do with the survival of the Jewish race—in other words, it was a racial issue. The argument will therefore be that under such conditions one has the moral right to behave indecorously.

But these are precisely the same reasons that the defendants in Chicago behaved similarly. Like the Congressmen, the defendants were genuinely angry. They had a serious moral concern, and the issues at the trial were very fundamental ones involving the most important sections of the Constitution, such as the guarantee of free speech. Race was also very basic to the trial.

Decorum

144

It is equally untenable to argue that, unlike the defendants, the Congressmen who walked out on the French President did not disrupt the meeting. If, as Julius Hoffman did, Georges Pompidou had taken verbal notice of them as they walked out, there most certainly would have been a scene. Some have even argued that the defendants could have simply walked out or never showed up in court. Had they done so, they would have been charged with contempt of court and jailed.

The decency of language. Savor the following delicacies from some of the leading standard bearers of the "well-kempt-clean-language society."

Spiro Agnew (describing the defendants): These weirdos . . . these malcontents, . . . these handful of oddballs . . . these social misfits.

Richard Daley (talking to Senator Ribicoff, according to the Defense): Fuck you, you Jew son-of-a-bitch, you lousy mother fucker, go home.

Thomas Aquinas Foran, the government prosecutor, called the Peace Movement a "freaking fag revolution", described Dellinger as a "sneak", Abbie Hoffman as "scummy but clever", the defense lawyers as "mouthpieces", and said of all the defendants, that Bobby Seale "was the only one [of them he did not] think was a fag".

The Judgeship. A judge does not lose his temper in court or get vengeful, vindictive, or punitive. He does not throw temper tantrums like a spoiled child whose ego has been hurt. It is silly to argue that a judge is only human. A judge must live up to certain professional standards. A thief does not oversee the federal mint. A nervous man does not practice surgery. A sadist should not be a policeman.

Ethics and Justice. Here again the law and order establishment has standards which if adhered to could not produce what they demand of the defendants. First, if the President is hardpressed to find one man of impeccable principle and integrity who can command enough respect to be nominated to the Supreme Court, what is this great standard that the defendants are being asked to emulate? If the President is so stubborn as to risk destroying the prestige of the Supreme Court simply because his misguided ego would not permit him to admit error, how then can we turn around and accuse the defendants of threatening the judicial system? Or consider many of the nation's lawyers. Their initial reaction was to flood the market with new ideas on how to gag more unruly defendants rather than how to censor the misbehaviour of the Court. The national council of the Bar Association in the heat of this controversy and in complete disregard of the supreme principle of universal justice advised the United States government not to sign the international Genocide Treaty on the highly immoral and disgustingly nationalistic ground that such a treaty might implicate American GIs involved in the My Lai massacre in Vietnam. Where then are the ethics that the defendants are supposed to preserve?

The question of *courtroom politics* is even more absurd. The expression "the court should not be used as a forum for politics" has recently joined "the silent majority" in the archives of simplistic rhetoric. The very fact that the law is made by politicians and interpreted by judges makes every issue before the courts a potential political issue, not to mention the fact that judges and district attorneys are either elected or appointed by politicians. So not only is there politics in the courts but politics does belong in the courts. The issue then is not that political ideas should not be expressed in court but rather that it should not be made a crime to have political ideas.

THE NEW POLITICS

The average young American today, is far more sophisticated politically than the average middle-aged American. Consequently, contrary to the common assumption, the young American is far more competent to judge the behaviour of the nation's politicians than his parents are. A clever administration will welcome this very healthy situation and strengthen the nation by responding to the challenge of a knowledgeable young generation. An incompetent and insecure administration, however, will be intimidated by the existence of an informed group which it cannot deceive. A competent well-meaning administration will accept the challenge and encourage the growth of a sophisticated public; an insecure and confused administration will see red (the pun is accidental) when faced with a sophisticated public especially one that has the energy of youth and the drive of idealism.

As one contemplates the panicky effort of an unsophisticated Nixon/Mitchell/ Agnew administration to wipe out this fresh offshoot of an awakening public, one cannot help but be amused at the vivid parallel between this troika and Samuel Beckett's

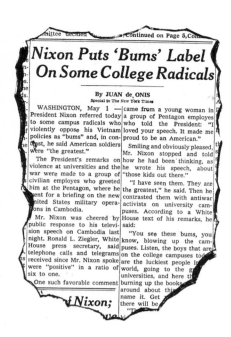

Nixon Puts 'Bums' Label On Some College Radicals

By JUAN de ONIS
Special to The New York Times

WASHINGTON, May 1 — President Nixon referred today to some campus radicals who violently oppose his Vietnam policies as "bums" and, in contrast, he said American soldiers were "the greatest."

The President's remarks on violence at universities and the war were made to a group of civilian employes who greeted him at the Pentagon, where he went for a briefing on the new United States military operations in Cambodia.

Mr. Nixon was cheered by public response to his television speech on Cambodia last night. Ronald L. Ziegler, White House press secretary, said telephone calls and telegrams received since Mr. Nixon spoke were "positive" in a ratio of six to one.

One such favorable comment came from a young woman in a group of Pentagon employes who told the President: "I loved your speech. It made me proud to be an American."

Smiling and obviously pleased, Mr. Nixon stopped and told how he had been thinking, as he wrote his speech, about "those kids out there."

"I have seen them. They are the greatest," he said. Then he contrasted them with antiwar activists on university campuses. According to a White House text of his remarks, he said:

"You see these bums, you know, blowing up the campuses. Listen, the boys that are on the college campuses today are the luckiest people in world, going to the greatest universities, and here they are burning up the books, storming around about this issue, name it. Get rid of the war, there will be another . . .

The challenge of young American politics

145

HAMM in his play, ENDGAME. In fact the play provides numerous fascinating parallels with America today. What we have is repression by the inadequate, out of a resentment at having their weakness exposed. Only sixteen years ago, under similar circumstances, Senator Symington was forced to recommend to Senator Joe McCarthy that he see a psychiatrist. There is much here for the psychoanalyst.

REVOLUTIONARY RHETORIC

Silly as it is, people are being destroyed today by the simple inability of those in power to understand the dynamics of revolutionary rhetoric. The authorities, by refusing to take the trouble to learn the language of the younger people, see a traitor in an honest man, an assassin in a joker, a communist in a serious man and an anarchist in a happy young man. Thus with the paranoia of high officials, a man who, after listening to a press conference, honestly criticizes the President's rhetoric is promptly branded a traitor. A man who, after attending a Vietnam Peace rally regarding which the President has chosen to stay home and watch television, jokingly says "that man should be killed", is promptly arrested and put on trial for plotting to assassinate the President. Nobody remembers that in America where sloppiness of language is not uncommon, hundreds of people use "he should be killed" or "I will kill you" to mean anything from "that's disgusting" to "I rather like you".

One day during the trial in Chicago, Julius Hoffman routinely ordered the marshals to evict sympathizers of the defendants from the courtroom. Anita Hoffman on the way out is reported to have cracked a slightly impudent but rather clever and perhaps even affectionate joke: "Julie, we will dance on your grave". The next day the defendants were deprived of having their families in court to hear their last statements before being sentenced. When counsel objected, Julius Hoffman explained that someone had threatened his life the previous day by saying that she would dance on his grave. Poor Julie. Even he forgot the simple logic that Anita could only dance on his grave after he was dead and buried!

The situation becomes increasingly serious with the increased deterioration in the use of English language in America and the simultaneous increase in the government's free-for-all wire-tapping of even the most innocent private conversation. As more Americans begin to read more books other than the Holy Bible and the American Constitution, their language is apt to be more colorful. Under the Chicago rules of the game, this means that the country is in for a large number of conspirators in the years to come.

HUMOR

Put briefly, one crucial problem of the country today is the lack of humor on all levels. Humor is a prerequisite for objectivity. Humor is a prerequisite for understanding. Humor is a prerequisite for empathy. Humor is a prerequisite for insight. Humor is absolutely necessary for the identification and comprehension of complexities. Without humor, the smallest problems take on gigantic proportions. Without humor the most complex issues will fall prey to simplistic interpretations and corresponding abortive solutions. It is this simplistic vein, predominant even in the highest echelon of society, which has been primarily responsible for a good deal of the unnecessary confrontation that now threatens the nation. It is ironic that it is America that is badly in need of humor; it is critical that humor be restored in order that a mature understanding be restored to the dynamics of American politics.

THE "REVOLUTION"

There are two kinds of mass social upheavals, one is a civil war and the other, a revolution.

In the first case, we have a system in which there is a privileged majority such as the middle class, and a disenfranchised minority such as the poor and the young. Here, the majority, with their electoral power, can adequately take care of themselves without government protection. The primary commitment of the government is, therefore, to the protection and enhancement of minority rights. When the government, in blind rejection of political common sense, chooses to support the majority against the already helpless minority, conflict arises. The minority loses all confidence in the ability of the system to represent their interest. Disillusionment sets in. If at this point the government reacts with a call to law and order, the gap widens and the situation is set for civil strife. All it takes is enough disillusionment, frustration and a sense of helplessness for a few of the minority to resort to tactical outbursts of violence. Such a situation soon becomes pregnant with a great disposition to suicidal

The dearth of humor

146

heroism. It is irrelevant whether this martyrdom is misguided or not. The end result is the same—undersirable violence. An incompetent government will retaliate with punitive measures. The entire machinery of repression is set into operation. The effect is only greater resentment. There is more violence and increased polarization. When this happens, an insecure government, feeling its grip on the people begin to slip, will become desperate and will resort to even more repression, including witch-hunts and name-calling. In political polemics, it will charge that "law and order have broken down" and will seek political gain by promising to "crack down" on dissidents. Very soon "dissidents" expand to cover practically anyone who in any way exercises his right to differ with the government. In America today, it has even come to include college professors, television networks, leading newspapers, the "effete snobs" of the Northeast and all those Senators, even Southerners, even respected Republicans, who voted against the confirmation of G. Harrold Carswell.

In such a situation the government posture is characterised by "get tough" slogans or variations on the theme. The relevance of legitimate dissent or obvious official shortcomings becomes obscure. Public debate, rather than center on the validity of the issues raised, is focused on the peripheral facades which are all too transparent. Thus, time is wasted debating the long hair, colorful attire or the admittedly peculiar language of those involved. What gets lost is the fact that when a government has to "get tough" and when armed police and national guardsmen become as common a sight as the mailman, the claim that democracy is functioning effectively becomes highly questionable.

What seems to have happened in this country is the "get tough" policy which was adopted many years ago by incompetent parents incapable of both the influence of exemplary behavior and the persuasion of love and understanding; the policy which resulted in the blowing up of the hitherto comfortable family situation, moved to the high schools and college campuses. There, too, with the growing professional incompetence of the faculty and the intransigence and "toughness" of the administration, the young were once again forced to explode the situation in order to bring about a responsive change. This policy has finally arrived in the government and the White House, and once again the "get tough" position reveals that the government did not learn anything useful from the preceding experiences in the family and on the college campuses.

It is unfair and rather unethical for anyone to claim that these young people have not tried all the conventional avenues of protest available to them short of disruption. Like the black movement before it, the young people involved in the Peace Movement and in the larger issue of healing social wounds, have done everything to express, explain and argue their positions. They asked questions about the issues. They talked about them. They wrote about them. They invited notable figures to their campuses to lecture on them. They travelled across the country to make speeches about them. They sang about them. And they even made movies about them. And in response, as if to tell them to "get lost", the President requests that Johnny Cash sing "Welfare Cadillac" and "Okie from Muskogee" in the White House.

Those who are still trying to avoid confronting the issues now find it fashionable to argue about whether or not the vocal dissenters represent the majority opinion among the young, just as they argued whether or not the so-called militant Blacks represented the majority of Black opinion. In a state of potential civil strife, it is not necessary for there to be a majority opinion in support of the claims of those who feel shortchanged. All that is necessary for the dynamics of civil strife to be set into operation is a handful of people who genuinely believe that the duly constituted government is irresponsive to their legitimate protest, and who are willing to risk personal harm in standing forth against them. It does not take a majority of the population to plant bombs in public buildings. This is why every democracy emphasizes minority rights in order to avoid situations of civil strife. In one way, this makes a democracy more vulnerable to minority frustrations than any other system of government. Yet this is not only unavoidable but desirable, and is the challenge every democracy must face in return for the freedoms and conveniences it otherwise enjoys.

It is therefore irrelevant for the press to emphasize that the Black Panthers are a minority rather than focus on whether or not the history of police brutality adequately justifies the existence of the Party. It seems that people are looking for the symptoms of a wrong disease in the society. People are asking whether or not there are signs of revolution when they should be seeking symptoms of civil strife. A revolution can come about only when there is a privileged minority, such as a functional aristocracy, and a disenfranchised majority. Such was the setting for the French

Revolution. The middle class in America, constituting a well-to-do majority, will never revolt and therefore the chances of a revolution in America are nil. But the chances of civil strife are great. And there is absolutely nothing to suggest that a civil strife is any less unpleasant and undesirable than a revolution.

In fact, those who are presently disturbed are not an insignificant minority. There are many who feel that things are seriously wrong in the country and that they are getting worse everyday, and that the government and the establishment, rather than working to improve the situation, only accentuate it and further polarize the country. Besides the traditional minority of the Black, American Indian and the Spanish-speaking American, this group includes countless young Americans in colleges and in High Schools. There is more political consciousness in the High School today than there was in the Universities only a few years ago, and in a democracy this should be welcomed. The group also includes countless liberals, conservatives, Northerners, Southerners, Congressmen, Senators, Democrats, Republicans, and even at least one former Chief Justice, and a current member of the Supreme Court. Unfortunately, in the traditional setting up of con men to divert the public, some have now moved to impeach Associate Justice William Douglas for writing *Points of Rebellion,* when they could have read the book as the considered opinions of a highly respected American who is not black, young, bushy haired and whatever else disqualifies people from opinions today. People like J. Edgar Hoover can of course scream "communist", "subversives", just as the President himself has called those who voted against his nominees regional 'racists'. But this only begs the issue.

Politics in High Schools

BOBBY SEALE

Bobby Seale was the most disciplined and best behaved of the defendants; yet he alone got the gags and shackles.

Bobby Seale was the least involved of the defendants in the Chicago Democratic Convention; yet he received the harshest punishment.

Bobby Seale was the only one who seemed to still have some faith, blind perhaps, in the judicial process; yet he was the only one who was not allowed legal representation of his choice.

Bobby Seale showed the most respect for Julius Hoffman; yet he alone was publicly humiliated by him.

Bobby Seale was the only black man.

THE NIXON-AGNEW-MITCHELL STRATEGY

The system of check and balance was destroyed with the election of Richard Nixon as President. This administration erroneously feels committed to gratify misguided whims by restoring the nation to a shameful puberty from which it had painfully and painstakingly begun to mature. Whatever his campaign strategy, a true leader will enlighten his campaign supporters to transform their partisan whims into a genuine national vision that embraces most of the delicate and healthy dreams of all segments of society. Mr. Nixon has not been able to make the transition from a presidential candidate to a president. Almost two years after his election, the President seems to be still running for the office.

Mitchell's Tango—Seven Steps

The strategy of repression of the present administration can be outlined in seven steps.

Step One—The Liberal Press

Spiro Agnew attempts to neutralize the influence of the press on public opinion. He separates TV from newspapers, taking TV on first and then the newspapers. The media protests, but only for a few days. Unfortunately, it is the nature of liberals to unwittingly aid and abet their own destruction by seeking refuge in nonfunctional objectivity. By believing that there is some virtue in neutrality in the face of gross vindictiveness on the part of a powerful rightwing, liberals stand aside while the less equipped make their shaky stand against glaring repression. It is only as an afterthought that liberals seem to realize that they are the ultimate target of the rightwing Establishment. It is only a matter of time before they are smashed by the momentum which they themselves, by default, have allowed to gather. Since Agnew's attack, the liberal press has, in fact, shied away from news analysis and adequate coverage of dissent, while guaranteeing full and uncritical coverage of Agnew, Nixon and the rest of the rightwing. For Agnew, step one was a complete success.

Step Two—Picking Scapegoats

By grouping together Bobby Seale, a Black Panther, Tom Hayden, an SDS member, Jerry Rubin, a veteran of the Berkeley Free Speech Movement, David Dellinger, an old pacifist, and John Froines, a college professor, Mitchell effectively establishes the prerequisites of guilt by association. And just in case the point was missed, the government overemphasizes crime in a move guaranteed to increase public insecurity and therefore create a more malleable public receptive to repression. In the meantime Richard Nixon honors a pet project of the liberals— anti-pollution —and in so doing effectively siphons off much of the liberal energy from the civil rights movement.

Step Three—Press Intimidation

Earl Caldwell and Mike Wallace are subpoenaed to release notes from confidential interviews with members of the Black Panther Party. Thus in the minds of the masses it is first falsely established that the Black Panther Party is subversive and violent; then by the trial, the SDS, the Yippies, and a sizeable proportion of young Americans are tied in to the "conspiracy" by association with Bobby Seale. Next CBS/TV and other liberal networks and newspapers are tied in once again by the specious implied association with Black Panthers. And even at this stage, the picture still seems unclear to the liberals.

Step Four—Provocation And Official Murder

While putting the pressure on the news media and softening them with empty promises of restraint, and leaving the Ku Klux Klan alone, the government launches Operation-wipe-out-the-Black Panthers in Chicago, with a repeat performance in Los Angeles. Hoffman sets up, for Bobby Seale, a situation in which any reasonable man worthy of his pride and integrity would be sure to get angry. The judge blatantly provokes unruliness in court. The effect is simple. Even those who cannot buy the propaganda line of law and order will buy the theory of decorum in court. As we are told by *The Village Voice,* the *New York Times* "unwittingly" aids this phase of repression by editing its reporters' copies to consistently make the judge "say" things while the defendants "shouted".

Step Five—Radicals Break With Liberals

The young radicals break ranks with the traditional liberals out of frustration with their insensitivity to the dynamics of the situation. For example, Jimmy Wechsler, under the slight pressure of rhetoric, finds himself asking Abbie Hoffman, Jerry Rubin and Rennie Davis why they do not go to Cuba if there is so much wrong with America. And the morning after, when it dawns on him how much like Barry Goldwater he must have sounded, he does not have the integrity of simply admitting that the remark was inadvertent. Instead, he excuses his embarrassing performance by calling Jerry Rubin a liar in his explanation to *New York Post* readers who may not have watched the television debate. Sadly, Jimmy Wechsler is one of the most reputable liberal journalists. And so we see the traditional liberals condemning the young radicals for making what only later will be recognized as the last stand against rightwing repression. The old liberals just as alarmed by the direction of the government but weary or less courageous, plead with the young to be cautious lest they provide the excuse to justify the repression. The young radicals, let down by what is tantamount to the cowardice of the once courageous liberals, condemn them as "sellouts", and dismiss them, to all intents and purposes, as no different from the rightwing. They say, and correctly so, that Mitchell needs no excuse for his high-handedness. The administration has abandoned justification as a necessary moral element in government action. This mutual frustration and disillusionment compels these two equally besieged segments to break ranks. Meanwhile the Nixon-Mitchell-Agnew battalions advance unchallenged against a broken and weakening liberal front.

And many liberals continue to theorize that such events as the disruptions at the Chicago trial can only help re-elect Richard Nixon and are therefore counter-productive. This, of course, is false. First of all, Richard Nixon was elected before the Chicago trial and, if anything, it was the behavior of the Democratic Establishment and not that of the young people which aided the Nixon campaign. Secondly, if the Chicago trial incidence is all it takes to make people support Nixon then the behavior of Claude Kirk, Republican Governor of Florida, should be more than adequate reason why such would-be supporters of Nixon should turn against him. But above all, there is the failure to realize that it is never the place of the underdog to be magnanimous and understanding. That would be a misplacement of responsi-

Scapegoat Melody

"Hey, Mike, what did Eldridge really tell you?"

Operation-wipe-out-the-Panthers

Poor Jimmy Wechsler, he must have had an excedrin headache.

bilities. Restraint is the option of the powerful, not of the weak; it should be demanded of the government and not of the defenseless resisters.

Step Six—Repression By Law

In the meantime, while the liberals pin their hopes on technicalities, the bigoted and the ignorant, encouraged by public government policy statements, attack defenseless black school children and overturn their buses. A coalition of grateful Southern Democrats and embarrassed "party loyal" Northern Republicans pass blatantly repressive laws that permit policemen to enter a premise without knocking; provide for preventive detention of suspects regarded as dangerous; allow indiscriminate wire tapping; prohibit resisting arrest whether such arrest is lawful or not, and provide mandatory life sentencing for conviction on a third felony. Once again, the excuse is that crime is on the increase although the government considers the increase in unemployment, a logical stimulant for crime, as healthy.

As with the illegal Rap Brown law, the embarrassed liberals falsely lay their hopes in the ultimate test at the Supreme Court. They ignore the fact that these laws could do irreparable damage long before they get tested in the Supreme Court. Even when they do get there, it would not be the Supreme Court of Chief Justice Earl Warren but that of Nixon-appointed Earl Burger, and others who "share (Nixon's) political philosophy". In other words, the liberals, looking only at isolated facts, are incapable of a broad perspective. They forget that it is not accidental that it is the same John Mitchell, the commander-in-chief of the anti-dissident forces, who recommended both Haynsworth and Carswell. They also ignore the implications of Nixon's desperate necessity to fill the Supreme Court vacancies only with people who fit into his overall power strategy.

Step Seven—The Politics Of Explosives

Some young people, driven against the wall by the establishment, are forced to resort to the use of explosives. Luckily they are still careful enough to do all in their power to prevent damage to life except, perhaps, their own. But property is damaged and in New York, some liberal property. And so liberal papers, reading as if their editorials were written by Mitchell and Agnew, only call for the use of the force of authority to seize and punish these people. What they also ought to be calling for is drastic action in the White House and Capitol Hill to eliminate the social forces that are causing these tragic acts of desperation.

No one can praise any act that jeopardizes life—be it that of the innocent bystander, or that of the culprit. But it is difficult to pass moral judgement on acts of desperation that involve the sacrifice of the participant's life. The line between heroic patriotism and misguided recklessness and suicide is much finer than some are willing to comprehend. It is just as painful to see these young Americans die in explosions as it is to contemplate the danger to innocent bystanders.

And so as the days wobble by, disillusionment of the young increases, the gulf between them and the liberal establishment widens and the authority of the repressive rightwing grows gigantic.

The government can now count on the liberals to be the ones to call for the repressive laws it already has up its sleeves. Thus it is a New York politician, Kelvin McGovern, who refers to young Americans as "shaggy bearded bomb throwers" and it is another New Yorker who asks for a summary death sentence for those caught with explosives.

THE PRESENT PICTURE

The state of the nation today should be disturbing to every American, no matter his political designation. In all of this seeming confusion there are certain incontrovertible facts:

1. Nobody likes the way things are in America. In particular, the young do not like the blatant lack of ethics of the system and the old do not like the disruption of the system.

2. It is possible and relatively easy to change the state of affairs to conditions satisfactory to all sides.

3. Short of violence, the government and the government alone is capable of bringing about such changes.

Digging absolutely

150

4. The government has not only refused to accept this responsibility but has, for misguided short-range political reasons, defiantly decided to ignore it. Instead, it has abandoned the role of government and gone in search of militant support against legitimate protest.

5. Liberals are in danger of being neutralized by a potentially powerful coalition of Southern Democrats and so-called loyal Republicans. If this trend is not stopped and the liberals are indeed neutralized, Congress may no longer be able to function effectively as a federal institution. Unless the liberals and the open-minded conservatives on Capitol Hill take the situation seriously and fight hard and openly, there is a threat that the coalition may be able to railroad its position through Congress whenever it chooses.

6. If the state of affairs in Congress gets to be such that the outcome of any issue can be predicted prior to any debate and when such outcome is guaranteed to be that desired by the same group, then democracy will cease to function. The right to vote is itself worthless unless it guarantees some influence in the ultimate decision making. Any minority group with representation in Congress is essentially not represented if the outcome of every issue is determined by an inflexible block vote by a majority. This is why there are built-in safeguards in any democratic system to give the minorities some power to influence the decision-making process.

THE THREE BRANCHES OF GOVERNMENT

The separation of the executive, the judicial and the legislative branches of government was intended to provide a check and balance for the protection of minority view point. For eight years under Presidents Kennedy and Johnson, the system worked. While the legislative branch could have remained independent and unpredictable, the executive was liberal, and the judiciary healthily controversial. So that those among the Blacks, the New Left and the young who had no confidence in the Legislature, could look up to either the executive or the judiciary for redress. This is one reason the country did not blow up in those turbulent years. There was violence within law, and the response of the executive and the judiciary was reparative not vindictive.

But the entire picture changed the moment Richard Nixon took over and flew his colors. With unusual access to pressing his own nominee for Chief Justice for the Supreme Court and with room for one more of his choice on the same Court; with a desire to control Congress through a Southern coalition; with the full backing of J. Edgar Hoover, who at last, after having been frustrated for eight years by the restraints of two cautious administrations, could now lay his hands on all those young American "communists" who often exist only in his imagination; Nixon seems to be attempting to control the legislative, the executive and imminently the judicial branches of government. Is there an opposition strong enough to reassure the young of its power to stop him? Perhaps the rejection of Harrold Carswell's nomination is reassuring, but only guardedly so.

GOVERNMENT BY INTIMIDATION

As the Nixon offensive against the process of government continues it is extremely important that Congress emphasizes its independence very clearly, and defends it openly. To act quietly behind the scenes and attempt to present a false united front under the guise of national stability will only serve to further increase the lack of confidence many young people now have in the government. It will also enable the administration to intimidate Congress and the people. In fact this has already begun.

The Vice President's appeal to the so-called "silent majority" to take up arms and protect themselves against the nation's leading networks and newspapers is intimidation of the press. So is the Attorney General's subpoena of the private notes of newspaper and television reporters.

The use of soldiers to break the letter carriers' strike in New York is of questionable implication. Of course, since it served the interest of big business— the soldiers delivered mail only to business and not to private citizens—there was no out-cry. The claim that the SDS was behind this protest of men whose annual salary after twenty-one years of service is roughly $8,000 is arrant nonsense and a continued insult to basic American common sense.

The administration has already forced the resignation of pro-civil rights employees of the Justice Department by frustration-intimidation.

The head, the hands and the legs
—the triple chase

The President's claim on the Carswell nomination that charges of racism, mediocrity and lack of candor levied against Carswell were "specious" is untenable.

"What is centrally at issue in this nomination is the Constitutional responsibility of the President to appoint members of the Court," said Nixon, "and whether this responsibility can be frustrated by those who wish to substitute their own philosophy or their own subjective judgement for that of one person entrusted by the Constitution with the power of appointment.

"The question arises whether I, as President of the United States, shall be accorded the same right of choice in naming Supreme Court justices which has been freely accorded to my predecessors of both parties."

This is a most dangerous attempt to intimidate Congress. It is quite serious when a President openly distorts known facts. The opposition to the nomination of Abe Fortas is still very fresh in the minds of many. The difference between Nixon and his predecessor is that Lyndon B. Johnson was capable of exercising discretion and judgement where Nixon had shown nothing but stubbornness. Johnson had enough confidence to be capable of admitting error in the interest of preserving the integrity and effectiveness of the Supreme Court, and subordinating his ego to the national interest. The effectiveness of the process of nominating and confirming candidates for public posts is based on the ability of the nominator to use discretion. If Richard Nixon cannot understand the embarrassment of his insistence on nominating increasingly inferior candidates for the Supreme Court, then perhaps there should be a limit on how many candidates the President can unsuccessfully nominate for a given position on the Supreme Court, after which he must forfeit the privilege of making such a nomination for the given position. This may serve to make the President more responsive to the considered opinions of highly qualified leaders and learned jurists.

The President by screaming "foul play" and demanding his civil presidential rights on this issue is only playing on the American people's sympathy for the underdog. It is only one step removed from calling on the people to defend themselves and the President against the Senate, just as they have been told to do against the press. It will not be long before Spiro T. Agnew will deliver such a speech in another of his now classic verbal exacerbations.

AN INSECURE PRESIDENT—AND HIS ASSISTANT

A President's insecurity is one of the most dangerous things to a country. President Nixon's underdog complex can cause all forms of witchhunts, paranoia, reckless exercise of police powers, and extreme repression. A president should not call on any segment of the people to defend him or themselves against any other segment of the people. In its ultimate effect, this is tantamount to instigating civil strife. More effectively than the allegations against the Black Panthers or the Students for a Democratic Society, Vice President Spiro Agnew has been crossing state boundaries every week to instigate riots. The attack on helpless black school children by white racists in South Carolina was in direct response to speeches of Agnew and the President's expressed opposition to school busing. It is therefore nonsensical to try the Chicago 8 or the SDS 12 when the Vice President, the chief violator of this unconstitutional federal law, is roaming the boondocks instigating "silent majority" violence and using the nation's networks to spread venom and encourage conflict.

(Actually the thought of Spiro Agnew going on a conspiracy trial in San Francisco or New York City for violating the Rap Brown law is most irresistible! I could see the scene. Haight-Ashbury or Greenwich Village. Stokeley Carmichael or David Dellinger as judge. If the judge must be a Hoffman, try Abbie. Kunstler would not mind being a prosecuting attorney. With a defense team of J. Edgar Hoover and William Hershey, and a jury of nine blacks and three young whites, the nation would see a trial far more like a carnival than Agnew saw in Chicago when he used the word. Joe McCarthy will turn in his grave and repeat what he said during his Senate trial, "Mr. Chairman, how much longer must I put up with this circus?")

It is not inconceivable that Mr. Agnew is not aware of the effect of his speeches. This will not be surprising in a man who in 1968 accused his predecessor of being "soft on communism" only to honestly say later, and in Chicago of all places, "If I'd known I'd be cast as the 'Joe McCarthy of 1968' I'd have turned five sommersaults to avoid saying it". And he added "I am not going to resurrect the days of Joe McCarthy". One wonders.

But it is of little more than sentimental importance how capable Agnew is of understanding the effects of his behavior. A naive leader who is honest and extremely

A boy once said to a girl,
"If you won't sleep with me
it is because you hate men."

Spiro T. Agnew vs. The Woodstock Nation.
Judge Carmichael: Mr. Kunstler, you have no objection to that?
Prosecutor Kunstler: Your Honor, . . .
Judge Carmichael: Sustained.
Defendant Spiro T. Agnew: But your Honor, . . .
Judge Carmichael: Mr. What's your name . . .
Defense Attorney J. Edgar Hoover: I . . .
Judge Carmichael: Objection overruled.
Prosecutor Kunstler: Thank you, your Honor
Judge Carmichael: Anytime Baby.
Defendant Spiro-you-know-Who: Your Honor, you are a black fascist, regional racist . . . what's the right animal . . . cat, yes, cat.

152

articulate and has easy access to power and to the media is the next most dangerous thing to an insecure President and a paranoid Attorney General. Add a panicky trigger happy police force, a frightened adult population and disillusioned youth; and you have what France might have looked like shortly before the Revolution.

PATRIOTISM

Patriotism should be sparingly invoked otherwise it can only erode the national self-confidence. Patriotism should never be used to intimidate public figures or to oppress outspoken citizens. Patriotism should never be used to camouflage the incompetence of a mediocre government.

A President's appeal to the people must take the form of calling on *all* of the people to devote themselves to solving social ills. John F. Kennedy called on *all Americans* to dedicate themselves to civil rights; he did not call on the black minority to support him against white racists. Lyndon B. Johnson called on all of the nation to support him in his search for a solution to the Vietnam war; he did not call on War Veterans to take to the streets to support him against members of Peace Movements. On the other hand, Richard Nixon called on the "silent majority" to speak out against the "vocal minority."

An appeal to some of the people against some of the people is a clear admission on the part of the government that it cannot represent all of the people. It is an admission of inability to function, and throughout the world when this situation arises, the government automatically resigns. This is precisely what Lyndon B. Johnson did by withdrawing from the 1968 presidential race after establishing that he had lost the confidence of a substantial segment, though by no means a majority, of the people. The loss of the confidence of a small segment of the public is sufficient to compel the government to question its usefulness. The best interest of the nation might demand that the government yield to others more capable of uniting the nation. It is such voluntary abdication that prevents civil strife in many countries.

THE SILENT MAJORITY

The government's reliance on a silent majority is the death-knoll of democracy. Silent men have no place in the functioning of democracy. As far as democracy is concerned, silent men are dead men and their voting options must be regarded as abstentions that may not be claimed by any one. Democracy is the rule of a majority of the expressive members of society and not that of a statistical majority of the population. If it were otherwise, there would be no need for voter registration. Candidates would be vying for votes of babies in their cradles or in their mothers' wombs. If it were otherwise, account would be taken in any election, of all those who register but do not cast their votes. This misconception of democracy as being based on a numerical majority probably derived from assumptions that all the people are well informed, capable of political thoughts, and able to exercise judgement. But this must be obviously false since Nixon and Agnew tell us that there is in fact a "silent majority". To have the support of the silent majority is to lead a non-functional segment of the body politic.

Spiro Agnew, probably because of his inability to comprehend the complexity of political reasoning and, perhaps, the implications of logic, has confused the concept of the unrepresented people with that of the silent majority. If all those who sing "Spiro is my Hero" form a silent majority, Nixon would never have been elected President. If those who elected the President are proud to be called "silent," they do not deserve the vote. And any one who claims to lead such people does not deserve to hold public office. Perhaps, there is a definite need to re-examine the theoretical basis of American politics in the light of these facts.

The image of Richard Nixon as a weak ineffectual man is dangerously misleading. This self-deception led the Democratic Party to disaster in 1968. It is human to confuse what we would like to believe about people with the truth. Somehow the Democrats went to Chicago believing that whoever won the nomination was guaranteed the presidency. Ironically, it seems the younger people knew better.

CIVIL VIOLENCE

Whenever a minority believes that it has recourse to redress, violence or the threat of it will be at a minimum. The casual flipping through of 1968 newspapers will confirm this. Never in the decade had young dissidents had more belief in the effectiveness of the system than when they used their campaign power in the New Hampshire primary. Never had the system been more responsive to them than when President Lyndon B. Johnson, in response to that primary, withdrew from the presidential race. It will probably be years for the country to recognize what a heroic and patriotic act that was on the part of the former president. It is extremely important that a national leader have enough conviction and principle to be willing to relinquish power if and when he thinks that he or the people would be unduly compromised. It is extremely unhealthy for a country to be led by anyone who would be president at all costs. On the one hand such a man will go to all length to be elected. On the other hand he will desperately hold on to power even long after he ceases to be effective and earns the disrespect and contempt of many of the people.

THE PRESIDENCY

Two such men were the presidential candidates in 1968. Hubert Humphrey— a man who once enjoyed the respect of many young Americans —was so desperate to be nominated that he allowed his party to create, in Chicago, what a younger Hubert Humphrey would have condemned outright. Even his refutation of President Johnson in the last hours of the campaign was a pathetic and unconvincing compromise. As for Richard Nixon, it was the story of a man who had worked so hard at becoming president and wanted the office so badly that a sympathetic nation figured, "might as well". The trouble is that the presidency of a country as complex and important as America should not be given to a man who begs longest for it. There was a time when the American motto (never really true anyway) that *anyone can be anything* might have had some appeal. At a time of complex national and international problems the requirements for the presidency should be so high that only the best would have the chance of getting it. The presidency of America cannot be an apprenticeship. Spiro Agnew should never have been nominated for the vice-presidency only for the world to be told that he was being given a "quickie course" in international politics by swimming and basking in the sun in a whirlwind tour of esoteric countries. Perhaps there should be qualifying tests for would-be presidential and vice-presidential candidates, as well as for cabinet nominees. If this were done, such accidents as Spiro Agnew would not happen.

Presidential Aptitude Test, PAT for short

ON BECOMING A GREAT PRESIDENT

Certain qualities are crucial for the presidency. There are different ways to be a great president: by taking on the challenges of the most pressing issues; by challenging the nation with the power of judgement and persuasion; by earnestly responding to issues that bother every segment of the society, no matter how small the segment; by being willing to risk a little loss of popularity now and then; by demonstrating such integrity that even those to whom he must say 'no' are convinced of the President's earnestness.

A president must have a talent for tireless initiative. Richard Nixon is highly mistaken when he argues, in his position paper on school desegregation, that he can only carry out the letter of the law—such as he sees fit to narrowly interpret. Not only is the President allowed to exercise initiative, the presidency *demands* tremendous initiative. Otherwise, the nation might as well have a computer in the White House.

One does not become a great president by watching football games on TV when thousands of citizens from all over the country are gathered a short distance away asking to be heard. Admittedly, presidents have been successful purely by refusing to risk being unsuccessful. The trouble, however, is that never before has America been in greater need of a heroic leader, a leader the people love, a leader the people hate, a leader the people abuse, a leader the people praise. But, all along, a leader the people respect and listen to. Ironically, no man more than Richard Nixon would want to be called a great leader. But no man is more incapable of attaining such heights.

And yet one cannot question the integrity of a man or condemn a man for not being what he is incapable of being. The trouble, however, is that while one cannot condemn the structural engineer for not being able to cure a heart disease, one must still admit that a heart disease needs a doctor. In so doing one must reluctantly imply that an engineer has no business risking the life of an ailing patient by keeping the doctors away, merely because he wants to go down in history as the world's greatest heart surgeon.

BEYOND THE PRESENT

After all is said and done, the question is, what can be done to prevent a disaster in the country. It will be presumptuous to pretend to have the answer. However, the matter is sufficiently important that every American, if only for selfish reasons of survival, must attempt to find an answer. No one would like to be blown to death in a public building, whether he sympathizes with Mitchell or the radicals.

At the time of writing this, the situation is very discouraging but perhaps not entirely hopeless. In spite of its appalling mediocrity, the present administration could, in fact, avert a catastrophe.

First, Mitchell must be informed that his job as Attorney General is to protect everybody, even the Washington Moratorium marchers who so tickled his wife's imagination. As Attorney General, Robert Kennedy was much tougher in his stand against civil violence than John Mitchell could ever be. He was capable of comprehending complex situations. Robert Kennedy was able to fight for civil rights and yet tell so called militant black Americans that he would not stand for riots. Ramsey Clark proved that one does not have to be a Kennedy to do that. If Mitchell had been Attorney General at the time of Watts it is a reasonable assumption that the country would have witnessed a vendetta. It is extremely important that a Democratic administration decided not to prosecute any of the Chicago 8 defendants in an incident that did much damage to that party.

Second, it is also important that someone convince Mr. Nixon that the 1968 election is over and, surprising as it may be to him, he is actually already the American President. He must now think and act on behalf of every American and must, especially, protect the rights and enhance the lot of the poor and the minority. He can do this without selling out to bigotry, mediocrity, and political insensitivity and immaturity. To lead is to uphold the ideal and to convince the generally reluctant majority to support the ideal.

The presidency is not identical to the Harris or Gallup poll. No matter what may be said about the so-called Southern strategy the fact is that Nixon does not need to prostitute what seemed like the newly acquired sense of justice in the nation in order to win another four-year term. In fact, the more intelligent and more successful strategy would have been to keep the southern support he already has and to woo the support of the North especially amongst those who have now been disillusioned by the Democratic party. Nixon cannot argue that the young did not give him a chance. Lyndon Johnson was treated with more derision and contempt by the young when he came to office than Nixon met when he took office, and that in spite of Johnson's very impressive record as a Senator.

Nixon had a unique opportunity for a new politics and could easily have given the nation a fresh start by pulling it together. By owing his election to the South, he was in a better position than Lyndon Johnson was to bring racists in the South into the path of light.

As long as racism persists in this country, there can be no peace. Not even if all the pollution is removed from the air.

Next, the separation of the different branches of government must be protected. Politics must be removed from the selection of Supreme Court judges. A president must nominate to the Supreme Court only those who enjoy the unquestionable respect of the entire country. Such men must be the best legal minds available. The President cannot afford to insist on imposing mediocre people on the nation and insist on holding fast even beyond the point of complete embarrassment to everyone. To do this is to dare segments of the society to do what they please: and Agnew has more than done this in his fund-raising arias. The claim made by Senator Roman Hruska that "there are a lot of mediocre judges and people and lawyers, and they are entitled to a little representation, aren't they? We can't have all Brandeises, Frankfurters and Cardozos" is untenable. The Supreme Court has absolutely no room for mediocrity. There are enough other places where mediocre people can find employment. Besides, it is an insult to the nation to suggest that the country cannot come up with one or two jurists of impeccable integrity and brilliant professional record.

The press must be left absolutely free to do its job as it sees fit just as the Stock Exchange is allowed to do its business.

In order to restore a sense of confidence and freedom and to dissipate the threat of repression, Mitchell must withdraw the FBI from college campuses and harmless night clubs and restore the use of the telephone to people who want to feel free to share a little sentimentality, without the fear of eavesdroppers. To make a citizen feel insecure and afraid to crack even the mildest joke is far more subversive than even throwing a bomb at a building.

The political parties for their part must restore the effectiveness of the two party system by regaining the confidence and respect of the young people. This will take the choice of truth over expedience at a time when most young people are sick and tired of a succession of expedient actions over the most blatant violation of ethics and principles. The nation must realize that to ask a man to vote for either of two candidates for whom he has no respect is not allowing him the use of his vote.

The old must stop dismissing the young as uninformed and unpatriotic if only because it is the young alone who bear the brunt of the nation's military entanglements. The old must open up to the young and be willing to listen to them. No nation of old people can survive more than one or two generations. It is the young who infuse society with renewed morality and renewed enthusiasm. Adult wisdom is worthless to society without the energy of youth to put it into good use. An administration that encourages the old to hate the young and lends its support to the misfortunes of ignorance under the pretence of a misunderstood silent majority can only lead a nation to disaster.

What is difficult to understand is why Nixon and Mitchell cannot see that it is so much easier, so much more enjoyable and so much safer to run the country with understanding, rather than with defiance as if they hated the people they led.

There may be sacrifices. Richard Nixon may have to abandon John Mitchell. But it seems worth it to dismiss one administrator in order to save the lives of many citizens. It is certainly worth it if that will help save the nation. Besides, it may be the only way to stop the increasing rate of bomb explosions throughout the country. Locking bathroom doors in offices and passing new laws will not do it. They only aid the lock industry and inconvenience people. Certainly the death penalty is not a deterrent since those who are frustrated enough to feel compelled to risk their lives in handling dangerous explosives would have decided to sacrifice their lives for their cause anyway, and will not be stopped by the fear of death. Besides, how many young people can the government hang before America decides that she has had enough of this?

Fortunately, some good old Americans are beginning to try to understand what it is the young have been trying so hard to say. Ironically, the first such sympathetic ears come from the least likely places.

Warren Hoge, writing in *The New York Post* of April 10, 1970, describes Dwight, Illinois:

A town of 3100, it sits astride the main Chicago-St. Louis line of the Gulf, Mobile & Ohio Railroad. It is a place where kids sneak cigarettes behind a warehouse for excitement by day and cruise the main street in rumbling jalopies at night.

On either side of the town is prairie and beyond that, more prairie.

Diana Oughton was born in Dwight, Illinois, 28 years ago. Now she lies there "in a quiet wooded graveyard." Diana was killed on March 6 in a bomb explosion on West Eleventh Street in Greenwich Village, New York City. This is how Dwight, Illinois, is trying to understand:

We are still groping for understanding. The great puzzle is the tremendous difference between the gentle character we know and the individual the newspapers describe.
— James H. Oughton Jr., the father

If we teach our children to care about others, we can't tell them how to implement their concern because there is no socially acceptable means.
— a sympathetic parent whose own son recently dropped out of school

Many of us from Dwight and towns like Dwight have decided there is too much wrong in America to simply accept it. Do not condemn her or what she did. Instead, try to see what turned her—what has turned thousands of people to protest, to civil disobedience and sometimes to death.
— a doctor's son, now living in New York

While I am a conservative, as you are, in much of my thinking . . . I am certain that Diana and the younger generation are trying to tell us something. While we may not accept their way, we must listen because what they are trying to say is worthwhile. This great country presents much opportunity for most of us but not all of us, and that is what is of deep concern to the younger generation.
— from a local friend of Diana's parents

And finally, a stranger wrote to the Oughtons:

Most of us find no one in our own social circle able to understand any of what these young people feel. These brilliant kids are not "nuts" or "effete snobs". They are serious, committed young people dedicating their lives to political change.

156

Only the young survive

Dwight, Illinois. Pop. 3100
In the heart of Middle America

And if there ever was a Middle America, Dwight, Illinois, is certainly part of it. Will Diana Oughton and her friends have died in vain?

That they have died in trying to come to grips with the contradictions of the country they must have loved is enough to make us listen. It is not important that they died violently. What of those who died quietly by burning themselves to death a few years ago? We have forgotten about them now. None of us can recall the names of the two lovers from a New Jersey High School who quietly asphixiated themselves in their automobile last year and left us a note saying they could no longer take the ugliness we have turned the world into. Will they too have died in vain?

On second thought, perhaps everything in the country is just fine and one is only merely complaining about the moral inconvenience of a negligible number of young people. If that is the case, all that has been said here is not more than an exercise in political thought. But even Richard Nixon, Spiro Agnew, John Mitchell, J. Edgar Hoover, John Stennis and the rest of that nondescript complex, suggest, perhaps unwittingly, that there is something wrong. Yet they too might just be indulging in another kind of exercise in political thought. On the other hand, there is the slightest chance that things are, in fact, very bad and that the future as seen from present trends is frightening. If this is the case, it is not too much sacrifice for anyone who loves America to stop for a moment and consider what is going on. There are many of us who love what this country could easily be. Perhaps, that is why many find the present state of affairs frustrating. This may come as a surprise to Mitchell and Agnew, but it is a fundamental truth that criticism may be born of the highest sense of affection and partiotism.

"I am a Super Patriot", Eldridge Cleaver recently said in Algeria, ". . . but not to the America I left. . . . I believe that there are two Americas. There is America of the American dream, and there is the America of the American nightmare. I feel that I am a citizen of the American dream, and that the revolutionary struggle, of which I am a part, is a struggle against the American nightmare."

This is the dilemma of many Americans today.

Musical chairs

Numbered, Numbered, Weighed and Divided

Jerry (to Leonard Weinglass): Take good care of it while I'm gone, Len. It's my favorite shirt.

158

ROLLINS

Myth in Surrealist Painting,
1929-1939

Studies in the Fine Arts: The Avant-Garde, No. 1

Stephen C. Foster, Series Editor
Associate Professor of Art History
University of Iowa

Kenneth S. Friedman, Ph.D.
Consulting Editor

Other Titles in This Series

Myth in Surrealist Painting, 1929-1939

by
Whitney Chadwick

umi
RESEARCH PRESS

Copyright © 1980
Whitney Chadwick
All rights reserved

Produced and distributed by
UMI Research Press
an imprint of
University Microfilms International
Ann Arbor, Michigan 48106

Library of Congress Cataloging in Publication Data

Chadwick, Whitney.
Myth in surrealist painting, 1929-1939.

(Studies in the fine arts : The avant-garde ; 1)
Originally presented as the author's thesis, Pennsylvania
State University.
Bibliography: p.
Includes index.
1. Surrealism—Themes, motives. 2. Painting, Modern—
20th century—Themes, motives. 3. Mythology, Classical,
in art. 4. Dalí, Salvador, 1904-   5. Ernst, Max, 1891-
1976. 6. Masson, André, 1896-   I. Title. II. Series:
Studies in the fine arts : Avant-garde ; 1.

ND196.S8C43 1979   759.06'63   79-26713
ISBN 0-8357-1057-2

Contents

List of Figures

Figure Credits

The author and publisher wish to thank the following individuals and institutions who have kindly granted permission to reproduce the indicated illustrations. Their cooperation is gratefully acknowledged.

Albright-Knox Art Gallery, Buffalo: 65; Archaeological Museum, Iraklion: 6; E.A. Bergmann, Chicago: 87; J. Bourjou, Brussels: 16; Salvador Dali, Cadaques: 60, 66-68, 70; Editions Cahiers d'Art, Paris: 9; Galerie der Spiegel, Cologne: 99-101; Galerie le Point Cardinal, Paris: 89; Erno Goldfinger, London: 86; Hanover Gallery, London: 59; Mr. and Mrs. Maxime Hermanos, New York: 3; Dr. Jerome Hirschmann, Chicago: 39; Edward James, Sussex: 27; Julien Levy, Bridgewater, Conn.: 88; Louvre, Paris: 84; André Masson, Paris: 1-2, 20, 23-24, 26, 28, 34-35, 37-38, 42-46, 52-57, 90-98; Menil Family Collection, Houston: 75; Moderna Museet, Stockholm: 82; Mr. and Mrs. A. Reynolds Morse, Cleveland: 12, 47, 58, 61; Musees royaux des Beaux-Arts, Brussels: 21; Museo Chiaramonti, Rome: 64; Museum Boymans-van Beuningen, Rotterdam: 15; Museum of Modern Art, New York: 8, 30, 62, 72; Museum of Modern Art, San Francisco: 29; Vicomtesse de Noailles, Paris: 73; La Reserve, Knokke-le-zonte: 63; Service Pictorial, Paris: 13, 14, 76-78, 80; S.P.A.D.E.M., Paris: 4-5, 7, 10-11, 17-18, 31, 74, 79, 81, 83; Mr. and Mrs. Jerome Stern, New York: 25; Richard S. Zeisler, New York: 49.

Preface and Acknowledgments

According to poet André Breton, Surrealism's charismatic and controversial leader, one of that movement's major goals lay in providing an appropriate *"mythe collectif"* for the twentieth century.[1] For Breton, this Surrealist
myth had to stand as a clear and unequivocal evocation of its age. Although
the legacy of Surrealism remains visible in all the arts—in theatrical cultivation
of absurdity and black humor, in literary manifestations of madness and the
irrational, in the tearing down of traditional barriers between art and life in
performance, process and body art as well as neo-Dada, Funk, Super-realism
and all the other "movements" that derive some part of their program from the
rich heritage of Dada and Surrealism—one can argue that there survives no
single myth identified with Surrealism and indelibly imprinted upon contemporary consciousness with the articulated set of images and psychological
content that distinguishes myth from the realms of folk tale, legend and story.
The true strength of Surrealism lay in the fact that, at its best, it sought to
raise consciousness and expand understanding of existence as a fluid state
in which chaos and contradiction are resolved by transformation and metamorphosis.

Before 1929, Surrealist literature contains only a few scattered and fragmentary references to myth. But by 1938, the year of the first major international Surrealist exhibition, mythological themes abounded in the paintings
and writings of Masson, Dali, Ernst, Breton, Eluard, Aragon and others and
filled the pages of the major Surrealist periodicals of those years—*Acéphale,
Minotaure* and *Le Surréalisme au Service de la révolution.* They range from
references to familiar classical cults like that of Dionysios, to sixteenth century
restoration of earlier myths like those of the Acephali and Leda, to Freudian
reinterpretations of the ancient content of myths such as Oedipus and Narcissus,
through the exploration of primitive cult, taboo and magic to the cultivation of
grander conceptions in the great "myth of love" or the "cult of the irrational."

Attempting to determine the relationship between these various myth
fragments and mythic survivals and the emergence of a more comprehensive,
but necessarily more abstract, collective Surrealist myth is not easy. There is
no single Surrealist iconography; there are only the productions of individual
Surrealists. But in looking at those productions in terms of a shared thematic
and imagistic content it is evident that many of these works, both literary and
artistic, confirm each other in their commitment to communicating Surrealist

principles and values through a set of recognizable images which have come to have a specific and shared Surrealist content.

During the 1930's, the years of the greatest concentration of themes and images drawn from mythological sources, the group was fragmented by a series of political and artistic quarrels among the members which resulted in various painters working relatively independently of Breton's strictures during some, if not all, of those years. The well known "excommunications" of 1929, which included Miro and Masson, are documented in the Second Manifesto. Yet Masson has related that during these years of "official exile" before he rejoined the group at the end of 1938 he was in almost daily contact with other members of the group and that this communication was marked by the constant sharing of important themes and ideas.[2] Without attempting to provide a comprehensive overview of Surrealist paintings that refer to myths, I have instead organized this study around those mythic themes that appear of greatest significance to individual Surrealist painters. It is hoped that a close analysis of specific myths will reveal more clearly the particular quality of the Surrealist imagination during these years and the meaning and function of myth in a Surrealist context.

I have been faced with all the methodological problems of any study of Surrealist painting. The literature on Surrealism, although vast, is in many ways unsatisfactory from an art historian's point of view. Although some fine critical studies of Surrealist literature exist, there has been almost no attempt to explore the themes and significance of Surrealist painting. Myriad surveys of Surrealist art yield little new information regarding the iconographic content of these paintings, and the painters' accounts are often obtuse and contradictory. This book in no way claims to represent a comprehenseive catalogue of the mythological paintings of Dali, Ernst and Masson. It is instead, I believe, the first attempt to explore the iconography of Surrealist painting using art historical method.

The original wealthy patrons and collectors of Surrealist art are widely scattered; many of their collections are currently in storage. The present whereabouts of other works is unknown both to the artists themselves and to the galleries which represent them. Catalogues of the works of Dali, Ernst and Masson are in preparation, and I wish to express my gratitude to their authors; Albert Field, Werner Spies and Françoise Will-Levaillant respectively.

This thesis is the result of almost three years of work and a great deal of assistance from other people. Without the continuing help of the staffs of the Museum of Modern Art in New York and the Bibliothèque Jacques Doucet Littéraire in Paris I would not have had access to a number of vital documents. Among the many people who have aided my research I would like to acknowledge with thanks the information, suggestions and introductions provided by Michel and Louise Leiris, Françoise Chapon, William Rubin, Julien Levy,

Nicholas Calas, Françoise Will-Levaillant, Salvador Dali, Lawrence Safire, Howard Limoli, André Masson and Gilbert Brownstone. Professor George Mauner kindly arranged the initial meeting with Masson and has seen this project through to the end. Special thanks go to my colleagues at the Massachusetts Institute of Technology, especially to Wayne Andersen with whom I have discussed many of these ideas and whose support and encouragement have greatly aided the project, and to Mary Daly who painstakingly typed this manuscript.

I

The Road to Myth

All myths are alive so long as men believe in them. Out of them come new deeds, new realities, because myth is creative.

View, 1944

Breton's demand that Surrealism enumerate the "collective" myth of its age underlines the movement's preoccupation with communal values and shared goals. In a sense *all* myths are collective, transcending individual perception and transmitting social realities. If there is a single connecting thread running among Surrealism's diverse personalities and productions between 1924, when the first manifesto appeared, and the early 1940's when Breton and others returned to Paris after the war, it appears in the unrelenting search for a new and shared reality communicable through the work of art. Myth does not tell the "story" of Surrealism; it reveals little about stylistic and historical developments. But it does provide one means of access to the often complex and obscure iconography of Surrealist painting. The myths of Surrealism are metaphors for all could not be directly stated; their symbols are the means of unravelling the Surrealist world view.

The Surrealist search for mythic expression really began in 1929 with Breton's recognition that Surrealism must have new guiding principles if it were to continue as a potent international political and artistic force. After five years of experimentation Surrealism needed a program that could spread the results of its explorations into the relationship between conscious and unconscious to an ever widening circle of initiates. But the seeds of this new direction lie in the history of the movement's first years, years which represented, in part, an attempt to establish the place of the work of art in the nexus of Surrealist theory.

In February of 1924 André Breton had purchased his first work by a young painter, André Masson, then living in Paris' Montparnasse district. Masson had executed the painting, entitled *The Four Elements* (Fig. 1), in late 1923, almost a year before the appearance of the first Surrealist manifesto. Exhibited in Masson's first one man exhibition at Henri David Kahnweiler's Galerie Simon in Paris, its mingling of mythic, alchemical and dreamlike images attracted Breton and anticipated many of the later concerns of Surrealist painting. For Masson the work marked the break with his earlier and more clearly Fauve and Cubist-inspired landscapes and still-lifes. Here, earth, air, fire and water and their myriad creatures mingled in a semi-illusionistic space that derives from the work of the Italian metaphysical painter Giorgio de Chirico. Masson's friend Michel Leiris accurately described the work: "In the distance, the ocean as a reminder of origins. Fire of the flame, air of flight, water of the waves and aquatic creatures, rotundity of the earth, the four elements are there indeed. Giving sense to it all . . . the indispensable human kingdom, hands occupied taking hold and letting go, distant silhouette of a desired being."[1] The painting, with its hermetic allusions, suggests the alchemical process, but Masson's primary source was the pre-Socratic Heracleitus of Ephesus, whom he had discovered through his reading of Nietzsche and whose view of a world in a constant state of flux and metamorphosis profoundly influenced his own search for a means of visually communicating a world stripped of absolutes. In an often quoted passage, Heracleitus had written, "Fire lives the death of air, and air lives the death of fire, water lives the death of earth, earth that of water."[2] "If it weren't for Nietzsche I do not believe I would have read Heracleitus," Masson later noted.[3]

Breton met Masson shortly after purchasing *The Four Elements* and invited the young painter to join with him in founding a periodical or a group. Sharing similar attitudes, the two disagreed about the importance of Dostoevski and Nietzsche, whom Masson had first read while living in Switzerland just prior to World War I. Nietzsche's Greece, the Greece of Orphic rites and Dionysiac cults, would provide a primary source for Surrealism's later re-evaluation of the classical tradition, but at this time Breton was still dismissing what he somewhat disdainfully characterized as the "mythe nietzschéen."

Eight months after the meeting, at the end of December 1924, the first Surrealist manifesto appeared with Breton's initial and now famous definition of Surrealism as ". . . pure psychic automatism through which the true function of thought might be expressed, either in writing or verbally, freed from any rational, aesthetic or moral considerations."[4] Born out of the ashes of Dada, Surrealism fought to overcome that movement's anarchism and nihilism by establishing a place for itself in the history of politically and artistically radical movements. Among Surrealist "precursors" in the search for a means of synthesizing all levels of human experience, Breton claimed Poe, Baudelaire, Nerval, Rimbaud, Bosch, Breughel and others. In the beginning he hoped for nothing less than the fusing of all the sources of human creativity—the dream, the unconscious, the conscious, the irrational—into a heightened reality that might alter the very shape of the world as well as man's understanding of that world. Deeply influenced by the lessons of Marx and Freud, Breton saw the new revolution occurring simultaneously on two fronts—the one political and external, the other exploring the deepest recesses of the human mind and unfolding its truths in the work of art.

Surrealism's first techniques for visualizing unconscious mental processes— automatic writing and drawing and the narrating of dreams—became the means of transcending reason and eliciting the profound connections that Breton believed existed among individual consciousnesses. Discussions of the spontaneous and unreasoned quality of these techniques often overlook the significant value attached to them as a means for establishing collective values.

The first manifesto mentions Surrealist precursors in painting ranging from Uccello to Seurat, Moreau, Matisse, Derain, Picasso, Braque, Duchamp, Picabia, Chirico, Klee, and "Man Ray, Max Ernst and—so close to us—André Masson," but is generally uninformative about the role of the visual arts in Surrealism. Discussing the graphic translation of the hallucinogenic image Breton noted that, "it is not a question of drawing, it is simply a question of tracing."[5] A few years later he recorded that ". . . it is impossible for me to envisage a picture as being other than a window, and why my first concern is then to know what it *looks out* on. . . ."[6] For Pierre Naville, even such a literalist understanding of the role of the artist was too much; he argued in the third issue of the newly founded periodical, *La Révolution Surréaliste,* that there could be *no* Surrealist art; "Neither pencil marks recording chance gestures, nor images representing dream figures, nor imaginary fantasies, of course, can be so qualified."[7]

The ensuing controversy over the role of paintings in a Surrealist world led to a series of essays by Breton, later published under the title *Le Surréalisme et la peinture,* in which he traced the development of the dream-like and automatic Surrealist image from the Synthetic Cubism of Braque and Picasso to the work of Max Ernst, Man Ray and Masson.[8] In the end the task of establishing a Surrealist visual imagery fell to the painters themselves and must be seen as fusion of Surrealist theoretical concerns with the vagaries of individual style and personality. As Rubin has pointed out, the first Surrealist works of art (Figs. 2 and 3) qualify as *peinture-poèsie.* Their roots in Symbolism and Cubism, they fuse interior and exterior reality into a fluid world in a constant process of transformation.[9] The first exhibition of Surrealist painting, held at the Galerie Pierre in Paris in 1925, included the work of Ernst, Miro, Arp, Man Ray and Masson as well as that of the three painters never formally affiliated with the movement but often recalled by Breton: Klee, de Chirico and Picasso. Regardless of individual style, which ranged from the Cubist-derived syntax of Masson to the first collages of Max Ernst, the works all derived their imagery from an interior source.

Surrealist paintings of the 1920's relied, whether implicitly or explicitly, on the technique of automatism to establish their specifically "Surrealist" content. The technique, to which Breton initially referred as the "pooling of thought," had both literary and psychological sources. Masson's method was close to pure doodling, Ernst's seems to have been formed through his reading of Freud while a student at Bonn University. Both the "monologue intérieur" first credited to Edouard Dujardin's novel *Les Lauriers sont coupés,* published in 1887, and Janet's essay of 1889, *L'Automatisme psychologique,* contributed. The most famous group of automatic productions of the 1920's, the *Cadavres exquis,* often demonstrated striking connections between the images of the various sections proving for Breton the existence of a "collective imagination" that could be visually tapped.[10] For Masson, whose automatic drawings and sand paintings are among the most spontaneous production of Surrealism's early years, automatism led directly to the fluidity of the metamorphic process.

Breton himself and others believed that the value of a work of art lay in the effort of the artist to encompass the whole psychophysical field, of which the conscious mind represented only one small part.

> La peinture, par exemple," wrote Pierre Mabille, "demande que l'oeuvre crée contienne à la fois une part de l'émotion individuelle ressentie par la réalité extérieure de l'objet représenté. Ce n'est que dans ces conditions qu'elle pourra se dire réussie. On voit qu'une telle peinture devient un symbole, que la main de l'artiste n'a été qu'un instrument d'expression de la nature. Le tableau en tant que symbole aura suivant les termes rapportés ci-dessus une vie propre et une action indépendente sur l'ambience.[11]

Like Dada, Surrealism made few distinctions between art and life; during the movement's first years social and artistic revolution were seen as proceeding hand in hand. The political situation of Surrealism before 1929 helped shape attitudes toward the work of art while, at the same time, laying the basis for the gradual shift of emphasis away from direct political action and toward an increasingly esoteric world view. Surrealist political activities during the 1920's reveal Breton's unwillingness to relinquish his autocratic control over the group. The first major crisis over contacts with the French Communist Party had come about in 1925 during the Morroccan rebellion which the Surrealists, still deeply affected by their personal experiences of World War I, perceived as a battle to prevent the liberation of a colonized people. Academics and the literary establishment in France generally supported the French government in its stand against the rebels; the Surrealists, who saw the struggle as a "war of liberation," endorsed the insurgents and their Communist Party allies in France.[12]

The alignment of various political groups in France during the Morroccan crisis brought the Surrealists into collaboration with the members of the *Clarté* staff, a literary and political journal published in Paris by younger members of the French Communist Party. The fifth number of *La Révolution surréaliste,* appearing on October 15, 1925, contained a manifesto signed by a diverse group of reviews including *Clarté* and *La Révolution surréaliste* and declaring that "Nous nous déclarons en insurrection contre l'histoire. . . . Nous ne sommes pas des utopistes: cette révolution nous ne la concevons que sous sa forme sociale."[13]

On other fronts the collaboration proceeded less peacefully. The previous year the Surrealists had published a pamphlet attacking Anatole France entitled: *Un Cadavre.* Here they had taken on a national hero: to the Right he was the guardian of *le style français;* to the Left he was the near socialist who had marched beside Juarès. The Surrealist denunciation was total: "Have you ever slapped a dead man?" asked Aragon. To the Surrealists whose literary radicalism outstripped their politics, France represented everything conservative and bourgeois; to a number of members of *Clarté,* perhaps more politically radical but less artistically *avant-garde,* the attack upon a venerated man of French literature appeared shocking.

The polarities that Breton viewed as fundamental to Surrealism demanded a dialectical revolution. The declaration that no mental revolution was possible without first effecting a revolution in social values distinguishes this first period of Surealist political activity. Willing to put Surrealism in the service of the revolution, but adamant in his refusal to allow the movement to be sacrificed to the sometimes incompatible goals of world revolution, Breton's intransigence ultimately brought about the collapse of the alliance with *Clarté.* With the publication of his "Legitime défence" in the eighth issue of *La Révolution surréaliste* he sharply attacked Communist intentions of monopolizing the revolution and argued the existence of two different problems: the problem of knowledge and that of an effective course of social action:

> I say that the revolutionary flame burns where it chooses, and that it is not up to a small group of men, in the *period of waiting* we are now *living through,* to decree that it can burn only here or there. . . . We believe that, having nothing to gain from placing ourselves directly in the political realm, we may, in matters of human activity, justifiably make use of the appeal to principles and thereby serve the cause of the Revolution. . . .[14]

In 1929 the major Surrealist periodical was retitled *Le Surréalisme au service de la révolution;* the first issue contained a telegram to Moscow in which the Surrealists reiterated their willingness to serve the revolution as long as it was understood that they did so by choice and in their own way. From this point on, Surrealism would pursue its goals along two parallel but separate lines: one of political revolution, the other of a deepening commitment to systematically exploring the forces of the unconscious.

When Aragon renounced Surrealism in favor of Communism in the early 1930's, relations between the two groups became even more strained. In 1933, Breton, Eluard and René Crevel were expelled from the Party for defending an article by Ferdinand Alquié in which he denounced "le vent de crétinisation systématique qui souffle d'U.R.S.S."[15] By that time Stalinist position on art had hardened and the final revolt occurred in 1935 during the *Congrès international pour la défense de la culture,* a Communist sponsored symposium which Breton had hoped to use as another forum for advancing Surrealism's position. In a letter to the organizers, the Surrealist writers argued that for them there could be no question in a capitalist society of the defense and maintenance of culture: "Cette culture ne nous intéresse que dans son devenir et ce devenir même nécessite avant tout la transformation de société par la Révolution prolétarienne."[16] And they demanded answers to the question of their right to pursue, in literature and in art, the search for new means of expression and the right of artist and writer to continue to investigate human life in all its dimensions. Ultimately, Breton provoked the Communist critic Ehrenbourg to a stinging denunciation of Surrealism. "Who are these Surrealists interested in Hegel and Marx and the revolution but unwilling to work for it?" demanded Ehrenbourg. "The example they set is one of studying pederasty and dreams among other aberrations!"[17] In the ensuing controversy, the Communist Party supported Ehrenbourg; Breton and others definitely broke with orthodox Communism but continued their commitment to a collective revolutionary action.

Meanwhile, however, the so-called "crisis of 1929" had also deeply marked the development of a Surrealist program leading finally to an extensive re-evaluation of Surrealism's artistic and political goals. The turning point for the movement came in 1929 with the publication in December of the Second Surrealist Manifesto in which Breton called for "the profound and veritable occultation of Surrealism."

In the second manifesto Breton argues first for the notion of the surreal as:

> . . . a certain point of the the mind at which life and death, the real and the imaginary, the past and the future, the communicable and the incommunicable, . . . will cease to be perceived as contradictions. It is in vain that one would seek in Surrealism anything other than the hope of determining this point. . . .[18]

He repeats that the activity of Surrealism demands a radical break with the world—both past and present. Everything must be done to destroy all notions of family, nation, religion. Let the undesirables leave Surrealism, cries Breton, "excommunicating" Artaud, Delteil, Gerard, Limbour, Masson, Souphault, and Vitrac, all of whom he feels have strayed from Surrealism's goals. The revolution, says Breton, must not be limited to politics. After the denunciations he turns to the question of Surrealism itself arguing that the movement has been negligent, that experiments into automatic writing and dream narration have too often failed to be rigorously pursued and have become merely passive entertainments. From now on, he says, Surrealism must devote itself to "human activity in all its forms." Later he would distinguish between Surrealism's "intuitive" and "reasoning" epochs, the latter representing a more considered use of the processes of the unconscious.[19]

In the pictorial domain the greatest impetus for the next few years would be provided by new converts like Salvador Dali, whose *paranoiac-critical method* moved Surrealism further into the realm of psycho-pathology. But the 1930's are also marked by increased Surrealist activity on a theoretical level. Gradually moving away from automation and the narration of dreams as techniques to stimulate the flow of thought, Surrealism now sought more controlled means for systematizing the unconscious.

Surrealist art had never pursued irrationality as an end; rather it attempted to synthesize the opposing but interacting states of objective fact and subjective fantasy in a dialectic of reason and unreason. Refusing to accept the work of art as an end in itself, the Surrealist artist admitted it only as yet another means to the exploration of mankind; "The single justification for a work of art . . . is to contribute to the enrichment of man, the transmission of values, the denunciation of social, moral and religious hypocrisy," declared Masson.[20] Discouraged by the realities of the European political Left in the early 1930's and by Surrealism's apparent failure to define itself from within as a social force, Breton turned toward more private and esoteric goals: the search to establish a language of Surrealism that could forge a new and vibrant relationship between oneiric, mythic and poetic thought.

Although reference to myth are scattered and fragmentary in Surrealism during the 1920's, the political and artistic situation of Surrealism in 1930 demanded new modes of expression. It is then that Breton commits the movement to subsuming all experiments in the language of the unconscious and the irrational under the general problem that Surrealism sought to raise: *"that of human expression in all its forms"* (Breton's italics).[21] Among the mythological themes that appear in Surrealist painting and writing during the 1930's are a group of pre-Classical and classical images: Dionysos, Oedipus, Theseus, Narcissus, Leda and Daphne, as well as specifically Surrealist images elevated to mythological levels: Gradiva and Loplop. The Surrealist reinterpretation of pre-classical and classical myth in the light of their own needs and desires is closely connected to the general shift in attitude toward ancient myth that occurred at the beginning of this century and replaced the formal and archaeological values of post-Renaissance Humanism with the anthropological views of the Cambridge school with its emphasis on the significant social role and collective content of ancient myth. Primarily *lycée* educated in the classical tradition, the Surrealists had inherited a set of nineteenth century attitudes that viewed myth as analogous to older forms of theology and metaphysics as a primary source for explanations for the origins of experience. Primitive myth was known mainly in fragments; these tended on the one hand to document supernatural interventions in the natural world, and on the other to establish intellectual continuity within the western tradition. Behind much nineteenth century French writing about myth lay assumptions about the evolutionary nature of knowledge and civilization; Classical Greece, the birthplace of democratic thought, was also understood as the source of the poetic imagination. Surrealist precursors among the Symbolist poets and painters had seen in myth a means of reaching universal, absolute Truth; "la matière du poème, c'est le mythe," wrote Mallarme.[22] And in the dream-like gazes of the classically draped women of Khnopf's and Moreau's painting the message is similar—follow us back into a poetic and Elysian past. The very conception of *patria* that the Surrealist revolt sought to vanquish was one that had found its symbols in the classical tradition and visualized them in the works of David and Ingres.

Myth, with its emphasis on feeling rather than thought, had long been associated in France with poetic expression. A tradition which encouraged the mingling of mythic elements in the arts had existed from the Renaissance well into the twentieth century. Among the School of Paris Surrealist interest in myth was certainly not the exception. During the 1930's Matisse's illustrations for Henry de Montherlant's *Pasiphaë: Chant de Minos* appeared, as well as Picasso's etchings for Albert Skira's luxury editions of the *Metamorphosis of Ovid, Lysistrata,* and the *Tauromachia.* In a more literary vein Gide's *Oedipus,* was well known as was Cocteau's *La Machine Infernale,* a transformation of the same theme.

One of the great repositories of classical themes in France was the ballet. The general repertories of both Diaghilev's *Ballet Russes de Monte Carlo* and the *Ballet de Paris* contained standard classical ballets: *Philomen and Baucis* was performed by the *Ballet Russes* in 1924, *The Triumph of Neptune* in 1925, *Oedipus Rex* in 1927—as well as more contemporary transformations of classical themes such as Cocteau's *Antigone* for which Picasso had designed the sets in 1922. Surrealist interventions in the ballet world met markedly different receptions between 1925 and 1933. In 1925 Breton had paid homage to Picasso for his designs for the ballet *Mercure;* it was Picasso himself who subsequently recommended Miro and Ernst to Diaghilev. The two produced a backdrop for the Ballet Russes production of *Romeo and Juliet* which opened at the Sarah Bernhardt theater on May 18, 1925. The curtain had scarcely risen when a group of Surrealists in the audience began a storm of whistles and cries accompanied by a flurry of leaflets thrown by Breton and Aragon asserting that:

the participation of the painters Max Ernst and Joan Miro in the productions of the ballet Russes by no means implicates Surrealism in such a betrayal of its basic ideas. These ideas are essentially subversive and can never come to terms with such enterprises, whose aim has always been to tame the dreams and rebellions of physical and intellectual hunger in the interests of the international aristocracy.[23]

The police were called, the offenders removed, and only the tactful intervention of Paul Eluard smoothed the rift between Ernst and Breton. Breton's view that the theater in general reflected the tastes of an effete aristocracy fueled his search for more direct and primitive forms of collective expression: "Plutôt la vie!," he wrote, "en brisant le masque en plâtre d'Eschyle pour le remplacer par un masque du Soudan ou du Nigeria."[24] By 1933, however, when Léonide Massine's new ballet, *Les Présages,* opened in Paris with sets and costumes by Masson the enterprise was hailed as an event of great significance although Masson was not at that time a Surrealist in good standing. Leiris wrote, "Avec le ballet des Présages, Masson, pour la première fois, a tenté de façon délibérée la création d'un mythe tragique. Jusqu' à ce jour, son art est resté dominé par cette tendance mythique."[25] Masson himself later noted that when the Cubist painters, and even Matisse and Bonnard, used Greek myth as a source for their work it was for purely sensual themes like the Rape of Europa but never because of a deeply felt identification with the tragic myths of ancient Greece. Myth in the nineteenth century—in the work of an Ingres or Cabanel— had often served as a device for screening an overtly erotic content and placing the spectator at an appropriate historical distance from an otherwise lascivious or titillating scene. Surrealist attitudes toward Classical and pre-Classical myth, shaped by the intellectual and historical situation of Surrealism, differ significantly from those of other members of the School of Paris.

Myth, a formal device which transcends the limitations of space-time and rational thought, served to communicate in much the same way that it had historically transmitted social values. In the area of Surrealist painting, where there exists no single and identifiable Surrealist "style" and where the value of the work is determined almost exclusively on the basis of its content, myth became one way of organizing and synthesizing Surrealist beliefs within a recognizable set of symbols. The creation of a Surrealist myth was never a quest for an idiosyncratic personal iconography but the search for a collectively understood means of conveying knowledge. In a lecture delivered in Prague in 1935 Breton remarked that, "In these conditions, thus, art is no longer a question of the creation of a personal myth, but rather, with Surrealism, of the creation of a collective myth."[26] Freud and Nietzsche had both used ancient myth to literally and metaphorically convey their understanding of the irrational; following their example, Surrealist literature and painting came to see myth construction as one way of establishing a historical continuity between Pre-Classical Greece, the Greece of Orphic rites and Dionysiac cults ignored by the rationalist thinkers of the classical tradition, and their own contemporary cultivation of irrationality.

Automatism, dream and myth mingled in Surrealism with the teachings of Freud and Nietzsche. Nietzsche, in *Ecce Homo,* comes close to describing automatism in art:

> C'est dans le cas de l'image, de la métaphore, que se caractère involontaire de l'inspiration est le plus curieux; on ne sait plus du tout ce qui est symbole, parallèle ou comparaison: l'image se présente à nous comme l'expression la plus juste, la plus simple, la plus directe.[27]

And from their reading of Freud the Surrealists were quick to realize that automatism, dream and myth all shared common characteristics: condensation, a displacement of the sense of time and space, a similar symbolism. Freud had viewed dreams as the residues of daily activity; myth as the collective heritage of centuries. For him the two modes of unconscious thought shared a symbolism that derived from their common origin in childhood, whether individual or cultural.

Various Surrealist's understanding of the relationship between myth, dream, the irrational, language and primitivism are an essential indicator of Surrealist attitudes during the 1930's. Surrealism's first contacts with Nietzsche came about through Masson who, struggling to imbue his own art with a sense of the full drama and tragedy of human existence, was naturally drawn to this thinker who saw Greek art as crystallizing man's deepest and most tragic spiritual impulses. In the January 1937 issue of *Acéphale,* editors Masson and Bataille publicly acknowledged a need for Surrealism to find sources in pre-Classical Greece. Toward this end, the issue was devoted to Nietzsche and contained an extract from his "Héraclite" in *La Philosophie à l'époque tragique de la grèce,* as yet unpublished in French.[28] Nietzsche's view of pre-Classical Greece intuitively anticipated what Fraser, Jane Harrison and other members of the Cambridge School would later establish irrefutably: the ritual origin of Greek tragedy and the interdependence of myth and ritual in all primitive cultures. Nietzsche, questioning the so-called "serenity of Greek art" inherited from Winckelmann and Goethe, had addressed his preface to *The Birth of Tragedy,* to Richard Wagner and, implicitly, to all artists for it is there that he claims that art, rather than ethics, constitutes man's essential metaphysical activity.

In declaring a view of art that places feeling above thought, irrationality above reason, Nietzsche laid the ground for later Surrealist beliefs. He argued that art owed its continuing evolution to an Apollonian-Dionysiac quality that distinguishes the separate realms of dream and intoxication. Apollo, the god of light who reigns over the inner world of fantasy, oversees the dream, the stimulus of all literature and art. It remains for the god Dionysos to break the self-contained individualism of the Apollonian way and return human life to a mystical experience of the collective. Setting up a dialectic between Apollonian and Dionysiac which extends through his exegesis of the origins and development of Greek tragedy, he argues that knowledge is insufficient, that only through the experience of the Dionysiac can the individual be shattered and fused with an original oneness. It is of fundamental importance to Nietzsche that man overcome the limitations of rational thought and he turned to Schopenhauer's *World as Will and Idea* for a description of the awe and ecstasy that seize the human mind when it begins to relinquish cognitive modes of thought. Extending this dialectic to the realm of the dream, he stressed its role as a source of artistic imagery:

> Although of the two halves of life—the waking and the dreaming—the former is generally considered not only the most important but the only one which is truly lived, I would, at the expense of sounding paradoxical, propose the opposite view.[29]

Nietzsche's work pointed the way to Sir James Fraser, whose *Golden Bough,* first published in 1890 served as an important source both for Freud, who quotes liberally from it in his *Totem and Taboo,*[30] and Surrealist painters like Ernst and Masson. Fraser's work, which opened up new frontiers in the interpretation of Greek religion and in the myths and rituals that accompanied it, also added further dimension to western understanding of the role and meaning of the dream in primitive society. Fraser remained bound by an essentially animist view in which the functions of the human mind, ancient or modern, remain the same but are simply used in an "undeveloped" way by primitive peoples. Likewise, Freud argues from the same position when, in *Totem and Taboo,* he suggests that the myths and dreams of primitive peoples are the collective wish fulfillments and unconsciously worked out conflicts of a social and cultural "childhood," stating in his preface that although taboos still exist among modern man, totemism, on the other hand:

> is something alien to our contemporary feelings—a religio-social institution which has long been abandoned as an actuality and replaced by new forms. It has left only the slightest traces behind it in the religions, manners, and customs of the civilized peoples of today. . . .[31]

Fraser shared with Freud an evolutionary view of human nature but he also tried to demonstrate how modern myths and superstitions still evident in the Europe of his day could be found in Classical themes as well as in primitive customs and beliefs. Believing in the existence of a common human mentality, Fraser's investigation of the function of the dream among primitive societies revealed primitive man's implicit belief that dreams were an integral and essential part of daily life; that, at times, dream life might even be regarded as a higher truth.[32]

Freud had insisted that dream material derived from everyday reality; Breton, in his *Les Vases communicants* of 1932, responded to the *Interpretation of Dreams* by arguing that in disavowing the existence of the prophetic dream Freud had failed to pursue his investigations far enough. But Breton eagerly embraced Freud's thesis that at the depths of the mind contradiction is absent, emotional tension due to repression is relaxed, sense of time is negated and external reality replaced by a psychic reality obeying the pleasure principle alone. And he argued for a view of the relationship between dream and waking in which both states are perceived as fluid, their contents ceaselessly intermingling.

Although automatism was the first Freudian technique used by the Surrealists—to resolve contradiction and incorporate into the poet's technique the free flow of unconscious thought—Freud's major contribution to Surrealism lay in his explication of the role of language in dream and dream interpretation. The heart of Freud's psychoanalytic theories—infantile sexuality and its role in the formation of the adult neurosis—played a far less important role in Surrealism than his writings on the dream and art. The formal structure of the dream—the condensation that results in a density of imagery, displacement of the senses of time and space and the importance of figurative language—are reconstituted in Surrealism. The night dream, according to Freud, approaches myth in that both are shaped by wish fulfillment and in primitive societies dream interpretation is based on symbols that play an important role in myth construction. Distinguishing between the conscious, governed by the ego and the center of logical thought and concepts of causality and identity, and the unconscious, governed by the pleasure principle and dominated by pre-logical or magical thought, Freud's understanding of the functions of thought, both conscious and unconscious, carried over to his analysis of the roles of dream and myth in primitive cultures. Karl Abraham, in 1931, pointed out these interconnections in *The Interpretation of Dreams:*

> I maintain this and formulate my view, in harmony with Freud's teachings in regard to dreams, as follows: the myth is a fragment of the repressed life of the infantile psyche of the race. It contains (in disguised form) the wishes of the childhood of the race.[33]

That the structure of dreams and myths and parallel structures in primitive culture can be regarded as similar manifestations of the unconscious mind was a fact often emphasized by Freud.

On a literary and theoretical plane it is in Surrealist publications of the 1930's that the relationship between dream, myth, primitivism and poetic language, and the significance attached to them in primitive cultures by Fraser, Freud, Nietzsche and others, is most fully explored. In 1933 Maxime Alexandre, in his *Mythologie personelle,* declares his intention of exploring myth through dreams, and vice versa, extracting from his own dreams four groups of myths: inherited mythological representations, contemporary myths, the new myths created each night in dreams, and the complex mythology of childhood.[34] Ten years later, Roger Colquehoun's "The Water Stone of the Wise" reaffirms the role of myth as a means of organizing the irrational at a time when Surrealist interest was rapidly shifting from myth to the occult:

> Myth is a volcanic force
>
> Myth must break through the crust, scattering a thousand new comets in the void
>
> Myth comes from the region between sleeping and waking, the multitudinous abyss, the unceasing cauldron rimmed with pearls
>
> No more tyrants and victims, no more the fevered alterations of that demon-star which sponsored the births of de Sade and Von Sacher-Masoch: but the Hermaphrodite whole
>
> Oedipus will be king no longer but will return to Colonnus. The new myth, the myth of the Siamese twins, will make of him a forgotten bogey.[35]

A special number of *Cahiers GLM* devoted to the dream appeared in 1938 and examined the relationship between dream, myth and the poetic imagination. In both modes of thought the rules which apply to normal behavioral patterns and courses of action are suspended. Both to some extent are irrational and contain dislocations of normal associations and connections, particularly in the perception of time and space. Both derive from the real world but neither is limited by it:

> C'est en cela qui la poésie est révolution: mise sur la voie par le rêve et tout ce qui s'y apparente, elle est un acte d'abandon volontaire à certains pratiques dont le but est toujours de désorganiser le monde tel qu'il est, pour en faire apparaître l'étonnante structure profond, celle qui nous concerne vraiment.[36]

For the mining of the rich poetic veins of dream and myth there existed lengthy historical traditions of which the Surrealists were fully conscious. Breton considered Surrealism the inheritor of the mantles of Romanticism and Symbolism; Masson listed among "La Poésie indispensable" Baudelaire, Heraclitus, Kafka, Keats, Mallarmé, Nerval, Novalis, Paracelsus, Jouve, and Rimbaud among others.[37] Freud himself was fond of pointing out that the first instance of the prophetic dream in literature occurs in the twenty-third chapter of the *Iliad* when the ghost of Patroklos appears in a dream to Achilles.

The belief, often emphasized by Freud, that the structures of dream and myth are parallel in primitive cultures and that both can be regarded as similar manifestations of the unconscious mind, stimulated the Surrealist search to identify the language of dream, myth and poetry and to seek antecedents for their relationship in primitivism:

> C'est à juste titre que les surréalistes accordent une importance primordiale à la vie concrète et mettent l'accent sur l'origine magique de la poésie dans l'élabora- tion des mythes qu'elle a crées et couvés pendant temps immémoriaux; ils soulig- neront plus tard le caractère essentiellement pratique et universel de la poésie au sense ou ils l'entendent et dont Lautreamont avait déjà dans ses poésies, jeté les bases théoriques.[38]

An emphasis on the power of the imagination and its correspondence with childhood and the primitive past had linked Breton to the Romantics from the beginning; Albert Béquin, in his *L'Ame romantique et le rêve,* remarks upon the similarities between Romantic theories of the dream and the un- conscious and the theory of the unconscious advanced by Freud and later taken up by Breton.[39] Both the Viennese analyst and the French poet shared an interest in the German Romantics and the French poets associated with them, especially Rimbaud, Nerval and Baudelaire.

The images of Surrealist paintings and poetry, springing from the imagi- nation and the unconscious, arise in that part of the human mind that also governs the construction of dream and myth. Ancient myth and Surrealist painting both contain fantastic figures—men and animals whose appearance undergoes a continual process of metamorphosis, magical occurrences and natural phenomena endowed with supernatural powers in a world dominated by a sense of mystery and the unforeseen. One means of access to the Surrealist Marvelous was through metamorphosis and the Surrealists were quick to note a corresponding interest in the metamorphosis of the gods as a means to com- municate a sense of a supra-rational quality of life among ancient Greek writers. Callois, in an article in *Minotaure* remarked that, "Il ne faudrait, surtout pas conclure que la mythologie est un sort de traduction poétique des phénomènes atmosphériques."[40] In his "Le Mythe et l'homme" he cites Schlegel's *Rede uber die Mythologie und Symbolische Anschauung,* reflecting that myth is, "Une expression hieroglyphique de la nature environnante sous la transfigura- tion de l'imagination et de l'amour."[41] And in *Acéphale* Jules Monnerot argued for a literary use of myth in which demonstrated facts and scientific "proofs" are replaced by powerful images. A contemporary mythology will find its fullest expression in the images of art; the role of modern literature, suggests Monnerot, is to rescue ancient heroes as is done, for example, in Blanqui's *Faust pendant quatre siècles* and de Bevotte's *La Legende de Don Juan.*[42]

The Surrealists viewed myth in the French sense, in which myths are con- structed from all the versions of a story, rather than the somewhat narrower English tradition in which a myth is identified as such primarily through its origins and historical meaning. Surrealist art contains both kinds of myths, however, and the desire to create a "collective" myth of Surrealism coexisted with Surrealist reworkings of older mythological themes. Masson's interest in the most somber myths of ancient Greece led to his founding, with Georges Bataille and Pierre Klossowski, a periodical entitled *Acéphale* (after the fabulous people reported by the ancients to have had no heads) and devoted to discovering the "religion that lies behind the political." The first issue contained an article by Marxist critic Max Raphael on the reconstruction of the pediment at Corfu. Identifying the declining influence of Greek art in its classical forms, Raphael acknowledges Nietzsche as the first to recognize the place of "Ancient" or pre-Classical Greece among those "primitive peoples whose thought will introduce a new epoch in European art." Tracing the influence of the near East on Greek art in support of his thesis that origins of western culture are to be found in pre-Classical Greece, he concludes that the current renaissance of Greek culture reveals the previous neglect of the most fundamental characteristic of Greek thought, ". . . la méthode dialectique que Héraclite, Platon et Aristotle ont si magnifiquement developée."[43] Raphael's article reveals the extent to which, by the mid 1930's, Surrealism had discovered an aspect of ancient Greek culture that appeared to support Breton's insistence that the Surrealist search for an extra-empirical reality was well within the traditions of western thought.

The early decades of the twentieth century had witnessed a general re-examination of the relationship between myth and poetry, symbolism and the irrational in several fields. Freud placed the cornerstone of psycho-sexual development on the Oedipus myth, excavating the dark underside of fate and incest. Classicists' attitudes toward myth in this century were dominated by the trends initiated by Fraser and Jane Harrison who applied new knowledge of comparative anthropology to the study of myth and religion and who tenaciously pursued the idea that the motives of custom and myth in primitive societies could illuminate those of more developed cultures. Kirk, in his *Myth: A Study of Its Origins and Development,* concludes that:

> At its best the anthropological approach brought a fresh vitality to the study of classical religion and myths, and enabled its followers to recover from the lethargy that had overtaken them once the nineteenth century fallacies of the animists, the Symbolists, the nature-myth School, the pan-Babylonians and the pan-Egyptians had been exhaustively laid to rest. It also freed them from the tyranny of Christian inhibitions and preconceptions in matters effecting the investigation of the sources of religious feeling; and opened up an immense range of new comparative material, some of which undeniably gave the clue to longstanding puzzles in the religion and sociology of classical antiquity.[44]

The gradual shift in emphasis from an archaeological to a more anthropological view of ancient Greek culture helped to break down barriers that had previously been erected between the primitive cultures of Africa and Oceania and those of western Europe and the Mediterranean. Breton himself believed in a pre-scientific and pre-rationalistic mode of thought; in 1928 he opened his essay, "Le Surréalisme et la peinture" with a call for a return to a primitive state of vision. The belief in a "primitive mentality," qualitatively different from that of industrialized Europe and less alienated from the human sources of myth and magic, had strong roots in French intellectual and artistic traditions. Out of Romanticism had come nineteenth century artistic revolts against "la vie bourgeois." "Là à Tahiti je pourrai. . . . écouter la douce musique de mon coeur en harmonie amoureuse avec les êtres mystérieux de mon entourage," Gauguin had written from Tahiti in 1890.[45] Fifty years later André Breton would allude to "all those mysteriously alluring entities that lurk beneath the surface of the creations of 'primitive' art."[46]

Breton had consistently demanded that the barriers erected before civilized man, barriers which ignore the worlds of the primitive, the child and the madman, be broken down. The social value ascribed to the dream in primitive societies was a powerful lesson for Surrealism:

> Je me propose de démontrer que la pensée dit 'non-dirigé' est à tel point la dominante de ce qu'improprement on a appelé 'la mentalité primitive' qu'il serait possible d'envisager un état pur de celle-ci où la Cassure que représente pour nous la passage de l'état de rêve à celui de veille disparaisse complètement," wrote Tristan Tzara in his "Essai sur la situation de la poésie."[47]

The "primitive" art collected by Breton and other Surrealists tended to be Oceanic rather than African as they had early noted Cubism's affinity for African masks but also perceived the work of Oceania as representing a more collective and therefore more "poetic" attitude:

> . . . l'auréole que nous evoquions s'attache en Océanie à la fois à une mythologie intacte, aussi violente qu' inspirée, et à une attitude créatrice en parfait accord avec la conception analogique qui fonde toute poésie aux yeux des surréalistes.[48]

The idea that there existed a "primitive mentality," significantly different from that of twentieth century France and characterized by a directness of vision and feeling that superceded the logical and rational, owed much to the writings of Lucien Levy-Bruhl, since 1925 director of the Institute of Ethnology in Paris. References to his pioneering work fill the pages of *Minotaure* and other Surrealist publications of the 1930's.

Levy-Bruhl's theory of primitive mentality rested on a belief that there exist significantly different modes of thought among various people. In this view he opposed Fraser and other anthropologists who saw the functions of the mind as the same everywhere but simply used in inferior ways by primitive peoples due to a lack of knowledge and a developed society. According to Levy-Bruhl, the difference is fundamental, not fortuitous; primitive peoples think differently and in order to understand them it is necessary to rid ourselves of our own sophisticated mental processes. He further argued that the problem is collective and therefore sociological and that it is possible to construct a collective psychology for each society.

Levy-Bruhl's researches had a number of important implications for Surrealist theorizing. Trained as a philosopher rather than an anthropologist, he did not make his first trip into the "field" until relatively late in his life and his early work was primarily concerned with establishing a new theoretical context for the understanding of anthropological data. He advocated studying those societies farthest away from our forms of thought, societies characterized by lack of abstraction or conceptualization in their thinking.

Stripping away the need for causal and logical connections between things, Levy-Bruhl argued that things could be simultaneously themselves and something else. In this system, every action appears as a revelation; nothing is fortuitous, though the mystical cause is often extra-spatial and extra-terrestrial. Supernatural powers, then, reveal themselves through luck and magic, dreams and visions. For Levy-Bruhl, myth is always creative and always characterized by a fluidity of images and by metamorphosis.

Under the influence of Levy-Bruhl and Michel Leiris, Surrealist poet and curator of ethnology at the *Musée de l'homme* in Paris, Surrealist researches into primitivism begin to appear in the 1920's. *Documents,* not itself a Surrealist magazine, but under the direction of Georges Bataille and with the collaboration of dissident Surrealists Masson and Leiris began in 1929 to publish archaeological and anthropological articles. On the cover of the first issue appeared the subheading: "Doctrines, Archáologie, Beaux-Arts, Ethnographie." Along with ruminations on the eccentric and grotesque appeared Leiris' "L'oeil de l'ethnographe," a record of his ideas about ethnography.

Articles appearing in other Surrealist periodicals during the 1930's drew liberally on the ideas of Levy-Bruhl; Roland de Rennéville, writing on the phenomenon of inspiration, fuses Levy-Bruhl's ideas with those of Freud, and concludes that it is only through myth that the primitive mind is able to generalize. A mythic representation replaces the general idea because, "un élément émotionel peut suppléer à la généralization logique."[49] The entire second number of *Minotaure* was devoted to the Dakar-Djibuti Mission of 1931-1933, an ethnographic and linguistic mission organized by the Institute of Ethnology of the University of Paris and the National Museum of Natural History. Leiris contributed an article on the sacrificial bull of Seyfore Tchenger in which he discussed Abyssinian beliefs about possession.[50] The study of primitive art intensified Surrealist interest in the concretization of the objects of dreams—the Surrealist object, believed to retain a profound and poetic connection between dream and reality, interior and exterior reality. An entire exhibition at the Charles Ratton gallery in 1936 was devoted to Surrealist objects as well as those of Africa and Oceania.[51] The major Surrealist exhibitions of the 1930's, Paris, New York, and London, contained numerous Surrealist objects both found and constructed. And immediately after the war an exhibition of objects (and some paintings) on the themes of myth, alchemy and esoterism was held at the Galerie Maeght in Paris.

Archaeological and anthropological sources colored all Surrealist attitudes toward myth. They find their fullest expression in the specific myths elevated and given pictorial expression by various Surrealist painters during the 1930's. And it is these paintings that reveal the transformation of theoretical views into specifically Surrealist statements.

II

Classical Myth
and the Painting of Dali, Ernst and Masson

Myth comes from the region between sleeping and waking . . .

Roger Colguehoun, 1944

The paintings of Dali, Ernst and Masson share several mythological themes
and heroes, among them Oedipus, Echo and Narcissus and Theseus and the
Minotaur. These shared myths, each of which finds its fullest expression in the
work of a single painter, transcend personal inclinations and indicate major
Surrealist preoccupations. An examination of these motifs reveals their meaning
for the individual painters, their transformations from the original source, and
their particular Surrealist content.

The Oedipus myth was one of the few Greek myths that found its way
into the Surrealist painting of the 1920's; Ernst's *Oedipus Rex* of 1922 (Fig. 4)
is often cited as his first painting with an overtly psychological content that
distinguishes it from his earlier Dada works. The painting depicts the juxtaposition of two bird-like heads that emerge from a hole in the ground with a
hand projecting through a window in a blank brick wall and holding a walnut,
the fingers pierced by a metal bow. *Oedipus Rex* has its immediate source
in a collage of the previous year (Fig. 5) and the two works share their strange
juxtaposition of unfamiliar objects and abrupt variations in scale. But the menacing quality, the suggestion of a veiled symbolic content evoked by the title,
is new with *Oedipus Rex,* and replaces the more forthright declamatory quality
of the Dada works. The collage, titled *The Invention,* depicts two fingers emerging from a window and holding between them a strange metallic press attached
to a severed bird's claw. The press appears as the means to transforming the claw
into a schematized linear print. Next to the mechanical device a small bud stands
above a line of these "prints," while underneath a tiny hand holding a bunch of
flowers emerges from a hole in the raised floor.

The most literal reference to the original myth lies in the piercing of the flesh by a metallic object. Laius had had the feet of the infant Oedipus pierced by a spike before he exposed the child; Ernst runs a metal rod through two fingers. Sala's strictly Freudian interpretation of the work rests on Ernst's well-known strained relationship with his rigid and fanatical father and Sala sees the hand of Oedipus pierced in punishment for touching the forbidden female sexual parts symbolized here in the nut with split shell. But Sala's interpretation, a literal application of Freud's writings on sexual symbolism to pictorial images, omits other major images from consideration and fails to probe deeply enough Ernst's peculiar transformation of the imagery.[1]

In the foreground appear two heads, the foremost that of a bird with human eye, the other transformed into a bull's head through the addition of nostrils and curved horns. The bull with human eye is a common image in Cretan art (Fig. 6) and the inclusion of bull's head, string, fence and human eye introduce another myth—one which would become of fundamental importance in Surrealism during the 1930's—into the Oedipus theme. It is in Sophocles' version of the Oedipus myth that Oedipus and Theseus meet, for it is Theseus who finally offers a home to the aged and exiled Oedipus. Both myths relate man's spiritual progress and his quest for knowledge; both embody the unknown in the form of monsters—one created from the passion of a woman for a bull, the other the half-human, half-animal virgin sphinx. The fence here suggests the Cretan labyrinth; it reappears in a painting of 1924 entitled *The Labyrinth* (Fig. 7). Around the bull's horns is tied Ariadne's thread, which disappears into the sky above.[2]

The Surrealist quest for knowledge, later overtly symbolized in the image of the labyrinth, took place internally and was committed to the creation of a "monde en fonction de la necessité intèrieure éprouvé par l'artiste," in the words of Breton.[3] The eye in this search was the visionary eye of Symbolist painting. In a lithograph of 1882 entitled *L'Oeil comme un ballon bizarre se dirige vers l'Infini* (Fig. 8) Odilon Redon had fused the images of eye and balloon, severing the eye from its human context and allowing it to ascend toward the heavens; in Ernst's painting a tiny balloon moves off into the distance. Ernst's identification of the eye with the visionary faculties came to be shared by a number of other Surrealists. In a strange self-portrait of 1931 Victor Brauner would depict himself with his right eye missing. In 1938 he lost that eye in a fight between two friends in which he had interceded as a peace-maker and he quickly came to associate the loss of the eye with an increase in his visionary faculties. In the Oedipus myth the blind prophet Tiresias foretells the myth's tragic future.

The Oedipus myth reappears in Ernst's work in the 1930's in a series of representations. His *Oedipus and the Sphinx* of 1935 (Fig. 9) was reproduced in a number of Surrealist publications after that date, and serves as an important example of the particular way in which Surrealism sought to amalgamate a series of pictorial images and an accompanying body of theory. Ernst's collage depicts a nude human body, its head replaced by the head, wings and breast of a sphinx. The front of the seated figure's torso has been removed, taking with it any indication of the figure's primary sexual characteristics. The body, due to its relative size and massiveness in relation to the sphinx, appears to be that of a young male, but alterations in the physical proportions (the arm and leg are significantly enlarged in relation to the upper body, the sphinx's head is reduced in scale) lend an androgynous quality to the composite figure.

We know from the original myth that at the time of his arrival in Thebes, Oedipus had just reached manhood, but Ernst's representation casts doubt on the distinctions which defined the roles of the protagonists in the Theban myth. The dislocations are first manifested physically and derive from the collage technique through which man and sphinx become a single creature. But the disjunctions which alter the shape of reality also have a psychological dimension, which imbues the image with its specifically Surrealist content. The fusing of male and female into an androgynous figure is extended here to the joining of human and sphinx, and suggests that the ancient confrontation between man and the virginal monster who holds his future in her hands has been internalized and is now as much psychological as physical. Breton had used the image of the Cretan labyrinth as a potent symbol of the unconscious into which man descended on a tortuous journey to self-knowledge. Ernst's representation likewise implies that the answer to the riddle of man's existence is psychological in origin.

The Oedipus theme had been a favored subject in Symbolist painting. In the works of Gustave Moreau, Fernand Khnopf and others the sphinx represented either the alluring fatal charms of the female or a mysterious muse-like figure who leads the poet to that otherworldly realm of being to which he is transported through sleep and the dream. Even Dada, militantly anti-historical, found a place for this image. Alain Mousseigne has convincingly demonstrated that Francis Picabia's *Sphinx* of 1923 has a visionary content in which Oedipus, a spiritual voyager capable of understanding the sphinx's most obscure riddles, is symbolized by the lidless eye.[4]

The Surrealist Oedipus is first and foremost a psychological being, born from a freudian parentage. But, like other Surrealist themes, its meaning varies as it is directed toward different ends by various Surrealist painters. Freud's Oedipus served to make plausible psychoanalytic assumptions about primitive incestuous wishes in the child. In reality, the original myth has somewhat different implications in that it reveals first and foremost the tragic consequences of seeking the truth behind appearances; the more one experiences truth, the more one knows, the unluckier one becomes. The theme of totemic sacrifice and the relation of the son to the father runs through the myth, a theme that obsessed Freud who, in *Totem and Taboo*, claimed that the meaning of the totem lay in its existence as a surrogate father. For Freud the doctrine of original sin was of Orphic origin. Mankind, it was said, were descended from the Titans, who had killed the young Dionysos-Zagreus and had torn him to pieces:

> At the conclusion, then, of this exceedingly condensed inquiry, I should like to insist that its outcome shows that the beginnings of religion, morals, society and art converge in the Oedipus complex. . . . This is in complete agreement with the psychoanalytic finding that the same complex constitutes the nucleus of all neuroses.[5]

Sala has argued that Ernst's *Oedipus Rex* (Fig. 4) alludes to this aspect of the saga and that there exists evidence of a powerful father figure in other of Ernst's paintings from those years. He cites *Ubu Imperator* (1924) (Fig. 10) with its dual sources in Jarry's *Ubu Roi* and a sexual spector of the father first glimpsed in a dream or nocturnal vision of 1897:

> In front of (an imitation mahogany) panel a dark shiny man begins to make gestures which are at once deliberate, buffoonish, and (here I rely upon much earlier memories) uproariously indecent. This curious personage sports my father's up-turned moustaches. Legs wide apart, knees bent, trunk leaning well forward, he carries out a number of leaps in slow-motion. Then he smiles and takes out of his pocket a large pencil made of some soft material which I cannot identify exactly. He gets down to work. Blowing heavily, he makes hurried black marks on the imitation mahogany. New shapes, as abject as they are unexpected, take their place on the panel. Animals, by turn ferocious and slimy, become so vivid, so life-like, that they fill me with horror and anguish. Well pleased with what he had drawn, the strange character rounds up his zoo and piles it into a kind of vase which he draws, for this purpose, in the empty air. He turns them all round and round in the vase with ever faster and faster movements of his pencil until eventually the vase itself begins to spin round and turns into a top. The pencil turns into a whip, meanwhile, I realize that this strange painter is my own father. Now he lays on the whip with all his might, accompanying each stroke with a terrible gasp and heave of his breath, like a blast from some enormous and furious steam engine. Beside himself with the effort, he sends the loathly top spinning and jumping around my bed . . .

> One day (Ernst continues) I was examining the problem—I was an adolescent already—of how my father must have conducted himself during the night of my conception. Suddenly there arose within me, as if in answer to this filial question, the memory, exact in every detail, of this waking dream which, till then, I had entirely forgotten.[6]

The double moustached figure reappears in a work entitled *Pietà or Revolution by Night* (1923) (Fig. 11), where the father holds the son in a pose of presentation while in the background the languid figure of a young man hangs on a wall.

The motif of the sacrificing father also appears in the work of Salvador Dali in the early 1930's; he selects for his Oedipus the figure of William Tell. "Comme Freud a fait revivre Oedipe, ainsi Dali a fait revivre Guillaume Tell," writes René Crevel.[7] According to Dali, in an inversion of Freud's thesis, the father sees the son as a rival for the mother's affections and slays him. Freud had concentrated his analysis on the incestuous marriage between Oedipus and his mother; Dali focuses on Laius' decision to kill the infant in order to prevent the fulfilling of a prophecy in which the child will slay the father.[8]

Dali's interest in the Oedipus/William Tell figure can be traced to a personal experience—his expulsion from the family by his father during the 1920's. When William Tell appears in his work, as for example in the drawing *Figures After William Tell* (ca. 1932) (Fig. 12), it is in the guise of a bearded patriarch. William Tell's apple becomes, for Dali, a "symbol of the passionate, cannibalistic ambivalence which ends with the drawing of the atavistic and ritualistic fury of the bow of paternal vengeance that shoots the final arrow of the expiatory sacrifice—eternal theme of the father sacrificing his son."[9]

The motif of the young man turning away in shame which appears in Dali's various versions of the William Tell story is identified with the castration that he sees at the heart of the William Tell story. In *William Tell* (1929) the bearded father, his sexual organs revealed, stretches out a pair of scissors as the son turns away, his sex replaced by a leaf. As Rubin notes, the interpretation of the bearded man as a father figure emerges both from the William Tell context and from the motif's sources in Ernst and de Chirico:

> In Ernst's *Pietà* this same figure is depicted holding a son in his arms—the origin of Dali's young man. To the right in the Ernst, drawn on a wall, is an enigmatic standing figure with full beard and mustache and bandaged head. It is this auxiliary figure, who in Dali's mind became associated with the father holding his son in the same picture, that is the *exact model* (Rubin's italics) of the father figure in the Dali's of 1929-30.[10]

The Oedipus myth in Surrealism takes on various psychological colorings for, as Roger Callois noted in 1935:

> Les situations mythiques peuvent alors être interpretées comme la projection des conflits psychologiques (Ceux-ci recouvrant le plus souvent les complexes de la psychanalyse) et le heros comme celle de l'individu lui-même: *image idéale de compensation* que colore de grandeur son âme humiliée.[11]

If among certain Surrealist painters filial relationships are played out under the symbolic guise of Oedipus, the myth also reveals a powerful psychological content through the interchange between Oedipus and his chief protagonist, the sphinx.

Ernst's Oedipus confronts the sphinx who holds in her hands the power of life and death. The sphinx's riddle, the answer to which reveals Oedipus's understanding of the nature of human existence, often becomes in Surrealist hands a query about love, a primary obsession among the group. She appears in Breton's essay "Le Chateau étoilé" of 1936 as a guardian beast before whom all who wish to enter the chateau (the Surrealist world) must answer a question about the future of love. Her riddle tests each Surrealist's commitment to love's liberating power. "Every time a man loves, nothing can prevent his taking on himself the feelings of all men," Breton himself answered.[12]

On another level Ernst's *Oedipus and the Sphinx* serves to symbolically translate historical fact into Surrealist substance. The lion's head appears in a number of collages from his *Une Semaine de Bonté,* published the previous year. In each representation it is attached to a human figure in military dress. In one (Fig. 13), the inclusion of a Napoleon-like figure strengthens the military association. Ernst identifies the lion as the *Lion de Belfort,* a reference to the bronze statue of a lion standing in the Place Denfert-Rochereau in Paris and commemorating the siege of Belfort during the Franco-Prussian War. The territory of Belfort had a long and complex military history as an area claimed by both France and Germany. Recognizing the military significance of this image, it is not surprising that Ernst included it in his representation of *Oedipus and the Sphinx,* since when Oedipus first encountered the sphinx, the city of Thebes was under control of this strange monster. Belfort, fought over by German and French armies, did not finally come under French control until after 1871. Among the Surrealists, Ernst and Paul Eluard were fond of relating that during World War I, while still strangers to each other, they had fought on the same front but for different sides. A few years later they would become friends and brothers under the aegis of a movement that sought to transcend the territorial and nationalistic concern that it viewed as inimical to its goal of mental liberation.

But the image of the sphinx also existed as a powerful symbol of the female principle: the source and destroyer of man. She had entered Greek mythology carrying with her the earth/mother/female/life/death association of her near Eastern origins. Under her domain the earth lay fallow and drought covered the land. In one representation from Ernst's *Une Semaine de Bonté* (Fig. 14) she appears at an open train window surrounded by images of decay and desolation; an arid desert, rotting corpses and the rats that fill the lifeless carriage.

It is also in this role of destroyer that she appears in Dali's satiric *Shirley Temple, the Youngest Monster sacred to the Cinema* (Fig. 15). A plaque underneath the figure reads, "Shirley . . . at last in technicolor," a fitting epitaph, as Dali has given her a scarlet body, perched a violet bat on her head, and rippled the background with the variegated shades of a full color sunrise. The sphinx's long curving claws are as white as the bleached bones scattered around her; the skull lying face up between her front feet adds a final grotesque touch. In the distance, the skeletal hull of a sailing ship rests on the sand, and several tiny human figures make their way across the beach. Dali emphasizes the female attributes on the body of this child/woman with sphinx-pointed breasts and long curved fingernails—and then surrounds her with images of death which contradict the image of childhood innocence embodied in the young Shirley Temple. But the red of the body and the sharp line that separates it from the flesh-colored portrait head suggest that this is merely a costume—innocence playing the role of the man-eating sphinx. In fact, we know the child idol only through the roles she plays, and Dali's representation seems to summarize all of his ambivalent feelings about this child and the woman she will become.

Surrealist attitudes toward woman, as expressed in the imagery of painting and poetry, fluctuate between viewing her as goddesslike muse and *femme fatale*. In her study of this dominant aspect of Surrealist imagery Xavière Gauthier isolates and explains these contradictory attitudes toward the female and explores the multiple roles assigned her in Surrealist productions: muse, virgin, child, celestial creature on the one hand; prostitute, devourer of men, object of sexual perversions on the other. In organizing these variegations along lines which, either openly or by implication, idealize or debase the woman, Gauthier concludes that the imagery which reflects the woman's destructive power invariably arises in a sexual context in which she is unconsciously perceived as a physical threat to man's potency. "This need to desexualize the female arises as a defense against a severe castration anxiety," she writes.[13] It was Freud who had thrust woman into the psychological role of the castrating female who, with her penis envy unresolved, fights back sexually in a vain attempt to regain the social, economic and political power that she fails to possess, but sees symbolized in the male organ. His own ambivalence toward women had its roots in the same nineteenth-century attitudes that formed the theoretical basis of Symbolist, and later Surrealist, imagery. "What sorceresses you women are," he wrote to Martha Bernays in 1882,[14] and in "The Theme of the Three Caskets" of 1913[15] he further developed what he saw as the source of woman's dual nature—her incompatible roles as mother and the bearer of life, and as harbinger of death and destruction.[16]

Gauthier reiterates Freud's formula for the rise of the male fear of castration from a fear of violating the incest taboo, a theme consciously developed among the Surrealists by Dali.[17] The male Surrealists' search for the ideal woman/love object was conducted, at least in part, independently of their wives, mistresses and liaisons: real women whose needs and fears could not be mythologized away. The language of love in the poetry of Breton, Eluard and others remains constant, while the names of the specific women invoked change frequently. The often-cited Surrealist "cult of love" is, on one level, a theoretical abstraction—a male escape from another more immediate and less metaphysical reality.

A careful examination of the Surrealist idealization of the female image reveals other literary, psychological and cultural forces affecting the development of Surrealist attitudes. Gauthier's conclusion provides only one of many explanations for the Surrealists' attitude toward the female. It cannot explain the particular symbolic transformation of female imagery that pervades the writings and paintings of Breton, Eluard, Dali, Masson, Bellmer, Brauner and others. Nor does it explain why so much of that imagery is, at least symbolically, directed either toward the womb or toward denying woman her biological procreative function, precisely that aspect of the female which would allow the "uterine Nirvana" to which Gauthier sees the male artist seeking to return.[18]

The Surrealists gradually redefined the creative process so that they presented themselves as competing with woman's biological function as a creator of life. Birth and womb imagery, a stunning metaphor for the process of the creative act, pervade Surrealist painting and writing as relentlessly as references to the *femme fatale*. David Gascoyne's poem "Charity Week" celebrates "the great bursting womb of desire. . ."[19] while Dali's *The Bleeding Roses* of 1930 (Fig. 16) replaces the traditional metaphoric "fruit of the womb" with a bouquet of bleeding roses, with their symbolic associations of passion, pain and death. Victor Brauner's sculpted *Number* of 1943 (Fig. 17) depicts a composite male/female figure containing a tiny figure in a box-like womb. Breton himself referred to the maternal woman as "a place sacred above all where lies the mystery of life, of procreation, of birth. . . ."[20]

The role of the artist, Ernst had written, was to "assist like a spectator at the birth of the work."[21] Yielding to the dictates of the unconscious, the artist theoretically allows his imagery to develop spontaneously in response to associations provoked by the results of various automatic or semiautomatic techniques. Ernst's *One Night of Love* (1927) (Fig. 18) evokes both the unique potency of amorous love and the generation of specific images by means of Surrealist techniques. His "night of love" produces yet another image—the bird that struggles forth from the abdominal area of the reclining figures. The act of love, then, gives birth to the work of art and also, symbolically, to the artist himself, depicted here in the form of a bird, Ernst's well-known alter ego.

But if the image of woman extended through Surrealism as a potent symbol of creation, the source of both life and art, the Surrealist attitude toward her in this role was somewhat ambivalent. Throughout the 1930's and early 1940's, a number of Surrealist artists would struggle with their conflicting attitudes toward the procreative female. The imagery of birth and that of the "vagina dentata," the devouring female, meet in Victor Brauner's *Totem of Wounded Subjectivity* (1948). Here a small fetal figure is caught between two rows of sharp tooth-like projections and the spread legs of the fantastic creatures which project above and below. In addition, both creatures, composed only of arms, legs, heads and teeth, grasp and squeeze disembodied womblike breasts from which milky fluid flows forth. Brauner explains, "Two evil Victors preventing the 'little' Victor from living."[22] Brauner confronts the images of the life-giving breasts and womb directly, if negatively; at other times Surrealist hostility toward the female found only symbolic expression as in recurrent images of the female praying mantis which post-coitally devours her mate,[23] or in references to de Sade's *Justine* and *Juliette,* in which sustained physical abuse is heaped upon the unfortunate female victims.

One of the most violent attacks on the female's natural procreative functions was that motivated by the writings of the Marquis de Sade, to whom Breton referred in the Second Manifesto as "Surrealist in Sadism." De Sade, who regarded the female body as an instrument on which to provoke a divine ecstacy of destruction, favored sodomy, the most anti-female of the perversions in that it obliterates physical distinctions between the sexes and most directly replicates animal copulation. The abuse heaped on the bodies of de Sade's victims renders them objects, their wombs and breasts tortured and destroyed, their bodies torn apart and recreated. From its earliest days Surrealism had sought ways to transcend the particular, to define a level of existence in which the contradictions of everyday life were resolved. Drawn to de Sade for the same reasons that they were drawn to the Orphic cults of Dionysos and the erotic excesses of Don Juan—the search for an all-consuming passion that would carry within it the seeds of a new reality—they managed to abstract a philosophical message from a frenzied lust.

The Surrealist's attachment to de Sade is dependent on the wish to debase and torment women's bodies—an essentially male philosophy which underlies all de Sade's writings, and which the Surrealists never questioned.[24] The ravaged female, denied her normal sexual, emotional and procreative functions, became the theoretical basis of the Surrealist object and the word-images of Magritte. In both cases the traditional relationships between word and image or object and function/meaning are destroyed in order that a new, more poetic meaning might emerge.

In the *Dolls* of Hans Bellmer, the idea of corporeal metamorphosis finds its most concrete and literal expression. Stimulated by the writings of de Sade, Bellmer began in 1934 to transform the bodies of dolls into frankly erotic reconstructions. The first *Doll* contained a hollow womb filled with a series of six "scenes," which could be activated by pressing a button in its breast, among them, a boat sinking through the ice of the North Pole, a handkerchief supposedly adorned with the spittle of little girls, and several illuminated pictures. Bellmer added the panoramic womb to the first doll in order to overcome his distress at the figure's stiffness and lack of an "inner life."[25] The articulation of the figure around a "central sphere" in the second *Doll* (1936) provided Bellmer with a means of rendering his dolls mobile and thus more life-like and derived from an experience in which:

. . . Bellmer discovered at the Kaiser Friedrich Museum in Berlin a couple of dolls, of the school of Durer, which were articulated around a *womblike sphere* (author's italics. . . . Bellmer seized upon this type of mobile joining in order to construct his second doll in defiance of nature: around this central sphere he could articulate two pelvises and two pairs of legs while the reversible pelvis can itself evoke either the tops of thighs or breasts, surmounted, or not, by a head.[26]

Bellmer's second *Doll* focused attention on the origin of form in a womb-like structure. The general preoccupation with this particular female organ and a series of themes which are specifically directed toward the symbolic trans-ference of the control of the procreative process from the female to the male, or from a biological to a spiritual plane, isolates this problem as one of central concern to Surrealism. Surrealist ambivalence toward the process of birth and gestation clearly springs from deeper sources than the sexual libertarianism they frequently extolled as a means of freeing man from the constraints of family and bourgeois parenthood. At issue is the whole question of the source and mechanisms by which artistic creation is made possible in a Surrealist con-text. As early as 1928 Breton, in his essay "Surrealism and Painting," clearly elucidated what by that date had become the primary impetus in the domain of pictorial Surrealism—the replacing of the image derived from nature by that drawn from an *interior* model (Breton's italics). The work of art would exist, not as an aesthetic end, but only as a means to the exploration and expression of an inner psychic reality. By 1929 all of Surrealism's concerns had been sub-sumed under the general problem that the movement sought to raise: "that of human expression in all its forms."[27] Automatic writing and drawing, the narration of dreams, collage, the object functioning symbolically, and other Surrealist techniques of the earlier years were to serve as the means of liberating the image from its traditional relationship to the objects of the exterior world. These means generated new psychological and emotional forces which intensi-fied that image. The validity of the painting or poem lay not in its independent existence as an object of aesthetic contemplation, but in the extent to which it revealed the psychological state of mind of its creator. It is precisely this fact which distinguishes the collages of Max Ernst from those of Braque and Picasso, as the aesthetic of Cubist painting gives way to the Freudian techniques of juxtaposition, displacement, and the condensation of images, all serving to free the image from conventional reality.

From a historical point of view, the concern with the work of art brought into being through a process closely identified with that of childbirth is not unique to Surrealism. But the self-consciousness with which that movement attacked the problem of the sources of artistic creation isolates this factor as one of paramount importance in a growing body of theory.[28] Among the Surrealists, Arp had chosen the generation of life itself as a metaphor for the creative process, writing in 1948, "Art is a fruit that grows in man, like a fruit on a plant or like a child in its mother's womb."[29]

The Surrealists had generally accepted Freud's model of psycho-sexual development—a model which sees artistic creation in terms of the pleasure principle and the therapeutic release of repressed material into fantasy and art. And although they were less interested in Freud's explanation of infantile sexual development than in his writings on the dream and the unconscious, they shared with him, and turned to their own artistic ends, what the analyst spoke of as "the most lovely thing the world has to offer us: our ideal of womanhood."[30] But the biological determinism that had shaped Freud's theories about the role of the penis in both male and female development was replaced in Surrealism by a more intuitive preoccupation with generative forces. An idealized view of woman as muse and mediator did not resolve their conflicting responses to her spiritual role as an inspiration for male creativity and her biological role as the actual generator of life. No evidence has emerged to suggest that Breton and others were aware of existing psychoanalytic writings on the phenomenon of birth envy, writings which generally view intellectual or artistic creation as a specifically male response to an inability to create biologically.[31] As Fromm explains:

> In order to defeat the mother, the male must prove that he is not inferior, that he has the gift to produce. Since he cannot produce with a womb, he must produce in another fashion; he produces with his mouth, his word, his thought.[32]

A series of recurrent themes—among them Pygmalion, the myth of the androgyne, Oedipus and the sphinx—reveals Surrealism's continuing attempts to resolve artistically some of the issues surrounding the polarization of the female image and the conflict between male and female creativity.

For the Surrealists, the myth of Pygmalion functioned as a metaphor for the transforming process which wedded dream and waking, the conscious and the unconscious, life and death. Masson's *Pygmalion* of 1938 (Fig. 20), a disjointed and unsuccessful painting from an artistic point of view, is nevertheless one in which the artist's ideas about fertile eroticism, generation and artistic creation are contained within this larger mythic structure. The gaping shell-like vagina and the raw beefsteak torso metaphorically attest to the animalistic vitality and regenerative potential of human sexuality. In a somewhat different context Masson would argue that the practice among many contemporary painters of attempting to reduce the world to a series of disconnected objects is only a way of stripping that world of the forces of life, growth, metamorphosis and death: "What do we see if not the generalized undertaking of a Pygmalion in reverse, striving toward total inanimation? In stripping away all references to the physical world he removes all spirituality."[33]

In the ancient Greek myth Aphrodite interceded in response to the prayers of the sculptor Pygmalion and breathed life into his beloved marble creation. But in the same theme, as executed by the Belgian Surrealist Paul Delvaux in

1939, the sculpture is that of a young boy carressed and held by a nude female figure. Here the lifeless image of man is implicitly brought to life in response to a woman's embrace. Delvaux's *Pygmalion* (Fig. 21) visually reveals two prominent Surrealist attitudes toward the female: her power to intercede dramatically in the life of man and her specific qualities as a salvationary heroine.

In Surrealist hands, the Pygmalion myth takes on new meaning, since the power to bestow life and to move the male Surrealist artist toward greater and more responsive creativity is removed from the realm of the goddess Aphrodite and bestowed on those mortal women loved by various male Surrealists. Manifestly a myth of metamorphosis, the Pygmalion theme also functions as a myth of creation, in which man produces the forms of life with his own hands and woman intercedes spiritually to breathe life into his creations. In removing woman to this level in the creative process, man both excludes her unique biological role (one which he is physiologically denied) and gives her spiritual creative powers of a kind which he may also share, since creation by thought or mind already lies within his powers.

The shifting of the creative act from a physical to a spiritual realm also forms one element of the long Surrealist search for the perfect androgyne, a myth that haunted Breton for many years. The eleventh issue of *Minotaure,* which appeared in the spring of 1938, contained an article by Albert Bequin on the history of this double being.[34] The Surrealists were attracted to the idea of the androgyne as a means of resolving the duality of the sexes and as a celebration of love and fecundity. "My wife and I always the same," Aragon would write of his lifelong love for Elsa Triolet.[35] And Breton, describing one of his own amorous encounters suggests that it was:

> Chosen perhaps
> From man and from woman. . .
> This meeting
> With everything that from a distance is fatal in it
> This rushing together of two systems considered separately and subjective
> Sets off a series of very real phenomena
> That take part in the formation of a distinct world
> of a kind to bring shame on what we would perceive
> Without it.[36]

Although the Surrealist androgyne had its original source in Plato's description of the third sex, it was also clearly identified with alchemical and nineteenth century transformations of the ancient myth. A reference to Balzac's Seraphita/Seraphitus accompanied a reproduction of *The Androgyne* published in the *First Papers of Surrealism* in 1942, and identifies one of the nineteenth century literary sources for this particular aspect of the Surrealist myth of love.[37] Throughout that century the myth of "the man/woman" figured prominently in the works of Balzac, Gauthier, Sar Peladan and the Dumas brothers in France, and the German Romantics for whom it emblemized the perfect man of the future. Ritter, describing it in his *Nachlars eines jungen Physikers,* does so in alchemical language, relating the androgyne to the double nature of the "rebis" or Philosopher's Stone.[38] Geoffrey Hinton has convincingly demonstrated the psychoanalytical and alchemical sources of the joined male/female figure in one of Ernst's first Surrealist paintings, *Of This Men Shall Know Nothing* of 1922 and notes that: "A copulating couple suspended in space is a common alchemic symbol of the *coincidentia oppositorum* and they are often represented together with the sun and the moon."[39] Ernst's *The Couple* of 1924 also refers to this myth with the position of the figures indicating the sexual joining of the male and female figures as the source for their metaphysical transformation into one being.

Balzac had derived the myth of the androgyne from Swedenborg and developed the character of Seraphita/Seraphitus into a dual being who lived only to purify himself and to love. It is this aspect of the myth that later attracted Paul Gauguin, who wrote in 1903, ". . . Seraphitus, Seraphita, fertile souls constantly coupling, who leave their boreal haze in order to travel through the universe learning, loving and creating."[40] The final stage in an evolutionary process, Balzac's androgyne is incapable of physical reproduction, but the author concludes that man can, through the power of poetic transformations, metamorphose himself. As a glorification of spiritual fecundity, the myth of the androgyne becomes a celebration of spiritual procreation. Unsatisfied with the human condition, Balzac puts all his hope into the gestures of love and the poetic imagination into which he assumes the human as the creator of life.[41] Unsatisfied with the exclusively spiritual generative potential of the androgyne, Brauner presents, in his *Number,* a gravid androgynous figure. Here male and female sexual organs are attached to the ends of a boxlike womb, in which resides a tiny sculpted figure. For Brauner, as for the other Surrealists, the metaphysical fusion of male and female into the perfect being had a physical and spiritual counterpart in the sexual act—an ecstatic union which blurred the distinctions between the sexes and moved the male artist to greater and greater creativity and the female into the cycle of gestation and birth.

The androgyne functions in Surrealism as a symbolic fusing of male and female powers; the sphinx is the symbolic expression of female power, but often expressed destructively as in Dali's work. It is Breton and Masson who finally use this theme to explore the existence of woman as primordial life principle in Surrealism. The flaying of Oedipus in the presence of the sphinx formed the subject of at least one Masson painting and links this figure with other frenzied and murderous mythological images of the 1930's such as *The Horses of Diomedes,* 1934 (Fig. 22). The painter explains:

Oedipus is flayed, he tries to enter a sort of vessel which is like an immense skinned beef, surrounded by flames. At the bottom appears the face of a very beautiful and alluring woman. And, in the background, there is the butterfly sphinx Death's Head; that is the game of symbols.[42]

For Masson, the ceaseless play between fertile eroticism and death lay at the very foundations of all life, and during the 1930's he increasingly came to view erotic or sexual struggle and combat as inevitably tied to the mythical conflict between male and female principles. He has indicated that he saw in the Oedipus theme the playing out of Bachofen's thesis tracing the development of ancient Greece from haeterism to a matriarchal system characterized by the primacy of the blood relationship, the equality of all men, and a fundamental respect for human life and the power of love.[43]

In Bachofen's view the social organization of a matriarchy rested upon the primary kinship of the blood relationship between mother and child. The male, unable to participate fully in that relationship, could control the offspring only by possession or "owning" the female. As man gradually evolved political and social power, blood ties were replaced by the ties between man and wife, ruler and ruled. The resulting patriarchy became one of order and authority, obedience and hierarchy.

In a number of representations during the 1930's Masson graphically illustrated his belief in a powerful earth/mother/female principle which he traces to Bachofen's writings. *The Earth* (Fig. 23), an automatic drawing of 1939, depicts the sensuous contour of a female body that is also that of the earth itself. The skeletal hand that squeezes fluid from one breast reinforces the female's double nature, simultaneously nourishing mother and harbinger of death. That same year Masson executed a painting entitled *Paysage matriarcal* (Fig. 24). Again the woman's body, reclining in a pose redolent with sexual associations, appears as if literally constructed of the earth itself as a monumental brick edifice. Implicitly, Masson suggests that the female principle has been institutionalized, erected now as a permanent structure, through the development of a matriarchal social organization out of an earlier and more primeval conflict.

Bachofen's thesis, altogether not widely acknowledged during the twentieth century, served as the basis for Erich Fromm's reinterpretation of myth in the early 1950's. Fromm chose to focus on the Oedipus trilogy as the key to the struggle between opposing patriarchal and matriarchal systems of social organization. He concludes ". . . in various formulations of the original Oedipus myth the figure of Oedipus is always connected with the cult of the earth-goddesses, the representatives of the matriarchal religion."[44] In his answer to the sphinx, Oedipus defined man as the savior of the world and humanity, freeing him to rescue Thebes from the sphinx's control.

The Surrealists were not unaware of the existence of the Oedipus theme as a myth of the ancestral hero. Ernst's 1934 sculpture, *Oedipus II* (Fig. 25), is a totemic representation with the sphinx worn jauntily like a hat.[45] The heroic nature of the Oedipus saga is stressed by Otto Rank, whose *Trauma of Birth* had shaped Cocteau's reinterpretation of the myth in his *La Machine Infernale* of 1934. Rank's views of the Oedipus myth, which also influenced Fromm, concerned the attempt to understand in a broader context why great culture heroes are largely held to be immaculately conceived changelings. Attacking Freud's Oedipus complex he argues that Oedipus is not hostile to his father (whom, as Bachofen had pointed out, Oedipus did not actually know) or abnormally in love with his mother (who he is not yet aware *is* his mother). It is Rank who links Oedipus with his Christian offshoot, Judas Iscariot, as well as with Moses, Sargon, Paris, Perseus, Tristan, Romulus, Hercules, Lohengrin and other motherless heroes.[46]

Fromm's writings on the Oedipus myth also reveal an attitude toward the subject very close to that of the Surrealists some fifteen years earlier, the similarities arising from their common source in Bachofen. But the Surrealists remained haunted by the matriarchal possibilities in the myth: Ernst's fusion of male and female into a single being, Dali's and Masson's concentration on the female principle that lay behind the original myth, and Breton's replacement of the question about man by one about the role of love.

Bachofen's ideas seem to have entered Surrealism by several different paths. Masson had read the German author and identified him as an important influence on both Sartre and Jacques Lacan, a friend of several of the Surrealists whose psychoanalytic writings on paranoia published in *Minotaure* influenced the development of Dali's *paranoiac-critical* method. But Bachofen's ideas had been anticipated by both Hegel and Goethe, and the Surrealists were also familiar with them from these sources. Hegel viewed the two orders as the thesis and antithesis of a dialectic for which his philosophy would provide the synthesis. Writing about the conflict which he recognized in *Antigone*, he remarked that, "the gods, however, which she worships are the gods below, the gods of Hades, the minor gods of emotion, of love, of blood, and not the gods of the day, of the free and self-conscious life, of the nation, and the state."[47] Similarly, Goethe, in *Faust*, writes of the dread of the mysterious mothers who belong to an ancient world which is now banned from the light of day, from consciousness. In a 1942 article on Yves Tanguy, Breton invoked Goethe's mothers, suggesting that "painting and poetry, each in its own sphere, had inevitably to make an attempt one day to rediscover the path leading to the Mothers in the very deepest depths.[48]

Bachofen's description of a social organization based on the principles of equality, respect for human life and the power of love, advanced one alternative to the deeply entrenched patriarchal social and political order which had shaped the Surrealist revolt. Freud and Marx offered Surrealism new forms of psychological and political indoctrination; Bachofen seemed to hold forth historical precedents for the mental liberation the Surrealists so eagerly sought. Since Bachofen's analysis was primarily historical, it remained for the Surrealists themselves to formulate a contemporary solution—to unite the patriarchal and matriarchal models so that life and art might flourish.

For the Surrealists, the female principle governed creation. Breton's insistence that painting and poetry must belong to the "inner gods" forced man to find a way to participate in this inner, more fecund, realm of being. It is in his last major work, *Arcane 17*, written during the summer of 1944, that Breton finally defined the artist as the unifying figure in the male/female polarity.[49] *Arcane 17* became Breton's final synthesis, a mystical and alchemical homage to the redeeming power of love and the final reconciliation of opposites.

Combining the themes of love, war and resurrection, he drew his analogies from myth, science and the occult. Again invoking Goethe, he clarifies the need to resolve the inherent conflict between male and female principles. Finally, it is the artist who will effect the synthesis, for he (Breton clearly refers here to the *male* artist) alone has access to both realms of being:

> . . . the time will come when the ideas of woman will be asserted at the expense of those of man, the failure of which is already today tumultuously evident. Specifically, it rests with the artist to make visible everything that is part of the feminine, as opposed to the masculine, system of the world. It is the artist who must rely exclusively on the woman's powers to exalt, or better still, to jealously appropriate to himself everything that distinguishes woman from man with respect to their styles of appreciation and volition.[50]

The need to establish constantly fluid boundaries between various stages of being also results, in Surrealist painting of the 1930's, in a gradual mythologizing of the metamorphic process, symbolized finally in the figure of Narcissus. Dali, Ernst and Masson each devoted a major painting to this theme. The myth, originally selected as a paradigm example of the idea of metamorphosis, finds physical and metaphysical expression in the work of Masson, psychological expression in that of Dali.

The Narcissus myth confirms ideas about the metamorphic process derived originally from Heraclitus and the German Romantics and present in Surrealist theory prior to the appearance of several paintings on the theme. Masson's *Narcissus* of 1934 (Fig. 26) represents a brief moment of stylistic calm during a period when his work was almost exclusively devoted to themes of violence and death, the paroxysmal qualities of which were heightened by the frenzied brushstroke. His *Narcissus* depicts the youth at a moment of physical calm but extreme psychological tension, the moment just preceding the death and metamorphosis. The boy lies on his back on a grassy bank, the upper half of the body twisted around and straining toward the elusive image in the water. The nymph Echo, a silent spectator, crouches in the background. The instability of the male body, apparently sliding down the hillside and momentarily arrested, suggests the figure's metaphysical instability, caught between the worlds of illusion and reality, life and death. Likewise, the fact that the upper and lower halves of the body face in opposite directions reinforces the myth's dualistic content. The Narcissus myth is the myth of love. In Masson's representation the lower half of the male figure shares the grassy bank with that of the nymph who loved Narcissus. But the upper body turns away from the defining of self through heterosexual love, an idea that had permeated Surrealism from the movement's inception. Instead, the upper body leaves that world, turning and falling toward the illusory reflection of self in the water. The stark simplicity of Masson's representation reinforces the irrevocable fate of Narcissus as, transfixed by his own reflection, he moves toward death and metamorphosis.

Masson's painting anticipates Dali's large *Metamorphosis of Narcissus* (Fig. 27) but he has indicated that the theme held none of the personal fascination for him which it did for Dali.[51] In fact, the Narcissus myth merely reinforced Masson's view of a world constantly in a state of metamorphosis. To Heraclitus' and Novalis' ideas of elemental transformation Masson added his belief in the physical transmutation of the animal and vegetal worlds.[52] His reading of Fraser's *Golden Bough* confirmed his belief that the animal and vegetal fragments that compose the universe may be interchangeable. He found additional support for his ideas in ancient Greek literature, especially that relating to the metamorphosis of the gods, but his commitment to a totality of existence subsumed in a fluid and essential relationship between microcosm and macrocosm, finds its immediate source in German Romanticism.

The Narcissus myth symbolized physical metamorphosis for Masson, and it led to several paintings on that theme, works that attempted to communicate the metamorphic process directly using the technique of automatism as a source for the emerging imagery. The earliest of these, his *Metamorphosis* of 1939 (Fig. 28), illustrates the progression from human to plant form and vice versa within the context of anthropomorphic representation. The left figure, its head replaced by a leaf, displays legs which twist and branch.[53] The figures retain a skeletal human structure, but the individual parts of the body contain both animal and vegetal forms. The right figure, its skeletal structure still basically intact, exhibits an insubstantiality indicating its potential for transformation. This same insubstantiality allows figure and ground to flow into one another, both equally animated, both part of the same greater whole. The flower that blooms in the pelvis of one figure and the coiled genitalia of the other suggest their respective sexes and the means to their fusion and transformation. Within the right figure's pelvis a small eyes is also visible: and Masson, in his writings, stresses what he felt to be the cosmic implications of the theme of metamorphosis, symbolized here through the presence of the single eye.[54] At the bottom of the painting pairs of praying mantises engage in active combat. The life cycle of the mantis fascinated Masson, and the fascination was shared by the other Surrealists, who spent many hours during these years watching the female mantises in Paul Eluard's collection devour their mates after copulation. For the Surrealists, and particularly for Masson, the essential and cyclical relationship between *Eros* and *Thantos* lay at the heart of the metamorphic process.

Masson's painting of the 1930's has been widely criticized for its literary content and lack of formal coherence. The problem is one of a painter caught in the conflict between his commitment to a representational style and his desire to express both philosophically and physically a *process* of change in his works. The works of the 1930's above all demonstrate his failure to find a pictorial form which would adequately express the emotional paroxyms and physical transformations essential to his art. The painting *Narcissus* represents an attempt to symbolically communicate the idea of metamorphosis by drawing on a existing myth. Unsatisfied with the result (the painting was apparently too static for Masson), he moved to works like *Metamorphosis* in which he attempted to physically illustrate, by means of form and brushstroke, the *process* of change. That he himself recognized the failure of his representational mode of painting in this regard is suggested by a later work entitled *Combat and Metamorphosis* (Fig. 29) in which the automatism of the early 1920's replaced the figurative style of the following decade. Here all the energy of the encounter is contained in the metallic line which twists, turns and crosses itself. The short violent strokes contain both passion and tension. It is the technique of automatism now set to a specific end. The combining of automatism with a consciously recognized, and often symbolic, psychological force, would influence American abstract painting during the early 1940's.[55]

Both Masson and Dali used the Narcissus theme as an image of metamorphosis, but the idea of metamorphosis had very different implications in their respective world views, and, therefore, in their works. Masson's view of a world activated by violence was derived in large part from experiences during World War I. Gravely wounded and later hospitalized again as a result of the intensity of his emotional reaction to the events of war, the young painter carried these experiences into his first encounters with Surrealism, unleashing his passion and fury in his paintings. Dali, the son of a prosperous Catalan notary, and enough younger than the other Surrealists to have escaped the traumas of war, saw metamorphosis as the physical product of a contrived psychological process, the paranoiac-critical method. Based on a number of psychoanalytic studies of paranoiac dementia, the method remained for Dali—himself not a true paranoiac—a consciously adopted guise by means of which the content of his paintings became charged with psychological meaning.

The Narcissus myth appealed to Dali on two levels. Through Freud the myth had become synonymous with self adulation; Dali's egocentrism and self-aggrandisement are as well known as his paintings. And the theme accorded perfectly with the concept of the double image fundamental to the paranoiac-critical method. A long poem written by Dali to accompany his painting of 1936 (Fig. 27) reveals both aspects:

When the clear and divine body of Narcissus
leans
down to the obscure mirror of the lake,

When his white torso folded forward
fixes itself, frozen,
in the silvered and hypnotic curve of his desire,
when the time passes
on the clocks of the flowers of the sand of his own flesh

Narcissus loses his being in the cosmic vertigo
in the deepest depths of which
is singing
the cold and dionysiac siren of his own image.

The body of Narcissus flows out and loses itself
in the abyss of his reflections,
like the sand glass that will not be turned again . . .

Man returns to the vegetable state
by fatigue-laden sleep
and the gods
by the transparent hypnosis of their passions . . .

When that head splits
When that head splits
when that head bursts,
it will be the flower,
the new Narcissus,
Gala—
my Narcissus.[56]

His painting entitled the *Metamorphosis of Narcissus* (Fig. 27) depicts a fantastic landscape filled in the background with tiny figures, a road which winds toward distant hills, a standing figure mounted on a pedestal and placed on a checkered gameboard and a cloud filled sky. In the foreground an abstracted and petrified Narcissus crouches in a reflecting pool. Next to this figure a stonelike hand holds an egg between its thumb and forefinger. From the egg a small narcissus breaks through the shell. The configuration of the fingers and the egg formally repeats the pose of the crouching Narcissus. Tiny ants swarm over the hand and next to it an emaciated dog chews on a small skeletal rib cage. The tiny secondary images which comprise the Narcissus are all drawn from other works of these years: figures placed on pedestals appear in *The Lugubrious Game* of 1929[57] and the *Invisible Man* (Fig. 66): groups of tiny figures in *Perspectives* of 1936-1937[58] and Spain (1938);[59] the hand holding the egg reappears in *Inventions of the Monsters* (1937).[60] The ants which crawl over the hand and the emaciated dog chewing bones are persistent Dalinien symbols of putrification and decay, images pointing to the rich pictorial world which he saw lying behind "the three great simulacra: excrement, blood and putrefaction."[61] The fossilization of the major images has its origin in Freud's writings on the ancestral sexual aggression.

Dali's poem and his painting on the theme of Narcissus reiterate the Surrealist's belief in desire as the means to effecting the transformations of the real world leading to the *surréel*. Dali insists that if one stands about four feet from the canvas and stares fixedly at it, the figure of Narcissus will appear to merge with the surrounding landscape and disappear from view.[62] For Dali, the metamorphosis of Narcissus occurs at this moment: the figure is replaced by the simulacrum of a hand holding a new narcissus. The paranoiac-critical method results in a visual transformation of the exterior world, a psychological and perceptual application of the fact of physical metamorphosis contained in the original myth. Dali explains that he showed the work to Freud when they met in 1938 and explicated its significance:

> Exposer pedogogiquement le myth du narcissisme et l'illustrer littéralement par un poème écrit en même temps. Dans ce poème et ce tableau il y a mort et fossilisation.[63]

The *Eros/Thanatos* polarity inherent in Surrealism is reflected in Dali's Narcissus. The image of Gala, through whom Dali claims redemption, opposes the images of death and fossilization. Like Oedipus, Narcissus functions as a Surrealist hero. Suddenly confronting himself he finds in confrontation the seeds of his death. But he is saved from the absoluteness of death by the process of metamorphosis, saved to live as a flower.

Freud explicated three stages in the evolution of the libido. The child's preoccupation with himself and his own body marks the first of these. During the second stage an erotic impulse intensifies that natural interest and the result is referred to as the narcissistic libido. Finally, in the course of the normal process of development, this desire is transferred to another person.[64] The Freudian Narcissus, then, is the individual whose development is arrested at the second stage of this sexual and emotional cycle. Thus, Narcissus is the myth of love which, because it is self-love and has no procreative potential, is really death. As a denial of heterosexual love, the Narcissus myth conflicts with Surrealism's fundamental commitment to the idea of love and the redemptive power of woman. Dali circumvents this problem by making the image of Narcissus interchangeable with that of Gala ("Gala—my Narcissus' "), just as he considered himself and Gala to be one, often signing his canvases Gala/Dali. In this way Dali bypasses the Freudian duality of male and female. Freud had seen both sexes as possessing characteristics of the opposite, to a greater or lesser extent; the resulting conflicts form the basis of neurotic compulsions. Dali's psychological absorption of Gala suggests his inability to deal with Freud's sexual polarities but is also part of the larger Surrealist search for the perfect androgyne. The sexual confusions underlying Dali's works form the basis for a future chapter devoted to the application of the paranoiac-critical method to Millet's *Angelus.*

The Surrealists were quick to see other applications of the Narcissus myth. In an article in *View,* Wallace Fowlie concluded that the myth found its most complete modern poetic expression in the figure of Stendhal's Julien. The Romantic self-preoccupation of Stendhal's character was shared by the Symbolist poets:

> The swan, a symbol white, pure motionless and dying, is a new reincarnation of Narcissus and Julien, and a new development of the pride which attached them to their destiny of frustration. Narcissus kneeling in his childlike pose of self-adoration, and Julien, seated on his rock and contemplating himself in the flight of the hawk, prefigure Mallarmé's swan which, this time, is not held down by his dream or relegated to the limbo of the darkest subconscious. He is immobilized, not by himself, but by the hard cold substance of the ice, exiled in the kingdom of frost and snow . . . [65]

By the 1940's the Narcissus myth had undergone its own Surrealist transformations. The emphasis placed on the idea of metamorphosis in the first Surrealist representations of the theme shifted to a later preoccupation with the sexual aberrations arising from a Freudian interpretation. In other words, although originally selected for its ancient content, within ten years Narcissus as a myth of metamorphosis had been replaced by the Freudian Narcissus. Freud's analysis of the myth had certain negative implications for Surrealism, since it applied to sexual development arrested at a pre-heterosexual stage and it is not surprising that the Narcissus theme finally acquired rather derisive connotations in Surrealist hands. Parker Tyler's "Christ, Socrates, Stalin and the Role of Narcissus," attempted to prove that the three, although ostensibly committed to a world outside themselves, were in fact completely egotistical in their implicit views of themselves as instruments chosen for some greater purpose. The article contained lengthy and aggressive attacks on the idea of love as embodied by these persons:

> The metamorphosed self-image is the hidden keynote of platonic love, which primarily is the passionate love of physical beauty by those who cannot countenance their own external homeliness. (Socrates)

It was because he lacked quantity, not quality, of love that he wished to possess the love of the earth's population. (Christ)[66]

References to the Narcissus myth occurs again in two paintings by Ernst devoted to Echo, the wood nymph who had loved and lost Narcissus. In his 1936 painting on the theme (Fig. 30) she appears as part of that primeval landscape immortalized by Ernst in other paintings of those years.[67] The painter has spoken at length of the predatory nature of his forests, metaphors for the origins and processes of life itself:

> They (forests) are, it seems savage and impenetrable, black and russet, extravagant, secular, swarming, diametrical, negligent, ferocious, fervent, and lovable, with neither yesterday nor tomorrow. From one island to another, over volcanos, they play cards with incomplete decks. Nude, they wager only their majesty and their mystery.[68]

In the *Garden Airplane Trap* (Fig. 31) the forest, much like a Venus Fly Trap, seems to attract the airplanes as if they were giant metallic insects and then transform them into vegetable matter. The same attenuated vegetable forms create a protective glade for the nymph Echo in the painting of that title. The nymph, with her human hand, bird's throat and head and beak which resemble some strange variety of trumpet flower, is as visually a unique creation as the airplane plants of the previous year. But the light in her eye and the thumb that jauntily points toward an opening in the dense foliage, suggest that she alone understands this forest creation of the artist's and that she alone can indicate the way out. That Ernst himself saw her in this light is suggested by the context in which she makes her first appearance in his writings:

> I see barbarians looking toward the west, barbarians emerging from the forest, barbarians walking to the west. On my return to the garden of the Hesperides I follow, with joy scarcely concealed, the rounds of a flight between two bishops . . . voracious gardens in turn devoured by a vegetation which springs from the debris of trapped airplanes . . . with my eyes I see the nymph Echo.[69]

Ernst's Echo is more than just a voice; the painter has given back to her the body she lost as punishment for offending Pan.[70]

The publication of the first issue of *Minotaure* in the spring of 1933 marked the re-emergence of a mythological theme which would assume increasing importance for Surrealist painting after that date. The theme was already popular in French literature and art prior to that date. Matisse had illustrated Henry de Montherlant's *Pasiphae: Chant de Minos*, first published in 1928. Montherlant's reworking of the myth seemed to anticipate Surrealist preoccupations in its assertion of the act of love as an act of choice freed from all pre-existing moral codes.[71] Gide's *Thesée* of 1946 is well-known, as is Ernst's

Labyrinth (1924) (Fig. 7), which alludes to this myth, as do de Chirico's many representations of Ariadne.[72] Much of the credit for the resurgence of interest in the Minotaur saga has been given to Picasso, whose etchings for Skira's *Metamorphosis of Ovid* (1933), *Tauromachia* (1934), and *Minotauromachia* (1935) remain perhaps the best known of all Twentieth Century representations of the theme. Masson has argued, both to me personally and to others who have published his accounts, that it was he and Bataille who selected this myth in the early 1930's for its symbolic implications for the modern artist:

> en realité c'est Bataille et moi qui avons réintroduit ce 'personnage' peu familier et qui est devenu avec le labyrinthe un thème de la mythologie surréaliste.[73]

According to Masson, the Minotaur first appeared in a series of drawings which he exhibited at the Jeanne Bucher Gallery in the spring of 1933. The revue *Minotaure* did not yet exist, nor, asserts Masson, had Picasso begun to execute the drawings and prints which would later clearly associate his name with this subject. On June 1, 1933, the first issue of *Minotaure* appeared. Masson and Bataille provided the title, over the objections of some other Surrealists, who wished it be known as *l'Age d'Or* after Bunuel's movie:

> Mais Bataille et moi, qui nous occupions des mythes grècs les plus sombres, en particulier les mythes dionysiaques et celui de labyrinthe de Crète, avons souligné que notre époque etait tout à fait 'minotaurèsque' et nous l'avons emporté.[74]

Masson was to design the first cover, but the offer was later withdrawn due to Skira's desire that the name of the better known Picasso appear on the cover of the first issue, and not until Number 13 was a cover of Masson's design used. The painter insists that up until this time, Picasso had executed some centaurs, but no minotaurs; that, in other words, it was the Surrealist dominated periodical that sparked his interest in the theme. In fact, the Zervos catalogue contains a painting of 1928 entitled *Minotaure courante,* consisting of a contour drawing of human legs and back to which is attached a horned bull's head with open mouth. The work contains none of the aggressive ferocity associated with Picasso's renderings of the theme after 1933, but it nevertheless proves the existence of the image in his *oeuvre* prior to the appearance of *Minotaure.*[75] It also seems clear, however, that the Surrealists' interest in the theme provided a strong impetus in this direction for Picasso, as the series of drawings and prints beginning with the *Minotaure et nu* date from June 24, 1933, according to the Zervos chronology.[76]

With the publication of *Minotaure,* the Surrealists announced a new myth. In 1924 Breton had explicated the relationship between the Cretan labyrinth and man's psychological imprisonment in the convoluted passages of the unconscious.[77] But it was Freud's teachings rather than Ariadne's thread which provided the means to psychological liberation. Only the imagination could shape and give expression to the unconscious. Surrealist writings of the 1940's reveal the symbolic implications of the Cretan saga for Surrealist theory. Daedalus, possessed with the idea of the subconscious principle as an element of architecture, would become a personification of the artist as creator, himself lost in a mental labyrinth. Finding in Pasiphae's moral calamity an opportune means of expressing himself, he ultimately unleashed the myth's tragic *dénouement:*

> Microcosmically, it is the tragic destiny of genius in relation to human daring and moral commitment. Sophocles and Aeschylus were aware of it. Oedipus Rex is the Minotaur.[78]

Before discussing Masson's interpretation of the theme, it is worth considering other Surrealist renderings, as they reveal the ease with which the theme was absorbed and bent to the artistic ends of certain individuals. Dali's cover for the eighth issue of *Minotaure* (Fig. 32) reveals the same eclectic borrowing and repetition of imagery that characterized his paintings of these years. The minotaur's human body derives from the *Venus de Milo of the Drawers,* and related drawings of 1936. Dali's minotaur is not only half-human/half-animal in form, but also represents a fusion of male and female elements reflecting the androygynous qualities of much of Dali's current pictorial imagery.[79] Other aspects of the work: the compartmentalization of the body, the presence of carefully delineated cloud forms and the specific images of glass, bottle, and key reveal Dali's iconographic debt to the Belgian Surrealist René Magritte at this time.[80] The bull's head with lolling tongue and white rimmed eye appears less as an image of animalistic ferocity than as an effete literary transcription of its mythical source. The creature's effected pose, with hand on out-thrust hip, suggests a sexual coquettishness fundamentally opposed to the somber content of the original myth. The fabulous monster who seemed to Masson to be the personification of all that he found "monstrous" in his own age, becomes in Dali's hands a merely decorative piece of book illumination.

Magritte's own design (a black cloaked figure with a bleached bull skull on top) (Fig. 33) conveys the same sense of mystery and enigma which pervades his paintings, but its existential loneliness is far removed from the ritualistic drama contained in Masson's first representations on the theme of the sacrificial bull. Like Picasso, Masson had been deeply affected by the drama of the *corrida.* But his stay in Spain also coincided with the tensions leading up to the outbreak of civil war, and he quickly associated the elemental passions felt in Spain with his earlier views of pre-Classical Greece:

> La période espagnole signifie pour Masson la fusion définitive de la force créatrice et de l'angoisse mythique qui l'animent. Son langage de peintre acquiert une simplicité de maître.[81]

The theme of the bullfight provided Masson with his first opportunity to express the intimate relationship between rite and myth in a context redolent of the essential struggle between life and death. *Rêve tauromachique* of 1937 (Fig. 34) represents an early attempt on the part of the painter to fuse the eternal and the present in a single work. The painting depicts the goring of a horse and matador while a fourth figure stands to the right holding a cape and apparently futilely attempting to distract the bull from his charge. Striving for stability at a moment of frenzy the right hand figure and the horse are frozen in vertical positions providing a fixed point around which the thrusting bull's haunches and the swirling figure of the tossed matador rotate. Iconographically the work recalls the imagery of Picasso's passionate statement on the horrors of the Spanish Civil War, the *Guernica* executed the same year. But although the animal images of both works derive from the same source and both painters use the images of the bullfight which both saw as a quintessential element in the passionate struggles which they identified with Spain at this time, Masson's painting conveys a sense of ritual dance more like that of the ancient images of Cretan bull vaulting than Picasso's symbolic recreation of the horrors of war. In Masson's work the bull ring appears as a stage: there are no spectators present as man and animal play out a centuries' old drama. Ultimately, however, the distinction between man and beast is rendered unclear as the standing figure on the right wears a horned headdress and his raised right arm suggests a waving tail recalling the mythical fusion between man and beast of the minotaur legend. The work suggests that Masson's attitude was shaped and reinforced by his understanding of the *corrida*.

The following year Masson executed what he now feels to be his major statement on the Theseus theme, *The Labyrinth* (Fig. 35). On an emblematic level, the image of the labyrinth became for the painter an essential cosmic symbol communicating through its cyclical structure the principles of unity within diversity, order within apparent chaos. Derived initially from the geometric mazes placed in the naves of certain Gothic cathedrals, Masson found further philosophical support for his formal structure in Chinese ideograms, particularly that of the yin-yang. Death, in the form of the minotaur, surrounds his labyrinth. In *The Labyrinth* Masson attempts to use the principles of the original myth as iconographic indices of his own metaphysical conception of the universe. But the conception is ultimately too grandiose and too philosophical for the pictorial means at the painter's disposal and fall into a kind of confused fussiness. The dominant form, a bull's head attached to a basically human structure, must also support architectural structures and imagistic references to animal, vegetal, and mineral worlds. The attempt to communicate the essential unity and interrelatedness of all aspects of the natural world through a single symbolically charged image ultimately leads to an unfortunate over-literalness on the painter's part.[82]

The minotaur head from *The Labyrinth* became the basis of Masson's design for the thirteenth number of the periodical (Fig. 36). Now, the head alone serves as a microcosmic presentation. Within its biomorphic form, tiny images suggest macrocosmic references, a bleached horn, steps which lead nowhere, a seashell. In the middle of what might be the forehead in a more naturalistic representation, a single cosmic eye shines forth, Masson's reference to the inclusive quality of myth as an artistic device.

In 1939 two more paintings by Masson on the Minotaur theme appeared. In the first of these, the *Childhood of the Minotaur* (Fig. 37) the creation of the monster becomes a metaphor for the creation of form from elemental chaos. Here a swirling fleshy mass gradually begins to differentiate into recognizable forms; limbs take shape, a head with flame-like tongue appears at the top. Although the forms are modelled there is no attempt to render them in any logical spatial relationship to one another. As in the *Metamorphosis* (Fig. 28) and *The Labyrinth* (Fig. 35) the interior of the body is opened up and exposed. At the moment of ecstatic coupling corporeal distinctions are abolished and at the center of the pulsing thoracic cavity a tiny bull's head appears. Masson's free painterly handling reinforces the work's ideational content and the result is a strong pictorial statement about the birth of a new figure through the violation of conventional forms. In Heraclitus, fire and water combine to make steam; in Pausanius the joining of woman and bull results in a strange hybrid; in Surrealism objects are conjoined to create a new poetry. Lautréamont's famous metaphor, "Beautiful as the chance encounter on a dissecting table of a sewing machine and an umbrella," has often been cited as the source of all Surrealist juxtaposition, literary and visual. But although the metaphor serves as an immediate exemplar, the philosophical dialectic which allows these conjunctions has its roots in the pre-Socratic tradition. Masson particularly was well aware of the path between Heraclitus and Novalis and Lautréamont.

The bizarre turbulent form comprising the *Childhood of the Minotaur* appears again in *The Workshop of Daedalus* (Fig. 38). Here it serves as but one element in a set of symbolic images. The central image is the large metallic forge, the gaping orifices and pointed arrow of which convey strong sexual implications. On the left behind the wall a spiral brick structure symbolizes the unity of life. The image derived originally from Dante's cyclical cosmos in the *Divine Comedy.*[83] On the right the skull resting on top of a guillotine connotes death, but also, in conjunction with the faceted gem atop the forge, refers to alchemical teachings on the origins of matter. The tiny figure of Daedalus works at fashioning a hollow animal mold, watched over by the wraithlike Pasiphae for whom it will become the means to a union with Minos' sacrificial bull. The foreground of the painting is filled by a huge semi-formless mass, the image of the Minotaur from the *Childhood of the Minotaur*. Small human figures work to bring life and substance to the fiery mass. The condensation of images is that of dreams, but it becomes here the vehicle for Masson's telescoping of the events of the original myth with his Romantic *weltanschauung*. The creations of Daedalus' workshop function as microcosmic metaphors for the creation of life itself, which Masson significantly places between the static images of birth and death. The mechanism which brings life into being, in this context the forge, also serves as an image of sexual potency in the essential and cyclical struggle between *Eros* and *Thanatos,* the struggle of life itself.

By 1943, when he executed his last painting on the theme of the Minotaur, *Pasiphae* (Fig. 39), Masson had abandoned the rather fussy naturalism of the earlier representations. Returning to his earlier experiments with automatic drawing, he now depends primarily upon the work's title rather than a collection of specifically symbolic images to convey the painting's mythical referents and content. Among the network of interwoven lines and colors, the images of Pasiphae, the Minotaur and the Labyrinth are discernible. Removed from any specific literary context, they are presented as isolated images, Surrealist totems. Paintings by Masson, Dali and Ernst based on Classical myths reveal above all else the painter's desire to use myth as a device for legitimizing their personal imagery and proving that surrealism, or the surreal, did in fact exist before Breton's group was formed, that present and past could be telescoped into a single eternal reality. The next step was to mythologize their own images.

The Tragic Myths

III

Dionysos: The Myth of Ecstasy

Je suis mythologue depuis toujours. Les mythes grecs, surtout les mythes sombres de la Grèce m'ont toujours frappé . . .

André Masson

Zeus, disguised as a mortal, had a secret love affair with Semele and jealous Hera advised Semele, then already six months with child, to make her mysterious lover a request: that he would no longer deceive her, but reveal himself in his true nature and form. Semele followed this advice and, when Zeus refused her plea, denied him further access to her bed. Then, in anger, he appeared as thunder and lightning, and she was consumed. But Hermes saved her six months son; sewed him up inside Zeus' thigh, to mature there for three months longer; and, in due course of time, delivered him. Thus Dionysos is called "twice-born," or "the child of the doubledoor."

At Hera's orders the Titans seized Zeus's newly-born son Dionysos, a horned child crowned with serpents and, despite his transformations, tore him into shreds. These they boiled in a cauldron, while a pomegranate-tree sprouted from the soil where his blood had fallen; but, rescued and reconstituted by his grandmother Rhea, he came to life again.

On April 13, 1933, a new ballet choreographed by Léonide Massine opened at the Monte Carlo theater in Paris. Titled *Les Présages,* the work had as a musical score Tchaikovsky's Fifth Symphony; Masson designed the costumes and sets and the entire production represented a collaboration between the arts of music, dance and painting similar to earlier efforts at the Ballet Russes de Monte Carlo that had included visual effects and staging by Picasso, Miro and other painters. In this case, however, the ballet was not a transformation of an older work but an original production written by Massine and based on ancient architectural motifs at Selinus, Agrigento and Paestum. The ballet was presented in four parts: first, life with its ambitions and temptations; then passion and the contest between sacred and profane love; thirdly, frivolity; and lastly, the culmination of man's tragic destiny through conflict.[1] The protagonists, conceived as entities rather than personnages (Action, Fate, the Heros) developed their dramatic presence through the combined movements of several dancers organized into complicated patterns of movement against a striking backdrop intended by Masson to shock the audience through its intensity; the design (Fig. 40) introduced a note of cosmic instability as whirling suns and flamelike stars shot across a sky marked by brilliant zones of color.[2] The effect was one of drama and heavenly turbulence. The costumes (Fig. 41) symbolically affirmed the dancer's roles as personifications of tragic forces. Through its design and choreography the ballet evoked vague and general ideas about joy, love and suffering stripped of the more conventional narrative content of much classical ballet. The work moved Masson's close friend Michel Leiris to comment that, "Avec le ballet des Présages, Masson pour le première fois, a tenté de facon deliberée la création d'un mythe tragique. Jusqu' à ce jour son art est resté dominé part cette tendance mythique."[3]

Masson was drawn to the Ballet *Les Présages* because it reflected his own struggle to evolve a style and iconography in painting that could adequately convey his profound sense of the emotional and spiritual trauma that underlay the life experience. Out of the fusion of his personal experiences after entering the French army as an infantryman in 1915 and his earlier reading of Nietzsche's *Birth of Tragedy* with its exaltation of the process of a poetic spirit caught between the painful shattering of the soul and its mystical rebirth into collective wholeness, he evolved the vision of a world caught in a ceaseless and metamorphic struggle between life and death that characterizes his work of the 1920's and 1930's. Gravely wounded in the offensive of the Chemin des Dames in April 1917, he later recalled the experience as a moment of cosmic madness that indelibly stamped his artistic development:

> The indescribable night of the battlefield, streaked in every direction by bright red and green rockets, striped by the wake and the flashes of the projectiles and rockets—all this fairy tale-like enchantment was orchestrated by the explosions of shells which literally encircled me and sprinkled me with earth and shrapnel. To see all that, face upward, one's body immobilized on a stretcher, instead of head down as in the fighting where one burrows like a dog in the shell craters; constituted a rare and unwonted situation. The first nerve-shattering fright gives way to resignation and then, as delirium slips over you, it becomes a celebration performed for one about to die.[4]

The images and experiences of war were quickly transformed into the dramatic and intense calligraphy of Masson's first automatic drawings and paintings. After 1924, and under the influence of the Surrealist group, he gradually evolved a series of automatic drawings and sand paintings based on the themes of combat and metamorphosis. His *Battle of the Fish* of 1926 (Fig. 2) and related works reveal his combining of a violent subject matter and impassioned attack on the canvas with an almost ritualized color sense. It is as if the passions could only be contained by ritualizing them, but it remained for Masson to discover the conceptual framework within which his imagery could be most effectively organized.

The gradual transformation of Masson's iconography of violence and erotic death into specific mythological themes occurred during the early 1930's and was shaped by both his reading and his close personal involvement with Georges Bataille and Michel Leiris. Bataille was instrumental in publishing, with the aid of Masson, Leiris and other dissident Surrealists, a series of periodicals devoted to pushing the limits of the irrational to the extreme. His *Documents* series of the early 1930's contained articles and photographs on de Sade, bizarre human and natural forms, and Paris *abattoirs* which he viewed as the descendants of temples originally functioning as places of religious offerings and animal slaughter. Ideas of slaughter and sacrifice obsessed Bataille and drew his interest to ritual and tragic myth in ancient Greece. Masson's own paintings of slaughter with their pictorial sources in Rembrandt and Chaim Soutine, contain images of animal dismemberment that would reappear in the mythological paintings. Meanwhile Leiris, now director of ethnology at the Musée de l'homme, had begun his studies into ritual sacrifice among certain African tribes.

The years from 1929-1933' were years of great personal instability for Masson; they were also the years during which he dropped his formal reliance on cubism and came to increasingly rely on an all-over net of gestures to organize his picture space. *The Rope* of 1928 (Fig. 42) anticipates the mingling of love and combat that would characterize Masson's work of the early 1930's. In the introduction to a one man exhibition at the Galerie Simon in 1929 George Limbour remarked:

> As for love, hasn't he manifestly represented it in a painting called *The Rope?* The serpentine, the flagellant, perhaps even the mortal dance at the side of the woman, beautiful victim who uncoils on a bed of obscurity her curves and her talents as seductrice, revealing a simple undulation the darkest and usually most hidden of her treasures . . . voluptuous dialogue of love and combat. It's no sure bet which of the two lovers will better knot around the other, but if anger lands the blows of this coarse whip, I incline to think that the submissive rope will lose no time hanging itself on the woman.[5]

Battles between animals and themes of animals devouring themselves fill Masson's work of 1929. Themes of murder, battle and rape appear with increasing frequency during that year, the year in which his own marriage ended in divorce and he passed from orthodox Surrealism.

Just prior to executing the designs for *Les Présages* he had produced a series of drawings for which Bataille wrote a text. Published under the title *Sacrifices* ("the gods who die") they include five subjects for which Masson engraved illustrations, *Orpheus* (Fig. 43), the *Crucified One* (Fig. 44), *Mithra, Osiris,* and the *Minotaur.* The works are based on Masson's reading of Fraser's *Golden Bough* and three of them are associated with the concept of the sacred bull. In the cult of Mithra all the beneficient things of the earth were supposed to have sprung from the deity's capture and the sacrifice of a sacred bull. The soul of Osiris was thought to have inhabited the body of Apis, the Bull of Memphis. The Minotaur was the terrible half-man half-bull that waited at the center of the Cretan labyrinth, soon to assume importance as a potent Surrealist symbol of the unconscious.

In 1933, the same year that he executed the designs for *Les Présages,* Masson also produced two paintings that are seminal indicators of the direction of his mythologizing during these years. Titled *Bacchanale* (1933) (Fig. 45) and *Petite Tragèdie* (1933) (Fig. 46) they introduce into his work the image of the ancient god Dionysos, to whom he had been introduced by Nietzsche. In the *Bacchanale* the god appears in symbolic form as the god of ecstatic love, his sign a bunch of grapes held up by a central female whose body undulates across the plane of the canvas. Around her two other couples and her mate engage in various acts of love. The richly painted background assumes the whirling patterns of a world mad with erotic excess while the fluid line that delineates the figures appears charged with powerful erotic currents. Stripped of the overt imagery of death that characterizes so much of Masson's painting, the *Bacchanale* is a celebration of life and love, albeit under the sign of the tragic god. The god Dionysos appears here in his incarnation as the god of the vine, of fertility, drunkenness and erotic passion.

It is not surprising that the image of Dionysos would be associated in Surrealism with ecstatic love; ecstasy as a means of redefining the nature and social significance of eroticism lies at the heart of much of Masson's art, but also of the Surrealist world view in general. Surrealism departed from Symbolist ideas about the nature of reality through Breton's insistence that reality was not something to be escaped through dream, trance or hallucination but was rather a state in constant process of redefinition. Insisting that the marvellous be perceived through the objects of the real world, Breton suggests that in the world as we know it the supreme human experience comes about through the act of love.[6] His treatise on the subject, *L'Amour fou,* first published in 1937 is a hymn to the idea of a love that has the power to transform: "La beauté sera érotique-voilée, explosante-fixe, magique-circonstancielle ou ne sera pas," he concludes.[7] As a metaphor for a love impulse that transcends time and space Breton turns to classical mythology in *L'Amour fou,* concluding that myths such as that of Venus revealing herself on earth express an eternal truth which translates into allegorical language a series of observations that lead beyond the realms of human existence.

Eros appears in Surrealism in many guises: the Sadean concept of corporeal metamorphosis that activates Hans Bellmer's *Poupées* (Fig. 19) and Bataille's *History of the Eye,*[8] the narcissistic and onanistic sexuality of Dali's paintings of the early 1930's, the ethereal female muses of Surrealism, among others. But it is in ecstatic love that the Surrealist finds the greatest liberation. The call to ecstatic love in Surrealism becomes a means to reinfuse the entire world with a sense of passionate commitment; ecstasy, following the Dionysiac model, is a means of circumventing reason: "ignoring ecstasy, one is reduced to analysis," remarked Bataille.[9] Dionysos, the liberator, is also the transcendant seer. Socrates, in the *Phaedrus,* identified prophecy and madness for the first time; "Our greatest blessings come to us by way of madness," he remarked.[10] Moreover, he distinguished between prophetic madness, the ritual madness of Dionysos, poetic madness inspired by the muses, and the erotic madness of Aphrodite and Eros. For Plato it was through Eros that the two sides of human nature—the animal and the spiritual—were brought together in harmony and it was Eros which supplied the dynamic force driving the soul forward in its quest of a transcending earthly experience.[11]

In Surrealism, Eros and Ecstasy are also intimately connected, with one another and with madness. The concept of ecstatic love always carries with it implications of transcendance and mystical fusion; from the beginning Surrealism celebrated the subversive power of Eros erupting into the world of everyday reality with an explosive force. But the erotic in Surrealism is always viewed as an aspect of interior experience and it is this that distinguishes it from mere sexuality—this conscious interior struggle to break free of the bonds of individuality in order to merge with the loved one. Michel Leiris' *Miroir de la Tauromachie* viewed eroticism as an essential life experience—profound, passionate and poetic while Bataille suggests that "De l'érotisme il est possible de dire qu'il est l'approbation de la vie jusque dans la mort."[12]

The equating of erotic ecstasy and madness in Surrealism derives from the Dionysos myth but finds contemporary expression in studies of the erotic component of hysteria by Charcot and Freud; "La plus grande découverte poétique de la fin du xix siècle," affirmed Breton and Aragon.[13] Dali's *L'Arc hystérique* of c. 1931 (Fig. 47) refers to this phenomenon, as did a Surrealist tableau at the 1938 International Exposition of Surrealism in Paris (Fig. 48): "Précédée d'un marécage et d'une végétation aquatique, la chambre à coucher pour hystérique fera rêver les jeunes émancipées de nos provinces."[14] In 1928 Breton and Aragon had decided to celebrate the cinquantenaire of hysteria, which formed the basis of Charcot's and then Freud's studies of neurosis. In the "attitudes passionelles" revealed in photographs taken from the archives they perceived a pure poetic state and they proposed a new definition:

L'hystérie est un état mental plus ou moins irréductible, se caractérisant par la subversion des rapports qui s'establissent entre le sujet et le monde moral duquel il croit pratiquement relever, en dehors de tout système délirant. Cet état mental est fondé sur le besoin d'une seduction réciproque, qui explique les miracles nâtivement acceptés de la suggestion (ou contre-suggestion) médicale. L'hystérie *n'est pas un phénomène patholigique et peut à* tous égards être considerée comme *un moyen suprême d'expression.*[15]

The Surrealists had demanded an open forum for their discussions of love and the erotic; in 1924 *La Révolution surréaliste* published the results of an inquiry into the role of love in each Surrealist's life; Breton's advocacy of free love rings from the pages of *Nadja* and *L'Amour fou.* And yet the society in which Surrealism flourished frequently inhibited Surrealist demands for free love and the wholehearted pursuit of erotic alliances. The results of these social constraints are, moreover, evident in a certain sexual conservatism in Surrealism when it came to the question of the lived experience. In *Nadja* Breton pits the unfortunate woman against a wife who clearly waits at home with patience if not total fidelity. Marriage, however frequently embarked upon, remained the major form of extended liaison among members of the group while Breton's vehement denunciations of homosexuality were well known. Inhibited by a social and cultural milieu from which there was no total escape, Surrealist explorations were increasingly displaced onto the place of mythology. Breton notes, in his own paen to ecstatic love published in 1937, that "le choix initial en amour" may be incompatible with an existent social system and he affirms that only a destruction of the economic basis of society will allow "à faire triompher, sur le plan de la vie réele, l'amour réciproque."[16]

Images of women drawn from the Dionysos myth offered a symbolic and artistic means of transcending the limitations of contemporary social mores. Masson found in J.J. Bachofen's *Mother Right,* first published in 1861, a sympathetic reassertion of the primary role of woman increasingly overwhelmed by the patriarchal biases of twentieth century culture. More recently, Kerenyi, in his analysis of Dionysiac cults, has recorded, "the magic power with which the phallic lord of exuberant, natural life revolutionized the world of women."[17] Kerenyi, following Walter Otto's lead, views the Dionysiac cults as a powerful religious experience satisfying sensual as well as transcendant needs rather than as playing the poetic and metaphoric role to which they had been relegated by writers more concerned with perpetuating the "noble calm" of classical ages:

Throughout its development the Dionysian cult preserved the character it had when it first entered into history. With its sensuality and emphasis on sexual love, it presented a marked affinity to the feminine nature, and its appeal was primarily to women; it was among women that it found its most loyal supporters, its most assiduous servants, and their enthusiasm was the foundation of its power. Dionysos is a woman's god in the fullest sense of the word, the source of all woman's sensual and transcendant hopes, the center of her whole existence. It was to woman that he was first revealed in his glory, and it was women who propagated his cult and brought about its triumph.[18]

By their nature, and by the content of the Dionysiac myths which shape them, the women of Masson's painting are tied to the earth—part of an endless cyclical drama of eroticism and death. His *Bacchanale au volcan* (1932) confirms the identification of woman with the earth, sexuality with the forces of nature; "la nature est aussi forces secrètes, violences invisibles, les germinations, les métamorphoses, les bons et les tristes présages, la mort, le sang, les merveilles de la nuit et les mauvais rêves."[19] In this pregnant nature the volcano becomes an image of orgiastic joy, of liberation and creation. An essential element in the ancient Dionysiac rites was the cave of fire which it was believed attended the god's rebirth. Breton, in his essay "Le Chateau étoilé," published in the eighth number of *Minotaure* invokes one such image of volcanic sexuality when he cites an episode in Sade's *Nouvelle Justine* concerning Mt. Etna: "Un jour, examinant l'etna dont le sein vomissait des flammes, je désirais être ce célèbre volcan. . . ."[20] A mystical celebration of the ejaculatory power of the volcano recurs in Masson's writings from Antille in the winter of 1944. In a prose poem he writes of the:

> Fourrure arborescente de la terre éventrée éventail de désir élan de sève oui c'est la roue de lourde feuille dans l'air fruité. Interroge la sensitive elle répond non mais rouge au coeur de l'ombre vaginale règne la fleur charnelle du balisier—le sang s'est coagulé dans la fleur insigne. Lave spermatique il t'a nourri pétrissant le verre banal la main de feu l'irisait de mortelle nacre. Le grande main caresse le sein du morne à moins que ce ne soit ta croupe Vénus d'anthracite elle irrite le crin des palmes soulève la plume des frondaisons et se glisse sous la toison amoureuse de l'énorme Sylvie.[21]

The fire, source of passion and life and capable of transforming vast landscapes, is a recurrent motif in Masson's painting of the 1930's. In 1934 he embarked on a walking trip through Andalusia with Rose Maklès, who would become his second wife. He returned to France briefly at the end of 1935, then went back to Spain where he remained until December 1936. On a night in January, 1935 that he spent alone and unprotected at the top of Montserrat he had his second violent experience of nature, one that inspired two cosmic paintings: *Landscape of Wonders* (1935) (Fig. 49) and *Dawn on Montserrat.* In the *Landscape of Wonders* a cowled figure from a nearby monastery passes through a landscape activated by passionate energy. Against a backdrop of whirling suns and stars that has its pictorial source in the backdrop for *Les Présages,* a serpent coils and tongues of flames reach into the rocky crevisses of the barren landscape. The work is theatrical in its intensity, dramatic in its brilliance:

The sky itself, I thought, appeared an abyss . . . the vertigo of heights and the vertigo of depths both at once. I found myself in a kind of maelstrom . . . there were shooting stars the whole time . . . the world entirely under a cover of clouds. The only place clear was the place where we were. And the sun rose. It was sublime. We were on our summit like Moses awaiting the arrival of the lord.[22]

Pagan and Christian sources fuse in Masson's representation in the image of the snake, sign of evil and the Christian fall from Grace but also tied to the Dionysos cult through the god's mother Persephone, seduced by her father who came to her in the form of a snake.[23] In ancient myth, the snake leads the boy Dionysos to the grape; in the cult, the maenads of the late period used harmless snakes as a barbaric adornment of their bacchantic dress.[24] Masson's more immediate source for the fusion of Christian and pagan is Nietzsche who had opposed Dionysos to Christ.

The ancient Greek sense of a *marvellous* communicated through a metamorphic process in which man and god participate in other forms of natural life combines with the imagery of Masson's personal and mystical experience of nature in his poem, *Du Haut de Montserrat:*

Tout doit revenir au feu originel
Tempête de flammes
Ainsi parlait HERACLITE
Levant et couchant de l'homme lucide et dur.
    Tu dois voir le flux et le reflux
Des passions méprisables
    Tu accepteras l'humide comme on aime
La mère qui nous engendra.
    Hommes et femes vous êtes voués aum
Feu de lave immatérielle.
Ca et la légère, écrasante
Toujours mortelle
Toujours vive
N'aimant que ce qui viendra
Toujours jetés aux volcans de vie et de mort.
Et *Paracelse:* Les dieux mains appuyées
Sur l'epée de la sagasse
En intimité avec les astres et les pierres
Amoureux des cavernes de l'homme
Due ventre de l'univers.
Et toi ZARATHOUSTRA oeil de lumière
Au centre d'un monde terrible et joyeux
Je vous salue des hauteurs
Du Montserrat.[25]

In 1936, after visiting Masson in Spain, Georges Bataille wrote several articles stimulated by the painter's account of the night on Montserrat. In one, published in *Minotaure* in June, he argues that the only path to reality lies through religious ecstasy: "La vie a toujours dans un tumulte sans cohésion apparente, mais elle ne trouve sa grandeur et sa réalité que dans l'extase et dans l'amour extatique."[26]

It was during a visit in Spain that Masson and Bataille had decided to found a review with the stated aim of "unmasking the religious behind the political." The result was *Acéphale,* the first number of which appeared in June 1936. The cover (Fig. 50) designed by Masson, included a Surrealist version of the *acephali,* a fabulous race described by ancient writers as having no heads:

> He was headless, related Masson, as was proper (his decapitated head in the form of a skull had taken refuge where his genitals should be), his body upright, his legs firmly planted apart in the earth, arms outstretched, in his right fist a flaming heart, in his left a dagger-shaped flower. His body is studded with stars but the entrails show through: the center of the body is a labyrinth constructed like a palace. . . .[27]

Or, in the words of Bataille's introductory essay,

> Man has escaped from his head as a convict has from prison. He has found, beyond himself, not god, who is the prohibition of crime, but a being unaware of the prohibition. Beyond what I am, I run into a being who makes me laugh because he has no head. . . . In one eruption he unites birth and death.[28]

The second issue of *Acéphale* was devoted to Nietzsche and Heraclitus, the third and fourth to the god Dionysos in his aspect as the frenetic and possessed god of death and rebirth. Masson executed four drawings for this issue: *Dionysos* (Fig. 51), *La Grèce tragique, L'Univers dionysiaque,* and *Le Taureau de Numance* (a reference to Cervantes Numance for which he had previously designed costumes.[29]

The third number of *Acéphale* took as its inspiration Walter Otto's *Dionysos: Myth and Cult* first published in 1933.[30] Otto's work furnished an important impetus to the direction taken by Nietzsche in his reexamination of Dionysiac beliefs. Attacked by more conventional analysts of Greek religion such as Martin Nilsson, Otto set out to study Dionysiac beliefs from a theological rather than historical point of view. He argues that Dionysos is not a projection of man's psyche on the world but that he *is*–a divine reality, "an intoxicated god, a mad god,"[31] who is finally given the highly significant title of "the liberator."[32] It was Otto's view that Dionysos' divine nature was madness, a madness inherent in and essential to the world itself. He sees this madness not as sickness or degeneracy but as a companion to perfect health. Nietzsche had stressed the *eruptive* character of the Dionysian; however, in one of his rare mentions of this god, refers to him as the "mad god" because of his effect on women. More recently, Kerenyi concludes that:

It is obvious that Otto was concerned not with a medical definition of what the Greeks call *mania* . . . but with a kind of visionary attempt to explain a state in which man's vital powers are enhanced to the utmost, in which consciousness and the unconscious merge in a breakthrough.[33]

Otto had stressed that Dionysos's role was not merely that of a dispenser of wine, but of a frenetic who possessed man and rendered him a savage—the god of the persecuted, the suffering and the dying. As the child of Zeus and a mortal Dionysos participates in two worlds, but is bound by neither of them. According to Otto the essence of the myth is contained in the circumstances of the god's conception and birth. The terrestrial and celestial worlds met in his conception, a meeting expressed in the double birth or rebirth. Otto suggests that the myth of Dionysos contributed to Greek thought a sense of frenzy so strong that thousands of years after the fall of their civilization it remains for a Nietzsche to communicate this feeling to modern man in the name of Dionysos:

Ariadne, the labyrinthe, the Minotaure, Theseus and Dionysos, all this mythic domain to which Nietzsche never ceased returning under an enigmatically ambiguous form, each time that he wanted to indicate the ultimate secret of the truth: que la verité est la mort.[34]

The Dionysiac universe eternally creates and destroys itself—its goal nothing but the fulfilling of this cycle: "On voit que le problème de la fiction ou de la verité ne se pose pas à propos du mythe moderne et nietzschéen de Dionysos qui, prospectif non retrospectif, ne se par des couleurs d'un lointain passé que pour mieux étreindre l'avenir."[35]

Nietzsche's Dionysos was the god of tragic passion and he appears in this light in a number of paintings from the 1930's. In *Tragédie* of 1933 (Fig. 52) Masson depicts a ritualized killing. The god Dionysos appears as a bull-headed male figure (the bull is a common ancient form taken by this god) holding a flaming heart in one hand and in the other a dagger. The figure is the prototype for the later *Acéphale* cover drawing with its strong Dionysiac associations. At his feet lies a spread-legged figure with heart-shaped hole in his chest. Nearby a third figure shrieks in agony. "The being who is fulfilled by transgression after transgression—when the swelling vertigo has abandoned him to the void of the sky—has become therefore not simply *being* but *wound* and . . . *agony* for all that exists as being," Bataille would later write.[36]

Concerning the fate of the dismembered god Dionysos there were two Orphic traditions—according to one the Titans devoured all the pieces of his body except one which, for the uninitiated, was the heart. The most profoundly secret and mysterious aspect of the ancient cult concerned a secret piece that was set aside and kept when the sacrificial animal was dismembered. In dismembering the body, the sacrificers—the Titans according to Onomakritos' version of the scene—set the heart aside; in the last formulation of the Orphic books appears the phrase, "for they left only the knowing heart."[37] The heart became an essential feature of the literary mythology of Dionysos. Pallas Athena picked it up and brought it to father Zeus who from it prepared a potion that he gave Semele to drink. It is in this way that Dionysos was born a second time.

But there are others who argue that the secret part was not a heart but a phallus.[38] In a series of Masson's works on the Dionysos theme it is the genitals that are removed and replaced by images of death while the dagger thrusts are recorded as violently sexual gestures. In the cover drawing for *Acéphale* (Fig. 50) a skull appears in place of the genitals while the dagger is held firmly erect while in the *Dionysos* drawing (Fig. 51) a thrusting dagger pierces the heart of the headless figure while a snaky-locked Medusa head peers out from between the legs. The dagger itself appears in a ritualized series of violent drawings entitled *Massacres* that appeared in 1933, the years of the first paintings on the Dionysos theme. In *Murder* (Fig. 53) a group of figures engage in violent combat. The staccato-like strokes of the brush and the harsh dagger-like shadows rhythmically echo the knife that plunges toward the victim's breast. Likewise, the *Massacre* drawings of the same year (Fig. 54) depict the unleashing of murderous forces in hand to hand combat. The victims are often women, the thrusting of the dagger is strongly sexual. Lanchner writes of these drawings that they are:

> Among the strongest Masson has ever made. They are done with great speed— as the artist says, 'so spontaneous they are really automatic drawings'—and line is broken by abrupt, spasmodic changes of direction. These 'arrow lines' echo the knives and penises that are invariably present. Generally in the *Massacre* series the victims are women but in one representation a sleeping male figure is surrounded by harpy-like beings who call to mind the Bacchic festival on Mount Citheron at which King Pentheus of Thebes was torn to pieces by his mother and aunts.[39]

The murders and massacres that fill Masson's work of these years all derive from his interest in developing a tragic art that has as its guiding spirit the figure of Nietzsche's and Otto's Dionysos. The painter's increasing involvement with Greek myth can be seen in the titles of many of his paintings from 1932-1934—*The Silenuses* (1932), *Daphne and Apollo* (1933), *Orpheus* (1934), and *The Horses of Diomedes* (1934) among others. In May of 1934 his third exhibition opened at Kahnweiler's gallery. It included works on harvest themes (in which the solar theme is affirmed with the idea of death), some representations of classical myths, those of the horses of Diomedes, Narcissus and Echo, Apollo and Daphne, five watercolors inspired by Fraser (Mithra, Orphée, le Crucifié, Minotaure, Osiris: the gods who murder) with a text by Georges Bataille, and several recent works, including figures of Pasiphae, the

Minotaur, the labyrinth, Theseus and Ariadne. But it was Nietzsche's Dionysos who crystallized the painter's most violent and tragic impulses and whose spirit suffuses Masson's attitude toward his mythological sources.

Dali's *Mythe tragique de l'angelus de Millet* and the Paranoiac-Critical Method

It is not the unconscious that I seek in your pictures, but the conscious.

Sigmund Freud to Salvador Dali

For a few years in the early 1930's, until his obsession with Hitler precipitated a confrontation with Breton's left-wing politics, Dali and his widely proclaimed paranoiac-critical method served as the major stimulus toward finding a surrealist means of exploiting the rich imagery of the unconscious. His own writings on the origins and formal manifestations of an hallucinatory imagery are filled with glowing allusions to his powers as a myth-maker. Carlton Lake, author of perhaps the most lucid explication of the "Dalinian personality" has referred to the painter in conversation as a "mythomaniac."[1] The original compulsion on Dali's part to create myths seems to derive from general Surrealist preoccupations with the subject manifested after 1929, the year in which he first joined the group. But the ends to which Dali put the device of myth construction are uniquely his and form an integral element in his larger attempt to thoroughly systematize the workings of the unconscious. His major statement on the subject, *Le Mythe tragique de l'angelus de Millet*,[2] represents an attempt to apply Freud's analytical model contained in the "Gradiva" and "Leonardo" essays to Millet's famous painting.

In the early 1940's Dali wrote that he had composed an essay on paranoiac interpretation called *Le Mythe tragique de l'angelus de Millet*, a book which he considered "one of the fundamental documents of the Dalinian philosophy."[3] The work appeared in 1963 and Dali explained that although written in the late 1930's the manuscript had been lost when the painter fled Arachon before the German occupation and was not recovered until some years later. The work is significant both for its detailed exploration of the mechanics of paranoiac-critical association and for what it reveals about a single Surrealist attempt to mythologize the past. It is only when examined in the light of this publication that the series of paintings after the theme of Millet's *Angelus* (Figs. 58-62) executed during the 1930's take their proper place in Dali's icono-graphic development.

The origins of the painter's interest in Millet's famous picture remain somewhat obscure. The most logical of Dali's many explanations is that, like several generations of school children throughout the Western world, he first encountered the work through a reproduction hanging on a classroom wall.[4] In retrospect he attached strange feelings of anguish to this original encounter, feelings long forgotten and suddenly provoked anew in 1929 upon seeing another reproduction of the same painting. More important, however, are his reasons for seizing upon this particular image as paradigmatic of the paranoiac-critical method. Dali was quick to recognize that the work's universal appeal could not be fully explained by its overt content, two peasants bowing their heads at sunset as the Angelus peals from a distant bell tower. From classroom walls to silk scarves and tea services Millet's humble piece of *genre* had become a symbol of pastoral virtues for millions of people. But why this particular work when the annals of Nineteenth Century painting are filled with sentimental devotions? His earlier reading of Freud led Dali to an examination of the latent sexual content of a work which he saw as "the most erotic picture ever painted, a masterpiece of disguised sexual repression":

> If Freud were here, he would back me up. That image has obsessed millions of people ever since Millet painted it. Why? It has obsessed me ever since the summer of 1932 . . ! One day in June, 1932, without any visual reference or association of ideas or traceable memory, I suddenly saw that picture in my mind's eye, in full color, and I realized it was one of the most haunting, enigmatic pictures ever painted, with layer on layer of unconscious meaning.[5]

When, a few weeks later, a visitor to the Louvre drove a hole through the canvas Dali became even more convinced of the work's disquieting quality. Jacques Lacan, a psychoanalyst, friend of Dali's and other Surrealists, and frequent contributor to *Minotaure* with articles on the relationship between paranoia and artistic creativity, interviewed the vandal who explained that he had had trouble deciding whether to attack da Vinci's *Mona Lisa,* Watteau's *Embarkation for Cythera* or *The Angelus.* Dali was quick to note the presence of Leondardo da Vinci in this trilogy of potential pictorial victims; "After all that Freud has taught us about Leonardo, it's only too obvious that the *Mona Lisa* has an incestuous fascination for all Oedipus types."[6] Unable to satis-factorily explain the troubling and enigmatic aspects of *The Angelus* Dali set about examining the painting in the light of the paranoiac-critical method which he had developed a few years earlier. But the application of this method to Millet's painting owes at least as much to Freud's teachings on the symbolic eruption of repressed material in the work of art as it does to Dali's thesis regarding the obsessing image.

Freud had used the psychoanalytical device of free association to trace the symbolic meaning of dream imagery to its source in the unconscious. Dali applied the same method to pictorial imagery, and particularly to that imagery which arises as a result of the visual hallucinations which Dali had exploited since childhood.[7] It is the paranoiac state which is characterized by systematized hallucinatory delusions and it was to the writings of Kraepelin and Bleuler that Dali turned for his understanding of the creative potential of paranoia.[8] Freud had attempted to clarify the reasons for the systematized delusions of paranoia by suggesting that the delirium arose as a result of the patient's attempt to repress homosexual and narcissistic tendencies.[9] The thesis influenced Lacan, and in his *De La psychose paranoiaque dans ses rapports avec la personnalité* he explained that:

> Contrairement au rêves qui doivent être interprété le délire est par lui-même activité interprétative de l'inconscient. Et c'est là un sense tout nouveau qui s'offre au terme délire d'intérprétation.[10]

Lacan's distinction between the paranoiac state and the dream state allowed Dali and others to replace Surrealism's earlier, and by now somewhat exhausted, preoccupation with the dream with a more inclusive and organized unconscious vista. But the symbolic meaning of delusional images still had to be systematized. Lacan's thesis became the basis for Dali's demand for an active delusional interpretation to replace the passive states of automatism and the dream. By using the external world as the source and stimulus for the delusion and by rendering the hallucinatory results with the clarity and precision of Dutch Seventeenth Century still-life Dali hoped to destroy all belief in the idea of a stable external reality without recourse to abstraction which would violate the essentially figurative structure of mental images. Dali has insisted that, unlike a madman, he himself is not mad; the question remains as to whether the conscious simulation of aberrant mental states used as the basis for artistic creation doesn't in fact result in a kind of emotional forgery. Dali's imagery is neither dreamlike nor does it arise from spontaneous hallucination; the latter fact no doubt leading to the iconographic codification which Rubin and others have noted.[11] In many instances Dali's hallucinated imagery originates in natural phenomena of the landscape around Cape Creus. Subsequent transformations of the imagery are arrived at by a complex process of conscious visual associations on the original object. Dali has explained that:

> Le mécanisme paranoiaque, par lequel naît l'image à multiple figurations, donne à la compréhension la clé de la naissance et de l'origine de la nature des simulacres, dont la furie domine l'aspect sous lequel se cachent les multiples apparences du concret.[12]

The process, as noted in Chapter V of this thesis, relies heavily on the stimulus of desire. As a model for the creation of the simulacra Dali chose the decorative style known as Art Nouveau, a formal abstraction of the organic twisting shapes of nature:

> Aucun effort collectif n'est arrivé à créer un monde de rêve aussi pur et aussi troublant que ces bâtiments modern style, lesquels, en marge de l'architecture constituent à eux seuls de vraies réalisations de désirs solidifiés, où le plus violent et cruel automatisme trahit douloureusement la haine de la réalité et le besoin de refuge dans un monde idéal, à la manière de ce qui se passe dans une névrose d'enfance.[13]

Fundamental to Dali's method is the fact that finally, when simulated, the paranoiac state is both passive and unconscious (the hallucination itself which is usually provoked by staring fixedly at some object) and active and conscious (the symbolic translation and communication of the hallucination). Although Lacan had identified the paranoiac state as a complete system of delirious interpretation in and of itself Dali has never been content to allow the paintings to speak for themselves. The paranoiac-critical method was first worked out visually in the paintings of the 1930's of which the *Angelus* series forms but one iconographic theme; the paintings were followed in turn by Dali's verbal exegesis of Millet's *Angelus*. Since the verbal and visual products tend to confirm and clarify one another I have not attempted to treat them completely independently.

The imagery of Millet's painting makes its first appearance in Dali's work in a painting of 1932 entitled *Meditation on the Harp* (Fig. 58). That year marked the height of his paranoiac activities and the moment when the highly original iconography of 1929-1930 began to become repetitive. Here a ghost-like image of Millet's male figure confronts a female nude who reaches around his neck with one hand and with the other touches the head of a kneeling figure dressed completely in black. One of his hands points toward the standing male figure; the elbow of the other arm is elongated into a phallic image supported by a crutch.

In his *Le Mythe tragique de l'angelus de Millet* Dali explains the peculiar grouping of the figures and the symbolic implications of the imagery.[14] He begins with a long series of associations leading first to an attempted explanation of the work's latent content, which will in turn clarify both the painting's troubling effect on him and the reason for its immense popular appeal through the years. Seizing first on the painting's somber mood, the attitude of piety bordering on grief (according to Dali) with which the couple greet the ringing of the Angelus in Millet's version, Dali deduces a preliminary association with death and concludes that the couple are actually in mourning and bowing their heads over a child's grave. Since the father-son relationship is fundamental to Dali's own obsessions (his preoccupations with the Oedipus complex, for example) he assumes that the child is a male.[15] This conclusion forms part of the original manuscript. A prologue, added prior to the book's publication in 1963, relates Dali's request that the Louvre X-ray Millet's painting.[16] The X-rays, also published by Dali, do in fact reveal an oblong geometrical shape, partially off the canvas, at the feet of the female figure. But whether it is a coffin as Dali asserts seems impossible to verify. Dali then includes an unsubstantiated claim that Millet had consulted a friend in Paris about the advisability of leaving the coffin in the painting. It was suggested that the presence of the coffin was too melodramatic and it was subsequently painted out.[17] The association, however, explains the presence of the third figure in Dali's *Meditation on the Harp;* it is the son, and the patched jerkin suggests a youth of peasant origin. Shrouded and dressed in black he functions as an image of death interjecting himself between the embracing figures. Dali's own Oedipal fixation has already been commented upon in the context of the Oedipus and William Tell themes. Spector has argued that Freud was first drawn to the figure of Leonardo da Vinci because of his own unresolved homosexual feelings, but Freud's intellectual detachment from his subject prevents the kind of personalized transformation of the theme immediately apparent in Dali's treatment of Millet's *Angelus.* The significance of the gestures and deformations found in Dali's figures will be considered later.

In his book on Millet, Dali moves quickly to a consideration of what he sees as the work's erotic aspect:

> On sait que les paysans, dans la rudesse de leurs labeurs, accablés par la fatique physique, tendent à érotiser, par une sorte de cybernétique atavique, tous les instruments de travail qui tombent sous leur main, la brouette en constituent le phantasme suprême, aveuglant, à cause de sa structure anthropomorphe, et des ses possibilitiés de fonctionnement symbolique.[18]

What is at work here is the application of Surrealist ideas regarding the object as the crystallization of dream or erotic impulses to the pictorial imagery of Millet's painting. The Surrealist object had originally been intended as a means of stimulating desire, and it is not surprising that Dali follows his observations on the wheelbarrow with a long series of hallucinatory experiences each of which has served to evoke the images of *The Angelus* in his mind: peculiarly shaped stones from the sea, rocks at Cape Creus, praying mantises in tidal pools, a tea set decorated with reproductions of Millet's painting, among others. The richness of the hallucinated associations proves for Dali the obsessive power of Millet's work. They are accompanied by a critical commentary which emphasizes the intense emotional reaction evoked by the delusions.[19] Dali, a literal follower of Freud, ascribes sexual origins to the emotional responses. A conscious interpretation of the images always follows the original delusion; "L'idée délirante apparaîtrait comme portant en elle-même le germe et la structure de la systématisation."[20] Thus the apparition of *The Angelus* appears to Dali as a para-noiac image, requiring an associative system which coexists with the delirious ideas. As the paranoiac images change the *appearance* of the original, the ac-companying associations transform its content. In Dali's reading Millet's female figure is seen as an expectant image, immobile and awaiting some imminent act of violence. The interpretation is based upon his associations of the pose with those of a kangaroo in danger, defensive boxer and a praying mantis await-ing copulation and the subsequent cannibalistic devouring of the male by the female.[21] The previous hallucinated appearance of Millet's imagery in the stones and megalithic rocks of Cape Creus confirms for Dali Freud's hypothesis that fossilized remains exist as symbols of ancestral sexual aggression.[22] Then follows a dream of Dali's containing a scene of brutal sexual violation and sodomy accompanied by yet another appearance of the mysterious *Angelus*. Moreover, the approximation of the female figure's pose to that of the praying mantis suggests to Dali a traumatic childhood fear of having his penis eaten by his mother. The symbolic expression of the fear is the mother's milk, and this fact seems to explain the exaggerated emphasis of the breasts in his first version of *The Angelus*. Without elucidating all the secondary associations which affirm Dali's analysis of the work's latent sexual content and its relationship with other Nineteenth Century popular imagery, it is already clear that Dali has used the paranoiac-critical method as a means of exploiting Freud's ideas about the sub-limated content of works of art.

Part of Dali's argument that the two figures in Millet's *Angelus* are frozen in an expectant pose preparatory to a moment of immanent sexual aggression rests on his belief that the man's hat is held in such a way as to shield an erect penis.[23] This "classical" attitude serves as a preliminary to the implicit cruel coupling. In his own version of the painting Dali concentrates on what he per-ceives as the erotic elements, transforming the latent sexual content of Millet's work into the manifest content of his own. The female, now naked, reaches out to embrace the male figure. The hand placed on the son's head emphasizes his subjugation; "il reste 'cloué' à la terre, hypnotisé par 'l'exhibitionisme spectral' de sa mère qui l'annihile."[24] Two Freudian precepts are invoked. Freud had suggested the potentially traumatizing effects of the child's accidentally wit-nessing the sexual activity of his parents. Not understanding the act his first associations are with its violence and subsequently his fear of the mother's death at the hands of the brutal male aggressor.[25] And secondly, the nourishing mother may become an image of the all powerful female principle; she who creates also has the power to destroy.[26] With his tremendous talent for utilizing a wide variety of sources Dali has applied his reading of Freud to the creation of the sexual symbolism which lies at the heart of his own painting.

That the final coupling will be sodomistic is proved for Dali by the presence of the wheelbarrow in Millet's version. Dali's list of erection fantasies includes, among others, flying, skidding, rapid locomotion and pulling and, according to him, the most frequent sexual obsessions among painters concern horses drawing carts or chariots and symbolize the sexual act and the feelings of impotence, strain and sexual debility frequently associated with it. The wheelbarrow, then, functions as a variant on this theme and symbolically gives to the sexual act an element of insurmountable physical effort, the animal ferocity contained in the act of sodomy. Moreover, the sacks in the wheelbarrow symbolically represent the two figures in the act of coupling. Dali's first version of the theme contains no wheelbarrow but does include, and in approximately the same spatial relationship to the female figure, a crutch supported phallic extension of the kneeling figure's right elbow. This strange phallus is also placed behind the female figure in a position which suggests sodomistic intent.

Dali's sexual borrowings from Freud and Kraft-Ebbing are too eclectic and too overt to allow the critic to conclude that the sexual content of Dali's works originates with himself. There is, however, a vast series of paintings which suggest that an intense personal fear of sexual debility forms the basis for much of Dali's imagery. Interestingly it is this aspect of the works which has been obscured by much of Dali's own verbal analysis. Of his painting *The Persistance of Memory* (1931) the artist suggested that: ". . . the famous soft watches are nothing else than the tender extravagant, solitary paranoiac-critical camembert of time and space."[27] Marcel Jean has pointed out perhaps a more convincing explanation for the origin of the soft watches:

> The word *montre* is a word image with a double meaning: in French, it is the imperative of the verb *montrer* and the name of the apparatus *mentrant* the time. But there is a very common childhood experience: the doctor asks the sick child to 'montrer sa langue' which obviously is soft. The child, we may say, *la montre molle* (shows it soft: with the double sense that in French this phrase can also mean 'the soft watch').[28]

There is further support for this idea of Jean's in a later painting entitled *Uranium and Atomica Melancholica Idyll* (1945) which depicts among other things a watch that ends in a tongue.[29] The tongue is also a well-known Freudian symbol for the penis; in other Dali paintings other parts of the body take over the erective function of the penis. In *The Great Masturbator* (1929) the entire figure is supported by a rigid nose while a stylized female head, recognizable as that of Gala, caresses the flaccid genitals.[30] This monumentalized flaccidity carries over to a work of 1934 entitled *Average Atmospherocephalic Bureaucrat in the Act of Milking a Cranial Harp.*[31] Here a giant phallus rests on a crutch while a seated male figure "plays" the soft drooping testicles. Dali has written at great length about the origins of the "crutch fetish" and the various symbolic meanings attached to it. One of the most persistent of these directly relates the crutch to a penis. In one fantasy the naked Dali uses a crutch to stab a ripe melon hanging overhead in order to drink its juice. At the height of the erotic fantasy, as his gestures with the crutch becomes more and more frenzied, the melon breaks loose and falls on his head splitting as it lands.[32] In the Freudian pantheon of sexual symbols ripened fruit stands as frequently as a metaphor for the female sexual organs as do umbrellas and walking sticks for the male. Dali's writings are filled with oblique references to fears of impotence; *Le Mythe tragique de l'angelus de Millet* contains several passages relating adolescent sexual fears. As recently as the Spring of 1973 the painter reiterated some personal sexual feelings that perhaps clarify many of his earlier references:

> Le reason for this story of Hitler and everything is because Dali is impotent sexually. But no completely—myself exaggerate tremendously in my talking—sometimes some erection is possible. But no make love too much because . . . is easy. Never clear anything you know. All big artists, except Johann Sebastian Bach, qui create tremendous quantity of (offspring) . . . (are impotent). Si your sperm is easy, you'll never create nothing, because you'll get childs and everything. But si your sperm is difficult, in this moment you start le surrealisme, you create fantastic things, or you like it making visions of things que Hitler . . . Alexander . . . Every important people is impotent.[33]

For the Surrealists the problem of the role of sublimation was apparently unresolvable. The dilemma surfaces most succinctly in the ambivalent attitude toward woman and love. Both the love object (woman) and the sexual act in provoking desire stimulated the release of repressed impulses which in turn gave birth to Surrealist works of art. The preoccupation with the fertile imagination and the unconscious sources of creativity also gave rise to a certain resentment of the female's natural procreative role. But that resentment could not be manifested directly and finds its expression only in certain symbolic images, like the Sphinx, which contain pre-Surrealist references to the idea of the destructive female. In Dali's works this fear is less often transferred to a specifically female image than it is internalized and covertly manifested in male images suggesting impotence or sexual debility.

Dali's paintings reveal that at the source of sexual fantasy and hallucination lies this fundamental fear of impotence. The sexual aggression which he reads into Millet's *Angelus* and which appears in his own *Meditation on the Harp* (Fig. 58) then, represents a form of fantasized overcompensation. That the paranoiac-critical method tends to reveal again and again this same concern suggests both the strength of the fear and the reasons for the repetitiveness of so much of Dali's imagery. Freud himself recognized the essential weakness of Dali's method as early as 1939 and conveyed his feelings to the painter in the course of an interview conducted in London that same year:

It is not the unconscious that I seek in your pictures, but the conscious. While in the pictures of the Masters—Leonardo or Ingres—that which interests me, that which seems mysterious and troubling to me, is precisely the search for unconscious ideas, of an enigmatic order, hidden in the picture. Your mystery is manifested outright. The picture is but a mechanism to reveal it.[34]

In the three or four years after completing *Meditation on the Harp* Dali executed several more paintings on the same theme. The later works reveal the particular manner in which the paranoiac-critical method served to provide a proliferation of pictorial imagery without significantly transforming the content of the ensuing works. A. Reynolds Morse has convincingly demonstrated through a comparison of certain paintings with photographs of the natural land formations around Cape Creus the extent to which Dali's supposedly mental imagery actually derives from the specific landscape with which he was most familiar. In this manner he has isolated one of the rock forms comprising Dali's second painting on the theme of Millet's *Angelus, The Architectonic Angelus of Millet* (1933) (Fig. 59) and photographed its source.[35] But, as is usually the case with Dali's works, the imagery has multiple sources and associations. In *Le Mythe tragique de l'Angelus* Dali had related that while playing with two small stones on the beach he unconsciously juxtaposed them in such a way as to form a miniature sculptural version of *The Angelus*. The stones, some washed smooth by the waves, others sharp and reminiscent of bones or animal skeletons, suggested to the painter the savagery of a primitive past. When combined to form *The Angelus* they served as reminders of that earlier age which Freud had characterized by its sexual aggressiveness. But the play with stones is a secondary association or source in the imagery of Dali's painting and the smooth precariously balanced stone with its several pointed projections has its natural source in a large rock near the painter's home. *The Great Masturbator,* executed the previous year, also makes use of this same form although here it has been forced into the shape of a human head recognizable as a self-portrait of Dali.

In the *Architectonic Angelus* (Fig. 59) smooth stone-like forms replace the human figures of the earlier works. The smaller of them, easily identified as the male principle by its sharp phallic-like projections, is supported by a crutch. Only the placement of the crutch prevents it from falling to the sand below as it thrusts a rigid prod into a hollow channel in the second form. The latter, by now unrecognizable as human, still retains certain characteristics which emphasize its female and maternal qualities; qualities which Dali had insisted were essential to his original interpretation of the theme. Its curvaceous shape and the pregnant bulge on the front of the figure serve to emphasize the essential difference between the two forms. Dali suggests that the original stones with which he played were very small; in the course of their translation into pictorial imagery they have become monumentalized in relation to the landscape and the two tiny figures who pass hand in hand between the monoliths. These tiny figures, identifiable as the child Dali and his father,[36] reinforce the work's Freudian content. The relationship of trust between father and son will be broken when they become competitors, first for the mother's affections, later through the son's sexual revolt symbolized by the crude scene of penetration symbolically enacted by the two stone figures. As if to emphasize the sources of his hallucinations in the natural world Dali's most bizarre creations are placed against, or formed from, the landscape around Cape Creus.

The majority of Dali's paranoiac-critical paintings retain a vast natural landscape, often identifiable as the beach at Cadaques or bay of Port Lligat. Originally derived from de Chirico, Dali's sweeping landscapes serve a similar function to those of the Italian metaphysical painter. Freud had often commented on the sense of stillness that pervades dreams, which tend to be far richer in visual than aural imagery. By placing his figures against such panoramic vistas, Dali attempts both to intensify the works' dream-like mood and to stress the function of the landscape as the original source for the hallucinated imagery.

In 1934 Dali transformed the imagery of *The Architectonic Angelus* into a new work entitled *Atavistic Ruins After the Rain* (Fig. 60) in which the "male" stone is now isolated as the painting's major image. Here the imagery is almost entirely drawn from other paintings and particularly from *The Architectonic Angelus*. The sandy beach, the town of Port Lligat viewed across the bay, the father and son with clasped hands and the crutch-supported stone-like form all function as persistent reminders that Dali's world is constantly undergoing a kaleidescopic process of change and transmutation, a process in which the past constantly imposes the ghosts of its forms upon the present. Here an oval shape, reminiscent of the opening cut through the "female" figure in Dali's *Architectonic Angelus,* has been removed from the rock. The rock, still precariously balanced on one point and supported by a crutch at the other end, now forms an arch though which the man and child, identified by the painter as "Dali et son père," can pass. In the background appears the familiar Catalan landscape: ". . . ma plaine chérie de l'Ampurdan qui devait, par la suite impregner de sa géologie si rare l'esthétique entière de la philosophie du paysage dalinien."[37] Reference is made to yet another painting through the two cypresses which seem to spontaneously generate behind the smooth stone. They derive from a work of the same year entitled *Apparition of My Cousin Carolinetta on the Beach at Rosas* in which a cypress sprouts from the inside of a small rowboat and before that from Böcklin's famous *Isle of the Dead.*[38] Both Dali and Ernst were drawn to Böcklin for the same reason: the Nineteenth Century painter's ability to create, by means of the fusion of nature and the imagination, a mood of withdrawal and dissociation from the world. Böcklin himself had seen the painting as a picture about which to dream and it is not surprising that Dali, in his unceasing attempt to find survivals of the past erupting into the present, would seize upon Böcklin's mysterious and elegiac landscapes. Once again the imagery of Böcklin's painting is condensed; two lone cypresses serve to evoke a memory of the past. But slight transformations in the imagery of Dali's later versions of Millet's *Angelus* fail to transform the content of the paintings in any significant way and the banality of the message is superseded only by the triteness of the titles.

That same year saw the appearance of still another work on the theme of *The Angelus,* again containing an obvious reference to Böcklin. At the feet of the two figures in the *Archaeological Reminiscence of Millet's Angelus* (Fig. 61) cypresses and the skeletal remains of architectural structures appear. Dali has also conveyed the mood of somber desolation contained in Böcklin's work. Here the setting sun casts long dramatic shadows across the beach, deserted except for the by now ubiquitous image of the father and son. The father reaches out an arm and gestures toward the towering figures. The figural images, recognizable through their poses as descendants of Millet's pious peasants, have been transformed into vestiges of monumentalized brick structures. It is as if Dali had transformed the architecture of Böcklin's work into the architectural figures of his own *Archaeological Reminiscence of Millet's Angelus.* The title *Isle of the Dead* was first applied to the painting by Böcklin's art dealer and was the name under which Dali must have known the painting. His inclusion of "atavistic references" to the idea of death in two works which derive their *raison d'être* from the violent eroticism of Dali's paranoiac-critical interpretation of Millet's *Angelus* suggests a reference to the Surrealist preoccupation with the essential and cyclical relationship between *Eros* and *Thanatos.* According to the paranoiac-critical method, that which is past, dead and present only as fossilized remnants, may be manifested as simulacra. The extent to which Dali depends on the work of other painters and writers for his themes and imagery indicates that the quality of his self-induced delirium is far from self-sustaining. The works which appear most bizarre after 1933, in fact, all have pictorial sources.

In 1935, in his *The Angelus of Gala* (Fig. 62) Dali returned to a more literal presentation of Millet's imagery. Here the imagery of Gala seated on a wooden block, her back to the spectator, confronts a frontal simulacrum of herself seated on a wheelbarrow. Behind the ghostly figure a painting of *The Angelus* hangs on the wall. But now the peasant couple are shown seated on an elongated wheelbarrow with heads bent and hands clasped, their poses echoing those of the two representations of Gala. Dali explains "Die Unbeweglichkeit Galas, die Gala betrachtet, muss im Vordergrund stechen, um den tragischen Mythos des Angelus von Millet anzukündigen."[39] Dali's own views concerning Gala's erotic powers are well known. Here he reinforces them by transferring to her Millet's imagery; by association she becomes the expectant female of Millet's painting.

In his study of Millet's *Angelus* Dali attempted to apply the methods of Freud to the interpretation of a single work of art. Freud used the method of psychoanalytic inquiry which he had develcped as a means of piecing together Leonardo's sexual development, finding evidence for his conclusions in the Master's works. Dali used the paranoiac-critical method which he had originated as a means of resolving through the Surrealist image the dialectical relationship between the images of the mind and those of the visually perceived world to explain the strange power of Millet's painting. But their results are very different. Freud concludes his study by confessing his own hesitations about the results of his attempt. He indicates that the results of any biographical psychoanalysis rest largely on the completeness of the material available to the analyst:

> Where such an undertaking does not provide any certain results—and this is perhaps so in Leonardo's case—the blame rests not with the faulty or inadequate methods of psycho-analysis, but with the uncertainty and fragmentary nature of the material relating to him which tradition makes available.[40]

Freud's methodological errors have already been pointed out, but although the conclusions he reached regarding Leonardo are inadmissable from an art historical point of view and the work remains almost completely speculative, Freud makes clear distinctions between the analysis of paintings and that of their creators. The Freudian method, dependent upon the motive forces of the mind and their subsequent transformations and developments uses works of art in the same way that it uses dreams; as symbolic recordings of mental processes. Dali, on the other hand, all but ignores Millet's motivations in his attempt to imbue the painting with a psychological life of its own. The result is the projection of his own fantasies, rather than those of the original painter, upon the work of art. *Le Mythe tragique de l'Angelus of Millet* ultimately says a great deal about Dali's method of working; almost nothing which can in any way be verified about the original work. His speculations are interesting, touching as they do upon an area of investigation into visual imagery which would later be exploited by segments of the advertising world.[41] Dali quickly transferred his energy from the analysis of Millet's painting to the creating of new images which through their associations with the original would hopefully succeed in conveying a similar erotic message to the spectator. But the supposedly erotic content of these images is either inaccessible through formal analysis and lost without Dali's accompanying verbal explication, as in the case of the *Archaeological Reminiscence of Millet's Angelus,* or expressed by means of a clichéd and superficial Freudian symbolism, as in the case of *The Architectonic Angelus.* Perhaps no Surrealist painter has written so exhaustively about his own works as Dali; perhaps no Surrealist painting has suffered more from an almost completely literary or descriptive content. Upon first glance the works retain their power to shock through their bizarre imagery and often explicit sexual content.

But any subsequent analysis reveals them as mere excuses for the continuing elaboration of the "Dalinian cult."

It remains to examine Dali's particular role as a myth maker. In order to exist as myth rather than a purely narrative recounting of some event a story traditionally had to explain some practice, belief, institution or natural phenomenon. Any myth has always had the additional function of serving to *unite a group* around some belief. Dali's *Mythe tragique de l'Angelus of Millet* provided a symbolic structure through which the paranoiac-critical method could be communicated. Dali found support for his attempt to mythologize the paranoiac-critical method through the images of Millet's *Angelus* in his belief that the method could be used to explain the appeal of a diverse group of paintings:

> L'histoire de l'art est donc spécialment à refaire d'après la méthode de 'l'activité paranoiaque-critique'; d'après cette méthode, des tableaux aussi differénts, apparement, que la 'Joconde,' 'L'Angelus' de Millet et 'L'Embarquement pour Cythère' de Watteau, représenteraient exactement le même suject voudraient dire exactement la même chose.[42]

The problem is, of course, that these works represent "exactement le même sujet" only for Dali and only by virtue of the imposition of a preconceived and very limited analytical model on their pictorial imagery. It is possible, on the other hand, that Dali's method could equally well be applied to any number of other works with the same result and, on the other, that another person using the same method would arrive at a very different conclusion. The highly idiosyncratic nature of Dali's paranoiac-critical method precludes the extension of his mythologizing to a larger public. Surrealism's sense of community, the idea of a collective imagination which found poetic and pictorial expression in collectively produced poems and *cadavres exquis,* drew the group naturally toward the device of myth construction. But although the paranoiac-critical method was widely extolled by other Surrealists when Dali first joined the movement in 1929 and did in fact help impel Surrealism toward a more conscious re-evaluation of the role of the unconscious during the early 1930's the method remained quite specifically Dali's. Breton and Eluard, in *L'Immaculée Conception* (1930) had simulated various aberrant mental states in an attempt to enrich their literary productions but the experiments were subsequently abandoned. Only Dali attempted to codify one such method, and the results of this codification are readily apparent in the repetitiveness of his pictorial imagery after 1932. Thus the tragic myth of *The Angelus* of Millet remained largely a private myth, inacessible except through Dali himself.

The Love Myths

Gradiva:
The Metamorphosis of the Surrealist Muse

Just imagine my joy when, after being alone so long, I saw today in the Vatican a dear familiar face! The recognition was one-sided, however, for it was the 'Gradiva,' high up on a wall.

Freud, letter to Martha Freud

The most concentrated expression of the Surrealist cult of love is found in the image of Gradiva, drawn from Freud and frequently recurring in the paintings and writings of Breton, Masson, Dali, Eluard and others.[1] To these artists she became the Surrealist muse, the incarnation of Breton's collective myth.

When Masson rejoined the Surrealist circle at the end of 1937 his interests in myth coincided with those of other members of the group. Several months later he began work on a major painting on the theme of *Gradiva* (Fig. 63), deriving his composition from an unsuccessful painting of the previous year entitled *Pygmalion* (Fig. 20).

The painting depicts a huge woman, half-flesh, half-marble, sprawled on a marble plinth in an attitude that hovers between sleep and death. The base on which she sits crumbles beneath her sandaled, marble foot and her splayed legs reveal a raw beefsteak and a gaping shell-like vagina. A volcano is in eruption in the distance to the right of the figure; to her left a rift in the wall reveals a dark abyss. A vertical strip of panelling suggests the figure's division but the two halves are visually united by the repetition of marble and fleshy leg and the bees which swarm over the right knee, their curved pattern of flight reflecting the arc of the marble arm which, on the left, encircles the head. The entire painting is bathed in a flickering reddish light intensified in a bed of red poppies growing at the base of the wall.

The image of Gradiva derived originally from a short novel by Wilhelm Jensen entitled *Gradiva: ein pompejanisches Phantasiestück* (1903).[2] Jensen's novel drew on a Classical Greek relief of a young woman, a cast of which he had seen in a Munich museum.[3] The original relief is in the Museo Chiaramonti in Rome (Fig. 64)[4] and was the object of a trip to the Vatican by Freud in 1907. The novel concerns a young archaeologist, Norbert Hanold, who falls in love with a plaster cast of this same relief. He calls her Gradiva, "the girl splendid in walking," a feminine equivalent of the epithet accorded by the "ancient poets"[5] to Mars Gradivus, the magnificent god of war. Her unusual gait captivates Hanold, and he notes particularly the perpendicular position of one foot; his fantasies about her become delusions and he dreams that he witnesses her death in the eruption of Vesuvius in 79 A.D. Accepting the dream as fact, Hanold is drawn to Pompeii by the power of the delusion, meeting there a woman who closely resembles his beloved relief. He encounters her three times and each meeting reinforces his belief that she is the spirit of his lost love, freed from the grave and allowed to wander through the streets of Pompeii each day at noon. Recognizing his mental state the girl manages to effect his cure. She then reveals herself as a childhood playmate, Zoe Bertgang, whom the young man had completely forgotten but who still lived near him in Hamburg. Hanold's amorous feelings, previously repressed and able to find expression only through his devotion to archaeology, are restored to their rightful place and the inevitable happy ending ensues.

Jensen's third-rate fiction might quickly and deservedly have faded into obscurity had not the Swiss analyst Carl Jung read it shortly after publication. Although Jung and Freud had not met at the time, Jung had read *The Interpretation of Dreams* and in 1906 began a correspondence with Freud which lasted for nearly a decade. In a letter of 1906[6] he recommended Jensen's *Gradiva* to Freud who became interested in the idea of analyzing dreams that have never been dreamed—dreams invented by an imaginative author and ascribed to fictitious characters in the course of a story. The result was Freud's *Der Wahn und die Träume in W. Jensen's Gradiva* (1907),[7] his first work devoted to literary analysis. Freud, who had visited Pompeii and climbed Vesuvius in September, 1902,[8] was fascinated by the analogy between the historical fate of the city (its burial and subsequent excavation) and the psychic mechanism which he himself had uncovered—burial by repression and excavation by analysis.[9] Subjecting the novel to the psychoanalytical method, Freud discovered that the laws of the unconscious applicable to a patient's behavior were manifested in the conscious actions of Jensen's characters.

Hanold's anxiety dream, the dream in which he saw Gradiva perish, expanded his fantasy about the existence and death of this girl into a delusion in which their life in ancient Pompeii is equated with Hanold's repressed memories of his childhood friendship. Meeting Zoe/Gradiva in Pompeii, he incorporates her into the delusion and, intuitively accepting her role in the fantasy, she manages to lead him back from a distorted reality. She thereby cured him.[10]

The delusion, characterized by Freud as a condition which produces no direct effect on the body and is manifested only in delusions that influence action, represents the struggle between Hanold's repressed erotic feelings for his childhood friend and the strength of the forces repressing them. In this way the potential strength of repressed passion is demonstrated. Despite its dynamic intensity it is unable to enter consciousness. Hanold, therefore, unconsciously transfers his amorous feelings for Zoe to the marble relief and, through the intervention of the living woman, is brought back to reality by a circuitous but unconsciously logical path.

Freud beautifully reveals the different economy of the unconscious, its relationship to conscious action, and the role played by dream in this nexus. He concludes that both scientist and artist arrive ultimately at the same understanding of the unconscious; one proceeds through the conscious observation of abnormal mental processes in others, the other directs his attention to his own unconscious and gives it artistic expression. The Surrealists were quick to seize on Freud's conclusion that science and art confirm rather than contradict one another in their explication of the unconscious. They found in Freud's essay an explicit justification for their own attempt to determine the tortuous relationship between artistic expression and the unconscious. Freud's *Gradiva* was a significant guide during the 1930's.[11] Breton recognized that the imagination provided the key through which the artist could unlock and give artistic expression to the mind's recesses and he integrated Freud's conclusion into his own study of the dream, *Les Vases communicants.*[12]

Freud's essay furnished many of the themes of Surrealism's second decade: the myth of love, the primacy of desire, the mechanism of repression and the dynamism of the repressed. But their explication of the unconscious could not be unmediated. Only the artistic symbol could provide the necessary link between the real and the surreal. The image of Gradiva became such a symbolic mediator and it is in this guise that she appears in Surrealist paintings.

The first representations of the image, in two drawings of 1930 entitled *Gradiva* and *Andromeda* (Figs. 68 and 65),[13] in a painting of the same subject the following year[14] and in *The Invisible Man,* 1929-33 (Fig. 66), coincide significantly with Dali's initiation into the Surrealist movement.

That the figure of Gradiva, first used by Dali, was immediately taken up by other Surrealists is no accident. Rather, it reflects a developing predisposition toward the Freudian explanation of the sources of artistic creativity.[15] The crisis of 1929 and subsequent expulsions and additions to the Surrealist group had moved Surrealism to an increased reliance on myth construction. Mythology released them from the constrictions of an order based on space-time; a mythology employing specific pictorial symbols fleshed out the abstractions of Breton's theorizing. The techniques used by the group during these years—the paranoiac-critical method, the manufacture of objects functioning symbolically, the simulation of mental diseases, the automatic message and the analysis of the interpenetrating states of dream and waking—were means of objectifying desire, psychological devices which would enable the mind to effect the necessary synthesis between contradictory states of being. It was Freud who had first demonstrated the dynamism of unfulfilled desire, projected individually as dream, collectively as myth. This is precisely the point of Breton's exegesis of the myth of Venus which he saw as an allegory of surreal love revealed to the everyday world.[16] For the goddess Venus the Surrealists substituted the muse Gradiva, she who could help the artist penetrate the barrier between the real and the surreal, she whose face was the "perceur de murailles."[17]

Her dual nature is most fully explored in Dali's works where she is both corporeal reality (Zoe/life) and mythical woman (Gradiva). For more than thirty years Dali equated his wife Gala with the Gradiva figure, substituting the living woman for Zoe Bertgang, "the double of the mythological image of Gradiva."[18] and transferring to her the qualities ascribed by Jensen and Freud to this bimorph. Of his *Three Apparitions of the Visage of Gala*, 1947 (Fig. 67), he suggested: "Gala is trinity. She is Gradiva the woman who advances. She is, according to Paul Eluard, 'the woman whose glance pierces walls.' " The painting derives its composition from Dali's 1929 work, *Accomodations of Desire*,[19] and like its predecessor, depicts rocks bearing hallucinatory figures on the barren beach at Cadagues. Gala's classicizing face appears three times, the petrified representations becoming more life-like as they emerge from the background. Gradiva's dual nature is rendered by the depiction of Gala first as a living being and then as a shade. But if Gala is Gradiva, Gradiva is also Gala and Dali's representations of the mythical woman, for example his *Gradiva* of 1930 (Fig. 68), are recognizable as portraits of Gala.

Dali personalizes the image of Gradiva and identifies her with the specific image of Gala; other Surrealists turned to the devices of classical mythology to suggest that their image belonged to another realm of being. According to Breton's theory of immanence, surreality resides in reality itself and is perceived through the objects of the real world.[20] Myth became one means of suggesting the integral relationship between the particular and the universal. Sometimes called "the Surrealist muse,"[21] Gala had originally been married to Eluard and is the object of his love poetry, "à Gala ce livre sans fin," he wrote in 1926, dedicating to her his newly published volume *L'Amour la poésie*.[22] Eluard had re-named her Gala and Dali referred to her as Galatea,[23] the ivory maiden brought to life by Aphrodite in response to the prayers of the sculptor Pygmalion. This mythical sculptor is a figure widely used by the Surrealists during these years and resembles the Gradiva theme in its blurring of the distinction between life and death, the animate and the inanimate.[24] The intensity of Pygmalion's love for his creation moved Aphrodite to intercede and transform the image into flesh and blood. The Surrealists, fascinated by the relationship between image and reality, immediately recognized the analogy between the legend and Hanold's marble relief. Like Gradiva, Pygmalion represented the unique potency of amorous love.

For the Surrealists, the presence of woman is proof of man's redemption and it is she who gives life meaning by her power to "mediate between man and the marvellous."[25] In Dali's eyes the initial meeting with Gala in Cadagues in 1929 was the culmination of a life-long pursuit of an ephemeral fantasy the images of which now "mingled in the indestructible amalgam of a single and unique love-being. . .[26] She (Gala) was destined to be my Gradiva, 'she who advances,' my victory, my wife. But for this she had to cure me, and she did cure me!"[27] Jensen's Zoe-Gradiva had effected Hanold's psychological cure: Dali credited Gala with saving him from the paralyzing attacks of hysterical laughter from which he was suffering when they met, enabling him to resume painting and achieve his "Surrealist glory."[28] Moreover, the fact that the "cure" was brought about solely through the power of a woman's love identified this particular aspect of the feminine psyche as the most powerful. Jensen's Gradiva, "the girl splendid in walking," became Breton's and Dali's "celle qui avance," a timeless being who leads the artist in his unceasing attempt to glimpse what lies ahead, beyond the real.[29]

Freud had indirectly suggested a second attribute of Gradiva. She differed from the other inhabitants of Pompeii in that she was not buried. She not only rose from the dead (marble made flesh), but rose therapeutically into Hanold's consciousness. His childhood love was no longer repressed; the muse was freed and again effective.

Although Gala was the best known of these muses, there were others. Breton, when he opened his Surrealist gallery on the Rue de Seine in 1937 (Fig. 69), inscribed their names on the facade. He later acknowledged that the gallery, which specialized in Surrealist and primitive art, had rescued him in a moment of extreme financial privation. In memory of Jensen's salvatory heroine he gave the name Gradiva to the gallery.[30] Above its glass doors, designed by Marcel Duchamp, as the silhouette of a conjoined man and woman,[31] her name was spelled out above those of other Surrealist "women" of the decade. The word *comme,* used as a copulative, subsumes among others, Gisèle Prassinos, the fourteen year old poetess adopted by the group in 1934; Dora Maar, Man Ray's photographer companion; Alice Paalen, the Surrealist poet and member of the group from 1935; and Violette Nozières, a young French girl condemned to death for poisoning her parents under bizarre circumstances and extolled by the Surrealists as a modern Electra.[32]

The image of Gradiva is not confined to the traditional concept of the muse. Although she appears as an isolated figure in several of Dali's drawings (Figs. 65 and 68), she also functions as a uniquely powerful erotic symbol in several of his most important works of these years, among them *The Invisible*

Man, 1929-33 (Fig. 66) and the finely executed drawing *Gradiva, William Tell and the Bureaucrat*, 1932 (Fig. 70). Each of these works pursues Dali's paranoiac-critical method. The attempt at a visual crystallization of unconscious images required by the method was, for Breton and Dali, largely dependent on the stimulus of desire.[33] The initial impulse was released by an external object, most frequently woman, the feminine repository of the love impulse closely associated if not identical with desire. The results of that stimulus are then projected onto her. As Freud had demonstrated, it was repressed memories and current fantasies of Zoe/Gradiva which stimulated Hanold into the expression of his delusion by awakening in him a desire to locate his repressed love-object. And it was this image which symbolized for the Surrealists the same essential stimulus.

She appears in *The Invisible Man* (Fig. 66) no longer the Surrealist symbol in isolation, but rather as part of that landscape each figure of which specifically serves, as Freud had generally elucidated, to release repressed eroticism. The man's torso, created from natural forms by erotically stimulated delirium as part of the paranoiac's imposition of the ego's desires on the natural world, is cradled by three erotic symbols: the vaginal heart with its stylized crown of thorns, the onanistic motif connecting the paranoiac figure with the artist's personal symbol of the lion, and the dual image of Gradiva in the right middle ground, the personification of desire. The deep perspective and sharply delineated shadows derive from de Chirico whose influence on Dali at this time has been noted by both Soby and Rubin.[34] Although the various images which surround the central figure appear consistently in a number of other works, the composition itself suggests this work's meaning. The painting is divided into three vertical registers by the alternation of light and dark forms; the central third is then bisected by the meeting of the pearl-encrusted hands and the stylized testes. An onanistic cycle connects the artist, depicted as a lion in the foreground, with the paranoiac figure above. The "invisible man" becomes visible through an imposition of erotic fantasy on the landscape of the mind. But the open and receptive heart attests to the fact that the onanistic stimulus is not exclusively genital. Likewise, the two Gradivas,[35] recognizable as depictions of Gala, define the delusion's origin as clearly as does the vaginal heart.

The juxtaposition of the "invisible man" and the Gala/Gradiva figures may also have an external reference. Dali worked simultaneously on this painting and *La Femme Visible*, a written account of his current method of painting dedicated to Gala who was, for him, the visible woman.[36] The relationship between eroticism and the paranoiac-critical method is depicted in both with unmistakable reference to their Freudian origin and to the implications of the Gradiva motif.

Dali's symbolic iconography is, however, limited by the fact that it never transcends its personal origins. It is ultimately restricted to a limited and repetitive set of symbols the meaning of which is nonetheless consistent within the body of his work. When Gradiva next appears in *Gradiva, William Tell and the Bureaucrat* (Fig. 70), she is again the mythical female caressed and held against the breast of William Tell, Dali's persistent symbol of repressive authority.

In 1934 Breton reiterated Surrealism's desire to deepen the foundations of the real, to bring about a greater consciousness of the world perceived by the senses and to present interior and exterior reality as two fluid states in the process of unification. The image of Gradiva became the symbolic expression of this unification, the being who existed in Jensen's novel and Freud's study both as dream image and corporeal being, belonging to the worlds of death and life, madness and sanity, fantasy and reality. Limited neither by space nor time, she participated in some form in each of these states but was bound by none of them. It is hardly surprising, therefore, that the projection of desire onto actual objects, the concrete realization of the images of dreams, the Surrealist *objet* so favored during this decade, would also find expression in the figure of Gradiva. The Surrealist object, existing as an image in the mind and as a phenomenal body, effected a final synthesis of the Surrealist dialectic. In 1937 Breton's essay "Gradiva" and Dali's Freudian analysis of the Catalan fairy-tale "The Wax Mannikin with the Sugar Nose,"[37] explained the theoretical basis of Surrealist objects as the ultimate objectification of desire. The heroine of Dali's tale is saved from death at the King's hand by substituting a wax image of herself. Dali explains:

> The wax mannikin with the sugar nose, then, is only an 'object-being' of delirium, invented by the passion of one of those women who, like the heroine of the tale, like Gradiva, or like Gala, is able, by virtue of the skillful simulacrum of their love, to illuminate moral darkness with the sharp lucidity of 'living madmen.' For me the great problem of madness and of lucidity was that of the limits between the Galuchka of my false memories, who had become chimerical and dead a hundred times through my subconscious pulsions and my desire for utter solitude, and the real Gala whose corporeality it was impossible for me to resolve in the pathological aberration of my spirit. And it is these very limits, which were peculiar to me, which are defined with a materialized symbolism in the form of a veritable 'surrealist object' in the tale I have just told—where the wax mannikin ends, where the sugar-nose begins, where Gradiva ends and where Zoe Bertrand (sic) begins in Jensen's Delirium and Dreams.[38]

This final projection of desire onto things and objects became a means of effecting the link between subjective and objective. It is the idea of love, and its erotic corollary, desire, which enables the mind to give form to formless psychic phenomena. Just as the dream is always the expression of unfulfilled desire, so the Surrealist object is the projection of these same desires onto actual objects. It is in this final guise as Surrealist objects that the Gradiva-like mannikins created by Ernst, Arp, Tanguy, Man Ray, Masson, Duchamp, Dali, and Miro (Fig. 71) stood on "la rue surréaliste" at the entrance to the Paris International

Surrealist Exposition in 1938, desirable simulacra of women waiting to usher the visitor into the surreal universe.

Dali was willing to accept Freud's mechanistic schema of cause and effect (repression: release: sterility: creativity) thereby reducing Hanold's delusion to repressed *personal* sexuality, but it was Masson who explored the *social* implications of the Gradiva theme.

His representation depicts the climax of Hanold's dream, August 24, 79 A.D. The heavens are black with smoke and the city bathed in a blood-red light. As Hanold stands at the edge of the Forum he sees Gradiva a short distance ahead of him. Appearing not to notice the impending destruction she walks across the flagstones of the Forum to the Temple of Apollo where, ignoring his cry of warning, she mounts the steps and sits down. She assumes the appearance of a marble statue and, calmly submitting to her fate, is soon obscured by the falling ashes. On one level Masson's iconography is drawn directly from Jensen: he reproduces the vertical position of Gradiva's foot described in the novel, the rift in the wall through which Hanold believed she returned each day to the grave, the poppies growing in the courtyards of excavated Pompeiian houses, the tomb and the volcano.

But the painting is more than a visual translation of its literary source. Subtle adaptations of the text in the form and placement of images suggest other levels of meaning. The rift in the wall becomes a rifle with fixed bayonet, an emblem of modern warfare intensified by the poppies growing underneath. Thus Jensen's "path to the tomb" became, for Masson, war itself. Implicit in the painting is the concept of holocaustal destruction, the sources of which may be natural: the volcano, or human: war. Gradiva, the most prominent element, suffers both of these destructive forces.

This compression of images, the type of condensation found in dream imagery, contributes to the painting's spatial dislocation. The background of painted panelling suggests the interior of a Pompeiian house, but the tomb on which Gradiva rests, the growing poppies and the volcano confuse the distinction between interior and exterior.

The figure of Gradiva is finally the mythological heroine who connects the cycle of myths that relate the development of Greek mythology from the Dionysos cults to the encounter of Theseus and the minotaur at the heart of the Cretan labyrinth. Masson's *Gradiva* is placed against a backdrop of painted panelling that replicates that of the Villa of the Mysteries at Pompeii, devoted to the secret rites and rituals of the Dionysiac cult. Her pose, with head flung back and encircled with bent arms, derives from representations of the sleeping Ariadne found at Pompeii as well as in a series of later representations, among them Poussin's wax copy of the famous Vatican *Sleeping Ariadne,* which had been in the Louvre since 1855, and de Chirico's *The Afternoon of Ariadne*

(1913) which was reproduced in the sixth issue of *La Revolution surréaliste* in 1926.[39] Ariadne, the wife of Dionysos after her abandonment by Theseus on the island of Naxos, is also the mistress of the labyrinth who, outside Crete, sometimes takes the form of the Great Goddess of Love. The mystery rites in Minoan Crete were celebrated with the early rising of Sirius in connection with honey, wine and light. In Masson's representation the key image of death and rebirth is the volcanic fire with its implications of sexuality and impregnation, the ancient mystery rites took place in the glow of the cult fire which emerged from a secret cave. Kerenyi relates that, at Knossos:

> the way to the 'mistress of the labyrinth' and back again was danced publicly in a certain dance ground. The mistress was at the center of the true labyrinth, the underworld; she bore a mysterious son and conferred the hope of a return to the light.[40]

Moreover, Dionysos was said to have invented honey and with representations associated with his cult bees figure prominently.[41] In Masson's *Gradiva* they swarm toward the honey that streams from her breast. There Rhea gave birth to Zeus. At a certain time each year a great fiery glow is seen emerging from the cave. According to the myth, this occurs when the blood remaining from the birth of Zeus runs over. The cave is inhabited by sacred bees, the nurses of Zeus. The central image in the *Gradiva* figure is a large beefsteak. The stripped animal flesh suggests both the *abattoir* which Bataille had viewed as the modern inheritor of the ancient sacrificial spot, and the ancient mystery rites associated with Dionysos and rebirth. According to Vergil, Aristaios sacrificed four bulls and four cows. He let the bodies lie for nine days; then bees swarmed from the entrails which had become liquid. It is the awakening of bees from a dead animal that signals the beginning of the rites of fertility and rebirth.

The poppies, which Masson substitutes for the asphodel mentioned in Jensen's story, carry significance as the symbolic images of dream and vision dating back as far as the ancient rites. Female idols bearing poppy heads as head ornaments and attributes and dating from the late Minoan period have been found at Gazi near Heraklion while inscriptions on clay tablets also attest to the cultivation of poppies on Crete during the late Minoan period. Kerenyi concludes from this evidence that: "It may be presumed that toward the end of the late Minoan period, opium stimulated the visionary faculty and aroused visions which had earlier been obtained without opium."[42] Recognizing the significance of the ancient goddess Ariadne, Masson transfers her attributes and significance to the Surrealist goddess *Gradiva*.

Masson's and Dali's paintings, Breton's essay and Freud's paper all use the Gradiva theme as a myth of metamorphosis—from death to life, from dream to wakefulness, from the unconscious to the conscious, from the mundane to the transcendental. The iconographic elements of the theme persisted throughout the 1930's. Pompeii, Freud's image of repression, appeared in Dali's *Dream of Venus,* an underwater exhibit prepared for the 1939 New York World's Fair. Looking through glass walls into large tanks, the visitor watched a series of marine tableaux and Surrealist objects. Living mermaids floated through the water against a background of ruined Pompeii while, in another section, Venus lay dreaming on a bed of glowing coals.[43]

From Leda to Loplop: Max Ernst's Muse

Max Ernst died the first of August 1914. He resuscitated the eleventh of November 1918 as a young man aspiring to become a magician and to find the myth of his time. Now and then he consulted the eagle who had hatched the egg of his pre-natal life. You may find the bird's advices in his work.

Max Ernst, *Beyond Painting*, 1948

In 1930 Max Ernst announced his first visit from Loplop, the "Superior of the Birds": ". . . Fantôme particulier d'une fidelité modèle, attaché à ma personne. Il me presenta un coeur en cage, la mer en cage, deux petales, trois feuilles, une fleur et une jeune fille."[1] A series of collages on the theme of *Loplop Introduces* (Figs. 86-89) followed the announcement. Neither the technique of collage nor the presence of bird images were new in Ernst's art at this time and the image of a bird called Loplop had appeared through the celebrated collage novel *La Femme 100 têtes* published the previous year.

Transformations in the psychological content of his bird images clearly mark each stage of Ernst's artistic life. His *Oedipus Rex* (1924) (Fig. 4) and *Two Children Menaced by a Nightingale* (1924) (Fig. 72) both mark the shift in attitude that characterizes his transition from Dada to the concerns of the Surrealist group which he joined in Paris in 1924. The latter work, with an overtly Freudian symbolism drawn from the *Interpretation of Dreams,* comes closest in Ernst's painting to illustrating the psychoanalyst's ideas. The work depicts the effect of a nightingale's appearance on two adolescent girls. A combination of painting and wood construction, it incorporates the sharp discontinuities in scale characteristic of Ernst's work during these years. The orthagonal wall and free standing arch in the distance are reminiscent of de Chirico's vast perspectives but the swinging hinged gate, the little wooden house with its enormous keyhole and the doorknob attached to the picture frame on the right destroy logical relationships in scale. Wall, gate, keyhole and frame reinforce the ideas of containment so prevalent in Ernst's work during these years.[2] As the nightingale, persistent image of male persuasiveness,[3] flies overhead one of the girls responds by collapsing on the ground, the other by attacking the intruder with a knife.[4] On the right a male figure "perches" on the roof of the house, protectively encircling a small female child with his arms. The nightingale seems to represent the symbolic incursion of sexual lust into the world of man, a "threat" from which the smaller child is protected by the encircling arms of the male figure.

At other times during the 1920's the bird serves as an emblematic signification of liberation or containment. The hieratic *Monument to the Birds* of 1927 (Fig. 73) suggests a Renaissance Ascension and the birds, neither at rest nor in flight, appear suspended against the sky. In another version of the same subject, several entwined birds rise heavenward with flapping wings, leaving below a roosting group.[5] The idea of the bird as an image of containment finds its counterpart in works like *Dove* of 1927 (Fig. 74), a collage in which a small delicate bird stares wistfully through the bars of its cage.

In 1929 the bird image merged with the idea of sight in a series of oval paintings called *The Interior of Sight* (Fig. 75) and Russell has suggested that here the egg is identified with the images fostered by the eye.[6] For Ernst, the interior of sight, the eye turned inward, rather than outward, is the metaphor for artistic creation; he notes in *Beyond Painting:*

> Max Ernst died the first of August 1914. He resuscitated the eleventh of November 1918 as a young man aspiring to become a magician and to find the myth of his time. Now and then he consulted the eagle who had hatched the egg of his pre-natal life. You may find the bird's advices in his work.[7]

The year 1929, marked by the publication of the collage novel *La Femme 100 têtes* and the appearance of the Bird Superior Loplop, stands out as the year in which the varied but anonymous birds which had nested, fought, teased and flown their way through Ernst's work of the 1920's begin to assume a single and articulated identity. But who is Loplop? What are the sources of Ernst's feathered friend and what role does the Bird Superior play in the work of the 1930's?

Described by the artist as his *alter ego,* the image of Loplop quickly assumed symbolic value as a herald of the unconscious sources of Ernst's imagery. The painter himself has written extensively on the origins of the image and, in an often quoted passage, traces the mythic figure to a childhood experience of 1906 in which he confused the death of a beloved pink cockatoo and the birth of a younger sister:

> Der Vogelobre Hornebom (Loplop). Ein Freund namens Hornebom, ein Kluger, buntgeschechter, treuer Vogel stirbt in der Nacht; ein Kind, das sechste in der Reihe, kommt in selbiger Nacht zum leben. Wirrwarr im Hirn des sonst sehr gesunden Junglings. Eine Art von Ausdehnungswahr, also ob die eben geborene Unschuld,

Schwester Loni, sich in ihrer Lebensgier des lieben Vogels Lebenssafte angeeignet hatte. Die Krise ist bald uberstander. Doch dauert in des Junglings Phantasie erne freiwillige–matinelle Vorstellungs–Vermegung von Menschen mit vogeln und anderen lebeweser, und dies spigelt sich wieder in den Emblenen seiner Kunst.[8]

The collages of *La Femme 100 têtes* (Figs. 76-78), with their accompanying verbal legends, visually fix a series of freely associated images and themes derived from the original experience and the succeeding hallucinations provided by it: the worlds of day and night, light and darkness, birth and death, suspended falling or flying figures (generally female), the eye, the egg, conception, torture, powerful and menacing male figures, little girls, nightmare, hallucination, violence and sexual confusion. The sexual nature of the experience was not lost on the adolescent Ernst though the fact that he was fifteen at the time has been often overlooked in later accounts and casts some doubts on the childhood innocence and ingenuousness with which he has surrounded the experience. His hallucinatory response to the parental sexual encounter which led to the birth of a sister becomes an essential ingredient in these collages, several of which refer to "Un Immaculée conception manqué." In one of these (Fig. 76) a woman crouches on a crib-like bed gazing fearfully toward a standing male figure while a child in the foreground turns away crying and a rabbit leaps across the room. Elsewhere (Fig. 77) the bearded image of the "père éternel" reaches through the bars of the cage that imprisons him while in the foreground, a young girl with one bared breast sits amidst a collection of books and other nursery objects and holds the mask-like head of an identical girl in her lap. In and out of these scenes flies the bird Loplop: image of mystery and night, of lust, scientific curiosity, and succour. Ernst's accompanying reference to "perturbation, ma soeur, la femme 100 têtes," "Loplop," and "L'Oeil sans yeux," reinforce the novel's origins in the sexual experiences, fantasies and hallucinations of his adolescence.

La Femme 100 têtes, unlike the earlier *Fiat Modes* collages of 1919 and the frottages of the *Histoire naturelle* (1927), derives its images from specific psychological sources. Its visual and verbal structure is far from random in spite of the apparent spontaneity and lack of logical development of the imagery. Underlying the apparently non-causal juxtapositions of image and image, and image and text, are an artistic self-consciousness and an adherence to Freud's theories regarding the consistency and structure of irrational mental processes. Yet its most concrete personnage, Loplop, remains its most elusive image. Only Ernst's identification of the bird as Loplop distinguishes it from the many bird images which had occupied the painter in the paintings and collages executed prior to 1929. Not until the series of collages entitled *Loplop Presents* (Figs. 86-89) is this bird physically differentiated from the other birds in his *oeuvre* and assigned a specific role in the painter's creative life.

Ernst has been identified with the development of two of Surrealism's most significant visual techniques—frottage and collage. Neither originated with him; both achieved new meaning and significance in his hands. Moreover both, though collage more strikingly than frottage, have close connections with Freud's writings on the structures of dream and the language of the unconscious. Unlike the collages of Braque and Picasso, essentially still-lifes incorporating bits of material from the studio world and worked upon by artistic sensibilities still committed to the creation of beauty, those of Ernst use photomechanical reproductions of the exterior world as a means of violating conventional ideas about the rational structure of that same world.

His accounts of the discovery of the techniques of collage and frottage are remarkably similar. In "An Informal Life of M.E." he relates the events leading to the first collages:

> One rainy day in 1919 in a town on the Rhine, my excited gaze is provoked by the pages of a printed catalogue. . . . Here I discover the elements of a figuration so remote that its very absurdity provokes in me a sudden intensification of my faculties of sight—an hallucinatory succession of contradictory images . . . superimposed upon each other with the persistence and rapidity characteristic of amorous memories and visions of somnolescence.[9]

The *Histoire naturelle* of 1927 contains the first results of Ernst's experiments with frottage. In his "Histoire d'une histoire naturelle" the painter relates that while trapped in a country inn one rainy summer day in 1925 he became obsessed with the texture of the well scrubbed wooden floor which at first reminded him of a childhood experience when, ill and feverish, he experienced a series of hallucinations while staring at a false mahogany panel; "oeil menaç ant, long ne, grosse tête de'oiseau à épaisse chevelure noir," etc.[10] The childhood experience had played the role of an optical provacateur and, in 1925, determined to explore the symbolism of this obsession and to strengthen his meditative and hallucinatory faculties, Ernst made a series of rubbings of the wooded boards. Staring intently at the drawings obtained in this way, "les parties sombres et les autres de douce penombre," he was astonished by the subtle intensification of his visionary faculties, ". . . de la succession hallucinante d'images contradictoires, se supreposant les unes aux autres avec le persistence et la rapidité qui sont propres aux souvenirs amoreux."[11]

From the day of his discovery of frottage, Ernst insisted that the role of the artist had become that of a spectator assisting at the birth of his works and he was quick to point out that this approach had clear historical antecedents. Some centuries earlier Leonardo da Vinci had noted:

> I will not refrain from setting among these precepts a new device for consideration which, although it may appear trivial and almost ludicrous, is nevertheless

of great utility in arousing the mind to various inventions. And this is that if you look at any walls spotted with various stains or with a mixture of different kinds of stones, if you are about to invent some scene you will be able to see in its a resemblance to various different landscapes adorned with mountains, rivers. . . . You will also be able to see divers combats and figures in quick movement, and strange expressions of faces, and outlandish costumes, and an infinite number of things which you can then reduce into separate and well conceived forms.[12]

He concluded his passage by remarking that, like the clanging of bells, these walls and stones were of a visual power strong enough to directly affect the imagination. Ernst, acknowledging his debt to Leonardo, introduced his "Histoire d'un histoire naturelle" with the words, "c'est comme le tintement de la cloche, que fait entendre ce qui'on imagine."[13]

Ernst had read the *Treatise on Painting* at least as early as 1912 when he was studying art history at Bonn. His *Histoire naturelle* contains a series of rubbings of natural objects—leaves, stones, wood, etc.—all of them subsequently elaborated into figurative drawings based on the suggestibility of the original textures. *Histoire naturelle* acknowledges Ernst's debt both to Leonardo, and his visual cataloguing of flora and fauna, and to Pliny whose detailed cataloguing of the natural world forms the conceptual basis of Ernst's own *Histoire*. In an entry dated August 10, 1925 (also the date of the alleged rainy day incident), Ernst makes note of an incident related by Vasari in which Botticelli had attacked the value of landscape paintings by asserting that the loveliest landscape could be obtained by merely throwing a paint soaked sponge against the wall. Leonardo responded, in a crucial passage cited by Ernst, that the role of the artist lay in consciously structuring the results of these and other chance gestures so that they might provoke certain associations in the viewer.

By the early 1930's Breton also had recognized the inherent "Surrealist value" of Leonardo's reflections on the stained wall. He suggests this source as a historical antecedent for the elaborate transmutations of reality currently being supplied by Dali's *paranoiac-critical* method. Breton concludes, however, that any two individuals, when confronted with the same wall, will interpret the visual phenomena differently, these differences deriving from the distinctive unconscious desires that each brings to the encounter.[14]

Ernst continued to stress the significance of Leonardo's remarks. In 1929 he played a small role in Bunuel's film, *L'Age d'or* and in one of the opening sequences he appears in the guise of a beggar making drawings on the walls of a hovel. In a conversation with Robert Lebel, the painter explained his interest in these textures: "J'étais donc de nouveau devant le fameux mur de Leonard de Vinci qui a joué un si grand role dans mes 'Visions de demisommeil.' "[15]

Leonardo's influence on Ernst was iconographic as well as theoretical and can be detected throughout the Surrealist work of the 1920's. *The Beautiful Gardner* of 1923, now destroyed,[16] and the *Sacra Conversazione* of 1921 refer to Renaissance themes common in the sixteenth century.

Both works contain standing female figures with a white dove perched on the upper thigh and partially obscuring the abdomen and pubic area. This joining of woman and bird occurs in a more exaggerated form in *La Parole* of 1921 (Fig. 79), a work in which the sexual associations are strengthened by the tight clasping of one of the bird heads between the upper thighs. The female figure emerges from a pod-like shell containing at its center, and between her legs, a single flower growing on a long stalk. In the background stands a bifurcated male figure, his sexual organs concealed or removed. This type of physical joining of bird and woman reappears on a page from *La Femme 100 têtes* identified by Ernst as "Loplop et la belle jardinière" (Fig. 78). Here a young girl (related perhaps to Ernst's "Perturbation, ma soeur"), her head totally obscured by the large bird that perches on her shoulder, walks in front of a small pond in an enclosed conservatory. Luxuriant foliage all but obliterates the tiny figures of a young man and woman that cross a miniature bridge in the background.

The intermediary stage between the bird images of the 1920's and the image of Loplop as it appears in the collages of the *Loplop Presents* series is provided by several drawings of 1929 entitled *Human Figure* (Figs. 81-82). In one of these (Fig. 81) a bird's head emerges from the center of an ornate flower. Leaves attached to the base of the flower form a dancer's skirt from which two human-like legs and feet project. The small drawing was then pasted onto a larger sheet of paper overlapping a pencil drawing of a vaguely anthropomorphic bird, greatly simplified and formally related to the flower/bird image. Essential to the series of *Human Figure* drawings is the anthropomorphic bird and the use of a small framed image placed in front of another, larger, figure. The two images—the presenting figure and the interior framed image—then become the subject of the whole in a manner reminiscent of Magritte's "paintings within paintings" of the 1930's.[17] Leonora Carrington has brilliantly characterized Ernst's metamorphosis from man to bird, writing:

> The bird superior ties fear to the flames of the fire by her tail and dips his feathered arms in the colour. Each feather immediately begins to paint a different image with the rapidity of a shriek. . . . The Bird Superior, with all his feathers painting different images at once, moves slowly around the room evoking trees and plants out of the furniture.[18]

When the first collages of the *Loplop Introduces* series appeared the following year Ernst retained the device of organizing images within images, images which are then "presented" by the Bird Superior; the painter recalls that the Bird Superior, "my private phantom," presented the artist with "a heart in a cage, the sea in a cage, two petals, three leaves, a flower and a young girl."[19] In *Loplop Introduces a Young Girl* (Fig. 83) the central image is a painting on plaster. A playful anthropomorphic bird, complete with gold bow tie, holds a rectangular frame within which are contained metal, string, and stone objects surrounding the medallion of a young girl's profile.

The work represents a condensation of images and ideas found in earlier collages, particularly those of *La Femme 100 têtes* concerning "Perturbation, ma soeur" as well as the derivation of images from the objects of the natural world and direct reference to Leonardo's famous plaster wall, the source of much of Ernst's hallucinatory imagery in the collages and the frottages. Since the drawings obtained by frottage yield naturally to a series of suggested images and transformations, the technique functions in much the same way as automatic writing and drawing. The figurative imagery of the collages, stripped of logical connections, brings the imagery into the realm of Freudian dream image with its reliance on displacement, condensation and alterations of the sense of time and space. The suspension of reason, the reliance on chance, and the negation of aesthetic considerations identify both frottage and collage as visual realizations of current Surrealist explorations in literature and the function of language. Ernst's account of the origins of both bear striking resemblances to the model for artistic creation presented by Freud—a model in which an actual experience triggers an old memory that may be elaborated into artistic form through the mechanism of wish fulfillment. Freud first presented the model in "Creative Writers (Poets) and Daydreaming" (1908), but it received its fullest treatment in the celebrated study of Leonardo da Vinci published in 1910.[20] In that work a childhood memory/fantasy recorded in one of Leonardo's notebooks is elaborated by Freud into the cornerstone on which rest both that artist's adult sexuality and his artistic genius.

In a 1942 article entitled "The Legendary Life of Max Ernst Preceded By a Brief Discussion of the Need for a New Myth," Breton acknowledged Freud: "The vulture whose unsuspected presence in Leonardo's *Virgin of the Rocks* has been detected, pursued its own course (it was already, Loplop in the Fifteenth Century)."[21] Breton's remark referred to a widely circulated theory, first advanced by Freud's follower Otto Pfister, that the form of a vulture might be discerned in Mary's blue robe in the Louvre version of Leonardo's *St. Anne With the Virgin* (c. 1483) (Fig. 84). According to Pfister, the bird's head appears on the left; toward the right the robe is stretched into the form of a vulture's tail, ending in the child's mouth.[22] Freud acknowledged this discovery by his analyst-disciple as an unexpected confirmation of his own explanation of the significance of this childhood memory (fantasy) on which he based his analysis of Leonardo's adult sexuality and artistic genius: "The key to all of Leonardo's accomplishments and misfortunes lies hidden in the infantile fantasy about the vulture."[23]

Freud's own analysis of Leonardo was motivated by his reading of Dimitri Merejkowski's fanciful *Romance of Leonardo da Vinci* which based the painter's life-long obsession with flying in a childhood memory related in one of the painter's notebooks:

> I recall as one of my earliest memories that while I was in my cradle a vulture
> came down to me, and opened my mouth with its tail, and struck me many times
> with its tail across my lips, as though to signify that all life long I would speak of
> wings.[24]

Freud seized upon the anecdote, applying to it the same method he had developed for explicating the symbolic content of dreams. Aware that paintings themselves cannot be psychoanalyzed he based his explication of Leonardo's psychological make-up, and ultimately his adult sexuality, on this single event. As several of Freud's critics have noted, the study contains a number of serious methodological errors, not the least of which was Freud's own mistranslation of the original passage, turning Leonardo's kite into the vulture whose presence in the unconscious he confirms by a personal dream in which he witnesses the death of his mother, her body attended by a group of vulture-headed figures.[25] Although his subsequent attempt to elucidate the mother symbolism of the vulture and relate it to the vulture-headed deity Mut, an Egyptian mother goddess who was fertilized not by a male but by the wind is demonstrably erroneous, it is the image of the vulture which enters Surrealist art, reflected in Breton's remark about Loplop and Dali's later analysis of the theme of St. George; "the vulture, according to the Egyptians and Freud, represents my mother's portrait."[26]

Freud's *Leonardo,* with its elaboration of a childhood experience into important material for the mature artist, provided the psychological model for Ernst's accounts of his discoveries of both frottage and collage. And it was to Leonardo's art that Ernst looked for a pictorial source for Loplop, the image to which accrued an increasingly powerful symbolic and psychological content during the 1930's. Leonardo's lost *Leda and the Swan,* well known to Ernst through reproductions, provided the artistic parentage for his Loplop. The Spiridon copy of Leonardo's *Leda and the Swan* (Fig. 85) is perhaps closest in physical form to the bird Loplop, as it appears in early representations of the *Loplop Presents* collages (Figs. 86-89). The two birds—one Renaissance, the other Surrealist—share long necks, attenuated and apparently mobile beaks and, most striking, the tufted crown of hair that lends both images a playful air. Ernst's Loplop undergoes several transformations in the course of its history, tending toward the increasingly linear and schematic. Yet even at its most stylized (Fig. 89), Ernst retained the crucial identifying characteristics that link his image with Leonardo's winged Zeus—the long beak and the short tufted crest.

Freud had overlooked the *Leda* when, applying his own theories of sublimation to Leonardo, he remarked on the absence of erotic works among Leonardo's paintings. The theme, however, reemerged in the Renaissance as one of the most powerful erotic subjects handed down from Classical antiquity. In the most common version of the ancient myth the god Zeus came to Leda, wife of King Tyndareus, in the form of a great white swan. The result of their coupling

was an egg from which hatched Helen and the twins Castor and Poly-
deuces.

Ernst's *Loplop Presents* collages acknowledge the myth's generative content (in Leonardo's version Leda and the Swan are surrounded by lush and
diverse plant forms and the earth itself appears to be in bloom). In two more
representations of the theme (Figs. 86-87) Ernst collages color engravings, paper
and pencil and crayon fragments over the mid-section of a bird/man. In the
first of these (Fig. 86) leaf and plant forms assume the contours of birds and
female legs. The images are the images of Ernst's paintings of these years—
animal and vegetal forms which evoke the forest landscapes that provided a
natural setting for his birds and fantastic creatures. In the Loplop series, Ernst
strips the images of their original pictorial contexts. Presented in isolated juxtapositions they become evocations of the painter's life and work. Through his
overlaid drawings, and the application of additional sheets of paper, Ernst
effectively confuses the spatial relationships between foreground and background, drawing and collage.

In his description of Loplop's sudden appearance in 1929 Ernst had noted
that the Bird Superior presented to him the fragments of the natural world that
became the basis of the *Loplop Presents* collages. Having assimilated Leonardo's
lesson about the inherent beauty and suggestibility of objects in the natural
world, Ernst has reduced them to a simple and striking series of small works
presided over by the figure of Loplop, the Bird Superior and *alter-ego*. Perhaps
more than any other Surrealist artist he manages to synthesize in this series two
often opposed sources of artistic creation—the natural world so avidly dissected
by Leonardo and the language of unconscious creation analyzed by Freud.

For Leonardo the bird had also served as a source for his scientific explorations into flying; he derived his designs for a flying machine from detailed
observation of the flight of birds. Freud based his essay on the sources of Leonardo's sexuality and artistic genius on the artist's memory/fantasy of the bird's
visit. Freud had originally been drawn to Leonardo through a fascination with
the relationship of art to science and the essay served as a kind of analytic
model for Freud's understanding of the artist's relationship to his works. As
Spector has pointed out, it also reflected Freud's strong personal identification
with the figure of Leonardo.[27] Leonardo, Freud and Ernst shared an obsession
with the linking of science and art. For Leonardo, with his synoptic mind, it
was necessary to prove painting a mental activity and a science, thereby affirm-
ing a new role for the artist. Freud's fear that psychoanalysis would be entirely
swallowed up by medicine (Science) led to his early attempts, in the "Gradiva"
and Leonardo essays, to assert the applicability of psychoanalytic method to
explicating the creative process. Traditionally, the artist has created, the scientist
has discovered. Historically their common point of reference was the natural
world, used by each as a starting point for their explorations. Ernst, finally,

uses the image of Loplop as a symbolic indicator that the sources of his art lie in the lessons of Leonardo and Freud. From the former he learned the necessity of a studied observation of the natural world, from the latter that of painstakingly observing his own mental processes. The fusion of these two methods, under the tutelage of the bird-muse Loplop, lies at the heart of Ernst's work.

Conclusion

The outbreak of war in the Fall of 1939 effectively dissolved Surrealism as a cohesive European movement. Since the middle 1930's Surrealist groups had sprung up in Eastern Europe, America, England and South America. The "internationalization" and diffusion of Surrealism continued throughout the war years. Breton, Masson, Ernst and others eventually found their way to America where they would exert a significant influence on American painting of the 1940's. Masson and Breton settled briefly in Connecticut; Ernst found his way to Sedona, Arizona with a new wife. A brief flurry of Surrealist activity in New York during these years marked, for all intents and purposes, the dying breath of Surrealism as a movement which had diligently worked for the transformation of man and his psychological relationship to his world. The New York based Surrealist periodicals of the early 1940's, foremost among them *View* and *VVV*, reveal a last paroxysmal attempt to capture that "mythe d'aujourd'-hui" for which Breton had been searching since the early 1930's.[1] Drawn first to Greek, and particularly pre-classical and Dionysiac, myth and later to the myths of Oceanic and African society, Surrealist myth during the 1930's had been largely characterized by its reliance on the Freud-oriented psychological content of myth and its structural relationship to dream and the poetic imagination. But as Surrealism gradually moved away from an almost completely literal application of Freudian principles to poetic and pictorial imagery the attitude toward myth shifted once again. The definition of myth was now extended to include all forms of magical, fantastic, legendary and totemic thought. By the early 1940's myth and the marvelous were one. In its final years as a movement, reflecting the profound disruptions and dislocations of the war years, Surrealist attention increasingly focused on the question of man's liberation; a liberation which could perhaps be best effected by moving away from the weighty theoretical constructions of the previous decade.

Trips to Mexico, Martinique, Haiti and other exotic lands combined with a reexamination of primitive magic and ritual and alchemical and occult theory to produce a new idea of myth which diverges significantly from that of the 1930's. Some indications for these new directions, though they remain outside the scope of the present thesis, can be found in the preparations for the first major post-war exhibition. Nearly ten years had elapsed from the time of the great International Surrealist exhibition of 1938 when, in 1945, the Galerie Maeght proposed sponsoring a major exhibition. Breton, who had returned to

France by way of Haiti at the end of 1945, thought that the exhibition should have myth as its theme. Marcel Jean, one of the participants, has described the installation in some detail. After passing through several rooms designed to conduct the visitor along a path of spiritual progression he entered a "labyrinth" dedicated to a being, a category of beings or an object capable of being endowed with a mythical life. Jean explains that:

> These objects or beings were: 1) the 'Worldly Tiger,' after a story by Jean Ferry about an imaginary animal training act; 2) *'La Chevelure de Falmer,'* described in *Les Chants de Maldoror* (last strophe of song IV); 3) the Gila monster; 4) Jeanne Sabrenas, the *cantinière* in Jarry's novel *La Dragonne;* 5) Léonie Aubois d'Ashby, from Rimbaud's poem *Dévotion;* 6) the Secretary-Bird, 'dear to Max Ernst' according to the letter of invitation; 7) the Concylura 'or Star-nosed Mole of Medieval authors;' 8) Duchamp's 'Gravity Manager'; 9) Brauner's object, the 'wolf-table'—an elegant little table furnished with a tail and a miniature wolf's head; 10) Raymond Roussel; 11) Breton's 'Great Invisibles'; 12) the window of 'Magna sed Apta' from George du Maurier's novel *Peter Ibettson* (the American film of this novel, made in 1935 had greatly impressed the Surrealists).—These myths of the future were each assigned a particular sign of the Zodiac.[2]

Works poured in from Europe and the Americas, paintings, sculptures, symbols and objects. A staircase of "sacred books" led to the Hall of Superstitions designed in the shape of an egg by the architect Frederick Kiesler which contained paintings sent by those Surrealists still living in America. Breton installed an altar, covered by a green net spotted with flies, in honor of Rimbaud's poem *Dévotion.* A bizarre series of esoteric objects and magical totems filled the gallery rooms. Missing from the exhibition, however, were the familiar mythical figures of the 1930's: Gradiva, Loplop and the sphinxes, centaurs and chimeras of the earlier years. The question of whether the eclectic objects of the post war surrealist world could be elevated to the level of mythical beings remained unanswered. Implicit in the plans for the exhibition was the suggestion that *any* object so labelled might play a mythical role. The catholicity of the exhibits was, in fact, some indication that in the course of its internationalization Surrealism had moved away from the intense soul searching and theoretical posturing that had characterized much of its earlier activity.

The catalogue anthology *Le Surréalisme en 1947,* published by Galerie Maeght, sought to answer some of the questions about the future of myth. Bataille, in his "L'Absence de mythe" argued that:

> Le mythe et la possibilité du mythe se défont: subsiste seul un vide immense, aimé et misérable. L'absence de mythe est peut-être ce sol, immuable sous mes pieds, mais peut-être aussitôt ce sol se dérobant.[3]

In the immediate post war years the question of liberty had emerged as a major Surrealist preoccupation and in an explanation which perhaps reflects the influence of current Existentialist thought Bataille suggested that only through the denial of God, myth and Being could man be set free on a path leading to liberty and truth: "Et aujourd'hui, parce qu'un mythe et mort ou meurt, nous voyons mieux à travers lui que s'il vivait . . . c'est la souffrance qui rend gai."[4] Pierre Mabille, Nicolas Calas, Jacques Brunius and Ferdinand Alquié all raised the problem of liberty in their respective essays.[5] When the Surrealists had returned to France in 1945 they found themselves suddenly in the somewhat awkward position of an "older generation." The young revolutionaries had become an establishment, replaced by Sartre and his followers, now rallied around the Existentialist banner.

In his "La Liberté surréaliste," Alquié reiterated Surrealism's demand for a reality formed from man's emotion and desires. The rejection of a transcendant reality, the negation of God, the affirmation that there exists no world but this one supposes some sort of surrender:

> la conscience religieuse, que l'on rejette ici, traduit en effet une aspiration positve: l'émoi que font naître en nous les mythes et les légendes, l'espoir secret qu'ils éveillent, en sont la preuve.[6]

Myth, then, belongs to a realm of transcendental thought which Alquié rejects as forcefully as he rejects a humanism which acknowledges nothing outside of man and finally fails to recognize whether the force impelling it toward life is one of hope or despair. Both Surrealism and existentialism reject God, an objective reality divorced from man and a transcendant reason. The subordination of reality to the domain of man, then, becomes liberty. This liberty manifests itself in Existentialism as despair, in Surrealism as dream. For Sartre, man is free everywhere, even in prison, because it is he who gives meaning to his situation; for Alquié man gives meaning to the world through the creative act, life and poetry at the same time. The Surrealist object frees man from the imposition of an objectively defined reality, automatic writing delivers him from the rigid exigencies of reason. The Surrealist, in transforming the wall of the prison into the walls of a palace, defines the path toward liberty in the totality of Being. The Surrealists were quick to attempt to refute Sartre's assertion that Surrealism, at best, remained only a linguistic game but in the face of this new philosophical onslaught they gradually became more wary of the charges of frivolity levelled at them by a generation less sympathetic to Surrealism's preoccupation with myth and magic.

Breton himself was not so quick to give up the ideas about myth which he had nurtured so lovingly for over a decade. But no longer would Surrealism concern itself with the adaptation or creation of specific myths. Instead, by its very existence and the all-inclusive character of its doctrine, it would become its own myth, the myth of the spirit set free along the path of liberty and truth. Throughout the history of the Surrealist movement the definition and purposes to which myth was put had changed as external and internal factors forced redefinitions of the movement's purpose and aspirations. Only one fact had remained constant: man must be brought to a clearer understanding of his psycho-physical existence. In his introduction to the 1947 exhibition Breton concluded, "On ne s'est proposé, dans le cadre de la présente exposition, que de donner un aperçu tout extérieur de ce qu'un tel mythe pourrait être–à la façon d'une 'parade' spirituelle."[7]

Between 1939 and 1948 Masson and Ernst published two last pictorial and poetic statements. That both took the form of a series of illustrations accompanied by short poems suggests a final attempt to tie together the literary and the pictorial under the aegis of myth. They differ from earlier mythical expressions in that both represent attempts to develop new and individual mythologies. Masson's *Mythologies of Nature and Being* and Ernst's *Paramyths* use myth as a means of communicating the painter's personal visions of the world, without the reliance on historical antecedents and justification that pervades much Surrealist myth construction of the 1930's, and without an overt reliance on models furnished by Freud.[8]

Masson's *Mythologie de la nature* consists of a short poem, each line of which is accompanied by a pen and ink lithograph (Figs. 90-95):

> A la source la femme aimé
> A la fois le piège et la proie
> Rejeté par la mer
> Apporté par l'orage
> Pose ta main sur la montagne
> Ecoute la pluie nourrice des abeilles
> Vois l'entre des Métamorphoses
> Il n ya pas de monde achevé
> Sur les rives de l'ennui
> Il y a le charme et le chêne enlacés
> Près des signes de feu
> Se reflétant dans l'oeil du marécage
> Assis dans ton jardin tu deviendras
> . . . Forêt.[9]

The drawings combine the short sharp strokes on which Masson had depended to convey a strong sense of energy and excitement in his painting of the 1930's and a more careful graphic description of the major forms. Almost exclusively linear, they often appear busy and confused in spite of the fact that they represent an almost completely literal translation of poetic ideas into pictorial form. For the previous ten years Masson had sought to define in his painting a world caught in a never ending process of flux and metamorphosis. Erasing the distinctions between man and nature, the animate and the inanimate, he presents a world in which there are no absolutes. All natural forms are caught in an unceasing and often violent cyclical struggle between *Eros* and *Thanatos.* Fertile woman becomes the source of all life, and he depicts the mountains themselves being torn from her pregnant body (Fig. 90). Earlier experiments with automatic drawing had given Masson a means to express the uninterrupted flow of mental images. He applies the idea of never-ending process of becoming which he had learned from that technique to the teachings of the pre-Socratics. Fusing those ideas with a deeply felt belief in the power of erotic violence he achieves a view of nature in which nothing is constant or immutable. The erotic and violent coupling of man and nature creates its own monsters. The dreaded Minotaur becomes a bizarre biomorph (Fig. 91) flung upon the sand. In nature "la femme aimé," the source of life, is the sea. The writhing amoeboid "child of the sea" carries onto land the forms which existed for Masson as pictorial symbols of his world view. The gaping shell at the end of one appendage is recognizable as the sea shell vagina which he had incorporated into his *Gradiva* as an erotic image. Carried by the storm the germinal image of life begins its metamorphosis. In a frankly erotic representation (Fig. 92) a hand reaches into the very source of life, the woman who is both human female and craggy mountain. The sexual content is made even more explicit through the waterfalls which cascade at the base of the mountain. The equating of the female body with natural rock formations, the *mons* Venus and the breasts, belongs to a centuries old tradition, but here Masson clearly identifies the entire human form with nature. The process of metamorphosis continues (Figs. 93 and 94) for there exist no absolutes. The Apollo and Daphne of ancient mythology entwine on Masson's "rives de l'ennui." The first three quarters of the poem lead the reader through Masson's creation of nature. But lest the spectator believe that he has escaped the invincible process the painter concludes by asserting that (you) "Assis dans ton jardin tu deviendras . . . Forêt." (Fig. 95) Even the most familiar domestic objects are not safe from the metamorphic process as tables and chairs violently transform themselves into trees and human forms. In Masson's view a table leg and a human leg are differentiated only by an accident of short lived rest. Caught in a momentary calm each will be caught up in the natural cycle of transformation. The endless and cyclical regenerations of the earth become the basis of Masson's personal mythology of chaos and violent metamorphosis.

As is the case with many of Masson's paintings these drawings suffer from the effects of an overliterary imagination. The poem, itself deeply suggestive, is finally weakened by a series of illustrations which leave little to the imagination. Through their lack of economy, they become finally pictorial absolutes, militating against a world view in which that which is absolute is denied.

Masson reiterates his essential theme in the "Mythologie de l'être," (Figs. 96-98):

Dans le pur néant
A la cime de l'être
Surgit la naissance
Rupture franche
Tu portes le poids de Narcisse
Gel et miroir mortel
Prisonnier du miroir
Transfigurant ta mort
Ton être s'angoissant
S'en retourne à la mère
Cet aigle solitaire c'est toi
Délaissé dans l'abîme du rien
Tu jaillis de ta gangue
Tu deviens dieu dansant
Quand la flêche d'existence
Atteint son but: la vie.[10]

Here the painter achieves greater clarity through the simplification of the imagery. Of prime importance in Masson's earlier mythological paintings had been the image of Narcissus and the painter evokes this hero once again to suggest the intimate relationship between death and the metamorphic process. In Masson's drawing (Fig. 96) reflection and reality fuse becoming first in death a single being, later life in a new form. As in the "Mythologie de la nature" the source of life is contained within a feminine image and again that female is both human and cosmic (Fig. 97).

A feeling of existential anguish pervades Masson's "Mythologie de l'être" and is reflected in the solitary placement of figures in a landscape (Fig. 98). Born from a gangue in a manner suggestive of the alchemical process, man becomes a "dieu dansant." Alchemical images, like the faceted stone (Fig. 98), suggest that the final end of the purification and transformation undergone by the stone in the alchemical process is the creation of life itself.

Masson's *Mythologies* represent a personal distillation and crystallization of the attitudes toward myth developed in his paintings and writings during the 1930's. Executed in 1938 and 1939 they anticipate the holocaustal destruction about to be unleashed across Europe. Premonitions of violence and transformation, they are also affirmations of life.

But if Masson used the device of myth construction to convey his view of chaos and destruction, rendering his personal *angst* in a series of illustrative works Ernst turned to myth construction in the late 1940's for quite a different purpose. His *Paramyths* set forth what he had learned about the technique of collage as a model for myth construction. If, as Freud had asserted, myth construction followed that of the dream in form and psychological content, then Ernst's collages must serve as prototypes for his own mythology. Essentially figurative, the collage depended on the devices of condensation, displacement and juxtaposition to create a visual world analogous to but not reflecting any known perceptible reality. With frequent allusions to antique prototypes (Figs. 99-101), Venus, Hercules and others, Ernst constructs his own pantheon of fantastic beings. In one of these collages (Fig. 99) a muscular Hercules appears, standing on a pedestal and holding in one hand three apples. A fringed shawl drapes his shoulders while, with one hand, he clutches a wooden club the end of which disappears beneath a lacy parasol. Beside him a figure, half bird, half female with a bird-like head, approaches. Making no attempt to explain his strange apparitions Ernst accompanies them with a short poem in which the words have undergone their own collage transformations:

> oh herkules oh fraukules
> oh fraukules oh frau
> oh ferkules oh haukules
> oh hercules und frau[11]

Throughout the poems a series of unrelated images follow one another; "the divine marquis, the emblem of pride, the burning iceberg, bird of paradise . . ."[12] and Ernst makes no attempt to contain them within a rational structure. Verbal dislocations, then, are as potent as their visual counterparts. The content of ancient myths could not be rationally explained or these stories ceased to function as myth. Likewise Ernst's *Paramyths* have a content which transcends logical analysis. Ernst's collages remain a paradigm for all Surrealist attempts to fuse the polarities of dream and reality, the conscious and the unconscious in a single image. In using the materials of the real world, illustrations, photographs, etc., as their imagistic sources they function like the dream, becoming finally not the residue of the day's experiences but the residue of its visual impressions.

But the late mythologies of both Ernst and Masson represent intensely personal visions, the results of years of artistic and philosophical inquiry. The extent to which the works of both painters influenced Surrealist theory and practise during the 1930's suggests that their mythological experiments were of primary significance for the movement as a whole. And yet Surrealist myth remains just that, a mythology for the initiate, for the viewer who was already schooled in the symbolism of Surrealist imagery. I have attempted to demonstrate in this thesis some of the ways in which myth of mythical thought found expression in the paintings of Dali, Ernst and Masson during the 1930's and some of the reasons for the Surrealists choice of myth as a communicative device. In conclusion it may be worthwhile to reexamine Surrealist myth construction in relation to more general theories of myth as a primary mode of imaginative thought.

There exists no single type of myth, and myth has been shown to encompass a variety of functions according to time, place and the structure of the society or group involved in the myth making process. Thus myth may reflect the attitudes of the myth makers themselves or may reflect specific human preoccupations attempting to resolve contradictions, explain origins or reflect the instincts or wishes of its progenitors. The Surrealist myths discussed in this work arise as a reflection of the preoccupations of individual Surrealists, but in order to function as myths must contain and promote Surrealism's major goals and aspirations. The adoption of pre-existent myths, Oedipus, Narcissus, Theseus and the Minotaur and others, and the subsequent attempt to imbue them with a specifically psychological and Surrealist content represented the initial step in Surrealist myth construction. These myths were valid first because they were already generally recognized as such and, in a sense, had been historically validated. Secondly, their use allowed Surrealism to claim a legitimate historical role; they effectively universalized Surrealist imagery. Moreover, they were capable of being transformed into specifically Surrealist statements about the relationship between man and the natural world. Drawn first to Greek myths which had already been restated, and thus to which accrued new levels of meaning, through the writings of Nietzsche and Freud, the Surrealists quickly turned to the creation of new myths, reinterpreting ancient myth in the light of Freud's writings on the psychological content of myth and its relationship to the dream. Freud provided the model for Masson's *Gradiva,* Ernst's *Loplop* and Dali's *Angelus of Millet.* But these myths also reflected specifically Surrealist preoccupations. Masson's *Gradiva* functioned as a major statement about the role of woman and the unique potency of amorous love in the context of Surrealism. And the *Gradiva* myth also served as an explicit justification for Surrealism's attempt to probe the workings of the unconscious. Ernst's *Loplop* functioned as a symbolic mediator between the Twentieth Century painter and the Renaissance Master whom he admired so greatly and whose works had inspired him to pursue the relationship between artistic creativity and scientific discovery. The problem for Surrealism was one of validating itself historically and at the same time preserving its place as a contemporary and revolutionary movement. Myth, which could not be submitted to completely rational explication, allowed the resolution of this contradiction. The image of Loplop functioned on several levels, as the artist's personal symbol, as an acknowledgment of his debt to Leonardo and as an admission that Ernst's own understanding of the psychological sources of creativity derived as much from Freud's exegesis as from the Renaissance painter. Likewise, Dali's *Mythe tragique de l'Angelus de Millet* applied Freud's model to the examination of a single work of art, a work which Dali viewed as containing a latent content inaccessible through conventional methods of formal analysis. But Dali's work never transcends its personal origins, gaining Surrealist acceptability only because for a few brief years Dali's exploitation of hallucinatory imagery provided a stimulus for other Surrealist experiments in this direction.

All Surrealist myths are, in a sense, myths of the hero. Oedipus, Narcissus, Gradiva, etc., function as Surrealist models for the final resolution of the polarities of existence. Capable of participating simultaneously in all states of being they and only they transcend the limitations of human consciousness. Breton had claimed Surrealism as the point at which the real and the imaginary, dream and wakefulness, the past and the present, the conscious and the unconscious would cease to be perceived as mutually exclusive. The imagination would provide the means for attaining this state. But unfortunately the point was beyond the ken of the Surealists themselves; only mythical beings could symbolically convey the attainment of true *surréalité*.

It is the particular function of Surrealist myth that accounts for its emphasis on the narrative and speculative aspects of myth at the expense of the practical and ceremonial. All myths are stories, dependent upon narrative for their creation and preservation. And in this respect Surrealist myths are no different from their ancient or primitive prototypes. When the Surrealists used Greek myths they accepted their pre-existent narrative structure and added to this structure Surrealism's own speculative content. Myths which are exclusively narrative, however, function as legend or folktale rather than myth. Moreover, the speculative content of Surrealist myths is always psychological in origin. Even the narrative structure of the *Gradiva, Loplop* and *Angelus* myths had been loosely established by Freud. It is in the application of these formal structures to the elucidation of Surrealist principles that the stories begin to operate as myths. Myth had traditionally been used to perpetuate through their ritualistic and repetitive use tribal customs and institutions. Surrealist myth, stripped of any associations with specific rites or rituals, served to support the movement's ideational framework. Breton depended on myth as a means to organize and transmit a growing body of Surrealist theory during the 1930's. Moreover the device of myth construction lent an air of authority to the abstract speculatons which characterized much Surrealist thought.

Another general feature of myth, and one which the Surrealists seem to have recognized, is the relationship between the complexity of the myth and the degree of abstraction of the paradox it attempts to explain. If the paradox can be submitted to a rationalistic explanation it is not dependent upon myth for its resolution. It is at this point that the Surrealists departed from Freud. Breton had suggested that the weakness of Freud's *Interpretation of Dreams* lay in the fact that it did not admit the possibility of the prophetic dream. But the prophetic dream, like the Surrealist object, depended upon the power of the unconscious to directly effect and transform the natural world. Freud's method was confined to explaining man; Surrealism sought an explanation for the world which would not be dependent upon logic. And myth provided the means to bridge the gap between man and the natural world. Since the problems posed by Surrealism could not be resolved logically they required a mythical solution. For Surrealism it was never enough merely to explain; the explanation had to become the means to transform the world. Once political revolution had failed, it was replaced by myth as the one formal structure which could encompass both man and his world. Freud's writings about the dynamism of repressed urges became the basis for the creation of myths which would erupt into the real world and bring about its transformation. If, as Freud had claimed, the dynamic force of that which was repressed could profoundly affect the individual personality, then myth must continue this process in a societal context. According to Freud, myths, like dreams, were partly shaped by wish fulfillment. For the Surrealists the universalizing of the structure and content of dreams took place in myth. In Chapter I of this study I examined the Surrealist theory of myth and particularly the relationship between myth, the dream and imagination.

Of fundamental importance to Surrealism was the role of the imagination in artistic creation. And the Surrealists were quick to recognize that both myth and fantasy had a number of points in common. Ancient myth and Surrealist painting both contained fantastic figures—men and animals whose appearance underwent a continual process of metamorphosis, magical occurrences, natural phenomena endowed with supernatural powers, all pervaded with a profound sense of mystery. If Surrealism existed as a state of mind not confined to any particular time, place or group of people then it gained part of its *raison d'être* from the fact that it shared certain features with the mythical expressions of other groups. In the first manifesto Breton had claimed a long list of Surrealist "precursors," who embodied the eruption of Surrealist principles in the past. Their contributions toward an art of mystery and fantasy became part of that "collective myth" sought after by Breton and others during the 1930's. Although it is possible to isolate specific Surrealist "myths." In the last analysis, I suppose, each of them merely contributes to the foundation of one major myth, that of Surrealism itself.

There is one additional reason for Surrealism's reliance on myth construction and that is the close formal relationship between myth and dream which Freud had noted. In both the rules which apply to normal behavioral patterns and courses of action are suspended, both are to some extent irrational and both contain dislocations of normal associations and connections. The dream with its dislocations of time and space and its often bizarre combinations of subjects, places and activities prefigures the structure of myth. And both dream and myth, although derived originally from the objects and events of the real world, are not limited by reality. The fact that although it has been demonstrated that man spends a large portion of his sleep engaged in dream activity upon awakening he remembers only a fraction of his dreams suggests that, consciously at least, the remembered dream represents a distillation of dream activity. Likewise, the content of Surrealist myths represents a form of condensation of Surrealist theory. But myth in Surrealism also represents a conscious process of organization and construction. Cassirer has noted that the simple equating of dream and myth fails to fully explain the origins and function of myth:

> The whole life and activity of many primitive peoples, even down to trifling details, is determined and governed by their dreams . . . the animistic theory which attempts to derive the whole content of myth from this one source, which explains myth primarily as a confusion and mixture of dream experience and waking experience, is unbalanced and inadequate in this form.[13]

Instead the Surrealists attempted to incorporate the understanding of the psychic mechanism of dreaming into the making of myth. By the mid 1930's automatism and the dream were seen as the means toward a more conscious exploration of the unconscious. Marcel Jean left a fitting epitaph to some twenty years of Surrealist experimentation:

> The greatness of Surrealist painting lies in its passion for discovery, in its appeal to the Marvellous, in its exact, legible, mysterious content. The labyrinth builds itself from the inside, but it can become as limitless as our need for liberty.[14]

And finally, automatism and the dream become subsumed in the creation of myths which would directly convey Surrealism's aspirations. Grandiose in its conceptions Surrealist painting generally suffers from an inability to evolve coherent formal solutions which satisfy pictorially its theoretical goals. More than any other Surrealist painter it is Ernst, in his collages, who achieves a major breakthrough in the development of an imagery which succeeds in welding together theory and practice.

The strength of Surrealist painting lies in its attempt to present a multi-dimensional view of man and the sources of artistic creativity. The Surrealist commitment to a total view of the human personality in its political, social, moral, rational and unconscious ramifications continues to this day. We are still far from any valid historical assessment of Surrealism's place in the history of western thought. The literature on Surrealist painting has all but ignored the thematic content of these works. The present book is only a first step in the tortuous process of determining the iconographic content of certain Surrealist works.

Notes

PREFACE AND ACKNOWLEDGMENTS

1. "Limits non frontières du surréalisme" (1937), *La Clé des Champs*, 24.

2. Masson, in private conversation with the author, May 1970.

CHAPTER I

1. See C. Lancher, "André Masson: Origins and Development," in *André Masson*, exhibition catalogue, Museum of Modern Art, New York, 1976, 102-103.

2. Cited in Lancher, 102.

3. Masson, *Entretiens*, 102.

4. Breton, *Manifeste du surréalisme*, in *Manifestes*, Paris, 1924.

5. Ibid.

6. *Le Surréalisme et la peinture*, Paris, 1928, 2.

7. P. Naville, *La Révolution surréaliste*, no. 3, April 1928.

8. See A. Breton, *"Le Surréalisme et la peinture*, Paris, 1928; also W.S. Rubin, "André Masson and Twentieth Century Painting," in *André Masson*, 13-15.

9. *Dada and Surrealist Art*, New York, 1968, 150.

10. The interior monologue, or stream of consciousness, differs from automatic writing in that the latter seeks to establish a direct link to the unconscious and recognizes the synthetic content of its imagery; the former is moved directly under the control of the ego; see J. Spector, *The Aesthetics of Freud*, New York, 1973, 152.

11. P. Mabille, "Notes sur le symbolisme," *Minotaure*, 8, 1936, 3.

12. For a fuller account see M. Nadeau, *The History of Surrealism*, trans. R. Howard, New York, 1965, 117-124.

13. "La Révolution d'abord et toujours," *La Révolution surréaliste*, 4, July 15, 1925, 32.

14. Breton, *Legitime défense*, Paris, 1926, 13.

15. Alquié, letter to André Breton, *Le Surréalisme A.S.D.L.R.*, 5, May 15, 1933, 41.

16. *Du Temps que les surréalistes avaient raison,* Paris, 1935. The tract was signed by Breton, Dali, Dominquez, Eluard, Ernst, Fourrier, Heine, Henry, Hughet, Itkine, Jean, Maar, Magritte, Malet, Mauoux, Mesens, Nouge, Oppenheim, Parisot, Peret, Ray, Singer, Souris, Tanguy, Valancay.

17. Ehrenbourg's letter is reprinted in *Du Temps que les surréalistes avaient raison,* 4.

18. At no time did Breton completely abandon the idea of political struggle, his attitude concerning the relationship between Surrealism and politics merely shifted. As late as 1938 he would journey to Mexico to talk with Trotsky. The result was their manifesto "Pour un art révolutionaire," Mexico City, July 25, 1938. The pamphlet is reprinted in Breton, *La Clé des champs,* Paris, 1953 (Diego Rivera's name appeared on the cover in place of that of Trotsky).

19. Breton, "Qu'est-ce que le surréalisme," Brussels, 1936.

20. Masson, cited in *Cahiers d'Art,* 14, 1939, 72.

21. Breton, *Seconde Manifeste,* 108.

22. Mallarmé cited in H. Watson-Williams, *André Gide and the Greek Myth,* Oxford, 1967, 28.

23. M. Jean, *History of Surrealist Painting,* 156.

24. Breton, cited in J. Baron, *L'Ane I du Surréalisme,* 132.

25. "Elements pour une biographie, in *André Masson,* Rouen, 1940, 14.

26. "Political Position of Today's Art," Prague, 1935.

27. F. Nietzsche, *Ecce Homo,* in *The Complete Works of Friedrich Nietzsche,* ed. Dr. Oscar Levy, vol. 17, New York, 1911.

28. "Nietzsche et les fascistes," *Acéphale,* January 21, 1937, 14-16.

29. Nietzsche, *The Birth of Tragedy,* trans. F. Golffing, New York, 1956, 32. First published as *Die Geburt der Tragödie oder Griechenthum und pessismismus,* Leipzig, 1886.

30. Compare S. Freud, *Totem und Taboo, Standard Edition,* XI, 3 and *passim.*

31. Ibid.

32. Compare note 29, above.

33. K. Abraham, *Dreams and Myths,* trans. W. White, New York, Nervous and Mental Disease Monograph Series, no. 15, 1913, 36.

34. M. Alexandre, *Mythologie personelle,* Paris, 1933.

35. R. Colquehoun, "The Water-Stone of the Wise," *New Road,* Bedford, England, 1943, 198.

36. A. Béquin, "Le Rêve et la poésie," *Cahiers GLM,* special number devoted to the dream, 7, March 1938, 9.

37. *Cahiers GLM,* no. 9, 1939, 61-62.

38. R. Gaffé, *Peinture à travers Dada et le surréalisme,* Paris, 1952, 28.

39. A. Béquin, *L'Ame romantique et le rêve,* Paris, 1939.

40. R. Callois, "Le Mythe et l'homme," *Recherches philosophiques,* 5, 1935-1936, 254.

41. Ibid., 254.

42. J. Monnerot, "Dionysos philosophe," *Acéphale,* 3-4, July 1937, 9-14.

43. M. Raphael, "A Propos du fronton de Corfu," *Minotaure,* 1, 1933, 6.

44. G.S. Kirk, *Myth: Its Meaning and Function in Ancient and Other Cultures,* Cambridge and Berkeley, 1970, 3.

45. P. Gauguin, *Lettres de Gauguin à sa femine et à ses amis,* ed. M. Malingue, Paris, 1946, no. 100, 184.

46. A. Breton, *Surrealism and Painting,* 78.

47. T. Tzara, "Essai sur la situation de la poésie," *Le Surréalisme au service de la révolution,* 4, December 1931, 19.

48. P. José, *Le Surréalisme,* Paris, 1967.

49. A.R. De Renneville, "Investigations," *Cahiers GLM,* 2, July 1936, 37.

50. *Minotaure,* 2, 1933, 75-82.

51. Ratton, a friend of Breton's, was also a dealer in primitive art and owned an extensive personal collection of African and Oceanic sculpture.

CHAPTER II

1. C. Sala, *Max Ernst et la démarche onirique,* Paris, 1970, 30 ff.

2. See W.S. Lieberman, in a note to Ernst's "Life of M.E. (as told by himself to a young friend)," in *Max Ernst,* exhibition catalogue, The Museum of Modern Art, N.Y., 1961, 10-11.

3. A. Breton, *Dessins symbolistes,* exhibition catalogue, *Le Bateau lavoir,* Paris, 1958.

4. A. Mousseigne, "Francis Picabia et le sphinx," *Gazette des Beaux-Arts,* 80, November, 1972, 305-311.

5. S. Freud, *Totem and Taboo,* 156.

6. Cited in J. Russell, *Max Ernst,* New York, 1967, 14; compare Sala, 30ff.

7. *Dali ou l'antiobscurantisme,* Paris, 1931, 14.

8. See *The Secret Life of Salvador Dali,* trans. H. Chevalier, New York, 1961, 319.

9. Ibid.

10. W.S. Rubin, *Dada and Surrealist Art,* New York, 1970, 226.

11. "Le Mythe et l'homme," *Recherches philosophiques,* 5, 1935-1936, 258.

12. *Minotaure,* 8, 1936, 25-39.

13. *Surréalisme et sexualité,* Paris, 1971, 271.

14. *The Letters of Sigmund Freud,* ed. E. Freud, trans. T. & J. Stern, New York, 1960, 9.

15. E. Jones, ed., *The Standard Edition of the Complete Psychological Works of Sigmund Freud,* London, 1957, vol. 12, 291-301.

16. Freud's references to the destructive power of woman are veiled by mythological references to her historical earth-mother underworld connections. In reality he saw the two opposites forming a unity in the unconscious when in puberty the male child learns about sex and prostitution and begins to think of his previously pure mother as a whore for sleeping with his father. See Freud, *Standard Edition,* 11, 165-175.

17. Gauthier, 192; compare Dali, *The Secret Life of Salvador Dali.*

18. Gauthier, 194.

19. The poem, written in the early 1930's, is dedicated to Max Ernst; it is reprinted in his *Collected Poems,* London, 1965, 9.

20. A. Breton, "Lettres aux voyantes," in *La Révolution surréaliste,* 15 October 1925, 20.

21. M. Ernst, "Histoire naturelle," *Cahiers d'Art,* special number, 1937, 22.

22. Cited in *Victor Brauner,* exhibition catalogue, Musée National d'Art Moderne, Paris, 1972, no. 90.

23. See W. Pressley, "The Praying Mantis in Surrealist Art," *The Art Bulletin,* December 1973, 600-615.

24. The cultivation of de Sade appears most strongly in the works of Georges Bataille who was in constant contact with the Surrealists without ever becoming a member of Breton's inner circle; see *Documents,* 7, 1929; Bataille's own erotic masterpiece *Histoire de l'oeil* is remarkable for its lack of objectification and sexual exploitation of the woman.

25. A. Jouffroy, *Bellmer,* William and Norma Copley Foundation, London, n.d.

26. C. Gelinski, *Les Dessins de Hans Bellmer,* Paris, 1966, 8.

27. "Seconde Manifeste du surréalisme," *Manifestes du surréalisme,* Paris, 1962, 108.

28. See R. Graves, *The White Goddess,* New York, 1948.

29. J. Arp, *Arp on Arp,* ed. M. Jean, trans. G. Neugroschel, New York, 1969, 241.

30. *The Letters of Sigmund Freud,* 76.

31. Though male envy has not gone unrecognized, it has received relatively little attention in psychoanalytic literature, at least in relation to penis envy, which remains the cornerstone of Freudian explanations of female sexuality. See M. Chadwick, "Die Wurzel der Wissbegierde," *Internationale Zeitschrift für psychoanalytische Pädagogik,* vol. 5, 1931, 178. More recently J. Bettelheim, *Symbolic Wounds,* New York, 1962, and M. Mead, "On Freud's View of Female Sexuality," in *Women and Analysis,* ed. J. Strouse, New York, 1974, p. 188 and *passim.*

32. Erich Fromm, *The Forgotten Language,* New York, 1951, 233.

33. A. Masson, *Metamorphose de l'artiste,* 2 vols. Geneva, 1956, 88.

34. A. Bequin, "L'Androgyne," *Minotaure,* spring, 1938, 10-13.

35. L. Aragon, *Le Fou d'Elsa,* Paris, 1951, 225.

36. "L'Air de l'eau," *Claire de Terre,* Paris, 1966.

37. A. Breton, "De la survivance de certains mythes et de quelques autres mythes en croissance ou en formation," *First Papers of Surrealism,* New York, 1942.

38. See M. Eliade, *Mephistolpheles and the Androgyne: Studies in Religious Myth and Symbol,* trans. J. Cohen, New York, 1965 98-103.

39. Max Ernst, *Les Hommes n'en sauront rien, The Burlington Magazine,* vol. 117, 1975, 294.

40. *Avant et après,* Paris, 1923, 223.

41. See M. Eliade, *Mephistopholes and the Androgyne,* 98-99.

42. Cited in J.P. Clébert, *Mythologie d'André Masson,* Geneva, 1971, 39.

43. Ibid., 38. J.J. Bachofen, a friend of Nietzsche's, first published his *Mutterrecht* in 1861; see Bachofen, *Myth, Religion and Mother Right,* trans. R. Manheim, Princeton, 1967.

44. Erich Fromm, *The Forgotten Language,* New York, 1951, 233.

45. Compare Ernst's 1920 collage *The Hat Makes the Man,* reproduced in *Max Ernst, Gewalde, Plastiken, Collagen, Frottagen, Bucher,* exhibition catalogue, Wurttembergischer Kunstverein, Stuttgart, 1970, 21.

46. See O. Rank, *The Myth of the Birth of the Hero,* Rank's work, though not widely discussed, was apparently known by Tzara as early as 1912 or 1913, according to Professor Howard Limoli of Sonoma State University.

47. Hegel, *Aesthetik,* Berlin, 1955, vol. 2, no. 2, Chapter 1.

48. A. Breton, "Yves Tanguy," (1942), reprinted in *Surrealism and Painting,* trans. S.W. Taylor, New York, 1972, p. 176; compare J.W. Goethe, *Faust,* trans. B. Taylor, Boston and New York, 1870, Part 2, Act. 1, p. 65.

49. André Breton, *Arcane 17,* Paris, 1957.

50. Ibid., p. 88 and *passim.*

51. Clébert, Mythologie d'André Masson, Geneva, 1971, 51.

52. Heraclitus said that fire is changed by the divine Reason that rules the universe into moisture on contact with the air. This moisture he calls the sea then becomes the seed of the cosmos and from it arise earth and heavens and all they contain; Heraclitus of Ephesus, *On Nature,* trans. G. Patrick, Baltimore, 1889, 90. Novalis' cosmology is contained in the "fragments" and in "Die Christenheit oder Europa," in Novalis *Gesammelte Werke,* ed. Karl Seeling, Zurich, 5, 9-62.

53. Directions Left and Right refer to those of the viewer.

54. Masson, cited in Clébert, *Mythologie d'André Masson,* 31 and *passim.*

55. See W. Rubin, "Notes on Masson and Pollock," *Arts,* 34, November, 1959, p. 41.

56. S. Dali, *Metamorphosis of Narcissus,* trans. F. Scarpe, New York, 1937, Pl. 32.

57. Reproduced in Rubin, *Dada and Surrealist Art,* Pl. 32.

58. Reproduced in *Catalogue of Works by Salvador Dali,* privately printed for The Reynolds-Morse Foundation, Cleveland, 1956, p. 47.

59. Reproduced in Rubin, *Dada and Surrealist Art,* no. 205.

60. Reproduced in *Catalogue of Works by Salvador Dali,* p. 41.

61. Dali, *Secret Life,* 103 and *passim.*

62. I personally saw no evidence of this when viewing the painting. The visual mechanism described by Dali clearly works in other of his productions. See, for example, his *Paranoiac Face* (interpreted photograph) of 1931; reproduced in M. Jean, *The History of Surrealist Painting,* trans. S.W. Taylor, New York, 1960, 217.

63. Cited in *Dali,* exhibition catalogue, Museum Boymans van Beuningen, no. 55.

64. Freud discusses the "narcissistic" libido and its relationship to sexual development in "Three Essays on the Theory of Sexuality" (1905), reprinted in the *Standard Edition,* 7, 125-230, 218.

65. "Narcissus: An Essay on the Modern Spirit," *View,* 3, 1943, 91.

66. *View,* 3, 1943, 75-76.

67. See for example *The Gray Forest* (1927) and *Europe After the Rain* (1940), reproduced in G. Gatt, *Max Ernst,* London, 1968, 33 and Plate 16. A. Bosquet discusses the significance of these and other paintings on the theme in his "Le Bonheur de Max Ernst," *Quadrum,* 5, 1958, 11-22.

68. Ernst, in "An Informal Life of M.D. (as told by himself to a young friend)," *Max Ernst,* exhibition catalogue, The Museum of Modern Art, New York, 1961, 17.

69. Ibid., 18.

70. Greek sources fail to agree as to which god severed the voice of the nymph Echo from her body. But for Ernst she ceases to be merely an echo and is revealed as a corporeal guide for the painter. H. Demisch, in his introduction to *Vision und Mythos in der Modernen Kunst,* Stuttgart, 1959, mentions Ernst's predilection for mythical personnages which would also function as archetypes; among them are Loplop the Superior of the Birds and Echo, an embodiment of the life force of the forest.

71. Henry de Motherlant, *Pasiphae: Chant de Minos,* Paris, 1928. Motherlant saw in the drama the possibility for the development of a new morality, a morality of choice created by the individual and free from all existing codes. Thus Pasiphae's act of love with the bull, because it is freely chosen, can be considered neither unnatural nor unhealthy. The Surrealists, on the other hand, believed destiny stronger than choice and saw no reason to strip the myth of its Nietzschean overtones or even to admit that man (or woman) caught in the grasp of desire was capable of making rational decisions about the exercising of his passions. Some indication of the tremendous influence of Nietzsche on Surrealist attitudes toward Greek myth is suggested by the fact that N. Katzantzakis' *Theseus* (1949) viewed the elements of the original myth as being charged with complex symbolic significance. Katzantzakis later acknowledged that his view of Greek myth had been shaped by his reading of Nietzsche. In a letter of 1949 Katzantzakis wrote: "Now, I'm beginning a tragedy with four characters: Minos, Theseus, the Minotaur, Ariadne. Minos, the last fruit of a great civilization. Theseus, the first flower of a new civilization. The Minotaur, the dark subconscious, wherein the three great branches (Animal, Man, God) have not yet become separated; this is the primitive, dark Essence containing everything"; reprinted in H. Kazantzakis, *Nikos Kazantzakis: A Biography Based on his Letters,* trans. A. Mims, New York, 1968.

72. Although Gide's last major work on a mythological theme postdates Surrealist productions, it is worth noting that he had been considering the project, and specifically the role of Theseus in the modern drama, at least since 1930; see H. Watson-Williams, *André Gide and the Greek Myth,* Oxford, 1967, 86 and *passim.*

73. Masson, cited in Clébert, *Mythologie d'André Masson,* Geneva, 1971, 37. The account also appears in M. Reis, "Picasso and the Myth of the Minotaur," *Art Journal,* 32, 1972, 142.

74. Clébert, *Mythologie,* 37.

75. Reproduced in C. Zervos, *Pablo Picasso,* 7, Paris, 1955, no. 423.

76. Ibid., 8, no. 112.

77. A. Breton, "Introduction au discours sur le peu de realité" (1924), reprinted in his *Point du jour,* Paris, 1970, 7. In this context Breton uses the myth as a literary metaphor without examining its inherent psychological or symbolic content.

78. O. Zadkine, "The Minotaur Lost and Found," *View,* 4, 1944, 44.

79. See, for example, *The Great Masturbator,* reproduced in Rubin, *Dada and Surrealist Art,* recognizable as a portrait of Dali but fused with the image of Gala who functions as the autoerotic stimulus.

80. Compare Magritte, *The False Mirror* (1928) and *Spontaneous Generation* (1937), reproduced in *René Magritte,* exhibition catalogue, Museum Boymans-van Beuningen, Rotterdam, 1967, 79 and 117. Magritte had not lived in Paris since 1930 but his works were widely circulated in Surrealist periodicals and he participated in several Surrealist exhibitions at the Galerie Pierre Colle in Paris during the early 1930's.

81. M. Landsberg, "André Masson et l'espagne," in *André Masson,* Rouen, 1940, 91. Landsberg also emphasized the influence of the bullfight and other Spanish rituals on Masson's growing interest in the subject of myth.

82. For a more complete discussion of the significance of this motif in Masson's work see W. Rubin and C. Lanchner, *André Masson,* New York, 1976, 51-57 and 149-151.

83. Masson, cited in Clébert, *Mythologie d'André Masson,* 36.

CHAPTER III

1. M. Leiris, "Eléments pour une biographie," in *André Masson,* Rouen, 1940, 14. Masson described the ballet as containing the same conflicting elements for which he was seeking a solution in his painting; "L'activité humaine, souvent interrompere par les distractions les désirs et les tentations . . . l'amour et la passion que le mauvais sort vient ébranler à plusieirs répreses . . . un divertissement où dominent la légèreté et la frivolité, telles sont les trois premières parties de ce ballet dont le sujet est la lutte de l'homme avec son destin; ibid.

2. It was Matisse, himself a collaborator with Diaghilev, who had proposed Masson for this project.

3. See note 1, above.

4. Cited in Rubin, *André Masson*, 31.

5. In the catalog *Exposition André Masson*, Galerie Simon, Paris, 1929; cited in Lanchner, 127.

6. A. Breton, *L'Amour fou*, Paris, 1937.

7. Ibíd., 14.

8. Paris, 1932.

9. G. Bataille, "Le Bleu du ciel," in *Minotaure*, 8, 1936, 51.

10. Plato, *Phaedrus*, trans. W.G. Helmhold and W.G. Rabinowitz, New York, 1956, 27.

11. See C. Kerenyi, *Dionysos: Archetypal Image of Indestructible Life*, trans. R . Manheim, Princeton, 1976, 129-40.

12. G. Bataille, *L'Erotisme*, Paris, 1957, 15.

13. Cited in Benayoun, *Erotique du surréalisme*, Paris, 1965, 81.

14. Ibid., 90.

15. Ibid.

16. A. Breton, *L'Amour fou*, 115.

17. C. Kerenyi, *Dionysos*, 1230 and *passim*.

18. Ibid.

19. Cited in G. Limbour, "André Masson et Nature," in *André Masson*, Rouen, 1941, 938.

20. A. Breton, "Le Chateau étoilé," *Minotaure*, 8, 1936, 37.

21. A. Masson, "Antilles," *Hemispheres*, no. 2-3, Fall-Winter, 1943-44, 21.

22. Cited in Lanchner, 141.

23. Ovid, *Metamorphoses*, Book V.

24. Plutarch, *Alexander*, in *Plutarch's Lives*, trans. A. Stewart and G. Long, London, 1906, III, 301.

25. A. Masson and G. Bataille, Montserrat," *Minotaure*, 8, 50-52.

26. *Acéphale*, 1, 1936.

27. "Some Notes on the Unusual Georges Bataille," *Art and Literature* (Lausanne), Autumn-Winter 1964, 107.

28. Ibid.

29. The works are reproduced in *Acéphale*, 2.

30. W. Otto, *Dionysos: Myth and Cult*, trans. R. Palmer, Bloomington and London, 1965; first published as *Dionysos: Mythos und Cultus*, Frankfurt, 1933.

31. Ibid., 49.

32. Ibid.

33. Kerenyi, 134.

34. Ibid.

35. J. Monnerot, "Dionysos philosophe," *Acéphale*, 3-4, July 1937, 9-14.

36. "Le Bleu du ciel," *Minotaure*, June 15, 1936, 51-53.

37. Kern, *Orphicorum fragmenta*, Berlin, 1922, fn. 210.

38. See Kerenyi, 260.

39. Lanchner, *André Masson*, 134.

CHAPTER IV

1. Lake used the term in the course of a telephone conversation in November 1973.

2. Paris, 1963. The work was actually written in the late 1930's.

3. S. Dali, *The Secret Life of Salvador Dali*, trans. H. Chevalier, New York, 1942, 64.

4. Dali, *Mythe tragique*, 17.

5. C. Lake, *In Quest of Dali*, New York, 1969. Dali explains that *The Angelus* is a para-noiac image because it provokes a series of associations which will finally provide the means to explicate the work's latent content. Thus, according to Dali, any work which provokes spontaneous association contains a sublimated content. But as Dali should have known from his reading of Freud, any event or image may function in this way, only the ensuing associations vary depending upon the individual.

6. Dali, *Mythe tragique*, 104-105. Dali explains; "*L'Angelus* s'associe donc d'une façon cohérente à la *Joconde* par le caractère oedipien qui leur est commun . . . Quant à *l'Embarquement pour Cythère*, qui complète la merveilleuse trilogie composée par le choix de l'aliéné, nous avons vu quelle fondamentale raison il a de s'associer ici à l'Angelus, mais nous sommes empressés de dire qu'une telle raison, d'ordre plutôt 'mecanique' n'était, bien entendu, pas le seule, ni même la plus frappante et la plus décisive pour le rapprochement des deux toiles; ibid., 105.

7. The richness of his personal hallucinations fills the pages of Dali's writings. See, for example, *Secret Life*, 75 and *passim* and *Mythe tragique*, 75 and *passim*, to cite only two of numerous examples.

8. Kraepelin had defined the paranoiac state as: "au développement insidieux sous la dépendance de causes internes et selon une évolution continue d'un système delirant durable et impossible à ebranlier, et qui s'instaure avec une conservation complète de la clarté et qui de l'ordre dans la pensée, le vouloir d'action"; cited in A. Breton, "Le 'Cas' Dali" (1936), in *Le Surréalisme et la peinture*, Paris, 1965, 130.

9. R. Ellenwood, *Breton and Freud*, 69.

10. Paris, 1932, 310. See also Lacan's "Le Problème du style et la conception psychiatrique des dormes paranoiaques de l'expérience," *Minotaure*, 1, 1933, 68-69. Lacan suggests that the paranoiac experience has a significance analogous to that of the mythical creations of folklore, 69.

11. See Rubin, *Dada and Surrealist Art*, 216. Rubin suggests that after 1931, "Dali's visions became functions of his readings in psychiatry, suggestions from which began displacing experiences drawn from his own psyche"; ibid. For one example, see Maurice Heine's clinical classifications of Kraft-Ebbing; M. Heine, "Note sure un classement psychobiologique des parasthesies sexuelles," in *Minotaure*, 3, 1933, 36.

12. S. Dali, "L'Ane pourri," *Le Surréalisme A.S.D.L.R.*, 1, 1933, 9. According to Dali the paranoiac activity must always begin with an external reality in order to validate the activity and render it communicable to others.

13. Ibid., 12. Art Nouveau seemed to him a stylized and fanciful style the products of which appeared almost as dream images, and he indicates that it is through observing images imitated in reality we are brought to desire the ideal objects lying behind his simulacra; "La réalité du monde extérieur sert comme illustration et preuve, et est mise au service de la réalité de notre esprit"; ibid., 10.

14. The painter set forth his objectives in examining Millet's *Angelus* as, among others, to explain the obsessing effect of *The Angelus* in the light of its insignificant appearance; to explore the reasons for the originality of the composition, according to Dali unique in the history of painting; to examine the work's psycho-pathological antecedents; to explicate the reasons for the similarity of mood between *The Angelus* and de Chirico's paintings of mannequins; and to reveal the treachery of involuntary thought as manifested in the works of Millet and Leonardo da Vinci; Dali, *Mythe tragique*, 15.

15. It should be remembered that, according to Spector, Freud's own unresolved feelings about his father were instrumental in his choice of Leonardo da Vinci and his homosexuality as a subject for study; *The Aesthetics of Freud*, 57.

16. I have not been able to locate the original X-rays which are apparently in Dali's possession.

17. Dali does not identify the painter who allegedly advised Millet that the coffin should be removed.

18. Dali, *Mythe tragique,* 7.

19. Ibid., 27.

20. Ibid.

21. The image of the praying mantis functioned as a highly significant Surrealist symbol; the implications of this image are explored by W. Pressly, in his "The Praying Mantis in Surrealist Art," *The Art Bulletin,* 55, December 1973, 600-615.

22. Compare Freud, *Standard Edition,* 13, 1.

23. Certainly one of Dali's more far-fetched assertions; there is no visual evidence to support Dali's claim. Compare Millet, The Angelus, reproduced in Dali, *Mythe tragique.*

24. Dali, *Mythe tragique.*

25. Freud explored the sources of neurotic behavior in the child's accidentally witnessing and misunderstanding the sexual activity of his parents in his "An Infantile Neurosis," *Standard Edition,* 17, 7-122.

26. Dali frequently uses the image of the sphinx to symbolically suggest this attribute of the feminine; see Chapter II.

27. Dali, cited in Jean, *History of Surrealist Painting,* 218. The painting is reproduced in Rubin, *Dada and Surrealist Art,* Dali explores the significance of the "melting" structures in his "Premiere loi morphologique sur les poils dans les structures molles," *Minotaure,* 2, 1936, 60-61.

28. Jean, *History of Surrealist Painting,* 218.

29. Ibid.

30. Reproduced in Rubin, *Dada and Surrealist Art,* 225.

31. Ibid., 233, Fig. 201.

32. Dali, *Secret Life,* 101. The crutch existed for Dali as a "found" object of his childhood and, in one of his fantastic experiences, he uses the crutch to poke the dead body of a hedgehog which, covered with a mass of worms, had been transformed into a frightful object, synonymous with death; ibid., 96.

33. Dali, cited in V. Raynor, "Dali and the Bathtub on the Ceiling," *Art News,* 72, May 1973, 53. Dali returned to this theme frequently. In a conversation with Alain Bosquet he suggested that; "Every creative person . . . fundamentally experiences a certain degree of abstinence. Now I'm not as impotent as I claim . . . Accumulated frustration leads to what Freud calls the process of sublimation. Anything that doesn't take place erotically sublimates itself in the work of art"; A. Bosquet, *Conversations with Dali,* trans. J. Neugraschel, New York, 1969, 95-96.

34. Cited in Rubin, *Dada and Surrealist Art*, 217.

35. See A. Reynolds Morse, *Salvador Dali: Catalogue of a Collection*, Cleveland, 1972, 125-177 and *passim*.

36. The frequency with which Dali depicts himself, often as a child sometimes in the company of his father, painted into his works as a spectator serves to reinforce the personal sources of the hallucinated imagery.

37. Dali, *Mythe tragique*, 36.

38. Reproduced in *Arnold Böcklin 1827-1901*, exhibition catalogue, the Arts Council of Great Britain, London, 1971, 31. Dali's interest in Böcklin was shared by de Chirico and Ernst.

39. Dali, cited in Dali: *Gemälde, Zeichnungen, Objekte, Schmuck,* exhibition catalogue, Staatliche Kunsthalle Baden-Baden, 1971, 100.

40. Freud, *Standard Edition,* 11, 135.

41. For example, the thesis is developed by V. Packard, in his *The Hidden Persuaders,* New York, 1957.

42. Dali, *Mythe tragique,* 105.

CHAPTER V

1. The theme was not confined to the immediate members of the Surrealist group and the image of Gradiva also appears in J. Cocteau, "D'un Mimodrame," 1946, in his *La Difficulté d'être,* Paris 1957.

2. Dresden and Leipzig, 1903; translated as *Gradiva: A Pompeiian Fancy,* New York, 1918.

3. E. Jones, *The Life and Work of Sigmund Freud,* 3 vols., New York, 1955, II, 342.

4. The relief, inv. no. 1284, was restored and interpreted by F. Hauser, "Disiecta membra neuattischer Reliefs," *Jahreschefte des Österreiches archäologische Institute in Wien,* Vienna, 6, 1903, 79-107.

5. Jensen, *Gradiva,* 4.

6. Cited in Jones, *Sigmund Freud,* II, 30.

7. Published in his *Schriften zur angewandten Seelenkunde,* Vienna, 1907; translated as "Delusions and Dreams in Jensen's Gradiva" in the *Standard Edition of the Complete Psychological Works of Sigmund Freud,* trans. J. Strachey, London, 1959, ix, 7-93.

8. Jones, *Sigmund Freud,* II, 23.

9. Editor's note, *Standard Edition*, ix, 51; the analogy between the burial of Pompeii and individual repression was used by Freud in *The Rat Man,* a case history published shortly after his analysis of Jensen's *Gradiva.*

10. Freud notes that Zoe's intuitive acceptance of Hanold's fantasy is an integral part of the actual method proposed by Josef Breuer and himself in 1895 for the cure of patients suffering from delusions. Thus the author intuited what the scientist has learned through experimentation; ibid., 88-89.

11. For example, the epigraph to Breton's *Les Vases communicants,* 1932, Paris, 1955, is a quotation from Jensen's *Gradiva.* P. Eluard, *Le Poète et son ombre,* ed. R. Valette, Paris, 1963, 37, cites the novel as among the body of "poésie indispensable."

12. Breton, *Vases,* 127. Compare Freud, *Standard Edition,* ix, 8.

13. This second drawing (Fig. 65) is exhibited at the Albright-Knox Gallery, Buffalo, under the title Andromeda. Dali, however, has stated in conversation that the work properly represents Gradiva.

14. Reproduced in the *Dictionnaire abrégé du surréalisme,* ed. A. Breton and P. Eluard, Galerie des Beaux-Arts, Paris, 1938, 60.

15. Freud's essay on Jensen's *Gradiva* was translated into French in 1931 by Marie Bonaparte. Since Dali did not read German it is most likely that his first representation of the themes date to 1931 or 1932; see J. Spector, *The Aesthetics of Freud,* New York, 1972, 156.

16. See A. Breton, *L'Amour fou,* Paris, 1937, 144.

17. P. Eluard, "Au defaut du silence," 1925, reprinted in his *Oeuvres complètes,* Paris I, 1968, 166. Eluard first uses the term in reference to his wife, Gala, whom the Surrealists regarded as their muse. Later Breton, Dali and Crevel refer this way to the muse Gradiva.

18. Dali, *The Secret Life of Salvador Dali,* trans. H. Chevalier, New York, 1961, 240.

19. Reproduced in *Salvador Dali 1910-1965,* exhibition catalogue, Gallery of Modern Art, New York, 1965, No. 245.

20. See Breton, *Qu'est-ce que le surréalisme?*

21. M. Harriman, "profiles: A Dream Walking," *The New Yorker,* 15, July 1, 1939, 26.

22. Paris, 1929.

23. *Diary of a Genius,* New York, 1965, dedication: "I dedicate this book to my genius Gala Gradiva, Helen of Troy, Saint Helen, Gala, Galatea Placida (sic)."

24. The theme also appears in Surrealism as part of the male myth of creation (see chapter II).

25. Matthews, *Introduction to Surrealism*, 163.

26. Dali, *Secret Life*, 91.

27. Ibid., 233.

28. Ibid., 349.

29. See Breton, "Gradiva," 1937, in his *La Clé des Champs*, Paris, 1953, 25-28.

30. Breton, *Entretiens*, 182.

31. Reproduced in R. Lebel, *Marcel Duchamp*, London, 1959, figs. 33-36.

32. See the pamphlet *Violette Nozières*, Brussels, 1933.

33. See J.H. Matthews, *Introduction to Surrealism*, 152-64, and R. Jean, "La Grand force est le désir," *Europe*, 475-76, 25-34.

34. Rubin, *Dada, Surrealism*, 113; Soby, *Salvador Dali*, 13 f.

35. See Fig. 68 and note 13, above.

36. Dali, *La Femme visible*, Editions Surréalistes, Paris, 1930.

37. The fairy tale is reprinted in Dali, *Secret Life*, 235-40.

38. Ibid., 240.

39. The *Bacchus* and *Ariadne* from Pompeii is reproduced in M.L. Barré, *Herculanum et Pompeii*, Paris, 1875, II, pl. 33. There is no evidence to suggest that Masson knew this work, but the Pompeiian pose persisted in later representations of the sleeping Ariadne. The Poussin copy of the Vatican *Ariadne* is reproduced in A. Blunt, *Exposition Nicholas Poussin*, Musée du Louvre, Paris, 1960, No. 241.

40. Kerenyi, *Dionysos*, 118.

41. Ovid, *Fastii*, III, 736.

42. Kerenyi, 26.

43. The exhibit was described in a press release dated June 15, 1939, for Dali's *Dream of Venus* exhibited at the New York World's Fair. The release is available at the Museum of Modern Art library.

CHAPTER VI

1. M. Ernst, "Au Dela de la peinture," in *Cahiers d'art*, no. 6/7, Paris, 1937, 24. The account is reprinted in translation in "An Informal Life of M.E. (as told by himself to a young friend)," *Max Ernst*, exhibition catalogue, the Arts Council of Great Britain,

London, 1961, 7-17; and *Max Ernst,* exhibition catalogue, the Museum of Modern Art, New York, 1961, 7-25.

2. See, for example, the wooden fence surrounding the bird head in *Oedipus Rex* (Fig. 4) and the barred cage that imprisons the small bird in *The Labyrinth* (Fig. 7).

3. The male nightingale is noted for the sweetness of his song during mating season. H.C. Andersen's famous children's story, *The Nightingale,* uses this bird as an image of desire; when the nightingale appears in T.S. Eliot's "Sweeney Among the Nightingales" it is associated with male lust. That Ernst was aware of similar associations in Chinese folklore is suggested by a collage of 1920 entitled *The Chinese Nightingale* (reproduced in J. Russell, *Max Ernst,* New York, Pl. 17).

4. A few days earlier Ernst had written a prose poem which began: "à la tombée de la nuit, à la lisière de la ville, deux enfants sont menacés par un rossignol. . . ." cited in *Max Ernst,* exhibition catalogue, The Arts Council of Great Britain, London, 1961, 11. See also S. James, "Journey into a Painting by Ernst," *View,* 2, 1942, 10-12.

5. Reproduced in Russell, *Max Ernst,* Plate 46.

6. J. Russell, *Max Ernst,* New York, 1967, 107. An analysis of the identification of the eye and sight/non-sight with sexual and creative powers is contained in Pierre Mabille's "L'Oeil du peinture," *Minotaure,* no. 12/13, May 1939, 53-56.

7. Ernst, *Beyond Painting,* New York, 1948, 29. First published as "Au Delà de la peinture"; note 1, above.

8. M. Ernst, "Biographischen Notizen," in *Max Ernst: Gemalde, Plastiken, Collagen, Frottagen, Bücher,* exhibition catalogue, Wurtembergischer Kunstverein, Stuttgart, 1970, 25.

9. "An Informal Life of Max Ernst," 10.

10. *Histoire naturelle,* Paris, 1927.

11. Ernst, *Au Dela de la peinture,* 18.

12. Leonardo da Vinci, Ms. 2038, Bibliothèque Nationale, 22 vol.; cited in translation in E. MacCurdy, *Leonardo da Vinci's Notebooks,* London and New York, 1906, 172-173.

13. Ernst, *Au Delà de la peinture,* 13.

14. A. Breton, "Le Chateau étoilé," *Minotaure,* 8, 1936, 33-35. Brèton suggests that Surrealism, by freeing thought from its previously rigidly defined functions, has created a language that might be shared by scientist and artist, both of whom incorporate into their methods natural laws, like chance. In support he quotes from M. Juvet's *La Structure des nouvelles théories physiques,* Paris, 1933. Breton's interest has its roots in Jean Arp's Dada exploitation of the law of chance which he understood as the natural law underlying artistic creation.

15. See R. Lebel in *L'Oeil,* August 1969, 33. As early as 1921 Breton had elucidated the mechanism of inspiration for the Surrealist; "Mais la faculté merveilleux sans sortir du champ de notre experience, d'atteindre deux réalités distantes et, de leur rapprochement, de tirer une étincelle; de mettre à la même intensité, au même relief que les autres; et, en nous privant de système de réfèrence, de nous dépayser en notre propre souvenir, voilà qui provisoirement le retient," *Le Surréalisme au service de la révolution,* 6, 1929.

16. Reproduced in Russell, *Max Ernst,* Pl. 27.

17. See, for example, Magritte's *The Human Condition* (1934), reproduced in Rubin, *Dada and Surrealist Art,* 203.

18. L. Carrington, "The Bird Superior, Max Ernst," *View,* 2, 1942, 13.

19. See note 1, above.

20. *Standard Edition,* 9, "Leonardo da Vinci and a Memory of His Childhood," *Standard Edition,* 11, 63-137; originally published as *Eine Kindheitserinnerung des Leonardo da Vinci,* Leipzig and Vienna, 1910.

21. *View,* 1942, 7; Breton further noted; "You see, I cannot grant you that mythology is only the recital of the acts of the dead: I who speak to you have lived to see disengaged from the banal transcription of his deeds the life of one of my dearest friends, Max Ernst"; ibid., 5.

22. See J. Spector, *The Aesthetics of Freud,* New York, 1972, 53-63 and *passim;* M. Schapiro, "Leonardo and Freud: An Art Historical Study," *Journal of the History of Ideas,* April 1956.

23. Freud, *Standard Edition,* 11.

24. D.S. Merejkowsky, *The Romance of Leonardo da Vinci,* New York and London, 1902, 377. According to Spector, Freud had read the work in a German translation of 1903; Spector, *The Aesthetics of Freud,* 55. Merejkowsky dwells throughout on Leonardo's attempts to overcome gravity and fly: "The prophecy (the vulture fantasy) was fulfilled: Wings for Humanity became the overriding dream of his life;" ibid. Leonardo's account of the childhood experience appears on the verso of a page of text devoted to observations on the flight of various birds, mainly of kites; see E. MacCurdy, *The Mind of Leonardo da Vinci,* London, 1928, 1122; for the original source, *Codex Atlanticus,* Ambrosian Library, Milan, 66 v.b.

25. Note 22, above.

26. Note 1, above.

27. See note 22, above.

CONCLUSION

1. A. Breton, "Devant le rideau," introduction to *Le Surréalisme en 1947,* Paris, 1947, 19.

2. M. Jean, *History of Surrealist Painting,* trans. S.W. Taylor, New York, 1960, 341, note 3.

3. *Le Surréalisme en 1947,* 65.

4. Ibid.

5. P. Mabille, "Considérations mineures sur la liberté," 94-97; N. Calas, "Révolte et liberté," 103-106; J. Brunius, "Certitudes sur la liberté," 122-124; F. Alquié, "La Liberté surréaliste," 125-127; in *Le Surréalisme en 1947.*

6. Alquié, 125.

7. "Devant le rideau," 19.

8. A. Masson, "Mythologie de la nature" (1938), and "Mythologie de l'être," (1939), published in *Mythologies,* Paris, 1946; and M. Ernst, *Paramyths,* Beverly Hills, Calif., 1949. The poems were then translated into German by the author and published by the Galerie der Spiegel, Cologne, 1945. A French edition was prepared by Ernst with the help of René Hughes. The three versions are bound together in a single volume published as *Pramythen, Paramyths, Paramythes,* Galerie der Spiegel, Cologne and Editions Gallimard, Paris, 1970.

9. Masson, *Mythologies,* 6-32.

10. Masson, *Mythologies,* 36-50.

11. Ernst, *Paramythen, Paramyths, Paramythes,* n.p.

12. Ibid.

13. E. Cassirer, *The Philosophy of Symbolic Forms,* 2, New Haven, 1955, 36.

14. *History of Surrealist Painting,* 361.

Figure 1

André Masson, *The Four Elements,* 1923-24,
Oil on Canvas, Paris, Private Collection.

Figure 2

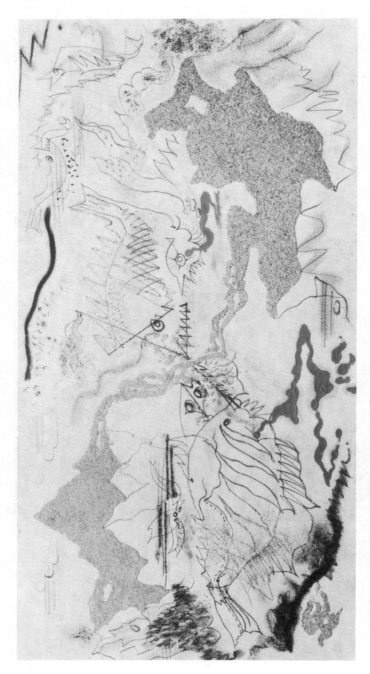

André Masson, *Battle of the Fishes*, 1926, Sand, Gesso, Oil, Pencil and Charcoal on Canvas, New York, The Museum of Modern Art.

Figure 3

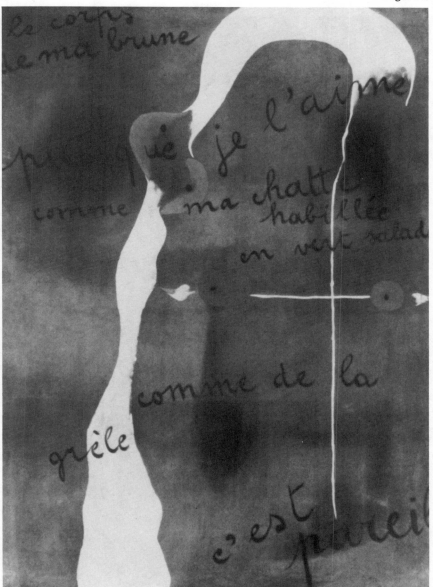

Joan Miro, *Le Corps de ma brune. . . . ,*
Oil on Canvas, New York, Collection
Mr. and Mrs. Maxime Hermanos.

Figure 4

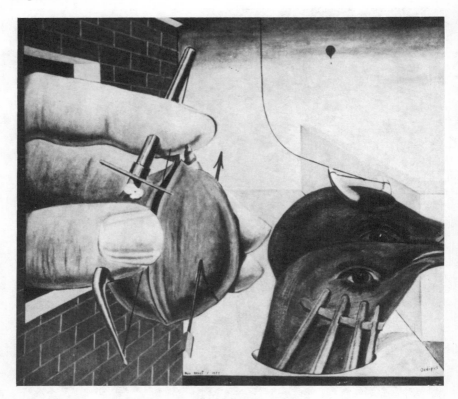

Max Ernst, *Oedipus Rex,* 1922, Oil on Canvas, Paris, Private Collection.

Figure 5

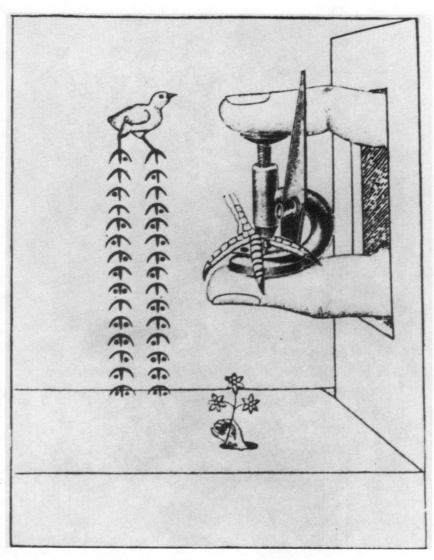

Max Ernst, *The Invention,* Collage from
Paul Eluard's *Répétitions,* Paris, 1924.

Figure 6

Bull's Head Rhyton, 16th cent. B.C.,
from Knossos, Crete, Heraklion,
Museum

Figure 7

Max Ernst, *The Labyrinth,* 1924, Oil
on Emery Paper, Paris, Collection A.
Mouradian.

Figure 8

Odilon Redon, *L'Oeil comme un ballon
bizarre se dirige vers l'infini,* Lithograph
from A. Edgar Poe, New York, The
Museum of Modern Art.

Figure 9

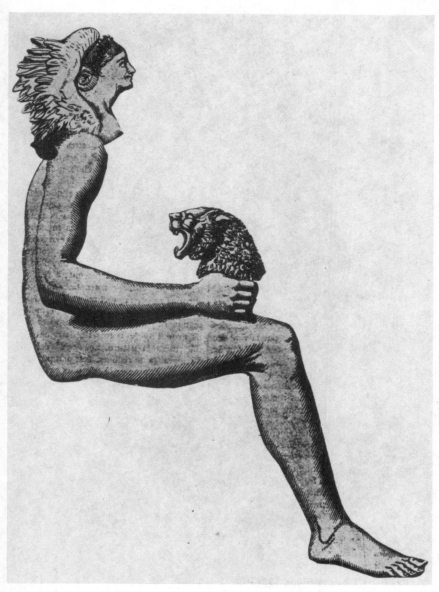

Max Ernst, *Oedipus and the Sphinx,*
1935, Collage, Paris, Editions Cahiers
d'art.

Figure 10

Max Ernst, *Ubu Imperator,* 1924, Oil
on Canvas, Paulhiac, Lot-et-Garonne,
Collection Hélène Anavi.

Figure 11

Max Ernst, *Pietá or Revolution by
Night,* 1923, Oil on Canvas, London,
Penrose Collection.

Figure 12

Salvador Dali, *Figures After William Tell,*
Ca. 1932, Pencil on Paper, Cleveland,
Collection Mr. and Mrs. A. Reynolds Morse.

Figure 13

Max Ernst, The Lion of Belfort, Collage of
Engravings from *Une Semaine de Bonté,*
Paris, 1934.

Figure 14

Max Ernst, Collage of Engravings from *Une
Semaine de Bonté,* Paris, 1934.

Figure 15

Salvador Dali, *Shirley Temple, The Youngest Monster Sacred to the Cinema of her Time*, 1939, Oil, Collage and Pastel, Rotterdam, Museum Boymans-van Beuningen.

Figure 16

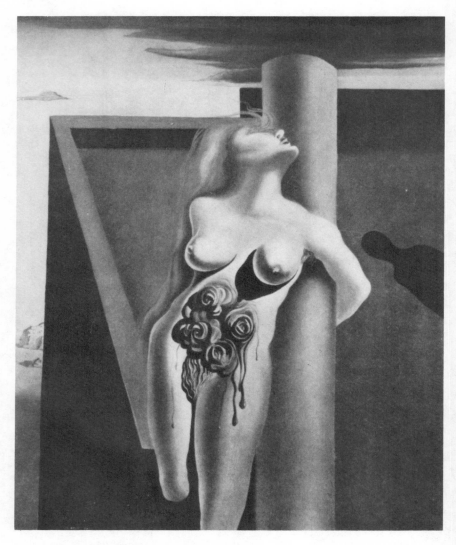

Salvador Dali, *The Bleeding Roses,* 1930,
Oil on Canvas, Private Collection.

Figure 19

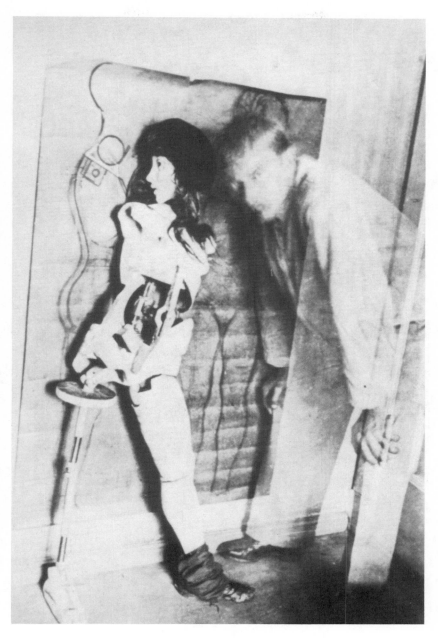

Hans Bellmer, *Doll,* 1936, View of *The Doll*
as arranged by the artist in 1936.

Figure 20

André Masson, *Pygmalion*, 1938, Oil on Canvas, Private Collection.

Figure 21

Paul Delvaux, *Pygmalion*, 1939, Oil on Canvas,
Private Collection.

Figure 22

André Masson, *The Horses of Diomedes*, 1934, Oil on Canvas, Paris, Private Collection.

Figure 23

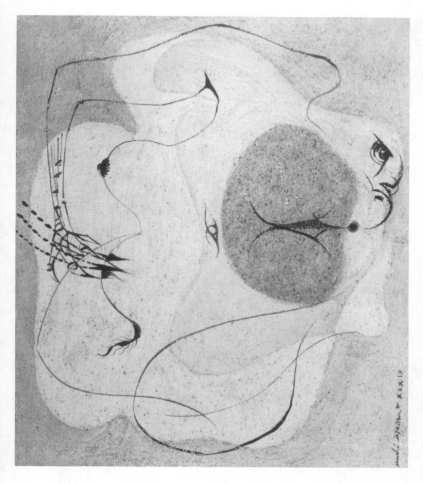

André Masson, *The Earth*, 1939, Sand and Oil on Wood, Paris, Centre National d'art et de culture Georges Pompidou.

Figure 24

André Masson, *Paysage matriarcal*, 1939, Oil on Canvas, Private Collection.

Figure 25

Max Ernst, *Oedipus II,* 1934
Bronze, New York, Houston,
Menil Family Collection.

Figure 26

André Masson, *Narcissus,* 1934
Oil on Canvas, Private Collection.

Figure 27

Salvador Dali, *Metamorphosis of Narcissus*, 1936-37,
Oil on Canvas, London, Collection Edward James.

Figure 28

André Masson, *Metamorphosis,* 1939,
Oil on Canvas, Paris, Galerie de
l'Ile de France.

Figure 29

André Masson, *Combat and Metamorphoses,*
1944, Oil on Canvas, San Francisco,
Museum of Modern Art.

Figure 30

Max Ernst, *The Nymph Echo*, 1936, Oil on Canvas, New York, Museum of Modern Art.

Figure 31

Max Ernst, *Garden Airplane Trap*, 1934, Oil on
Canvas, Collection the Artist.

Figure 32

Salvador Dali, Cover for *Minotaure,*
June 1936.

Figure 33

René Magritte, Cover for *Minotaure,*
Winter, 1937.

Figure 34

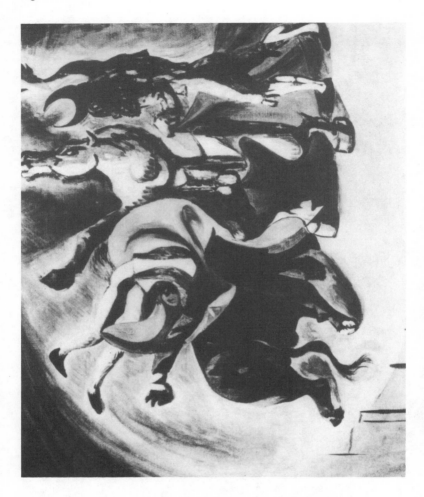

André Masson, *Rêve tauromachique*, 1937, Oil on Canvas, Paris, Formerly Collection Andre Léfevre.

Figure 35

André Masson, *The Labyrinth*, 1938,
Oil on Canvas, Rome, Private Collection.

Figure 36

André Masson, Cover for *Minotaur*,
May 1939.

Figure 37

André Masson, *Childhood of the
Minotaur,* 1939, Oil on Canvas,
Private Collection.

Figure 38

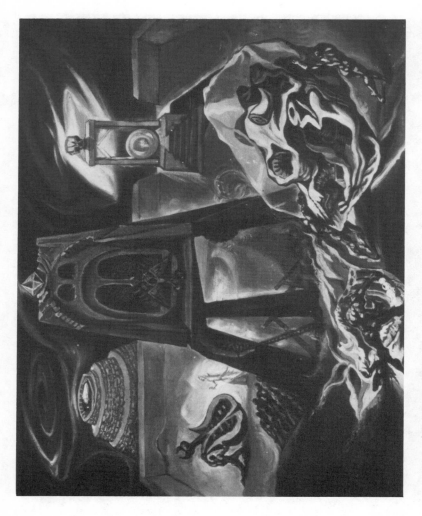

André Masson, *The Workshop of Daedalus*, 1939, Oil on Canvas, Private Collection.

Figure 39

André Masson, *Pasiphaë*, 1943, Oil and Tempera on Canvas, Chicago, Collection Dr. J. Hirschmann.

Figure 40

André Masson, Backdrop for the ballet *Les Présager*, 1933.

Figure 41

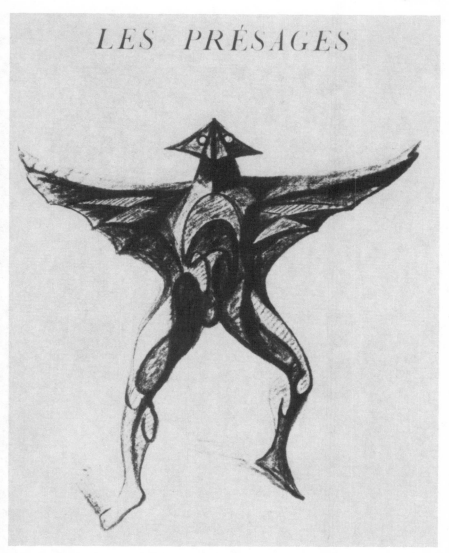

André Masson, Costume for the ballet
Les Présages, 1933.

Figure 42

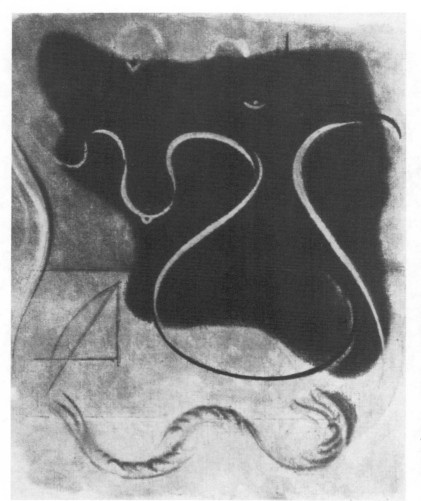

André Masson, *The Rope*, 1928, Pastel,
Aix-en-Provence, Private Collection.

Figure 43

André Masson, "Orpheus," 1933, Etching
from *Sacrifices,* published in 1936.

Figure 44

André Masson, "The Crucified One,"
1933, Etching from *Sacrifices,*
published 1936.

Figure 45

André Masson, *Bacchanale,* 1933, Oil
on Canvas, Private Collection.

Figure 46

André Masson, *Petite Tragédie*, 1933, Oil on Canvas,
Private Collection.

Figure 47

Salvador Dali, *L'Arc hystèrique*, 1937, Ink on Paper,
Cleveland, Collection Mr. and Mrs. A. Reynolds Morse.

Figure 48

Installation view, International
Surrealist Exhibition, Paris, 1938.

Figure 49

André Masson, *The Landscape of Wonders,* 1935, Oil on Canvas, New York, Collection Richard S. Zeisler.

Figure 50

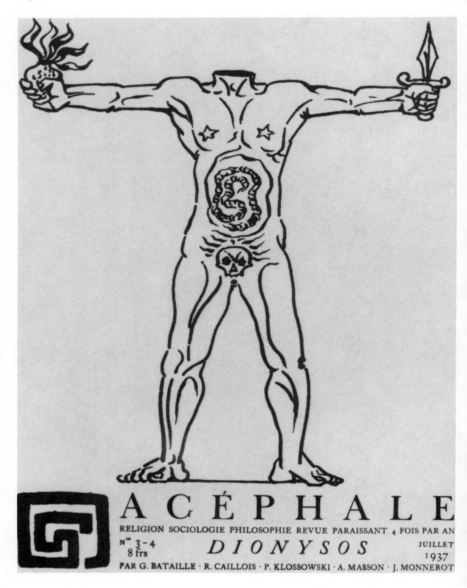

André Masson, *Acéphale,* 1937.

Figure 51

André Masson, *Dionysos,* 1933,
Ink on Paper, After *Acéphale.*

Figure 52

André Masson, *Tragédie*, 1933, Oil on Canvas, Private Collection.

Figure 53

André Masson, *Murder*, 1933, Oil on Canvas, Paris, Private Collection.

Figure 54

André Masson, *Massacre*, 1933, Ink, Paris, Antwerp, Collection Collette Dooms.

Figure 55

André Masson, *Massacre*, 1933,
Ink, Paris, Private Collection

Figure 56

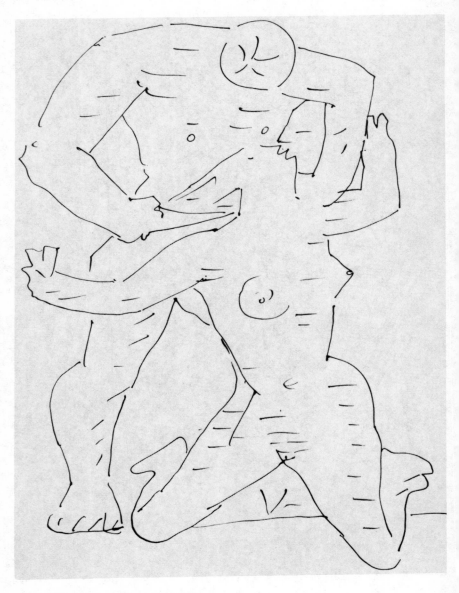

André Masson, *Massacre*, 1933,
Ink, Private Collection.

Figure 57

André Masson, *Massacre*, 1933, Ink, Private Collection.

Figure 58

Salvador Dali, *Meditation on the Harp,*
1932-33, Oil on Canvas, Cleveland,
Collection Mr. and Mrs. A. Reynolds Morse.

Figure 59

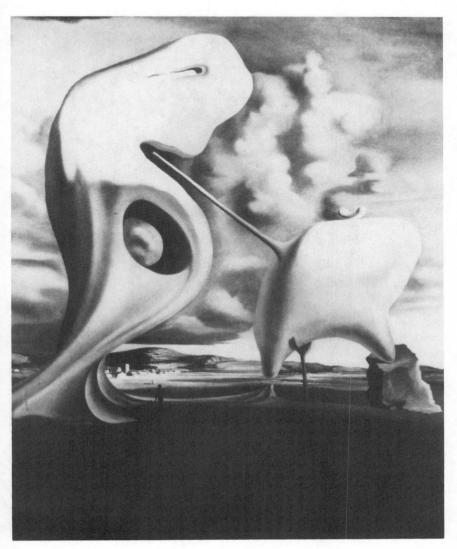

Salvador Dali, *The Architectonic Angelus
of Millet,* 1933, Oil on Canvas, London,
Hanover Gallery.

Figure 60

Salvador Dali, *Atavistic Ruins After
the Rain,* 1934, Oil on Canvas, Rome,
Collection Carlo Ponti.

Figure 61

Salvador Dali, *Archaeological Reminiscence of Millet's Angelus*, 1934-35,
Oil on Panel, Cleveland, Collection Mr. and Mrs. A. Reynolds Morse.

Figure 62

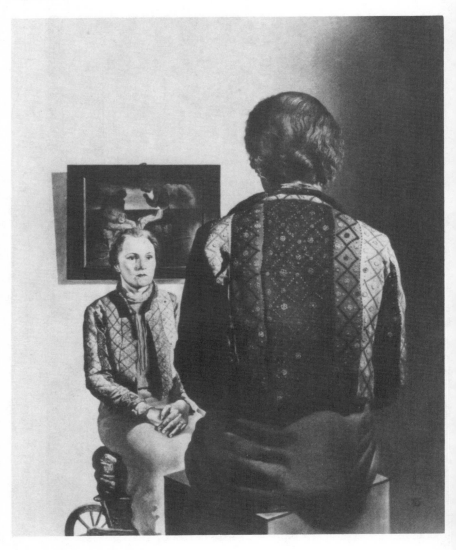

Salvador Dali, *The Angelus of Gala,* 1935,
Oil on Panel, New York, Museum of Modern
Art.

Figure 63

André Masson, *Gradiva*, 1939, Oil on Canvas,
Knokke-le-Zoute, Collection Gustave Nellens.

Figure 64

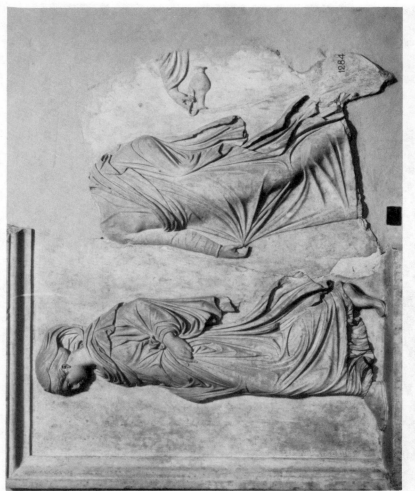

Marble relief, Vatican, Museo Chiaramonti.

Figure 65

Salvador Dali, *Andromeda* (identified
as *Gradiva*) 1930, Drawing, Buffalo,
Albright-knox Art Gallery, Gift of A.
Conger Goodyear.

Figure 66

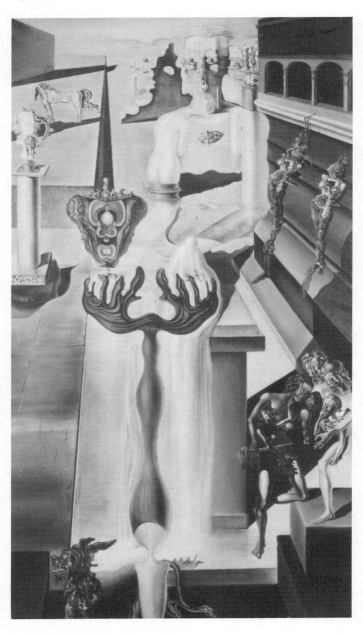

Salvador Dali, *The Invisible Man,*
1929-33, Oil on Canvas, Private
Collection.

Figure 67

Salvador Dali, *Three Apparitions of the Visage of Gala*, 1947,
Oil on Canvas, Port Lligat, Collection Salvador Dali.

Figure 68

Salvador Dali, *Gradiva*, 1930,
Drawing, Private Collection.

Figure 69

The Galerie Gradiva, Paris, as photographed in 1937.

Figure 70

Salvador Dali, *Gradiva, William Tell
and the Bureaucrat,* 1932, Drawing,
Private Collection.

Figure 73

Max Ernst, *Monument to the Birds*,
1927, Oil on Canvas, Paris, Collection
Vicomtesse de Noailles.

Figure 74

Max Ernst, *The Dove,* 1927, Oil and
Collage on Canvas, Paris, Galerie
le Point Cardinal.

Figure 75

Max Ernst, *The Interior of Sight,* 1929,
Oil on Canvas, Houston, Collection Jean
de Menil.

Figure 76

Max Ernst, Collage from *La Femme 100 têtes*, 1929.

Figure 77

Max Ernst, Collage from *La Femme 100 têtes,* 1929.

Figure 78

Max Ernst, Collage from *La Femme 100 têtes*, 1929.

Figure 79

Max Ernst, *La Parole,* 1921
Oil on Canvas, Private Collection.

Figure 80

Max Ernst, Collage from
La Femme 100 têtes, 1929.

Figure 81

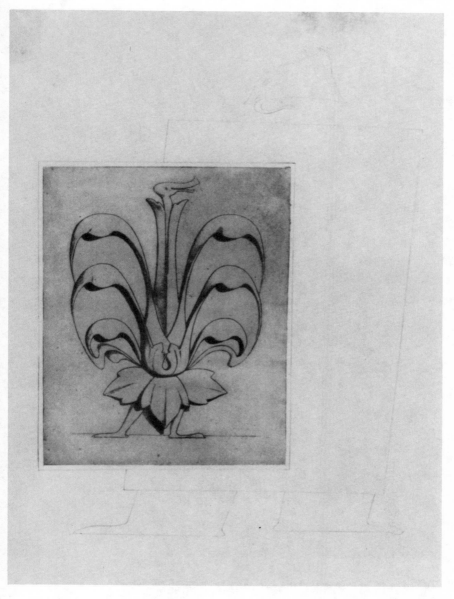

Max Ernst, *Human Figure,* 1929,
Drawing and Collage on Paper, New
York and Paris, Collection Alexandre Iolas.

Figure 82

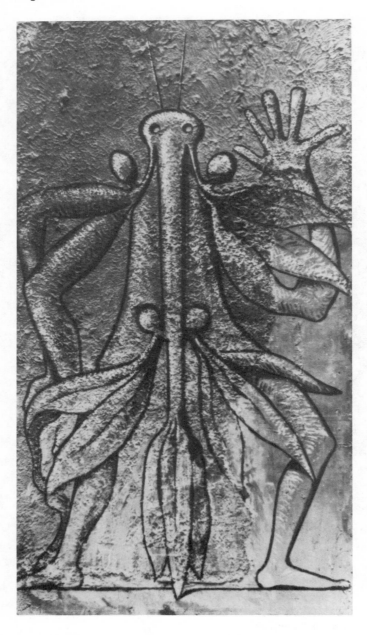

Max Ernst, *Human Figure,* Ca. 1929,
Drawing and Collage on Paper, Private Collection.

Figure 83

Max Ernst, *Loplop Introduces a Young Girl,* 1930, Plaster
and Oil on Wood, Metal, etc., Huismes
Collection the Artist.

Figure 84

Leonardo da Vinci,
St. Anne with the Virgin,
Ca. 1483, Paris, Louvre

Figure 85

Leonardo da Vinci, *Leda and the Swan,*
copy after, Rome, Spiridon
Collection.

Figure 86

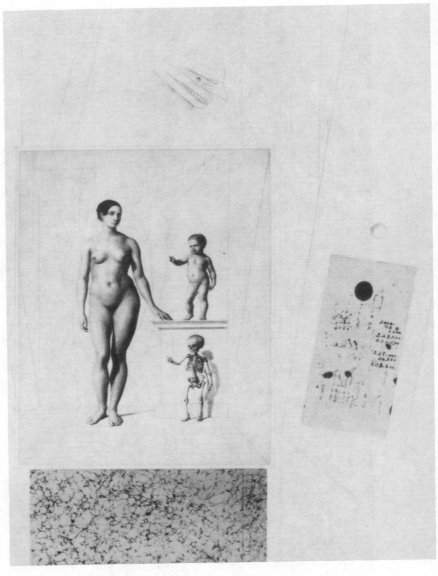

Max Ernst, *Loplop Presents,* 1931
Collage and Drawing, London, Collection
Ursula and Erno Goldfinger.

Figure 87

Max Ernst, *Loplop Presents,* 1930,
Collage and Drawing, Chicago, Collection
E.A. Bergmann.

Figure 88

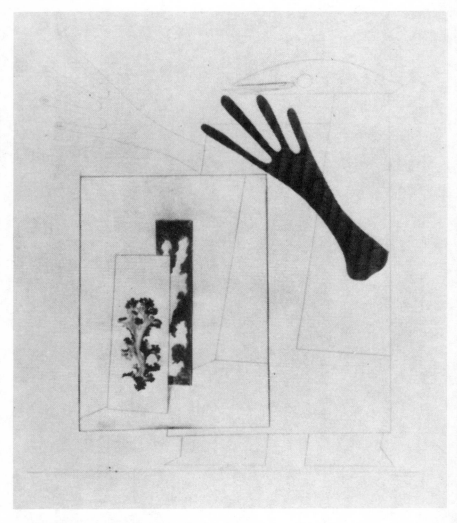

Max Ernst, *Loplop Presents,* 1931,
Collage, Frottage and Pencil, Bridgewater,
Conn., Collection Julien Levy.

Figure 89

Max Ernst, *Loplop Presents a Flower,*
1931, Oil and Collage on Plywood, Paris,
Galerie le Point Cardinal.

Figure 90

André Masson, Illustration from
Mythologie de la nature, 1938.

Figure 91

André Masson, Illustration from
Mythologie de la nature, 1938.

Figure 92

André Masson, Illustration from
Mythologie de la nature, 1938.

Figure 93

André Masson, Illustration from
Mythologie de la nature, 1938.

Figure 94

André Masson, Illustration from
Mythologie de la nature, 1938.

Figure 95

André Masson, Illustration from
Mythologie de la nature, 1938.

Figure 96

André Masson, Illustration from
Mythologie de la nature, 1939.

Figure 97

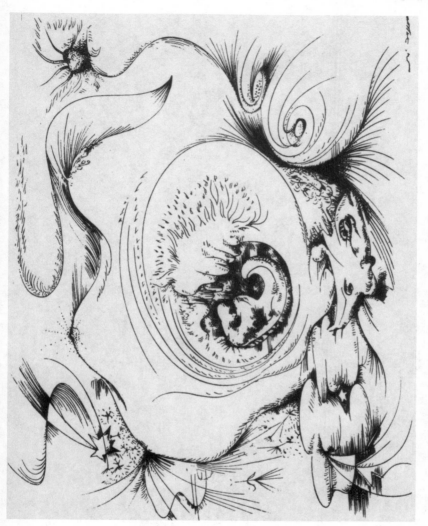

André Masson, Illustration from *Mythologie de la nature*, 1939.

Figure 98

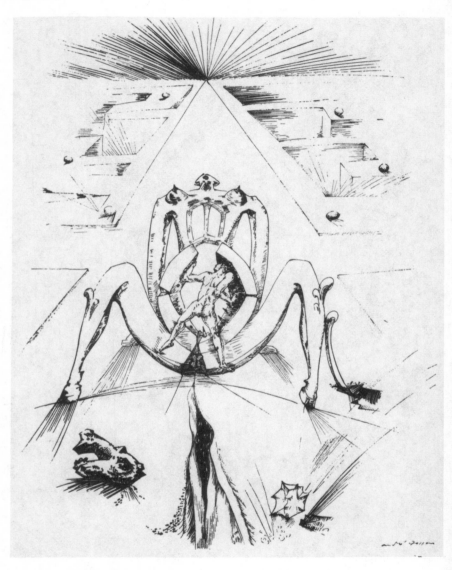

André Masson, Illustration from
Mythologie de la nature, 1939.

Figure 99

Max Ernst, Illustration from *Paramyths*, 1948.

Figure 100

Max Ernst, Illustration from *Paramyths*, 1948.

Figure 101

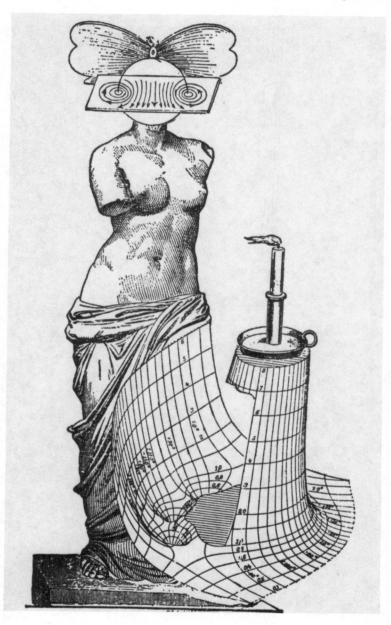

Max Ernst, Illustration from *Paramyths*, 1948.

Selected Bibliography

Good bibliographies of Surrealism already exist. See, for example, those of Herbert S. Gershman and J.H. Matthews mentioned below. I have not attempted to include here all books and articles consulted during the course of my research, but only those cited in the text of the thesis or containing material of relevance to it.

BOOKS AND ARTICLES

Alexandre, M. *Memoires d'un surréaliste,* Paris, 1968.
────── . *Mythologie personelle,* Paris, 1933.
Alexandrian, S. *L'Art surréaliste,* Paris, 1969.
Alford, G. "The Universe of André Masson," *College Art Journal,* 3, January, 1944, 42-46.
Alleau, R. *Guide de la France mystérieuse,* Paris, 1964.
Alquié, F. *Entretiens sur le surréalisme,* Paris, 1968.
────── . Letter to André Breton, *Le Surréalisme* A.S.D.L.R., 5, May 15, 1933, 41.
────── . *The Philosophy of Surrealism,* trans. B. Waldrop, Ann Arbor, Mich., 1965.
────── . "Le Surréalisme et la psychanalyse," *La Table ronde,* 108, December 1956, 145-49.
Aragon, L. *La Peinture au défi,* Paris, 1930.
────── . *Le Paysan de Paris,* Paris, 1926; reprinted 1966.
────── . "Le Surréalisme et le devenir révolutionaire," in *Le Surréalisme* A.S.D.L.R., 3, December 1931, 2-8.
────── . *Traité du style,* Paris, 1928.
Arco, M. *Dali al desnudo,* Barcelona, 1952.
Artand, A. *A La grand nuit, ou le bluff surréaliste,* Paris, 1927.
Artforum, 5, special number, September 1966.
Ausstellung Salvador Dali unter Einschluss der Sammlung Edward F.W. James, exhibition catalogue, Staatliche Kunsthalle Baden-Baden, 1971.
Balakian, A. *André Breton: Magus of Surrealism,* New York, 1971.
────── . *Literary Origins of Surrealism,* New York, 1947.
────── . "The Metaphysical Gamut of Surrealism," *The French Review,* 18, February 1945, 202-208.
────── . *Surrealism: The Road to the Absolute,* New York, 1959.
────── . "The Surrealist Image," *Romantic Review,* 44, 4 December 1953, 273-381.
Baron, J. Bousquet, J., Eluard, P., Leiris, M., and others, "Hommage à André Masson," *Cahiers du sud,* February 1929.
────── . *L'An I du surréalisme,* Paris, 1969.
Barr, A., ed. *Fantastic Art, Dada, Surrealism,* New York, 1936.
────── . *Masters of Modern Art,* New York, 1955.
Barré, M.L. *Herculaneum et Pompeii,* Paris, 1875.
Bataille, G. "André Masson," *Labyrinthe,* 2, May 1946, 8-9.
────── . "La Conjuration sacrée," *Acéphale,* June 24, 1936.

_____. "Le Jeu lugubre," *Documents,* 7, 1929, 369-372.

_____. *Oeuvres complètes,* 2 vols., Paris, 1970.

Bedouin, J.L. *André Breton,* Paris, n.d.

_____. "Eros et l'instinct de mort," *Médium,* 4, January 1955, 23-26.

_____. *La Poésie surréaliste,* Paris, 1964.

_____. *Vingt ans du surréalisme: 1939-1959,* Paris, 1961.

Beguin, A. *L'Ame romantique et le rêve,* Paris, 1939.

_____. "L'Androgyne," *Minotaure,* 11, Spring, 1938, 10-13.

_____. "Poetry and Occultism," *Yale French Studies,* 2, Winter 1949, 12-25.

_____. "Le Rêve et la poésie," *Cahiers,* GLM, 7 March 1938, 9.

Béhar, H. *Etude sur le théâtre Dada et surréaliste,* Paris, 1967.

Bellmer, H. "Naissance de la poupée," *Cahiers,* GLM, 1 May 1936, 20-21.

_____. *La Poupée,* Paris, 1936.

Benayoun, R., ed. *Erotique du Surréalisme,* Paris, 1965.

Berès, P. Inc. *Cubism, Futurism, Dadaism, Expressionism and the Surrealist Movement in Literature and Art,* New York, 1948.

Berg, P.C. *Bilanz de Surrealismus,* Coburg, Germany, 1951.

Bevotte, R. de. *La Legénde de Don Juan,* Paris, 1906.

Blanchot, M. "L'Ecriture automatique, l'inspiration," *La Nouvelle revue francaise,* 1, 3 March 1953.

_____. *Lautréamont et Sade,* Paris, 1949.

Blanquis, H. *Faust pendant quatre siècles,* Paris, 1924.

Bonne, J.C. "Art and Fantasy in Psychoanalysis: Freud's Analysis of Leonardo da Vinci," *Arts Magazine,* 47, April, 1973, 34-38.

Bosquet, A. "Le Bonheur de Max Ernst," *Quandrum,* 5, 1958.

_____. *Entretiens avec Salvador Dali,* Paris, 1966.

_____. ed. *Surrealismus, 1924-1949,* Berlin, 1950.

Brassai, "Du Mur des cavernes au mur d'usine," *Minotaure,* 3-4, 1936.

Breton, A. "André Breton (1896-1966) et le mouvement surréaliste," *La Nouvelle revue française,* 15, special number, April 1967.

Breton, A. *Misère de la poésie: "L'Affaire Aragon" devant l'opinion publique,* Paris, 1932.

_____. *Nadja,* trans. R. Howard, New York, 1960.

_____. *Les Pas perdus,* Paris, 1924.

_____. *Point du jour,* Paris, 1934.

_____ and Trotsky, L., *Pour un art révolutionnaire indépendant,* Mexico City, 1938.

_____. *Position politique du surréalisme,* Paris, 1935.

_____. "Pour Dada," *La Nouvelle revue francaise,* 83, August 1920, 208-215.

_____. "Prestige d'André Masson," *Minotaure,* 12-13, 1939, 13-15.

_____. "Prolégomènes à un troisième manifeste du surréalisme ou non," *VVV,* 1, New York, June 1942.

_____. *Qu'est-ce que le surréalisme?,* Brussels, 1934.

_____. "Situation du surréalisme entre les 2 guerres," *VVV,* 2-3, March 1943, 44-53.

_____. *Le Surréalisme et la peinture,* Paris, 1928.

_____. *Les Vases communicants,* Paris, 1932.

_____. Char. R., Eluard, P., *et al., Violette Nozières,* Brussels, 1933.

Brion, M. *Art fantastique,* Paris, 1961.

Browder, C. *André Breton: Arbiter of Surrealism,* Geneva, 1967.

Brownstone, G. Introduction to *André Masson,* exhibition catalogue, Galleria Schwarz, Milan, 1970.

Burgi, S. *Jeu et sincérité dans l'art,* Neuchatel, 1943.

Cahiers Dada-Surréalisme, 3 vols., Paris, 1966-1969.
Calas, N. "L'Amour de la révolution à nos jours," *Minotaure*, 11, 1938.
————. *Confound the Wise*, New York, 1942.
————. *L'Amour fou*, Paris, 1937.
Breton, A. *Arcane 17*, New York, 1944.
———— and P. Soupault, *Les Champs magnétiques*, Paris, 1920.
————. "Le Chateau étoilé," *Minotaure*, 8, 1936, 33-36.
————. *La Clé des champs*, Paris, 1953.
———— and P. Eluard, *Dictionnaire abrégé du surréalisme*, Paris, 1938.
———— Dali, Dominguez, Eluard and others, *Du temps que les surréalistes avaient raison*, Paris, 1935.
————. *Entretiens 1913-1952*, Paris, 1952.
———— and Duchamp, M. *First Papers of Surrealism*, exhibition catalogue, Coordinating Council of French Relief Societies, New York, 1942.
————. "Gradiva," (1937), reprinted in *La Clé des Champs*, Paris, 1953.
————. *De l'humour noir*, Paris, 1937.
———— and P. Eluard, *L'Immaculée Conception*, Paris, 1930.
————. "Introduction au discours sur le peu de réalité," (1924), reprinted in *Point du jour*, Paris, 1970.
————. *Légitime défense*, Paris, 1926.
————. "Limites non frontières du surréalisme," *La Nouvelle revue française*, 283, April, 1937, 613-615.
————. "Manifeste du surréalisme," (1924) and "Second Manifeste du surréalisme," (1929); reprinted in *Manifestes du surréalisme*, Paris, 1946.
————. *Manifestoes of Surrealism*, trans. R. Seaver and H. Lane, Ann Arbor, Michigan, 1969.
———— and A. Masson, *Martinique charmeuse de serpents*, Paris, 1948.
————. "Le Message Automatique," (1933), reprinted in *Point du jour*, Paris, 1970, 171.
————. *Foyers d'incendie*, Paris, 1939.
————. "Surrealist Intentions," *Transformation*, 1, 1950, 48-52.
Callois, R. "Le Complexe de Midi," *Minotaure*, 9 December 1936, 9-10.
————. "Le Mythe et l'homme," *Recherches philosophiques*, 5, 1936, 47-48.
Carrouges, M. *André Breton et les données fondamentales du surréalisme*, Paris, 1950.
————. "L'Avenir de la poésie ou la voyance," *Cahiers GLM*, 4, March 1937, 59-67.
————. "Surréalisme et occultisme," *Cahiers d'Hermès*, 2, 1947, 194-218.
Cassou, J., "La Jeune peinture espagnole," *Renaissance*, 16, July 1933, 162-163.
Caws, M.A. *The Poetry of Dada and Surrealism: Aragon, Breton, Tzara, Eluard, Desnos*, Princeton, New Jersey, 1969.
————. *Surrealism and the Literary Imagination: A Study of Breton and Bachelard*, The Hague and Paris, 1966.
Cazaux, J. *Surréalisme et psychologie: endophasie et écriture automatique*, Paris, 1938.
Chadwick, W. "Masson's Gradiva: The Metamorphosis of a Surrealist Myth," *The Art Bulletin*, 52, December 1970, 415-422.
Charbonnier, G. *Le Monologue du peintre*, 2 vols., Paris 1952 and 1960.
Cirlot, A. *La Pintura surrealist*, Barcelona, 1955.
Clébert, . *Mythologie d'André Masson*, Geneva, 1971.
Cocteau, J. *La Difficulte d'être*, Paris, 1957.
————. *Oedipe-roi*, Paris, 1928.
Connoly, C. "Surrealism," *Art News*, November 1951, 130-170.
La Conquête du monde par l'image, Paris, 1942.

Cowles, F. *The Case of Salvador Dali*, Boston, 1959.

Crastre, V. *André Breton*, Paris, 1952.

———. *Le Drame du Surréalisme*, Paris, 1963.

———. "Sur le suicide de Jacques Rigaut," *La Nouvelle revue française*, 203, August, 1930, 251-255.

Crevel, R. *L'Esprit contre la raison*, Marseille, 1927.

———. *Salvador Dali où l'antiobscurantisme*, Paris, 1931.

Dali, exhibition catalogue, Museum Boymans-van Beuningen, Rotterdam, 1971.

Dali, exhibition catalogue, Staatliche Kunsthalle, Baden-Baden, 1971.

Salvador Dali, 1910-1965, exhibition catalogue, Gallery of Modern Art, New York, 1965.

Salvador Dali, exhibition catalogue, Galerie Jacques Bonjeau, Paris, 1934.

Salvador Dali, exhibition catalogue, Galerie Pierre Colle, Paris, 1932.

Dali, S. "Communication: visage paranoiaque," *Le Surréalisme au service de la révolution*, 3, 1931, 40.

———. *Dali de Draeger*, Paris, 1968.

———. *Dali on Modern Art*, New York, 1954.

———. *Declaration of the Independence of the Imagination and the Rights of Man to His Own Madness*, privately published, 1939.

———. "I Defy Aragon," *Art Front*, 21, March 1937, 7-8.

———. "De la beauté terienne et comestible de l'architecture modern style," *Minotaure*, 3-4, October, 1933, 69-76.

———. *De la psychose paranoiaque dans ses rapports avec la personalité*, Paris, 1932.

———. "Derniers modes d'excitation intellectuelle pour l'été 1934," *Documents*, 34, June 1934, 33-35.

———. *Diary of a Genius*, New York, 1965; originally published as *Journal d'une génie*, Paris, 1964.

———. *50 Secrets of Magic Craftsmanship*, trans. H. Chevalier, New York, 1948.

———. *Hidden Faces*, trans. H. Chevalier, New York, 1944.

———. "Interprétion paranoiaque-critique de l'image obsédante *L'Angelus* de Millet," *Minotaure*, 1, 1933, 65-67.

———. *Journal d'un génie*, Paris, 1964.

———. *La Conquête de l'irrationnel*, Paris, 1935.

———. *La Femme visible*, Paris, 1930.

———. "La fotografia ura creacio de l'esprit," *L'Amic de les arts*, 2, September 1927, 90-91.

———. *L'Amour et la mémoire*, Paris, 1931.

———. "L'Ane pourri," *Le Surréalisme au service de la révolution*, 1, 1930, 9-12.

———. *La Métamorphose de Narcisse*, Paris, 1936; *Metamorphosis of Narcissus*, trans. F. Scarpe, New York, 1937.

———. *Le Mythe tragique de l'Angelus de Millet*, Paris, 1963.

———. *Les Cocus de vieil art Moderne*, Paris, 1954.

———. "Les Eaux où nous nageons," *Cahiers d'Art*, 10, 1935, 122-124.

———. "Les Nouvelles Couleurs du sex appeal spectral," *Minotaure*, 5, 1934, 20-22.

———. "Le Surréalisme spectral de l'éternel féminin préraphaélite," *Minotaure*, 8, 1936, 46-49.

———. *Lettre ouverte à Salvador Dali*, Paris, 1966.

———. *Manifeste mystique*, Paris, 1951.

———. "Notes pour l'interprétation du tableau," *La Persistence de la mémoire* (1931), Manuscript; photocopy in the library of the Museum of Modern Art, New York.

———. "Nous limits de la pinture," *L'Amic de les arts*, 3, February 1928, 167-169.

――――. "Objects psychoatmosphériques-anamorphiques," *Le Surréalisme au service de la révolution*, 5, 1933, 45-48.

――――. "Objects surréalistes," *Le surréalisme au service de la révolution*, 3, 1931, 16-17.

――――. "Première loi morphologique sur les poils dans les structures molles," *Minotaure*, 9, 1936, 60-61.

――――. "Psychologie non-euclidienne d'une photographie," *Minotaure*, 7, 1935, 56-57.

――――. "Rêverie," *Le Surréalisme au service de la révolution*, 4, 1931, 31-36.

――――. *The Secret Life of Salvador Dali*, trans. H. Chevalier, New York, 1961, 319.

――――. "The Object as Revealed in Surrealist Experiment," *This Quarter*, September 1932, 197-207.

――――. "Why They Attack the *Mona Lisa*," *Art News*, 62, 1963, 63-64.

――――. *Salvador Dali, vu par sa soeur*, Paris, 1960.

Decarnes, L. *Paul Eluard*, Rodez, France, 1964.

Demisch, H. *Vision und Mythos in der Modernen Kunst*, Stuttgart, 1959.

Descharnes, R. *Dali de Gala*, Paris, 1962.

――――. *The World of Salvador Dali*, trans. A. Field and H. Chevalier, Lausanne, 1962.

Desnos, R. *La Liberté ou l'amour*, Paris, 1927.

Duplessis, Y. *Surrealism*, New York, 1962.

Dupuy, H.J. "Bilan du surréalisme," *Renaissances*, 16 November 1945, 76-85.

Edwards, H. *Surrealism and Its Affinities: The Mary Reynolds Collection. A Bibliography*, Chicago, 1956.

Eigeldinger, M., ed. *André Breton: Essais et témoinages*, Neuchâtel, 1950.

Einstein, C. "André Masson: Etudes ethnologique," *Documents*, 2, 1929, 93-105.

Eluard, P. *Oeuvres complètes*, 2 vols., Paris, 1968.

――――. *Le Poète et son ombre*, ed. R. Valette, Paris, 1963.

――――. *Voir*, Geneva and Paris, 1948.

Ernst, M. *Beyond Painting and Other Writings by the Artist and His Friends*, Paris, 1948.

――――. "Comment on force l'inspiration," *Le Surréalisme au service de la révolution*, 6, 1933, 43-45.

――――. *Ecrits et oeuvre gravé*, Paris, 1963.

――――. *Ecritures*, Paris, 1970.

――――. *Histoire Naturelle*, Paris, 1926.

――――. *La Femme 100 têtes*, Paris, 1929.

――――. *Les Malheurs des immortels*, Paris, 1922.

――――. *Oeuvres de 1919 à 1936*, Paris, 1937.

――――. *Rêve d'une petite fille qui voulut entrer au Carmel*, Paris, 1930.

――――. *Une Semaine de bonté ou Les Sept éléments capitaux*, Paris, 1934.

――――. *View*, 2d series, no. 1, April 1942, Paris.

Max Ernst, exhibition catalogue, The Copley Galleries, Beverly Hills, California, 1949.

Max Ernst, exhibition catalogue, Musée National d'art Moderne, Paris, 1959.

Max Ernst: Malingar, Collage, Frottage, Techningar, Grafik, Bücher, Sculpturer, 1917-1969, exhibition catalogue, Moderna Museet, Stockholm, 1969.

Max Ernst, exhibition catalogue, Orangerie des tuileries, Paris, 1971.

Max Ernst, ed. W. Lieberman, exhibition catalogue, Museum of Modern Art, New York, 1961.

Max Ernst: Gemälde, Plastiken, Collagen, Frottagen, Bücher, exhibition catalogue, Württembergishcer Kunstverein, Stuttgart, 1970.

Max Ernst, Intro. by G. Bataille, Paris, 1959.

Etiemble, R. *Le Mythe de Rimbaud*, 2 vols., Paris, 1952 and 1954.

Evenson, N. "The Phantom Cart by Dali," *Yale University Art Gallery Bulletin*, 29, December 1963, 34-37.

"L'Evidence Surréaliste," *Les Quatre Vents,* special number, 1946.

Fowlie, W. *Age of Surrealism,* New York, 1950.

Freud, E.L., ed. *The Letters of Sigmund Freud,* trans. T. and J. Stern, London, 1960.

——. *The Standard Edition of the Complete Psychological Works of Sigmund Freud,* 23 vols., trans. J. Strachey, London, 1957.

Frois-Wittman, J. "L'Art modèrne et le principe du plaisir," *Minotaure,* 3-4, 1933, 79-80.

Gaffe, R. *Peinture à travers dada et le surréalisme,* Paris, 1952.

Gascoyne, D. *A Short Survey of Surrealism,* London, 1935.

——. "Premier manifeste anglais du surréalisme," *Cahiers d'art,* 5-6, 1935.

Gauss, C. "The Theoretical Background of Surrealism," *The Journal of Aesthetics and Art Criticism,* 2, 1948, 41-46.

Gauthier, X. *Surrealisme et sexualité,* Paris, 1971.

Gershman, H.S. *A Bibliography of the Surrealist Revolution in France,* Ann Arbor, Michigan, 1970.

——. "Futurism and the Origins of Surrealism," *Italica,* 39, June, 1962.

——. *The Surrealist Revolution in France,* Ann Arbor, Michigan, 1969.

Gershman, H.S. "Toward Defining the Surrealist Aesthetic," *Papers on Language and Literature,* 2, New York, 1966.

Gide, A. "Dada," *La Nouvelle revue française,* 79, April 1920.

——. *Oedipe,* Paris, 1931.

Giordine, Y. *Aragon prosateur surréaliste,* Geneva, 1966.

Glicksberg, C.I. "The Psychology of Surrealism," *Polemic,* 8, 1947.

Greenberg, C. "Surrealist Painting," *Horizon,* II, January 1945, 49-56.

Hahn, O. *André Masson,* London, 1965.

Harriman, M. "Profiles: A Dream Walking," *The New Yorker,* 15, July 1939, 26.

Hauser, F. "Disiecta membra neuattaischer Reliefs," *Jahreshefte des Osterreiches archaologisches Institut in Wien,* Vienna, 6, 1903, 79-107.

Heraclitus of Ephesus, *On Nature,* trans. G. Patrick, Baltimore, 1889.

Heine, M. "Note sur un classement psycho-biologique des parasthésis sexuelles," *Minotaure,* 3, 1933, 36.

Hercourt, J. *La Leçon du surréalisme,* Geneva, 1943.

Hodin, J.P. "The Future of Surrealism," *Journal of Aesthetics and Art Criticism,* 14, 1955-1956, 475-488.

Hugnet, G. "Dada and Surrealism," *The Bulletin of the Museum of Modern Art,* 4, 1936.

——. *La Septième face du dé,* Paris, 1936.

Hungerland, I. *The Surrealist Sensibility: A Study in Standards of Evaluation,* unpublished manuscript available at the Museum of Modern Art Library.

The International Surrealist Exhibition, exhibition catalogue, New Burlington Galleries, London, 1936.

Kayser, S.S. "Salvador Dali's Search for Heaven," *Pacific Art Review,* 2, 1942, 30-56.

Kazantzakis, H. *Nikos Kazantzakis: A Biography Based on his Letters,* trans. A. Mims, New York, 1968.

Janis, S. *Abstract and Surrealist Art in America,* New York, 1944.

Janis, H. "Paintings as a key to Psychoanalysis," *Arts and Arrchitecture,* 63, February 1945, 38-40.

Jean, M. "The Relationship Between Surrealist Artists and Writers," Lecture given at the Museum of Modern Art, March 1968, as part of the Dada and Surrealism Symposium sponsored by the Graduate Division of the City University of New York. The text is available at the Museum of Modern Art.

——. *The History of Surrealist Painting,* trans. S.W. Taylor, New York, 1960; originally published as *Histoire de la peinture surréaliste,* Paris, 1959.

Jensen, W. *Gradiva: A Pompeiian Fantasy,* New York, 1918.
Jones, E. *The Life and Work of Sigmund Freud,* 3 vols., New York, 1955.
Josephson, M. *Life Among the Surrealists,* New York, 1962.
Jouffroy, A. "La Collection André Breton," *L'Oeil,* 10, October, 1935, 32-39.
Jouhandeau, M. "André Masson," *La Nouvelle revue française,* 144, October 1925, 377.
Juin, H. *André Masson,* Paris, 1963.
Kerenyi, C. *Dionysos: Archetypal Image of Indestructible Life.* Trans. R. Manheim, Princeton, 1967.
Kirk, G.S. *Myth: Its Meaning and Function in Ancient and Other Cultures,* Cambridge and Berkeley, 1970.
Lacan, J. "Le Problème du style et la conception psychiatrique des formes paranoiaques de l'expérience," *Minotaure,* 1, 1933, 68-69.
Lack, C. *In Quest of Dali,* New York, 1969.
Landsberg, M. "André Masson et l'espagne," *André Masson,* Rouen, 1940.
Lautréamont, C. de *Lautréamont,* "Poètes d'aujourd'hui," 6, Paris, 1946.
———. *Oeuvres complètes,* Paris, 1956.
Lebel, R. *Marcel Duchamp,* London, 1959.
Leiris, M. L'Age d'homme (précédé de *De la littérature considérée comme une tauromachie*) Paris, 1946.
———. Limbour, G. *André Masson et son univers,* Geneva, 1947.
———. "André Masson," *The Little Review,* Summer 1926, 16-17.
———. *Aurora,* Paris, 1946.
———. "Eléments pour un biographie," in *André Masson,* Rouen, 1940, 14.
———. "Espagne 1934-1936: sur une exposition d'Andre Masson," *La Nouvelle revue française,* January 1937.
———. *L'Age d'homme,* Paris, 1946.
———. "Le Taureau de Seyfou Tchenger," *Minotaure,* 2, 1933, 75-82.
———. *Nuits sans nuit et quelques jours sans jour,* Paris, 1961.
———. *Simulacre,* Paris, 1925.
Lemaître, G. *From Cubism to Surrealism in French Literature,* Cambridge, 1941.
LeSage, L. *Jean Girandoux, Surrealism and the German Romantic Ideal,* Urbana, Ill., 1952.
Levi-Strauss, C. "The Structural Study of Myth," in T. Sebeok, ed., *Myth: A Symposium,* Bloomington, Indiana, 1958.
Levy, J. *Surrealism,* New York, 1936.
Levy, M. "Dali: The Quantum Gun at Port Ligat," *Studio,* 162, September 1961, 82-85.
Levy-Bruhl, L. *L'Ame primitive,* Paris, 1927.
———. *La Mentalité primitive,* Paris, 1922.
Lieberman, W.S. "Life of M.E. (as told by himself to a young friend)," *Max Ernst,* exhibition catalogue, The Museum of Modern Art, New York, 1961.
Limbour, G. "André Masson," *Arts de France,* 15-16, 1947, 51-59.
———. "André Masson et la nature," *Les Temps Modernes,* 61, 1950, 1938-43.
———. *André Masson et son univers,* Pais, 1947.
———. "André Masson: le dépeceur universel," *Documents,* 5, 1930, 286-289.
———. "L'Homme plume," préface au catalogue de la première exposition d'André Masson, Galerie Simon, Paris, 1924.
———. "Preface à la deuxième exposition d'André Masson," Galerie Simon, Paris, 1929.
Lippard, L. *Surrealists on Art,* Englewood Cliffs, N.J., 1970.
———. *The Technical Innovations of Max Ernst,* Unpublished Master's Thesis, Institute of Fine Arts, New York University, 1962.
Mabille, P. "Mythologie de la nature, par André Masson," *Cahiers d'Art,* 5-10, 1939, 105-135.

———— . "Notes sur le symbolism," *Minotaure,* 8, 1936.

Malingue, M., ed. *Lettres de Gaugin à sa femme et à ses amis,* Paris, 1946.

Man Ray. *Résurrection des mannequins,* Paris, 1966.

Marcuse, H. *Eros and Civilization,* New York, 1955.

Masson, A. "A Crisis of the Imaginary," *Horizon,* 12 July 1945, 42-44.

———— . *Anatomy of My Universe,* New York, 1943.

———— . "Antille," *Hémisphères,* 2-3, 1943-1944, 21.

———— . "Des Nouveau rapports entre peinture et regardant," *Mercure de France,* 334, October 1958, 193-207.

———— . *Entretiens avec Georges Charbonnier,* Paris, 1958.

———— . "La Poésie indispensable," *Cahiers GLM,* March 1939, 61-62.

———— . "L'Homme emblématique," *VVV,* 1, June 1942, 10-11.

Masson, A. *Le Plaisir de peinture,* Paris, 1950.

———— . "Le Surréalisme et après," *L'Oeil,* 4 April 1955, 12-17.

———— . "Life and Liberty," *Art in Australia,* 4, 1942, 11-17.

———— . *Métamorphose de l'artiste,* 2 vols., Geneva, 1956.

———— . "Monet le fondateur," *Verve,* 7 December 1952, 68.

———— and Bataille, G. "Montserrat," *Minotaure,* 8, 50-52.

———— . "Notes sur la peinture," *Cahiers du sud,* 315, 1952, 67-74.

———— . "The Bed of Plato," trans. C. Mills, *New Road,* 1943, 214.

———— . *Sacrifices,* Paris, 1936.

André Masson, exhibition catalogue, Baltimore Museum of Art, 1941.

Massot, P. *André Breton ou le septembriseur,* Paris, 1967.

Matthews, J.H. *An Anthology of French Surrealist Poetry,* London, 1966.

———— . *An Introduction to Surrealism,* University Park, Pennsylvania, 1965.

———— . "Forty Years of Surrealism (1924-1964)," *Comparative Literature Studies,* 3, 1966.

———— . "Gradiva ou la jambe artificielle," *Gradiva,* 1, May 1971, 9-11.

———— . "Literary Surrealism in France Since 1945," *Books Abroad,* Fall 1962.

———— . "Poetic Principles of Surrealism," *Chicago Review,* 15, Summer, 1962.

———— . "Surrealism and the Cinema," *Criticism,* 4, Spring, 1962.

———— . *Surrealism and the Novel,* Ann Arbor, Michigan, 1966.

Matthews, J.H. "The Case for Surrealist Painting," *The Journal of Aesthetics and Art Criticism,* 21, Winter, 1962, 139-147.

Miller, J.A. and Regnault, F. "André Masson n'existe pas," *XXe siècle,* 38, June 1972, 34-37.

Molleda, M. "With Salvador Dali at Port Liget," *Arts,* 37, February 1963, 64-68.

Monnerot, J. "Dionysos philosophe," *Acéphale,* 3-4, July 1937, 9-14.

Morse, A.R. *A Catalogue of Works by Salvador Dali,* Cleveland, 1956.

———— . *A New Introduction to Salvador Dali,* Cleveland, 1960.

———— . *An Evening with Salvador Dali,* Cleveland, 1966.

———— . *Dali,* Cleveland, 1954.

———— . *Dali: A Study of His Life and Work,* Greenwich, Connecticut, 1958.

———— . *Salvador Dali,* Cleveland, 1955.

———— . *Salvador Dali. A Catalogue of Prints, Lithographs, Etchings 1924-1967,* Cleveland, 1967.

———— . "The Dream World of Salvador Dali," *Art in America,* 33, July 1945, 110-126.

Henry de Motherlant. *Pasiphäe: Chant de Minos,* Paris, 1928.

Motherwell, R. "Concerning the Present Day Relative Attractions of Various Creatures in Mythology and Legend," *VVV,* 1, 62-63.

——— . *The Dada Painters and Poets: An Anthology,* New York, 1951.

Mousseigne, A. "Francis Picabia et le sphinx," *Gazette des Beaux-Arts,* 53, November, 1972, 305-311.

Mullahy, P. *Oedipus: Myth and Complex,* New York, 1948.

Nietzsche, *The Birth of Tragedy,* 1st published as *Die Geburt der Tragödie, oder Griechenthum und pessimismus,* Leipzig, 1886.

Nadeau, M. *The History of Surrealism,* trans. R. Howard, New York, 1965, 117-172.

New York, Museum of Modern Art Library, *Eluard* and *Dausse* collection, 1935. (Also typescript list of Dada and surrealist books, periodicals and ephemera.)

Nougé, P. *Histoire de ne pas rire,* Brussels, 1956.

Passeron, R. *Histoire de la peinture surréaliste,* Paris, 1968.

Péret, B. *Anthologie de l'amour sublime,* Paris, 1956.

——— . *Anthologie des mythes, legendes et contes populaires d'Amerique,* Paris, 1959.

Peyre, H. "French Poets of Today," *Yale French Studies,* 21, Spring-Summer 1958.

——— . "The Significance of Surrealism," *Yale French Studies,* 2, Fall-Winter 1948.

Pierre, J. *Le Surréalisme,* Lausanne, 1960.

Prévert, J. *Paroles,* Paris, 1946.

Rank, O. "The Myth of the Birth of the Hero," *Nervous and Mental Disease Monograph Series,* 18, 1917, 67-69.

Raphael, M. "A Propos du fronton de Corfu," *Minotaure,* 1, 1933.

Raymond, M. *De Baudelaire au surréalisme,* Paris, 1940.

Raynor, V. "Dali and the Bathtub on the Ceiling," *Art News,* 72, May 1973, 50-53.

Read, H. *Art Now,* New York, 1934.

——— . *Surrealism,* London, 1936.

——— . *The Philosophy of Modern Art,* London, 1952.

Reinach, S. *Statuaire grecque et romaine,* 2, Paris, 1909.

——— . *Répertoire de peintures grecques et romaines,* Paris, 1909.

Reis, M. "Picasso and the Myth of the Minotaure," *Art Journal,* 32, 1972, 142-145.

Revel, J. "Minotaure," *L'Oeil,* 89, 1962, 66-79.

Rennéville, A.R. de. "Investigations," *Cahiers GLM,* 2 July 1936, 37.

——— . *L'Expérience poétique,* Geneva, 1948.

——— . *"Le Surréalisme et la poésie,"* La Nouvelle revue française, 10, November 1909.

Rivière, J. "Introduction à une métaphysique du rêve," *La Nouvelle revue française,* 10, November 1909.

Robin, P. "Les Conférences littéraires: Dali," *Inquisitions,* 1, June 1936, 51-52.

Rosenberg, H. "Breton—A Dialogue," *View,* May 1942.

Rubin, W. *Dada and Surrealist Art.* New York, 1968.

——— . "Max Ernst," *Art International,* May 1, 1961, 31-37.

——— . "Notes on Masson and Pollock," *Arts,* 34, November 1959, 36-43.

——— and Lancher, C. *André Masson,* exhibition catalogue, Museum of Modern Art. New York, 1976.

Rutra, T. "André Masson," *Transition,* 15, February, 1929.

Sala, C. *Max Ernst et la démarche onirique,* Paris, 1970.

Sanouillet, M. *Dada à Paris,* Paris, 1965.

Schatten van het Surrealisme, exhibition catalogue, Knokke le Zoute, Casino communal, 1968.

Seligmann, K. "Oedipus and the Forbidden Fruit," *View,* 1, March 1944, 24.

Shattuck, R. *The Banquet Years,* New York, 1958.

Soby, J. *Salvador Dali: Paintings, Drawings, Prints,* exhibition catalogue, Museum of Modern Art, New York, 1941.

Solier, R. de. "Dali le fétichiste," *XXe siècle,* 36, June 1971, 157-159.

——— . *L'Art fantastique,* Paris, 1961.

Spector, J. *The Aesthetics of Freud,* New York, 1972.

Sur, J. *Aragon, le réalisme de l'amour, avec des notes marginales d'Aragon*, Paris, 1966.

Surrealism and its Affinities, The Mary Reynolds Collection, Chicago, 1956.

Sweeney, J.J. (A series of interviews with: Duchamp, Max Ernst, André Masson, Tanguy, *et al*) *Bulletin of the Museum of Modern Art*, 12, May 1946.

Tapié, M. *Dali*, Paris, 1957.

Tériade, E. "André Masson," *Cahiers d'Art*, 4, 1929, 41-45.

Topass, J. *La Pensée en révolte essai sur le surréalisme*, Brussels, 1935.

Torroella, R. *Salvador Dali*, Madrid, 1952.

Tzara, T. "Essai sur la situation de la poésie," *Le Surréalisme* A.S.D.L.R., 4 December 1931.

Vailland, R. *Le Surréalisme contre la révolution*, Paris, 1948.

Vitrac, R. "André Masson," *Cahiers d'Art*, 5, 1930, 525-531.

Waldberg, P. *Le Surréalisme*, Paris, 1962.

——. *Max Ernst*, Paris, 1958.

—— and Nacenta, R. *Le Surréalisme: Sources, Histoire, Affinités*, Paris, 1964.

Watson-Williams, H. *André Gide and the Greek Myth*, Oxford, 1967.

Zadkin, O. "The Minotaur Lost and Found," *View*, 4, 1944.

Zervos, C. "A Propos des oeuvres récentes d'André Masson," *Cahiers d'Art*, 7, 1932, 232 242.

——, ed. *Max Ernst: Oeuvres de 1919-1936*, Paris, 1937.

——. *Pablo Picasso*, Paris, 1955.

PERIODICALS

L'Amour de l'art, March 1934.

Bulletin internationale du surréalisme, 1-4, April 1935-September 1936.

Cahiers Dada-Surréalisme, 1, 1966; 2, 1968.

Cahiers d'art, 5 and 6, 1935; 1 and 2, 1936.

Cahiers du sud, 280, 1946.

Cahiers GLM, 1-9, May 1936-March 1939.

Contemporary Poetry and Prose, June 1936.

Crapouillet, special number, 1949.

Documents, 34, June 1934.

Europe, revue mensuelle, Paris, 1968.

Intervention surréaliste, 1, June 1934, special number.

Littérature, 1-20, March, 1919-August 1921.

Médium: informations surréaliste, 1-8, November 1953- June 1953.

Médium: communications surréaliste, 1-4, November 1953-January 1955.

Minotaure, 1-13, June 1933-May 1939.

La Nef: almanach surréaliste du demi-siècle, 7, special number, March-April 1950.

New York. Bulletin of the Museum of Modern Art, 13, May 1946.

New York Dada, April 1921.

La Nouvelle revue française: André Breton, 1896-1966, 172, April 1967.

La Révolution surréaliste, 1-12, 1924-1929; reprinted in one volume by Arno Press, New York, 1968.

La Revue europeénne, 1923-1929.

Surréalisme, October 1924.

Le Surréalisme au service de la révolution, 1-6, 1930-1933, reprinted by Arno Press, New York, 1969.

Le Surréalisme, même, 1-5, October 1956-Spring 1959.

Le Surréalisme révolutionnaire, 1, March/April, 1948.
This Quarter, 5, Paris, September 1932.
Transition, 1-27, April 1927-April 1938.
View, September 1940-March 1947.
XXᵉ Siècle, 1-7, March 1938-May 1939.
VVV, 1-4, June 1942-February 1944.
Yale French Studies, 2, Fall/Winter 1948; 31, May 1964.

Index